John

Happy New Year '06

Good Reading

Casey

The Science Before Science

A Guide to

Thinking in the 21st Century

Anthony Rizzi

Press of the Institute for Advanced Physics

*This book is dedicated
to my children:
John Marie, Giuseppe, Kateri, and Nicolo,
as well as their
brothers and sisters that may follow.*

CONTENTS

Acknowledgements

Writing a book that has percolated in my mind over many, many years means there are many people to thank. It would be an immense task to remember and list all the people that have contributed over the years to bringing me to clarity on this or that thought. I am grateful to them all and, yet, do not want to miss explicitly thanking the most obvious contributors.

So, I begin by expressing deep thanks to my parents, Dr. Anthony M. and Mrs. Anna Mary Rizzi, in particular my mother, for raising me in a strong, loving family, which is fertile soil for healthy thinking. In the writing of the book, my beautiful wife Susan's help was indispensable. She spent many long hours commenting in detail on the manuscript's content, style, grammar and punctuation, making the job of the IAP Press editor much easier. I am also grateful for her encouragement during the numerous long hours of work that inevitably goes into a book.

I was also aided immeasurably by ten people--scientists, philosophers, and laymen alike--who volunteered to read the book and make comments on each chapter as it was written. I thank each of them as well as those who made comments on the completed manuscript. Heartfelt thanks especially to Randy LaBouve, Joseph Martin, Daniel McLeod, and Raymond Rizzi. Particular thanks are in order for Fr. Benedict Ashley; his detailed and wise comments, as well as his friendship, were invaluable during the writing period. A special thanks to Michael Romalis, who was especially helpful in ironing out issues related to the exposition of Bell's theorem. Also, special thanks to James Stoner who gave in-person time to discuss his detailed comments.

In thanking all readers of the prepublication manuscript, I nonetheless retain all responsibility for whatever errors may remain; they were mine before their comments and remain so after.

This book was made possible by a grant from the Earhart Foundation. The year long writing period was also funded by the Discovery Institute which granted the remaining monies necessary for me to take the time off from my regular research activity. I am truly thankful to both organizations.

Galileo myth--that there is enmity between science and religion--may be the most important effect of this book. It would be wrong, however, to think that Rizzi is engaged in polemic, however important.

This book aims to place modern science in the wider context of human knowledge from which it can only escape by way of forgetfulness. Rizzi loves science and practices it with more than ordinary success. Reflection on the lacunae of scientific education and the deleterious effects on society of misrepresentations of science has made Rizzi a philosopher. He has written a book of fundamental importance, one that will earn and deserve a wide readership. Only a physicist could have written it. Almost anyone can read and understand it. To do so could be the beginning of wisdom.

Ralph McInerny
University of Notre Dame
April, 2004

Preface

*S*cience is increasingly important and, at the same time, less and less able to give a good defense of itself and has even spawned its own enemies. Sound philosophy, the sole remedy, is almost unknown. In our culture, only that which is "scientific" is considered truly known; indeed all else is considered mere opinion. Since science is such an integral part of our modern mindset, one ought to start with science to introduce both the need for philosophy and philosophy itself. Further, in our culture, ironically, only a scientist has the credibility to say where to look for these answers. In addition, a scientist who knows philosophy is uniquely aware of the problems that confront the modern mindset in relation to philosophy. When I was young, first learning science, I looked for a book with these ingredients to no avail. I had pressing questions and no single place to find the answers. Still today, all interested in science confront the same disturbing questions that I had. I wrote The Science Before Science to answer that need.

There are a growing number of people who believe everything is merely appearance. Through various interpretations of quantum mechanics, noteworthy scientists have said fundamentally the same thing. Science, the study of nature, is then the study of what? It is as if, after a long calculation of shifting things to one side of an equation, one gets "1 = 4" and says, "look

what I've discovered!" instead of, "yikes, what did I do wrong?"
Of course, scientists, while doing their science, implicitly take for
granted that what they study exists. But how is it that anyone can
deny so self-evident and foundational a thing as the fact that the
real is real? Sound philosophy is sorely needed today. Not a
branch of linguistics or mathematics or a descriptive science, but a
science that reaches the fundamental level of man's questions.

How does one read a book that is answering such
fundamental questions, a book that is basically about everything?
It is written to be read at multiple levels. Each must read the book
at his own level trying not to get pulled, by the many interesting
subtopics, into the next level too early; done at the appropriate
time, no level will appear too difficult to penetrate; done too early,
one will spend more time than necessary digesting the concepts.
Don't get bogged down; rather, allow yourself to experience the
joy of discovery as you encounter each new idea. A glossary is
provided to give quick access to terms. Also, footnotes are
provided to give further depth for those who are interested. Still,
this is an introductory book; to encourage you to go even deeper,
the Books of Interest section is provided at the end of the book.

The aim of this book is to relate wisdom. Wisdom ultimately
does not come from without. It can only come from within. The best
a book can do is put forward the ideas, the thoughts that will spur
the reader to look for himself and to give assent himself. One can
lead a horse to water...In more concrete terms, philosophy
requires much meditation, one must live with the ideas, test them,
fight with them, and finally make them one's own. This process
happens in the sciences all the time with each new generation of
students. We need it to happen also in the science before science if
science is to survive as the sincere search for truth.

In the book, I uncover the foundations of science; each
chapter builds on the previous. The plan of the book is to first
reemphasize the need for wisdom and make it known that much of
what we know is not knowledge at all but belief. This involves
many startling discoveries about our own thinking and even the

*need for trusting others. We then begin the task of seeing what we
do know and how to solidify it into true science.*

*In Chapters 3 and 4, you will encounter topics and
discussions that are little known. Though the subjects will be
familiar, the insights into them will be, for nearly all, completely
new. As Mark Schneider, MD, said to me, "I used to believe the
things you point to in your book, but now I know them and no one
can take them from me." Another reviewer said after reading
Chapter 3, "it seems I should have known all this, because they are
things I've encountered all my life, but I did not really know any of
it." The depth may seem vast, but again the reader should resist
the temptation to try to understand all at once. I utilize a spiral
approach to the topics so that the reader is not expected to grasp a
given concept completely in the first encounter. Terminologies and
concepts are revisited throughout the book. Again, the book is
written so that the reader, on the first read, can obtain a
fundamental understanding and on the second reading deepen that
understanding.*

*In Chapter 5, we apply this important new general
knowledge to fascinating sci-fi like questions about animal and
robotic intelligence, as well as to the possible engineering of
people and animals. In Chapter 6, we move back to more
fundamental ground to see how all knowledge fits together and see
what the place of modern science is. This chapter answers the key
questions about how arguably the major intellectual controversy of
all history started and why it continues.*

*In Chapter 7, we enter the fascinating realm of applying
our knowledge to problems in modern science. The six sections of
this chapter can be read individually or skipped on a first read.
However, I always recommend a light read (as earlier, though not
as strongly, as these subjects aren't absolutely needed for later
chapters) even if things seem to be beyond your current
understanding--just get what can be had and move on. For those
not as interested in the detailed questions, I recommend reading
the Big Bang and the Evolution sections, including those related to
chance, before moving on to Chapter 8.*

Once you've reached Chapter 8, you are in for a real treat as you've reached the top of the mountain. While you still have to walk to see the full view, the uphill travel is over.

Chapter 8 proves the existence of God, but be careful not to skip directly to it and expect to follow the proofs. There is a reason why there are seven chapters before it. Chapter 9 gives the basis for answering moral questions, like: What limits should be put on science's exploration and use of its findings? Chapter 10 brings to bear all our acquired knowledge on a question whose answer will decide the future of our culture: How should we do science?

If this question is not answered adequately, science will stay disconnected from, or worse answer via scientism, man's deepest questions, and the widespread feeling of displacement and malaise can only be expected to deepen. With no integrated balance, technocratic thought and devices will reign, and man will feel increasingly alienated as less and less room is allotted for his humanity. It is only by accessing the enduring truths that we can place our scientific knowledge in context and regain meaning in our increasingly chaotic and busy lives. It is my sincere hope that, in the pages to come, you will encounter these truths and experience the great joy they elicit.

A Note for My Scientific Colleagues

The *most* *formidable* *enemy* *of* *science* *today* *is* *subjectivism. Essential to science, as Einstein once observed, is the understanding that the world exists independent of us and of our understanding of it. Against science, subjectivists, especially in the form of deconstructionists, hold that everything is a construct made by us. Physicist Alan Sokal, as you will see in the first chapter, did much to manifest the power currently wielded by the movement. Unfortunately, scientists have not always answered the subjectivist's in a convincing manner. In some cases, scientists themselves, including leading ones, have for example, claimed via quantum mechanics that the world does not exist when we're not looking at it. What better way to feed subjectivist belief than to propound that their belief is given by science?*

The confusion about the meaning and foundation of science often starts inadvertently early. In my field of physics, for example, sophomore high school students are told to draw the path of an object on an x-y plot; the student plots time on one axis and position of the object on the other. If the object is moving at constant speed, the student draws a line representing the history of the object's motion as it moves, say, from the left side of the room to the right. But note: the student has drawn a picture which represents time as if it is all at once, because, after all, the picture is all at once. In the picture, the object is both at the left and right simultaneously. The path for not making proper distinctions about time is in place. It is the beginning of a process of habituation that can make one think time is reducible or "nearly" reducible to space. In the process one ignores and later forgets in varying degrees the things that one has deliberately left behind in order to facilitate analysis. These issues come to a head when one later studies Einstein's relativity theory, for example.

This book lays the foundation that answers the subjectivists and other objections to science as well as unravels the many misinterpretations of modern science that have arisen. Much of what is said will be readily accepted as obvious, but much also will be very new. The reader will be asked to step back from his particular field of interest and look at its roots and to be careful to distinguish starting points from conclusions. He will need to be willing to broaden his thinking, for each field has its own particular methodology and habits of thought that cannot go unchanged into other arenas. For example, in physics, I am used to thinking in terms of mathematics. I can relate to the sci-fi spoof, Hitchhikers Guide to the Universe, which asks, "What is the meaning of life, the universe and everything?" and gives the answer: 42. Part of the answer's humor derives from the fact that nearly all of what we, as physicists, do demands mathematical answers; yet we do not expect one to that question. In short, we frequently need broader means than the merely mathematical, yet we are not exposed and do not have facility with broader thinking, and so we instinctively withdraw from the unfamiliar and try to use our familiar tools. Other fields have parallel issues. Such tendencies, I think, bear close watching. In general, it might be helpful to bear in mind a statement that helped one of my scientific readers better understand how to approach such broader topics, "Don't dissect the argument down to nothing and try to understand it after you've killed it, let yourself understand it then dissect it." Or in other words, "Don't hone right away onto the detail, stay back and look for awhile first."

The book is written to develop the foundation of science in a logical manner that builds each chapter on the previous. In Chapters 3 and 4, one will encounter topics and discussions that are little known. Though the subjects will be familiar, the insights into them will be, for nearly all, completely new. The depth may seem vast, but one should resist the temptation to try to understand all at once. I utilize a spiral approach to the topics so that the reader is not expected to grasp a given concept completely in the first encounter. Terminologies and concepts are revisited throughout the book, including in a glossary. The book is written so that the reader, on the first read, can obtain a fundamental understanding and on the second reading deepen that understanding.

Chapter 1

Science without Wisdom

*W*e have been taught that the earth revolves around the sun. In fact, our world revolves around modern science. Modern science permeates our collective mindset. Think not? Consider what you actually know about the earth's motion. Do you feel as if the earth's surface is moving at 1,000 miles an hour due to its rotation? Do you feel like the earth is moving 67,000 miles an hour around the sun? Indeed, we still use language that indicates how strongly we do not sense any motion of the earth. Any of us might say: "It's getting dark, because *the sun is going down.*" Even among those with an advanced scientific education, many have not considered on what grounds they believe and say these things. Hence, for most, the motion of the earth is more than a matter of faith; it is a matter of *unconscious* faith. That is, it is one thing to trust an expert's word, but it is another level of faith completely to not even be conscious of the fact that one is taking another's word.

The medieval Christian took the Bible as true on faith, but he was conscious that it was faith. Yet, we identify with the conclusions of the science of the earth's motion to such an extent that we consider ourselves personally superior in *knowledge* to our predecessors if we think the earth goes around the sun. Ironically, we even consider with some disdain those who used to think otherwise, because we imagine that they were at the mercy of rigid systems of doctrine that did not leave room for personal independent thought. Of course, the fact that the earth moves around the sun is a valid conclusion of physics, but, for most, it is

1

not a personal conclusion at all. It is part of an unrecognized belief system attained during childhood.

The same arguments apply to the roundness of the earth. We all believe the earth is round. Why? Many have not even asked why. Why not? Unconscious (or blind) faith in science. After all, how many have done the experiments to verify the shape? How many have actually seen the earth from space? How many have flown all the way around the earth, watching to verify a continuous heading that would end in a great circle flight around the earth? Irony appears again when one discovers that most today think medieval men were victims of ideological strictures that kept them from knowing the earth was round. To add insult to injury, history tells us that medieval men knew the earth was round. For instance, sailors were long familiar with the effect of the curvature of the earth, allowing one to see ships at a distance when in the crow's nest, but not when on the deck.

Want still another example of science's influence on our thought? Consider what is said about the nothingness of the atom. We are taught that an atom is composed of electrons and a nucleus. The electron is point-like and most of the mass of the atom is in the nucleus of the atom. If the nucleus of the atom were such that it was the size of a basketball, the "edge" of the atom would be two *miles* away. It is thus said and believed that the atom is filled with mostly space. The inference is then drawn that since we are made of atoms, we are mostly nothing. From this, the atom becomes associated with a sort of underlying nihilism. We are made to feel that somehow our senses and our common sense have lied to us and are untrustworthy. Even more, we are left with the sometimes unarticulated thought that we are really, after all, relatively unimportant and worthless. Many adopt such attitudes as basic unchallengeable truths.

In reality, science makes use of our senses in its collection of data. We must, for example, trust our senses and logic to get conclusions. If one generates a scientific conclusion that is, in turn, used to nullify the trustworthiness of our senses, we destroy the scientific conclusion itself because it always depends on experimental data that in turn depend on our senses. This effect, in turn, of course, destroys the reason that we distrusted our senses in the first place. The conclusions of science are a second, third, or fourth level of knowledge that is dependent on a first level. In fact, the activity of science itself is a continual refutation of nihilism, because it continually trusts that the world is understandable; even more, that it is understandable by us. We are thus so far from nothing that we can understand in profound ways the things around us. Though the anti-common sense conclusion is demonstrably false, most believe it somehow a part of the lessons of science. For some reason, science, left to itself, seems to generate a nihilistic element in the culture.

Thus, even those who find science disagreeable must agree that it affects the way they think. Further, through technology, its close relative, science impinges on nearly every human activity. Some have argued that science has severely damaged both of these areas of human life: our thinking and our practical human activity.

They argue that science is the reason our thinking has turned very mechanical and unconcerned with the value of the individual man and his life. They further continue that science has introduced concepts like time dilation in relativity, the supposed non-causality in quantum mechanics, and evolution in biology, that have robbed us of our human patrimony. They say it has alienated modern man from himself. Many speak, with good reason, of a rift between two cultures: the humanities and the sciences; not a few place the blame with science. The present modern science-oriented culture has bred groups who deny that real knowledge is possible. These groups and others attack science as being purely a sociopolitical phenomenon; they say its findings only tell us about scientists and their culture, not the real world. Such ideas taken to heart will eventually undermine real science. It appears that science has hatched, or helped hatch, a culture with elements that are potentially destructive of science. The critics thus can lay claim that science is somehow suicidal.

Recently, the trend in a certain segment of the humanities became so prominently anti-rational and so obviously purely a tool for the promotion of ideology that a scientist, Alan Sokal, felt the need to respond. He wrote an article that purported to explain many already commonly accepted ideological (also called "politically correct") tenets by means of advanced theoretical concepts in mathematics and physics. He knew his arguments were completely unfounded, yet he knew that it would be accepted for publication.

A prominent humanities journal printed the long article and it received rave reviews. He then stunned the same academic audience by revealing in another journal some time later that the paper was a hoax. He packed the Princeton University physics department colloquium with people wanting to hear him and a humanities professor discuss the issue. The article also sparked an intense debate in the journal *Physics Today*. Many in Princeton and elsewhere were intrigued by the anti-rational attitude that had invaded the academy and that was so closely related to science as to appear to be spawned by it. It was also a spectacle of another fissure opening between science and the humanities.

In the arena of technology, the critics blame science and scientists for nuclear weaponry that can destroy whole populations. They blame science for pollution, for leaving us at the mercy of machines instead of people, and for overcomplicating our lives. The last sentiment can be elicited from almost anyone on the phone wading through endless voice programmed computers to get to an operator.

Of course, most people *do* recognize the benefits science has wrought. They cheer the new cures for old diseases and the striking increase in sanitary conditions. They note the convenience of modern homes, especially modern kitchens, laundry rooms, and bathrooms. The same appreciation is not missing for communications, transportation and computation.

The most zealous of the critics recognize that science cannot be the only problem. However, these facts do not make the negatives science has accrued any less real. In light of the criticism, we are prompted to ask the obvious question: what is wrong with studying nature? What's wrong with science? We are compelled to answer: nothing-- nothing, at least, with science as science. How can knowledge insofar as it is knowledge be bad?

What, then, is wrong? If it is not the study of nature per se, it must be something closely linked with it. Sort of. In fact, it is the absence of something that should be closely linked with science. We are missing a certain wisdom, a certain understanding that would properly integrate science into our intellectual life and our daily activities. We need philosophy.

Philosophy is that knowledge (in Latin, *scientia*) or science that seeks and studies first principles of all things. In a way analogous to modern science, philosophy does not directly satisfy any material need; man lived thousands of years without it. It satisfies our need to know. We all have a natural desire to know. Without "why" and "what," we would be a race of mutes; no, worse, we would be savage mutes. In science, we often have deeper "whys" after we get major discoveries; we have many questions about the scientific discoveries themselves. We need the science that comes before science to answer such questions. Literally, philosophy is love *(philia)* of wisdom *(sophia)*. Philosophy, in this literal meaning, is already giving us direction; it is saying it will give us these answers if we allot the effort required. We must want (love) to posses this "knowledge before science." One must activate the gift of wonder that Einstein praised as so good and crucially important.

Published by IAP Press, Baton Rouge, LA
In conjunction with AuthorHouse. 06/24/04
IAP Press: IAPpress@iapweb.org

ISBN: 1-4184-6504-6 (sc)
ISBN: 1-4184-6503-8 (dj)
Library of Congress Control Number: 2004093835
Includes bibliographical references, glossary and index.
Science/Philosophy
Q174 .R59 2004
501--dc20

Printed in the United States of America
Bloomington, Indiana

Chapter 2

A False Sense of Certitude

*T*o begin to awaken our sense of awe again, we must philosophize. In science, one's awe at nature is increased each time one makes a quantum leap in understanding. It is an experience that Einstein calls near religious. This experience is nothing other than the enjoyment of glimpsing something of the unity and order of nature.[1] One of the first times I had such an insight was when, as a teenager, I saw that the theoretical Maxwell[2] speed curve (calculated in 1859) plotted on the same graph with measured data (first taken at high precision in 1955), and the measured data all fell nicely along the curve (see Figure 2-1 that shows this plot).[3] Anyone who has had such an "Aha" or "Eureka!" experience knows that it makes you want to see more. The same happens at an even deeper level in philosophy.

---

[1] The same experience occurs in other fields with analogical but not identical meaning. For example, in a subfield of modern mathematics, one sees the unity of a given subfield rather than necessarily and primarily an order in nature. Here we speak of science in the sense as the study of nature.

[2] James Clerk Maxwell (1831-79) is a physicist in a class with Einstein and Newton.

[3] The order of the world (it has a particular order, otherwise the data would not consistently fall on any curve) and the seemingly miraculous ability of mathematics (in this case the derivation that led to the equation of the Maxwell curve) to describe the physical world (what renowned physicist Eugene Wigner called "the unreasonable effectiveness of mathematics") are two things that are seen in this plot.

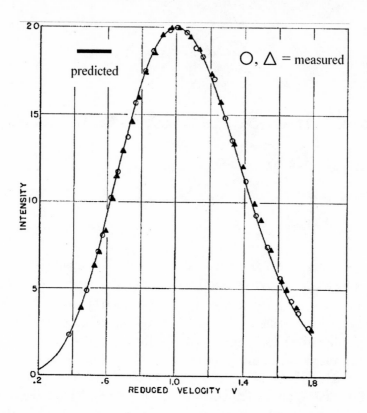

Figure 2-1: The solid line shows the predictions of Maxwell for the molecular speed distribution. The circles and triangles are measured values. Note the marvelous agreement between prediction and experiment![4]

In Chapter 1, we already began philosophic exploration at two levels. First, we examined the roots of our scientific "knowledge" in three examples (the motion of the earth, the shape of the earth, and the nothingness of the atom). Second, this examination--backed up by the cultural effects of science--revealed

---

[4] The experiment measures the distribution of the speeds of Thallium atoms at different temperatures. The circles represent the experimental data obtained at a temperature of about 1,100 F (870 K). The triangles are for about 1,240 F (944 K). The Intensity is in arbitrary units, and the reduced velocity is the speed divided by the most probable speed (that's why 1.0 is the peak). The chart is from Miller and Kusch, Physical Review, volume 99, page 1,344.

to us the need for something beyond science. We found we need a "science before science."

When we said something came "before science" we did not mean what a literalist might mean. He might say the only thing that came before science is many centuries without science. We did not mean a chronological "before"; coming first in time was not the issue we raised. "Before" in the sense that a cause precedes an effect is at issue. There is also a second sense in which we meant it. When one knows what a triangle is, he already has the idea of what a side is. So the idea of a side comes before the idea of a triangle. Note that it does not have to be in the order of time. They can be grasped simultaneously, yet the side will always be before the triangle, because the side is required in the idea of a triangle.

We cannot avoid philosophy. To attempt to show that one can avoid philosophy is itself philosophy. In this book, we have already learned some philosophy. The very recognition of philosophy (the science before science) is philosophy, and the above clarifications are further deepening our understanding, and thus are more philosophy.

We can continue such reflections by looking closely at not just our conclusion but at the examples that led to it. If the conclusion is so fruitful, we expect more yield from the field of information from which we harvested the conclusion. Let's look.

All three of the examples in the first chapter share one aspect. They make us note the distinction between knowledge and belief and that we do not often *know* where one begins and another ends.

In the case of the earth's motion (revolution and rotation), we saw that most of us do not *know* the real evidence for such motion; in fact, circumstantial evidence seems to belie such motion. We know what others tell us about it and we believe it to be true. This is belief; even more, it is belief that is mistakenly taken as knowledge. This type of belief is in a class by itself. In it, knowing and believing have not just been tangled up, they've both been reduced to belief. What both explains how such a thing can happen and demands particular concern is that the reduction completely escapes conscious thought.

In order to unwind the issues involved here, we have to be precise about the meaning of words. We don't want to logic chop and thereby leave out part of reality in the name of clarity, but we do want to make appropriate distinctions. An aside is appropriate here because of the importance of this point.

The temptation to sacrifice reality for clarity has trapped many an otherwise strong and competent thinker.[5] We can resist better if we recognize that reality is very complicated and that we are prone to error, especially in the philosophic arena. St. Thomas Aquinas[6] (1225? –1274 AD) noted, in the thirteenth century, that mathematics is much more connatural to us (in tune or sync with our innate abilities) than philosophy, and that it is much harder *for us* to reach certainty in philosophy than in mathematics.[7]

Figure 2-2: St. Thomas Aquinas holding Aristotle's work on fundamental physics.

(Drawing by Alejandro Ezcurra, copyright by IAP 2003)

Hence, we have to be careful not to require things to fall into the type of study that is easiest for us and thus most clear to us. In the domain of physics, Albert Einstein recognized the problem when he warned that as coherent, clear, and attractive as his theory

---

[5] The great mathematician Rene Descartes (1596-1650) is one notable example. See Chapters 3 and 6.

[6] St. Thomas Aquinas, a Dominican Friar, lived during the time of the coming of age of the University.

[7] We will discuss this more in Chapter 6 when we explore the scope, methodology, and definition of the various sciences.

of general relativity[8] was, only experiment (i.e. the real world) would determine its worth. Likewise, in philosophy, we seek the real. The history of philosophy is littered with corpses of eminently **clear** wrong theories. For example, Kant, Hegel, and Leibniz,[9] all great minds, fashioned great systems of clarity and force that, nonetheless, crashed against the rock of reality. For example, Kant's system demanded that Euclidean geometry was the only type of geometry that the mind of man could conceive; it was not long after him that Gauss[10] discovered non-Euclidean geometry. Hegel's way of thinking led him to think it mandatory that there must be only seven planets, not in the sense of a tentative theory, but in the philosophical sense of an overarching requirement. He ridiculed European astronomers when they looked for a planet between Mars and Jupiter, because it was "against reason" for a planet to be there— in fact, this is where the asteroid belt[11] was found. Of a different order, but still relevant, is Leibniz's system that made it mandatory that this be the best of all possible worlds. Hence, a clarity that appears too soon or is too broad and facile is likely to be a counterfeit achieved by ignoring the full depth and breadth of the reality under consideration. We thus have a related admonition: philosophy is a real science, a real discipline requiring real work; it is not an armchair discipline.

In common usage, knowledge can mean anything we take as relatively certain for whatever reason. We can call this knowledge in the *improper* sense. I have knowledge *proper* only when I come to conclusions based on facts and principles that I have personally "seen"[12] and, if required, based on a chain of reasoning that I have walked through myself. *Belief* in the generic

---

[8] The self-consistency and force of this grand theory are hard to overstate. It is the theory that gives us black holes and the big bang theory. It is the theory that superseded that great and beautiful theory of gravity of Isaac Newton…not by destroying it but by making it a very special case of a much bigger system.

[9] Kant (1724-1804) and Hegel (1770-1831) were philosophers; Leibniz (1646-1716) was a philosopher and a mathematician (co-discoverer with Newton (1642-1727) of calculus).

[10] Karl F. Gauss (1777-1855) was one of the greatest mathematicians ever.

[11] The asteroid belt is a "belt" of thousands of small planets in orbit around the sun between Mars and Jupiter.

[12] "Seen" is meant to include any sensorial data, not just sight, and in the case of principles, it refers to personal apprehension of them.

sense means having a level of probable, but not certain, conviction that is usually largely based on the word of another. In this sense, improper knowledge is thus a species of belief. *Belief* in the proper sense means trusting the word of another. If I say, "I believe the sky is blue" and I am looking at it and it is blue, then I am using the word *belief* improperly. One cannot know and believe the same thing at the same time and in the same manner. If I know something, someone telling me it does not change my state to one of both knowledge and belief. I do not, in the proper sense, believe the teller is correct; I know he is correct. If I say I believe in my friend and I know him, then I must be referring to different attributes of my friend. For example, I know his basic character and I believe that he will make good decisions.

Revolution and Rotation of the Earth

What then can be said about the common man's trust that the earth goes around the sun? Examine a likely scenario. The man in question is told during his childhood by one of his schoolteachers that the earth moves around the sun. He is then told how it happens and the history behind the discoveries. Yet, he does no experiment and no analysis; he simply accepts it because of the authority of his teacher. This is a belief hanging from a chain of beliefs. First, it involves trust that the teacher who told him is truthful and has transmitted the information accurately. Second, it involves trusting the authority that taught the teacher who, let us suppose, did the experiments and followed the arguments. Our man must trust that this final authority did the experiments right, interpreted them correctly, reasoned correctly, and passed the result on accurately. But, the chain is made strong over time as people of authority reaffirm the lesson that he was taught as a child. If all goes well, our man acquires experience that enables him to judge who are real authorities and who are not. But, in the end, what he has is not proper knowledge, but faith based on authority. The certainty of the belief here rests on the trustworthiness of the authority and its attending cultural structure. Of course, our man will have *infra-scientific*[13] experience, experience that has not been philosophically examined, that he will be unconsciously referring to and judging whether the motion of the earth really occurs or not, but this is not proper knowledge because it is below the surface.

Scientists who have *not* done the experiments also have faith based on authority; nonetheless, they have a degree of certainty that is lacking in the above case. They will have ancillary knowledge that gives the statement more believability. They will have studied the principle of inertia. They will have done the basic inertia-related experiments somewhere in their education and are *conscious* of the rather odd fact that when an object is thrown, it continues in motion after the force is removed. They also know of an effect related to this inertial effect, the tendency of an object to stay in its state of uniform *rotation* unless acted on by an outside force. With this background, they can *personally* understand something of explanation of the earth's rotation and revolution. What's more, they are conscious of the most relevant consequence of the law of inertia; they understand and observe it nearly every day. For example, a trained (or just thoughtful) observer in a moving vehicle will note that objects in the car behave the same as they do when the car is not moving. In fact, someone in a completely closed[14] train car that is moving at uniform velocity cannot tell he is moving.[15] Knowledge of these types of facts gives scientists reasons that interlock at multiple places with what they are told about the motion of the earth.

The above understanding of inertia, for example, partially explains why we do not feel the motion of the earth. Yet, the earth's motions are not linear, but rotational motions. Objects, like us in such a rotating frame, should feel other forces (centrifugal and Coriolis forces) due to our slow but real veering off of our

---

[13] The prefix "*infra-*" means, "under" or "beneath," as in infrared light, which is "under" red (less energetic than red). *Scientific* is used here in its generic sense that derives from its Latin root *(scientia)* meaning knowledge.

[14] "Closed" means one is not allowed any observation that gives information about things outside the car. For example, observing shadows that come through the windows is violating the "closed" assumption.

[15] Vibration can give a clue that one is moving, but it is an indirect sign only. Here we are speaking about a sensation of the linear motion itself.

natural inertial path.[16] The scientists can do the calculation to prove the effect is too small to be sensed by us. Such interlocking points give scientists valid reason to give greater weight to the conclusions given them by authority. Yet, it still remains that until they do the experiments (as simple as they may be) and follow the arguments through, they do not *know,* in the proper sense, about the motion of the earth.

Roundness of the Earth

The case of the roundness of the earth is less complicated, at least in principle, because we can talk to astronauts who have seen that the earth is spherical. This would be only one level of trust. One may say, as some have (a scientist among them), "Hold on. What about satellite pictures of the earth? I've seen these, so I *know* the earth is round." Once again our unconscious trust in science and its high authority in our culture is revealed. The satellite pictures seem to have the force of knowledge, yet a second look reveals that concluding the earth's roundness from a photo is at least two-tier faith.

First, one must trust the editor of the publication that the picture has been reproduced faithfully and is what it purports to be, a picture of the earth. Remember, most of us have not seen the shape of the continents revealed on that scale. Before high-altitude pictures, it was only the group of men who surveyed the costal lines of a continent who had proper knowledge of the shape of the continent on the appropriate scale.[17] The three pictures below, Figure 2-3a-c, show the changing view of the continents and our world; they make us note how little different than our ancient ancestors most of us are in what we *actually know.* When we see the satellite pictures of the earth, it is only because we have seen other similar pictures that we think, "Oh, there's the earth." The

---

[16] This description is a Newtonian one; the general relativistic description would be different, but it includes the effects discussed as well, although it accounts for them in a different way.

[17] This assumes, of course, that they surveyed *and* calculated *and* mapped the results. If no one did all these tasks then no one had proper knowledge of the coastal shape, because everyone was dependant on trusting the work of another.

sense of independent verification *only* comes from having seen yet another picture like the ones others have told us is the earth.

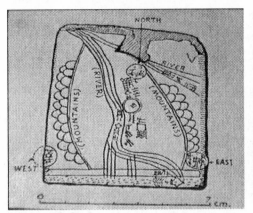

Figure 2.3a,b: (a) Left figure shows reconstructed map from Ga-Sur (2500 BC), believed to be earliest known map. (b) Right figure shows reconstruction of Homer's view of the earth (900BC). (courtesy of Jim Siebold)

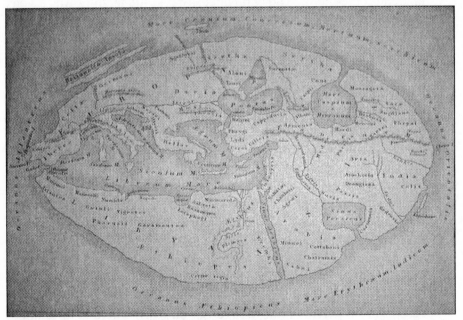

Figure 2-3c: Reconstruction of the world map according to Dionysius (124AD). All these maps show the evolving picture of the shape of the land masses on earth. (courtesy of Jim Siebold)

Second, one must trust that the device that took the picture was designed and made correctly, so it accurately portrayed what was there. Again, moderating factors like experience with and knowledge of cameras can supply ancillary knowledge that increases the degree of one's trust in the truth of what is seen. Also, taking information from an authority or individual whose accuracy and truthfulness has been proved out multiple times in the past increases the reasonableness of one's trust. Collaboration from multiple sources of authority does the same. But, this type of "knowledge" still does not fall under the sharp definition of knowledge proper. It is not knowledge but very reasonable and necessary human faith.

We do not have to look far for examples of photographs that give--deliberately or otherwise--misleading information. Even more interesting is the doubtability of videos and photographs. There have been claims, occasionally flaring up into full-blown controversial television and radio reports that America never landed on the moon. The claimants say that the landing was a hoax and that the pictures were generated on the ground by stagecraft and technical manipulation. The fact that it takes a significant scientific expertise to understand apparently simple pictures of the men on the moon worked in the favor of the claimants. Few have the requisite expertise and those who do don't spend their time investigating such things. Thus, it is not hard for the layman to fall into arguments that sound plausible. Specifically, the claimants made arguments that the things in the picture could not possibly be the way they appeared. They said, for example, that there should be many more stars in the sky than appeared in the moon shots. They worried about the dust sticking together too much in the footprints on the lunar soil. Interpreting such things takes scientific expertise that the average viewer could not learn and apply with any certainty in a short TV special. Yet, the claimants manage to show, quite unintentionally, that as necessary and important as it is to learn from well-informed, trustworthy authority, such learning is based not on personal knowledge but on trust. There is little doubt that men went to the moon; we have converging evidence from numerous diverse sources.[18] Such evidence makes the probability that it did not happen vanishingly small; yet it still remains true that it is not the type of "knowledge" that we have of the book in one's hand. We know the latter in the sharp, proper sense.

Of course, not all knowledge is what might be called direct knowledge, such as knowing that this object called a book is in front of me. There are things that one can deduce from such facts that create a chain from which a new piece of knowledge hangs. For instance, from the fact that I am reading a book, I can conclude that someone wrote the book. Yet, this knowledge is just as real knowledge as the first. However, as one proceeds to more complicated and multi-tiered reasoning, the possibility of error in reasoning increases and the need for care and rechecking increases. One must always proceed from what is more known to what is less known. Because of the time and effort that must be expended, it is clear that we cannot know everything.

All of us depend on knowledge in the improper sense. Because much of this type of knowledge has a virtual certainty, we can continue to use the word *knowledge,* but we should attempt to bring as many things as prudent under the umbrella of real knowledge. Prudence[19] demands that we bring first the most important things under the umbrella and then, in order of importance, as many of the rest as our abilities, time and station in life require and allow. It is a gain in (proper) knowledge to see that we depend on each other's truthfulness and accuracy to do what we do well and with minimum error.

Scientists have a particular burden in this regard, because if science is to progress they must be able to trust each other. **No scientist** can do every current experiment and follow every current argument, let alone try to repeat all that has been done up till now.[20] He must rely on others. Knowledge of this fact reinforces the need for us to always tell the truth.

---

[18] Also, we have all kinds of ancillary knowledge that interlocks with that evidence.

[19] See Chapter 9 on moral virtues.

[20] This not to say, of course, that a given scientific error will not be discovered in the end. Such errors will infect the community for a period, both in terms of the direct damage to real science and in the damage to the implicit trust that is needed for scientific work to proceed according to fact, not politics alone. The

The Foundations of Modern Science

In general, we have to be particularly cognizant of the foundations of modern science, so that false philosophies, like the one associated with the atom in the previous chapter, do not become associated with the otherwise trustworthy structure of science. If we are not cognizant, we can only expect the result will be the anti-rational, anti-science attitude we outlined in the first chapter. For, as in the example of the atom, people can draw nihilistic conclusions from a false understanding of what science is and then can take their conclusion as having the full weight of scientific authority.

In truth, one has a choice: the "science before science," or irrationality at the core of one's intellectual life. Of course, most people do not make an explicit choice; most make an implicit choice in favor of philosophy, *except* when they are asked about philosophy. They, thus, oscillate between unconscious acceptance and a conscious rejection. In the latter state, they deny that the title science "knowledge" belongs to philosophy. They think of philosophy as vague, feeling-oriented and subjective.

The "science before science," called philosophy, is the study of the first principles of all things. An unconscious (or, worse, an explicit) rejection of philosophy is rejection of the science of wisdom that alone allows one to consciously and intelligently assess one's own thinking.[21] Such a rejection leaves the root of one's thinking ungrounded, hanging in the air, where it is free to blow in the wind of one's will. One is left, at the core level, with no option but blind faith. Such faith, in turn, tends

---

real point is that science done as a community depends radically on being able to trust. If you could not trust anyone in *any* way, you could have no science as we know it, not even a limping science. To see this with clarity, think, for example, about publications. A completely dishonest publisher would not put anything resembling the original authors' papers in his journal; he would instead stock it full with misleading and wrong information. If all publishers were like this example case, so much for learning about what others do by reading.

[21] One can oscillate back and forth as stated above, but it remains true that one has no thought-out foundation for one's thinking.

towards one of two poles: the religious and anti-religious. The two poles are really one when sought in this way, because they both lead to anti-rational attitudes; they lead respectively to anti-rational fideism and anti-rational subjectivism; reason is lost in "God" or reason is lost in self.

The latter, for example, comes in many current interpretations of quantum mechanics, where it is thought the observer creates the reality. Of course, many scientists and laymen alike avoid falling into such holes by just not following the logic of their unarticulated positions to their unavoidable conclusion. Such is the case with anyone who wants to deny *fundamental* principles (see Chapters 3, 4, 5, and 9 for more on such principles); he can say the words of denial, but he cannot accomplish the denial without mental suicide (turning off his mind). For instance, to say that there is "no such thing as truth" is to say words without meaning. It is proclaiming the very thing you want to deny, for if the statement is true, it belies itself. It proclaims as truth that there is no such thing as truth. Such is the trouble with such fundamental error; by the very act of articulating it, one gives it more than its due. One assigns a group of words to the fundamental error that make it appear to have meaning. In fact, this problem appears with all error at different levels. When one tries to articulate an erroneous position, one can articulate what's true in it; that is, one can articulate what is not error in the given position. But, what is wrong in the position can only be presented by giving it a force that it really does not have. Hence, to explain the error itself, one, in some sense, always gives error what it does not have. Error as error is a *lack* or *privation* of order or unity in our knowledge; hence, of itself, it is nothing. When one tries to say what nothing is, one always ends in trouble, because nothing *is* not. Hence, only those things that are true have any real force.

A danger particular to our scientific culture arises because of the specialized nature of the modern sciences,[22] that is, sciences that require particular experimental, theoretical and methodological training. If people are unaware of the "science before science," they will think that the modern sciences are a closed system

---

[22] Examples of such sciences include what one, in ordinary conversation, now means by physics, chemistry, and biology.

sufficient unto themselves and exclusive of all else. If all sciences have the special nature of modern sciences, it becomes necessary to substitute belief for knowledge when crossing into many fields, because one cannot hope to obtain such specialized training in all subjects. While this will always be true at a technical level, it should not be true at the deepest level, because, being the study of one reality, all the sciences (fields of knowledge) are ultimately related to each other. In short, the science that is both the unifying underpinning and the general or "big picture" view of the various subjects, i.e. philosophy, will receive no attention. Absent conscious philosophizing, those in each field will tend to develop uncritical philosophical positions, which will usually not even be recognized as philosophical, from *within* that specialized science. More general experience and thinking will thus be excluded a priori.

Because of this, an expert in one field will be unable to truly critique the philosophical[23] position of an expert in another field. Hence, in such an environment or system, **philosophical error will tend to be compounded** rather than resolved. In other words, the system will be unstable, not self-corrective, with respect to such error. In such a system, particular error *within* a given field is stable, self-corrective, but this doesn't help our situation. Indeed, instability in any one field would not be cataclysmic like the system instability we are discussing. The system is unstable with respect to foundational error, error about the very ground on which the fields exist, error that can cause self-destruction of the system itself.

Sound philosophy is the remedy to such pitfalls. Recall that all the truth we have uncovered in this book so far comes *without* doing particular experiments or having *particular* expertise, experience or even training in analysis. Philosophy draws not on particular experience, but on what philosophers call *common experience*. It requires much particular effort, attention and even vocabulary, but it does not draw on expertise in a particular technique, but on a type of thinking that all men do spontaneously.

---

[23] Philosophy will still occur, but it will masquerade as part of a specialized science.

Nothingness and the Atom

How then does science without philosophy lead to conclusions like the one relating to the atom (from Chapter one), and how do we untangle the warranted belief in the conclusions of science from the unwarranted unscientific pseudo-philosophy? The conclusion looks inescapable. If the atom is mostly nothing, and we are atoms arranged in a certain way, how do we escape the conclusion that we are mostly nothing as well?

To find the answer, we can either start from the top and work down, or from the bottom and work up. By so stating the alternatives, we have already uncovered the seed of the answer. There is an order to our knowledge; some things we know immediately, and other things are derivative in varying degrees. It is the levels of knowledge that we brought out earlier in the comparison between the knowledge of the book in front of me and the derived (and proper) knowledge of the existence of an author of the book.

More specifically, we are much more certain of the existence of the book than in the atoms that make up the book. We can see and touch the book. [24] We cannot see or touch the atom. How do we even "know" atoms exist? How do we know what they are? These complicated questions, and related issues, will be addressed in detail in Chapters 6, 7 and 10. For now, it is enough to note two things. First, our knowledge of the atom is not *just* a third or fourth level of knowledge in the above sense. It is more complicated; one's knowledge of the atom is suspended by multiple chains in such a way that the loss of one component of the chain structure can completely change the way one would understand the atom. It is like a child's swing; loss of either support will end with the child on the ground. The type of knowledge that is conveyed up the chains is of a very specific, narrow type; to avoid misunderstanding the philosophical import of the message conveyed up the chains, one must be very careful and clear in moving from link to link. Second, because we know we are

---

[24] We can also hear it (by striking it) and even smell it—e.g., some have that new or old smell.

not "mostly nothing,"[25] the statement that "the atom is mostly nothing" cannot be correct, at least in the context in which the atom appears as a constituent of us and things. Saying that the atom is "mostly nothing" must be a way of stating something about the atom as seen by and exposed to our means and methods of scientific investigations. In other words, the premise must be wrong as interpreted, so we must reinterpret it. Again, the experimental facts and verified theories found by physics about the atom remain true, but we have to be more careful in our attempts to translate the layered, abstract and particular knowledge of physics into the direct, common knowledge of everyday language. Everyday language is by its nature laden with philosophical meaning. Hence, a translation of modern physics to everyday English that is *not* conscious of philosophical issues will tend to generate conundrums like the nothingness of the atom and of us.

Of course, scientists know they must, and do explain obvious things like the hardness of the table and the

---

[25] In the syllogism: "The atom is nothing, therefore we are mostly nothing, therefore we are of little value" (nihilism), there is an equating of the nothingness defined as "a vacuum" to the nothingness defined as "lack of reality" or void of being. This is strictly appropriate philosophically, because "a vacuum" means "nothing" in a philosophical context. However, although modern science often implies that vacuum means empty space, i.e., truly "nothing," the lack of sensitivity to philosophical issues has left us with some very ambiguous terms. At one moment, "vacuum" means nothing; at another, it means a sea of particles or a continuous field. So, even an isolated atom is not composed of mostly nothing in the way common parlance suggests. These issues will be discussed in Chapter 10.

The second point is that in any substance, especially man, much more is in play than what one sees in experiments on a "bare" atom or small group of atoms. To jump from an atom to man being "mostly nothing" (even if it were true of an atom) forgets that the situation of an isolated atom is qualitatively different from that of atoms in a macroscopic substance, for instance. In the latter case, many atoms of different types are acting together in a specific way. In the case of man, they act together not under the form of just life but of intelligent life. Thus, to conclude from one's belief about an isolated atom to man's mostly nothingness is even more outrageous. The tendency to do so comes from our underlying reductionist approach that assumes that everything can and really is just its components; that is, the whole is just the mathematical sum of its parts. As we will see in Chapters 6, 7, and 10, the reductionist approach (and generally all those approaches that we will later call empiriological) does have proper place in the *specialized* sciences.

impermeability of the skin. This is not the question. Explanation can occur at qualitatively different levels. Each modern science has become, by mode of practice, a purely special (in the narrowest sense) science. It works on one plane of explanation that is remarkably effective in its arena. But, its mode of explanation, which will be discussed in detail in Chapters 6 and 7, does not encompass philosophical questions; in fact, it deliberately excludes them in all but exceptional cases (and even there it's usually a reluctant admission of failure).

For example, science talks about man being made of atoms; actually a typical man contains 10^{28} atoms. [26] Science never poses the question: is man one thing or is he 10^{28} things? He cannot be in the same way and at the same time both 1 and 10^{28}. $1 \neq 10^{28}$. There is, of course, the explicit belief that the two do work together, but the question at the philosophical level is never addressed; it is left implicit...in fact, the reductionist philosophical conclusion that man is 10^{28} things, not one, is the unconscious position taken—a position that leads in turn directly to nihilism. The facts can only be truly reconciled by establishing how the two planes of explanation interact with each other. In short, one must understand how the philosophical fact that you are one, that you are not a multiplicity but an individual person, fits with the physics fact that you are 10^{28} atoms. This is a question for philosophy, not physics. We will deal with it in more detail in Chapter 10 when we have a clearer understanding of the issues involved. At this point, we can simply say the oneness of man's being demands that the atoms must be, in some way, subsumed (without destroying the atom's reality) by the being of the man. Here we begin to see reality itself is multi-layered. Reality is not a song with one voice, *univocal*, but

---

[26] It is illustrative of the special sciences to explain this calculation in detail. For purpose of calculation, assume a typical man is all water and is shaped like a cylinder 2 meters high and 1/4 meter in diameter (volume = .1 m^3). Using density of water =1g/cm^3 (gives 100 kg (220 pounds)) and weight of 18g/mole, he will then have approximately 10^28 atoms in his body. This simple calculation is a typical "order of magnitude" calculation in physics. Notice how much was abstracted away from what man really is in the calculation; it is a good metaphor for what is done in the special sciences. It gets a true and good result, but also leaves most of reality behind.

a song with multiple voices that can make up chords. Reality is not homogeneous but heterogeneous.

From *Blind Belief*
to
Proper Knowledge and Belief

To proceed further in understanding the meaning of the atom and similar problems, we need to establish more philosophic depth. How? We do what we have just done with the three examples of Chapter 1 (the motion of the earth, the shape of the earth, and the nothingness of the atom) with more of our infra-scientific thought and experience. This infra-scientific knowledge alluded to earlier is the experience of living; the older we are, the more of it we have. Each of us has it; I may have thought about these experiences here and there in a haphazard way, but they have never been subjected to the type of rigorous analysis that would qualify it properly as "science" *(scientia)*, as proper knowledge. The experience we are referring to is "common experience" that all people have. We all have it not because we share the same type of experiences by accidental fact (though this is no doubt true), but because we are all human beings. The amount and level of thought given to common experience will vary among individuals. It will require no special technique in thinking to mature the infra-scientific experience into philosophical nuggets, just thought and the development of habits of thought. Such habits will include a humility that concedes to reality--not self or thought--the place of primacy. It will also require the realization that philosophy is a real field requiring real work like any other field. Unlike other fields, the study is broad and deep; it is the attainment of wisdom. For so large a treasure, it is no surprise that it will have its own particular difficulties that must be overcome to attain it.[27] Only after infra-

---

[27] The great mathematician, Leibniz, said of ethics: "If geometry were as much opposed to our passions and present interests as is ethics, we would contest it and violate it but little less not withstanding the demonstrations of Euclid." Such a statement can help us see that the same danger accompanies the science of wisdom for similar reasons.

scientific experience is subject to deliberate reasoning and meditation, such as we have already begun, does one obtain philosophical results.

All three examples brought home the importance of distinguishing knowledge from belief. We also saw that the complexity of reality demands that we exercise great care in making distinctions without sacrificing reality for clarity.

We see more clearly the role of knowledge and belief in our intellectual life. We have also built up, by the very act of incorporating philosophical proper knowledge into our intellectual life, trust in the intelligibility of reality and our ability to grasp that intelligibility; this will continue as we bring more of our infra-scientific experience into the realm of knowledge proper. A great genius of the eleventh century, St. Anselm of Canterbury (1033-1109), said, "I believe that I may understand."[28] If belief is taken in the purely human sense[29] the words, in this translation, imply: I trust that I can understand things in the world. [30] Well, we do **not** have to trust that we can know; through philosophy, we know it. Yet, as we've seen through the examples, a culture, and hence the individuals who make it up, can avoid doing philosophy *consciously*,[31] and thus, such a culture can forget that it can and indeed in many cases does know. A radical sort of disbelief in the knowability of reality can set in. If we adopt an attitude and are in a milieu that denigrates our trust in our powers to understand, we will no longer seek understanding. One does not seek what he does not feel he can obtain. This applies to philosophy, science and all fields. Why would someone travel around the earth to get to the

---

[28] In the original Latin, the quote is: *"Credo ut Intelligam."* Also, he expressed this idea in a similar statement that he has "faith seeking understanding," or in Latin, *"fides quarerens intellectum."* In this form, it implies that beyond knowing that reality is knowable by us, we need the impetus to do the seeking. Renowned physicist Richard Feynman's statement that "One needs one's heart to follow an idea" captures it.

[29] St. Anselm was talking about Divine faith, not human faith.

[30] However, Anselm meant that he believes so that he can understand. It's only the translation that makes it seem to say something else. Yet, this meaning is not so different; we will discuss it in the next paragraph.

[31] That is, we can do philosophy without naming it and let it ride below the surface most of the time and thereby not let it have any directing power over our thinking and decisions.

other side if he thought it flat? He does not think there is an "other side" to get to and, worse, may think he would fall off an edge if he tried. In short, we cannot be skeptics at our core or we will lose our awareness of our ability to know and deaden our desire to know.

The examples also made us realize our dependence on improper knowledge. The original meaning of St. Anselm's quote comes to the fore here. His meaning is not so different from the meaning derived from the translation above. St. Anselm meant that he believes so that he can understand: "faith seeking understanding." The quote then means--at our level of discussion, i.e. human faith--that an ability to trust what you are told frees you. It frees you to probe your improper knowledge (the things you are told and believe) with confidence that they are true and thus that you will, with perseverance, finally succeed in converting some of this improper knowledge (belief) to proper knowledge.[32] Such a process feeds on itself, because a success increases one's level of trust. Since much of our proper knowledge begins with improper knowledge, it is very important to identify trustworthy sources. If we are unsuccessful in identifying trustworthy sources, we will either remain in a state of belief of erroneous things, or we will discover that our sources are erroneous and become cynical about our ability to learn from others.

The examples also brought home the need to sort out what we know first and what is derivative. In fact, most of our mistaken beliefs were about unexamined origins. Thinking we had knowledge of the motion and shape of the earth came from not having examined the origin of our information. False conclusions from the physics of the atom came from unconsciously forgetting that the atom did not come first in our chain of knowledge.

In order to delve further into reality, we must examine the origins of our knowledge more closely.

---

[32] Even if one cannot convert a particular element of improper knowledge to proper knowledge, one can have increased confidence in it by accumulating supporting evidences such as discussed for the motion and roundness of the earth.

Chapter 3

First Things First

An intelligent student of mine--let's call him Bill--once told me he was not sure reality was real. Everything, he said, is really appearance. Being, he went on, is not real. I pointed out that the science he studies depends on the fact that it is. He answered: well, one can just write all the science down and put an asterisk that it may all not be true. I reminded him that everything he knows came from something real; otherwise he would not know it. After all, he was a child once with no knowledge. Even the things that he had been told that were untrue came from real books or real people; otherwise, he would not have those things in his mind. Bill then had a look of recollection; he remembered what he already knew. But how did he forget so self-evident and foundational a thing as the fact that the real is real? Sound philosophy is sorely needed today. Not a branch of linguistics or mathematics or a descriptive science, but a science that reaches the fundamental level of man's questions. In particular, we need to start with the first things, the foundational things, to build the "science before science" on firm ground.

For those who think that only a very few could possibly think like Bill, remember that one does not start with ideas like "all is just appearance." One follows a path that ends with such ideas. One starts with seemingly innocuous principles that may only be slightly off the mark.

However, little errors in the beginning cause big errors later on. Such is the warning of the giants of philosophy: Aristotle (384-

27

322 BC) and St. Thomas Aquinas. History has demonstrated that fact over and over again.[33] Common sense agrees. If I shoot an arrow at a distant target, it only takes a slight error in my initial pointing to completely miss the target. We must correctly identify what comes first or risk huge mistakes like my student's. My student is not alone; he stands in the company of multitudes, especially with those with an advanced education.

Before we know anything particular about the essence of things, we know, as G.K. Chesterton[34] (1874-1936) said, "There is an 'is.'" Before we know self as self, we know that things exist.

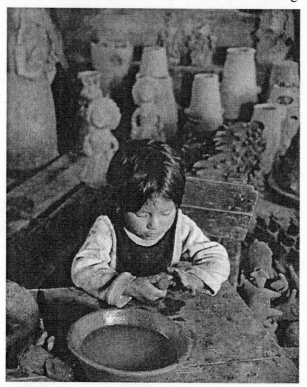

Figure 3-1: One can imagine this child in the third world somewhere, having grown with no formal education. Yet she knows a lot of things. And, the first thing she knows is that there is an is. (Photo by David Hiser/Photographers Aspen, courtesy of ARC Worldwide)

---

[33] See Etienne Gilson's *The Unity of Philosophical Experience*, where he shows history has been the great laboratory of philosophical experimentation.
[34] Chesterton is widely recognized as a writer and thinker of first rank.

Sometime when you were a child in your mother's womb, you had your first noticeable bump against the placenta, or you first felt the side of the uterine wall. You became aware of things. It was only much later that you became aware of yourself as a self.

Figure 3-2: Painting of Plato (left) speaking with Aristotle (right). This figure is a cut from the center of Raphael's work *The School of Athens.*

My student's mistake is the mistake of Rene Descartes who, wanting all things to have the clarity of mathematics,[35] thought he could doubt the existence of everything but himself. From self, Descartes "proved" God from which he, in turn, recovered everything or so he thought. Kant and others--my student among them--brought this thinking to its logical

---

[35] It is often thought that Descartes was in rebellion against his Catholic faith and culture. To the contrary, he thought Catholicism fundamentally true, but in need of a solid foundation that he thought it did not have because of its lack of immediate mathematical-like clarity.

conclusion. Namely, if I know only what is in my mind, how can I know that there is anything outside my mind? I cannot. If I start inside my head there is no way out.

In fact, of course, Descartes really knew a lot of things, things that were no longer open to doubt by him. He then implicitly used his knowledge of these things in seeing that he could not deny that he existed. He said, "I think, therefore I am." It is only in the act of thinking about something outside the self that one sees that one is a thinking self. Self is not accessible in the direct way Descartes thought. Try to observe yourself, as a self, (at the core that makes you, you) without observing yourself thinking something or doing something; it cannot be done. Knowledge of things comes first for us.

This is an important principle. It is paired with a closely-related principle that we glimpsed above; this principle can be stated as "existence precedes essence."[36] In summing up, we know things exist before we know self and before we know the essence of such things.[37] The verity that something exists is the first thing we know. In short, we know "there is an 'is.'" We will return to these principles, but let's get more specific first.

The Senses

How do we know things? We have gone through an example that imagined one's childhood before birth. Knowledge there occurred through sensorial perception, in particular, the sense of touch. The sense of touch has a primacy above our other senses, which we identify as seeing, hearing, smelling, and tasting.[38] Taste

---

[36] It does not have the meaning that 20th century Existentialists give it, for they deny essence. The Existentialists responded to a real over emphasis on essence. The emphasis on a narrow range of essences went so far (and still does) that not only was existence's primacy forgotten, but its very reality was lost.

[37] We will see later that existence precedes essence in a more profound sense. Confer chapters 4 and 8. Of course, as soon as we know something exists, we know something about it, but only in the vaguest way.

[38] This list is not exhaustive. There are senses that are qualitatively different: for example, when one is accelerating, one can sense it through the inner ear. We also sense when we need food...hunger. These senses seem to be both supplementary and "inner."

is restricted in an obvious way. [39] The remaining senses (sight, hearing, and smell) are mediated rather than direct. When we touch an object, we are in direct contact with it. However, when, for example, we hear the sound of an object, we are in contact with it through the sound that travels to us from it. Yet, whatever order we find among the senses, their commonality is the most striking thing about them. Through them, we know various qualities of things: hardness, pressure, temperature, color, sound, taste, and smell. The senses are the means through which we know everything. [40]

Well, most of us accept that we know things through the senses as "common sense." However, if pushed on the question, most would not be able to explain further. In other words, we have an incomplete and unformed understanding on this point. This leaves us without any guard against a fundamental skepticism about our senses that would attack the roots of our knowledge. What's more, such skepticism, ironically, is endemic to our scientific culture; we have been taught to doubt the senses at least implicitly by our use and mode of teaching the modern sciences. Also, remember that the work of philosophy is to transform our improper knowledge--which is really a species of belief--into proper knowledge. Finally, as we've seen, increasing our understanding will increase our "belief that we may understand," and thereby inspire us to seek to understand. So, let's take some time to better understand our sensorial knowledge and to quell doubts that have arisen about the trustability of our senses.

Through the senses, we know individual things. Those involved in the particular sciences, such as physics, must remember this. Our culture is involved--no, immersed--in the particular sciences, thus we all must be mindful of the primacy of the senses. As we have seen, we sometimes forget that the entities

---

[39] Only a narrow range of things are appropriate for bringing into contact with one's tongue.

[40] Like most philosophical knowledge, the primacy of sense knowledge leaves its presence in common language. For example, the primacy of sense knowledge can be seen in phrases like "that makes sense." The special place of touch in bringing one in closer contact (because it is not mediated) can be seen in the phrase "I felt" which is used when one wants to convey what is closest to his core self.

discussed by modern science, like the atom, are only known through experiments that in turn depend on our senses. The atom is not primary. The motion of the earth around the sun or around its axis is not primary. The shape of the earth is not primary for most of us. The sense-received fact that things exist is primary. The sensorial data that registers the relative motion between the earth and sun is primary. The sensorial data that registers the local flatness of the earth is primary. We then, of course, put the data together.

Are the Senses Trustworthy?

But, you may say, we have already shown the senses to be erroneous. They seem to indicate that the earth is at rest and that the earth is flat; these things are not true. This apparent contradiction is easily resolved by what already has been said. From our senses directly, we only know that the earth is locally flat. One cannot determine whether or not the earth is globally flat from direct sensorial impressions unless we fly, watching as we go, into space. As for the earth's motion, it is true that one does not sense the earth moving. However, from that fact, the conclusion that the earth is absolutely motionless is not sustainable, because we can only sense motion above a certain minimal acceleration. We cannot, as we already stated, sense uniform (zero acceleration) motion; recall the example of being in a completely enclosed train.[41] Further, we know that we cannot sense changes in uniform velocity, that is, accelerations, below a certain level. This fact is implicit in the experience of being in an enclosed car in a uniformly moving train, because we know that the train's motion is not completely uniform; it is only uniform enough to not be sensed. Sometimes the train will hit a big bump and remind us that it is hitting little bumps all the time.

Hence, the senses have not given us false information in either the case of the motion of the earth or the shape of the earth. We have erroneously deduced false information from them. Again, this must be the case because the senses put us in contact with the

---

[41] Recall also that this is illustrative of the principle of inertia.

reality, with the world; they are our only source of information about it.

However, you may go on to list similar "proofs" of the untrustability of the senses that "science shows us." Such proofs are paradoxes because they use the senses to make you doubt them. Think of a few; you most likely have some of your own.

You may, as an underclassman in college, have been shocked, as I was, by the following demonstration, which was calibrated to make one doubt his senses. My MIT professor tried to induce in us the feeling that colors are not quite real and in general that things are *radically* different than they appear. He showed us two "black and white" slides of the same scene on two separate projectors.[42] He pointed both projectors to the same screen and merged the images. Not surprisingly, the new image looked similar to the separated images. Then he put a red filter in front of one projector, and, like magic, the image acquired a whole range of colors. This demonstration introduced and *completed* our study of color for that course.

And, what about physicist Gustav Fechner's (1801-1887) color wheel? This wheel, when it is not rotating, looks black and white, but when it is rotated, after a while, one sees colors. Try it for yourself by using an enlarged photocopy of Figure 3-3 pasted to a piece of cardboard; poke a short pencil through the center and spin it. It works.[43]

Sticking with visual paradoxes, what about the television screen that looks like a picture but really is not? The television image is not on the screen all at once but only on the screen one small spot at any one instance. We "see" one screen.

Although all these paradoxes deal only with the sense of sight, they illustrate the *types* of attacks that are often made against the trustworthiness of ***all*** the senses. How do we resolve the paradoxes?

---

[42] I found out later that one slide had been taken with a red filter and one with a green filter.

[43] For those with easy Internet access, you might also try the site http://dogfeathers.com/java/fechner2.html. As of the writing of this book, it runs a nice "rotating" disk on your screen, with adjustable speed and direction.

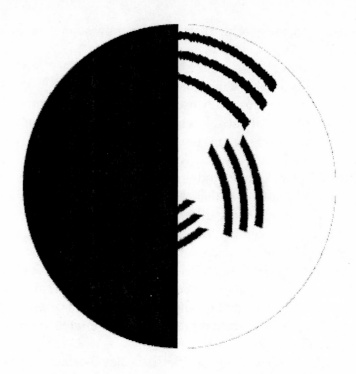

Figure 3-3: Fechner's disk appears to generate color when rotated.

Culturally attuned to the particular sciences as we are, our first tendency is to try to resolve them using modern scientific methodology and theory. To do this in a complete fashion would be a book in itself, because it would involve areas of research that, even after centuries, still have not established some of their foundational principles.[44] But, that is okay; we're *not* trying to do modern science. Remember we are doing philosophy, the science of the first principle of things (the science before modern science). Philosophy relies on *everyday experience,* not on specific highly-refined experimental methodologies and instrumentation. Philosophy uses ordinary thinking, not particular techniques involving theory and model building. Because of the latter, we have to be very careful of philosophical conclusions drawn from such sciences. Indeed, if we start down the road of the modern

---

[44] In particular, in areas like how the eye interfaces to the brain.

specialized sciences, we have abandoned philosophical explanation and have replaced that mode of explanation with a mode that is only proper to the specialized sciences. Also, we will not have laid the foundation to properly interpret the more detailed studies that we will later properly do in the specialized science.[45] In brief, to answer the paradoxes, we need to do philosophy. Since philosophy *will regulate*--but *only* in a general way--the interpretation and understanding of the particular sciences, we can prescind somewhat from the particulars.

Let's explore each of the optical paradoxes mentioning particular sciences only to distinguish them from the philosophical answers we're after. The paradoxes may seem to belong to the particular sciences, but this is so *only incidentally* because the paradoxes are artifices. Though they only exist in the controlled arena set by man, they are accessible to direct sensorial observation.

Take the paradoxes in order. First, the professor above really has just illustrated the complicated nature of our sight. He has not disproved the ability of our senses; he has just shown that it is not as simple as we might have thought. But, maybe even this is somewhat overstated for we have, no doubt, already seen color mixing, for instance, as a child mixing Easter egg dyes. We already know that colors combine in funny ways. He has only added a new type of mixing. Of course, he has also opened a fascinating arena for the study of the eye, light, and the properties of bodies in light. He has given us another reason to think that white light must be composed of colors.[46] The experiment can be tweaked to bring more complete and precise data, and we are on the path to the special sciences.

The spinning disk paradox is an example of a sense pushed to an extreme limit; yet even at the limit, the sense is still giving us more information about the object. But, we can get back to the

---

[45] By contrast, once the philosophical foundations are established, we will immediately see that philosophy will require the specialized sciences to proceed further.

[46] White light can be decomposed into the colors of the rainbow (this is fundamentally what happens in a rainbow). As our own composition of atoms doesn't mean we are *only* a bunch of atoms, one must be wary of reducing all color to *just* the colors of decomposed white light, i.e. the rainbow colors.

standard regime by stopping the motion and seeing that the paper is really black and white. For the specialized sciences, this produces more clues that white light is composed of multiple colors and points towards more interesting lines of experiment and thinking to follow.[47]

As for the television screen appearing as one picture, this is a species of a limitation of the sense of sight. Our sense of sight accurately reveals to us what is there, but it cannot resolve at the speed at which the dots are moving, so they blur together.[48]

Such paradoxes as the ones above are not too distant from optical illusion and the simple perspective encountered in drawing. The senses offer clues to their own interpretation in such cases. Here we see an example. One does not blame the senses for not seeing the back of a statue when you've only looked at the front. This is a limitation of the sense of sight; one cannot see all at once. Recall the example of the earth's shape: from our close-up vantage point, we cannot see the shape of the whole earth. In a similar way, the sense of sight has motion limits. It cannot distinguish things appearing faster than a certain limit. We also know this from experience; one can draw a stick figure in successive stages of walking on successive index cards, and by flipping the cards, appear to see the stick man walk across the card. We easily recognize this as a limit of the sense and not as the sense of sight giving false information. An analogous thing applies to the TV image. Try the following. In an otherwise dark room, focus your eyes a couple TV-screen widths to the right of the TV and sweep them a couple TV-screen widths to the left.[49] You will see various

---

[47] Some think that this phenomenon can be explained by saying the alternating black and white cause cones/rods to fire in such a way as to induce the equivalent colors. My own hypothesis, which is not backed by experiment, is that the persistence time of the cones varies from wavelength to wavelength, so that the wavelength(s) that persists (on short timescales that repeat) such that it is emphasized over the others shows up. Of course, this theory uses the fact from physics that white light is composed of a wide spread of wavelengths of visible light.

[48] This probably occurs in our perception, rather than in the eye itself. Philosophers make a distinction between perception, which is accomplish by the internal evaluative "sense" (what might be called, via an incomplete *metaphor*, processing systems), and the external senses.

[49] Experiment with different sweep lengths until you see the effect.

images of the TV screen as you do this. You are seeing the various frames sweep by. The various images are distorted because of the fact that the TV is scanning as described. Hence, the senses themselves, like seeing the back of the statue, can and must, in the end, be the instrument through which one finds out about the limitations of the senses.

Do these paradoxes mean our senses are unreliable? We've seen the answer is no. Let's look more purely philosophically for a moment. Remember, the senses are that by which we know things. They put us in contact with things. The basic error made above is in assuming these paradoxes mean our senses are untrustworthy. Its more sophisticated version is that only a highly refined science can tell you anything of what color really is and indeed if it is real. The truth is that the refined science can utilize what the senses give to increase our understanding, but it is the senses that provide that information.[50] The problem with the paradoxes above occurs when one tries to start with them. To understand something, one must start with the object in its natural state, not in an artificial or pathological state; only after the natural state is understood can the pathological cases be understood. It is only with reference to the natural state that the perturbed or pathological state is identified as perturbed or pathological. We recognize an object in its natural state, and only then do the pathological states create further questions. For example, in the case of color, we know there are colors such as the rainbow colors: Red Orange Yellow Green Blue Indigo Violet (ROY G BIV); everyone recognizes them.[51]

If we could not see colors, there would obviously be no science studying them. This means color as a *property of things* would not be studied, because light is the way we know colored things. If everyone were blind, the highly technical and abstract study of light would certainly not exist now, because there would be no *visual* properties to explain or wonder about. Sure, all the

---

[50] In fact, by mode of practice, most of the modern sciences attempt only a limited sort of explanation. This will be discussed in detail in Chapters 6 and 7.

[51] We don't see all colors (or said in a specialized science mode, we don't see all wavelengths of the electromagnetic spectrum), and of the ones we do see, we don't see all equally well. These are both *limitations* of the sense of sight. What we see is really there (in the non-pathological state), but it isn't everything, and we can be mistaken in our processing and interpretation of what we see.

effects of light on bodies would occur as they do. Thus, those properties would be available to us by their effects through our other senses. Such knowledge does not put us in contact with the property itself; it is an abstract substitute. We have to invent a sort of mythology using things we do know with our other senses to describe it.

Case in point: a blind man could sense the presence of a hummingbird. He could learn that a certain flower attracts the hummingbird to it and another does not. After checking that none of his other senses can verify a difference between the flower that attracts the birds and one that does not, he may thereby deduce a property of the flower which he may call color. One flower, the one others call "red," he notes attracts the bird and the other, the one called "black," does not. Note he has not made contact with the property called color; he has only deduced it from its effects on the bird. Further, he will have to do many checks, other experiments, and much reasoning to try to confirm color's presence. He *may* never be absolutely certain, never have proper knowledge of the existence of an actual non-sensed property, because of the network of hypotheses, deductions, and observations that he has to rely on. However, in our simple case, it seems he should be able to come to know color exists. Still, his knowledge of color would be only analogical knowledge, limited to *analogies* from sound and other sensorial data. Only a person born blind knows what it's like to not know color. However, the state of the blind man's knowledge of color is very like the state of our knowledge of atoms. The senses come first and we cannot sense atoms. Renowned physicist Sir Arthur S. Eddington (1882-1944)[52] expressed this fact in a physicist's language by saying, "Molar physics has the last word in observation for the observer is molar."[53]

To manifest one of the key issues at stake for the particular sciences, take the case of water waves. Consider a man who never has experienced waves in any way. Say he knows about atoms and

[52] It is an interesting fact that Eddington stated this, because in other ways, he--like most theoretical physicists--tended towards the philosophical idealism defined later in this chapter.
[53] In saying "molar physics" Eddington is referring to macroscopic objects, objects directly accessible to our senses. One mole is 6.02×10^{23}. So, for example, 1 mole of copper atoms weighs about 60 grams or 2 ounces.

calculates correctly how all the atoms in the water move when a rock is thrown into the center of a lake. The calculation outputs massive data corresponding to positions and velocities of an unimaginable number of the atoms. In such an array of numbers, one would have **scant** hope of finding the phenomenon of water waves; our man does not even know what he is looking for. The thing would be next to impossible if he knew what he was looking for, but the very thing one normally would want to explain by arrangements of atoms in such a calculation, he would not even know about. Such is the state of someone without sensorial knowledge in a particular arena.

Sensorial knowledge and our discussion about it are very important. A friend of mine thinks that magic and other sleight of hand techniques are somehow a refutation of the reliability of the senses and hence of the philosophy associated with it, that of St. Thomas and Aristotle. This is just one more example of specious argument that we've already seen. In fact, many think that one can go back and second guess the accuracy of sensorial knowledge, and postulate some system that is logically consistent that completely undermines what the senses have given us. Such a thing is impossible. In so constructing a system, we are doing what Descartes did; we are using knowledge (in this case, sensorial knowledge) that we have, but pretending not to use it to undermine the very knowledge that we used. Such systems of thought must forget that *all knowledge comes to us through the senses.*[54] Such systems of thought lock oneself in one's head. People who adhere to such systems are called *philosophical idealists,*[55] because, for *them* only ideas are real. As my student Bill learned, this ends up undercutting all reality.

Immanuel Kant codified the philosophical idealist's position, which now, unfortunately, is the default *declared*[56]

---

[54] As we'll see in the next chapter, not all knowledge is sensorial knowledge, though it all comes through the senses.

[55] The word *idealist* has two completely separate senses or definitions. In this book, I speak of philosophical idealists, which are defined above. These idealists should be distinguished from "idealists" in common parlance which means those who aspire to reach an ideal or ideals.

[56] For example, although in physics, chemistry, and biology departments, lip service is given to Kantian (more generally, philosophical idealist) thought,

position in academia and in nearly all other environs. Kant's success is partly explained by his tying his philosophical system to Newtonian physics and Newton's great and deserved fame. One of Kant's goals was to make Newtonian physics[57] have a certainty that it did not have. However, Kant thought that one could not know the thing itself. Hence, without in any way setting up a straw man, Kant and Kantians *must* say, "Kant doesn't know anything about anything." Such is always the end of the matter when one forgets that all knowledge in man comes through the senses. We non-Kantians can be simultaneously more accurate and kinder; we can say, "The foundational principles of Kant's philosophical system were wrong, but still he knew a lot of other things."

Sensorial Knowledge: A Radical Discovery

Now, we are ready to ask a quite crucial philosophical question. Is sensorial knowledge *just* the physical change that happens when I come into mediative or immediate contact with an object? Concretely, if I pick up a cold glass of water, the glass cools my hand down and I warm it up.[58] Is this the sum total of what happens? Obviously not. Something happens in me that doesn't happen to the glass; I am *aware* of the coldness of the

---

when it comes to the business of doing science, Kantian thought is ignored. After all, the study of nature would stop if one seriously believed he was not able to learn anything about nature. In fact, no one acts on this sort of thinking except in the sterile environment of abstract discussion.

[57]Many attribute to Kant a developed skill in physics. Physicist and renowned philosopher and historian of science, Fr. Stanley Jaki has shown that Kant's knowledge and ability in physics was minimal (though Kant considered himself another Newton). Jaki's thesis comes in the context of Kant's book, *Universal Natural History and Theory of the Heavens*. Jaki says that apart from two insights: 1) postulating nebulae as other galaxies and 2) his correct, though not completely original, explanation of the visual hue and shape of the Milky Way, "the book [*Universal Natural History...*] is a storehouse of inaccuracies, contradictions and amateurism and plain fancy." (cf. Jaki's translation of Kant's *Universal Natural History...* published 1981 by Scottish academic press).

[58] Physically, heat transfer occurs that we could describe in terms of the atoms whose existence is real but taken underneath the higher plane of existence of the substances of glass and man.

glass. I apprehend,[59] take hold of, the coldness of the glass. I "sense," among other things, the coldness of the glass. Here we have something very interesting to investigate. It will be our first look at an act of knowledge. In some real way, I have become coldness. I have changed in a unique way. Knowledge is a unique species of change.

What is Change?

Before we can better understand sensorial knowledge itself, we must reflect on *what* we know. After things themselves, the next thing we are aware of is change. Things are, but they also become. This fact of reality confused early philosophers and continues to confuse many moderns. Consider the two most instructive examples from the ancients. Heraclitus of Ephesus (c. 500 BC)[60] thought change was the only reality.[61] Parmenides of Elea (b. 540 BC) thought being was the only reality. These two define the two extremes of error in this arena. It is said, "Every error in philosophy that can be made has been made many times over." All of the current apparently radically new philosophies, including those that purport to spring from new discoveries of modern science are, truth be known, rehashes of very old philosophical mistakes. Indeed, the ones claiming necessity from modern science often involve the most simplistic mistakes.

Parmenides corrected the error of Heraclitus, but only by making an error in the opposite direction. Nonetheless, what Parmenides did is hard to overestimate. For the first time in history, a philosopher, Parmenides, had abstracted the notion of being. Unfortunately, Parmenides immediately jumped to pure Being. This Being is completely one, absolute, unchangeable, eternal, incorruptible, indivisible, and containing every perfection;

---

[59] "Apprehend" is an important word. Broaden it from the common *exclusive* meaning that is related to a policeman apprehending a criminal. "Apprehend" means, more broadly, to take hold of or bring to conscious presence; this broad meaning is the way it is used here.

[60] Heraclitus was thought to be in the prime of life in 500 BC. This gives a period of about 70 years between the prime of life of Heraclitus and Parmenides.

[61] Buddhism also espouses this idea.

this is the being most would call God. Parmenides jumped straight to Being Himself.[62] For Parmenides, everything was pure Being. Of course, we do not have such direct knowledge of God or even God's existence. The type of being we know is not complete and *unchanging*; it is changing. All change was an illusion for Parmenides, because Being is all there is. Parmenides is yet another example of a philosopher enamored with an idea (the most powerful idea), and who does not want to dim any of the clarity of the idea, even at the expense of not being in conformity with reality. Thus, having abstracted this powerful idea in its fullness, he tried to force all of reality into it. He rejected even one of the most evident parts of reality, the fact of change. Sound philosophy must neglect nothing, least of all what is most evident. We must account for both being and change. Both are undeniable facts.

We begin with being. Being, of course, does not mean what it means in science fiction, a self-conscious entity with a will and mind. The widespread use of only this meaning is an indication of the philosophical insensitivity that holds sway in our culture. Just as a living *thing* is anything that *lives*, a *being* is anything that "*be s*,"[63] anything that exercises the act of existing. How does change fit with being?

Let's analyze a concrete example to see how. At one point, an apple is a small, round, green fruit, but it matures into a larger, red fruit. It remains an apple throughout, but its size and color, among other things, change. We need vocabulary to discuss this. The change in the apple is like the change that occurs in the making of a statue. For instance, consider an unformed mass of bronze that is formed into a statue of Einstein. Now, we call the mass of bronze that persists through the change, "*matter*."[64] We identify the bronze as having two different "*forms*." At first, the *form* of the bronze was, let's say, a random blob shape, and then the *form* was the shape of Einstein. In an analogous way, we say

---

[62] A Being containing every perfection would obviously include intelligence and personhood; hence, one should use the generic personal pronoun ("He") for this being.

[63] Pronounced "beez."

[64] Later we will identify this type of matter as secondary matter, and only refer to it with the modifier "secondary," never as simply matter.

the apple changed from red to green, it kept its *matter* but changed one of its *accidental forms.*[65]

The color is called an "accidental" form, because it is not the essence of the apple, but only one of its properties; we will reserve the name essence or *substantial form* for the latter type of form. The use of the word "accident" (from the Latin *"accidens"*) is not meant here to imply an unintentional or random occurrence. Such is the common usage of the word "accident"; we say the child spilled the milk by accident. Be conscious that we are now getting into a technical vocabulary whose meaning is sharp and should not be confused with common usage. An *accident* means "that which of its nature must inhere in something else."[66] It is what we call a property. Furthermore, an accident is not necessarily something unimportant; it may be quite important. Case in point: the ability to move is an accident of a horse but obviously not the essence of a horse.

The statue example is very helpful, but it can be misleading. In transitioning from the making of a statue to the growth of an apple example, the word "form" undergoes a qualitative change in meaning. "Form" moves from meaning simply "shape" to a more general meaning that includes things like color. In the case of the apple, one says the apple lost the form of the color green and gained the form of the color red. The statue changed geometric shape. No geometry is involved in the apple's color change; here, the word *form* has been generalized to indicate a much broader concept. It indicates a property of the apple. So, one can say the same thing in two ways: "red is a property," or "red is an accidental form."

Aristotle identified nine categories of accidents. [67] They are:

---

[65] This description is only meant to convey a general idea of accidental change and not meant to be exhaustive. A more complete description would include the entire tree as well as the ground around its roots and the air. In the more complete description, in addition to the accidental change of the apple's color, some of the ground and air become part of the apple and the apple tree.

[66] Or, said another way, an accident is "that which of its nature must exist in another."

[67] The categories of accidents, with the Greek transliteration in parentheses, are: quantity (poson), quality (pion), relation (pros ti), action (poiein), reception

Those properties intrinsic to a *material* substance:

1)   *Quantity* (extension)

2)   *Quality* (what issues from a substance, such as color, temperature, pressure, sound, smell, hardness, and consistency)

Those properties involving relations in a strict sense:[68]

3)   *Relation* (pure relations such as equality, similarity, and causality)

4,5) *Action* and *reception* (often translated "passion" or "being acted on" or "affection") Respectively, changing and being changed.

6-9) *Place, orientation, environment, time*

We will be particularly concerned with the first two: quantity[69] and quality. Color, for example, falls under the category of quality. However, it can be shown that all changes of material substance involve at least these nine categories.

Because, as we've seen in the growing apple, accidental change must be change of something; a property is a property of something. Red is a property of the apple. Hence, we have already implicitly introduced the idea of *the subject of action* or "*substance.*" A *substance* is that which primarily exists; it is that which exists *per se* and not in another.

As we've anticipated by introducing the words *essence* and *substance*, accidental change, like that of the apple from green to red, is a very narrow type of change. It only involves changes of accidents (properties), not essences. Let's reflect on change of a more profound type.

Take a couple of examples. I pluck an apple off a tree and eat and digest it. What is the difference between the apple before and after these two actions? An animal dies. What's the difference

---

(paschein, often translated "passion" or "being acted on" or "affection"), place (pou or topos), time (pote or chronos), orientation (keisthai or thesis), environment (echein, sometimes translated "state"). Confer Aristotle's *Categories* c. 4, 1b 25 sq. or *Topics* c. 9, 103a 21 sq.

[68] Because of the oneness of the reality, everything is related to everything else in some sense.

[69] Quantity is distinct from all the other categories in two ways; it is the first accident, and it is the only one that does not admit degrees. We will discuss the meaning and import of these terse but important statements in Chapters 6 and 7.

in the animal before and after its death? In both these changes, something persisted through the change. However, whatever persists during such changes is minimal. After all, an apple as part of a tree is a completely different thing than an apple as part of me. In fact, after it has been integrated into my body, it is no longer an apple at all. Still, *any* type and number of changes can occur to an apple, and I would still "see" that there is something (call it a substratum) that persists through all the changes.[70] In spite of everything, it's the same "stuff" I started with. Yet, I have allowed "the stuff" any number of changes and any type of change, so I must say that this stuff, this substratum, is really very close to "nothing." In analogy with what was said above about accidental change, we call this underlying stratum that persists during change *prime matter*. *Prime matter* really has no existence *on its own;*[71] it only exists as part of material substances. From this point onward, we will mean by *matter* only *prime matter*. The previously mentioned type of matter that is involved in accidental change will now be referred to as secondary matter.

Further, the apple changed from one thing to another. It went from being a substance called an apple to being part of my substance. This is an example of substantial change. In our technical language, the substantial *form* of the apple was lost, and the prime matter was activated by the substantial *form* of the man, me. Similarly, in case of the death of an animal, the substantial form of the animal is lost and replaced by the substantial form of the inorganic[72] substance (or substances) that is a dead animal.

Since word usage can be a source of confusion, let's pause for a moment on the new technical vocabulary. The *essence*[73] of a

---

[70] There is a parallel here with what the modern physicist calls conservation of matter and energy. This is not the whole issue, because the modern physicist is concerned with a measure and quantity. We will discuss these types of issues in Chapters 6 and 7.

[71] For this reason, it is sometimes called pure potentiality, but potentiality only has meaning in reference to act.

[72] Note that here inorganic does not refer, as it does in chemistry, to substances without organic molecules. It refers to a substance that is not organic in the sense of not organized from within, not acting from within, which is the unique character of life.

[73] We will tighten the definition of essence up in Chapter 4.

thing is primarily the *substantial form* of the thing. Another word for essence is *nature*. Again, we should be careful about confusing this technical language with other everyday use of the words. For instance, nature is commonly used to mean all sub-human reality. One says "pollution can ruin nature." Then again, sometimes nature means what happens on the "average"; one says, "It's not natural to live without a phone."

Similarly, the word *form* is used in an analogy to the case of the form of a statue; however, its meaning is exactly the opposite of that found in other common usages. When one says that something is mere *form*ality, one means it is peripheral and external, not important, not the essential thing. In physics, mathematical "formalism" is important, yet it is considered the container for the real content. Similarly, the modern expression, one should not allow "form over function" means "don't let the way you want something to look drive what it can do"; in other words, form means, again, just an external garb. When one says, "I wrote down just what you said, but in a different form," one means that it is the same essential thing, but it looks different. In philosophy, form means exactly the opposite of these usages; form is what is essential. The statue analogy is the place where the common language and technical language best resonate. In the statue, it is the form that makes the difference.

A further caution is needed at a deeper level. When a philosophical issue is under consideration, it is important not to lean on one's imagination. The imagination is our ability to recall and manipulate[74] our *sensorial* knowledge. By it, we can recall

---

[74] We know by experience that the imagination has the ability to create new images from memories by adding, subtracting and substituting from other images; we will discuss this ability and its importance more in Chapters 4 and 5. In a fuller treatment, one would see that the external senses have a number of internal counterparts that carry out specialized activities. Since these powers are part of the sensorial system, they can be called internal senses. Those internal senses or powers are: 1) the *unifying sense* that brings together all the data of the individual external senses to fashion a phantasm by which one knows the thing under consideration; 2) the *sense memory* that allows recollection of an experience accurately and in proper context, including time, place, etc.; 3) the *evaluative sense* that, in turn, controls the 4) *appetitive power* which causes the animal to feel attraction or repulsion depending on whether the evaluative sense determines the thing under consideration to be helpful or harmful to the

what we have sensed. It is, in this way, the memory of the senses. These memories put us in contact with the original events by way of *phantasms* or *images*.[75] When someone recalls the road he takes to work every day, he gets an image in his mind of that road. When he remembers his girlfriend or wife, he "pictures" her in his mind's eye; he "sees" her. When one thinks, however, he does not necessarily need *images*. In fact, modern use of images and sensorial faculties, as we discuss later, is such that it impedes abstract thinking.

We've seen this fact already in our description of the "science before science." If one asks one's imagination about the meaning of the word "before," one imagines, for instance, a boxcar in line behind the engine in a train. We have seen that this is not what is meant. "Before" meant *prior* in an abstract sense; it meant: *required by* or *implied by,* as a triangle requires the notion of a side. And, so it is with accident and substance. When "accident" is defined as "that which inheres in another," the imagination tempts one to think of chocolate candy where the nuts "inhere" in the candy. Such a picture can make one believe that one can just take away the "accident," the nut, and still have the nut and the candy (just smaller). An accident is not an extrinsic thing attached to substance, the way images tend to make one think; an "accident" is a being that cannot exist on its own, makes no sense on its own, and can only be understood with respect to a substance. "There is a red…" begs the question, "A red what?" In the same way, saying, "There is a thing" begs the question, "What is it and what properties does it have?"

The relationship between form and matter is similar. We have seen that a material substance is a combination of form and matter. They are mutual causes of the substance. Without either, we would not have a substance; although it is the form that activates the matter and thus makes it prior to matter in the way just discussed.

---

organism; and finally 5) the *imagination* which is the ability to recall and manipulate the phantasms.

[75] We will see in Chapter 4 that one needs phantasms even while sensing something (e.g., as mentioned in the previous footnote, the unifying sense makes the phantasm available while one is observing (sensing)).

We are now ready to solve the problem of Parmenides: how does being fit with change? Foremost, why did Parmenides see such a problem in reconciling change with being? Because he was the first to understand, at some level, the first principle of all knowledge, which is called the principle of contradiction. **Something cannot *be* and *not be* at the same time and in the same way.** Note that this statement is much *more* than simply a statement in logic; it is a statement about existence, about being. It is not possible to think the opposite; it is a self-evident principle. If something *is,* Parmenides reasoned, for it to change (i.e. for it to acquire a form that it did not have) means it *is not* as well as *is.* This statement cannot be true; therefore, Parmenides concluded, change is not real. Of course, this is to deny the obvious. Change happens all around us constantly.

When it looks like one must choose between two hard facts of reality, one must look more deeply to see the resolution of the paradox. It is not reality that is inconsistent; I, who am trying to understand it, have failed to see reality as it is. Change does indeed imply that things are not pure being, are not *being* in its plentitude. Material being, changeable being, must contain an element of *potentiality.* Changeable beings must have the capability of acquiring different forms. We have already named this capacity or potentiality *matter* (prime matter). Now, something is only *potential* in respect to something that is *actual.* We say that the wood has the *potential* to be burned. Or, the apple has the *potential* to be eaten; that is, the apple has the *potential* of becoming part of my being. The apple has *potential* to take on my *form.* Note *potentiality* and *actuality* go together in the same way as *matter* and *form.* The substantial *form* actualizes the *matter* of a substance to be what it is. *Act* and *potentiality* are like two "sides" of the same sheet of paper;[76] a sheet of paper has a front and a back; neither makes any sense without implicit reference to the other. The great Aristotle was the first to explain these things. Fifteen

---

[76] Be careful of leaning on images in the wrong way. Images can be helpful in initially conveying a concept such as this, but such concepts are intrinsically understandable outside such physical imagery; so, this crutch should be dropped as soon as one's philosophical legs are strong enough to allow it.

hundred years later, St. Thomas[77] transfigured Aristotle's work not by altering his principles, but by unequivocally and explicitly taking them to their foundation in *being*.[78] He identified clearly the primacy of existence; the primacy of the act of being.

The renowned philosopher Jacques Maritain[79] (1882-1973), says, "Between Aristotle as viewed in himself and Aristotle viewed in the writings of St. Thomas is the difference which exists between a city seen by the flare of a torchlight procession and the same city bathed in the light of the morning sun." To the degree something *is*, that is the degree to which it is in *act*. To be *in potentiality* is in some way *to not exist*. Thus, changeable being, also called material being, has an element of nothingness in it. We already said as much when we said that *matter*, *prime matter*, is in some sense nothing. Matter limits what a thing is. It is because of matter that we can have more than one individual in a species. Because the same substantial form of a "dog" actuates different matter, we can talk of Lassie *and* Rin Tin Tin. They are different dogs because different matter is activated and limited or circumscribed in different ways.

The solution to Parmenides' problem with change is to recognize that not all being is being in its plentitude; there are beings that have an element of nothing in them.[80] They are closer to nothing. In fact, such being, changeable being, is the one we

---

[77] So high is St. Thomas's respect for this first rank genius, he identifies Aristotle as "the philosopher." Prof. John Saward has made the very interesting and likely correct statement that St. Thomas also uses "the philosopher" to mean the philosopher *par excellence,* the best man can do with purely human wisdom. This is confirmed by the fact that neither he nor I have come across a passage in St. Thomas's work where "the philosopher" is wrong. But Aristotle referred to as Aristotle is stated to be wrong on occasion.

[78] *Being* here refers to the act of existence, or in Latin *"esse"* meaning "to be" as mentioned.

[79] In my judgment, Maritain is the greatest philosopher of the nineteenth and twentieth centuries.

[80] This does not mean that they are "mostly" nothing, as claimed in the atom example of Chapter 1. To the degree something is, it is not nothing. The very phraseology "mostly" nothing is an error due to misuse of the imagination. The very idea that a fraction of the reality of a thing is nothing is a contradiction. Nothing is the absence of being. When we say changeable being has an element of nothing in it, this is just a way of speaking, indicating the capacity for change in material things; it does not literally mean that being can be non-being.

have direct experience of. Changeable being *is* by its *form* and *is not* by its (necessary) union with *prime matter*. Again, changeable (material) being is something but it *can become* (matter) something else. Changeable being *is* in one respect and *is not* in a different respect. So, the principle of contradiction is not violated.

Equivalently, one can say every material thing *is actually* something (form), and *is potentially* something else (matter). From this perspective, one sees the thing *is* in two different ways. Of the two, potentiality is a much harder one to get, as Parmenides and many modern people find.

What then is change itself? Change can be defined as "the actualization of the potential as such." Given a substance before and after change, one simply has a form in act with the potential (its union with matter) to become other forms. Thus, change is not act *and* potentiality. Change is potentiality in the process of becoming actuality.

What Is Sensorial Knowledge?

Finally, given this knowledge of material change, what can we say about sensorial knowledge? Recall that sensorial knowledge necessarily involves a bodily organ like the skin on one's fingers. The bodily organ underwent a physical change. My skin changed when I picked up my ice water. Specifically, the temperature of my skin (a property belonging to the category of quality) decreased in magnitude; the skin got colder. So far, this is exactly the type of material change we've described above. Such change was called an accidental change. In technical language, the form of the skin changed; the change was a modification of a quality of the skin. However, we also identified a more profound type of change that occurred in sensorial knowledge; in fact, it is the core of sensorial knowledge. When I touch the glass, I am aware of the coldness of the glass. I am conscious that the glass is cold. I, in some way, become coldness. This change is not like the accidental changes of the cooling of my hand and the warming of the glass. Those physical (material) changes and other similar ones occur during the process, but they are not conscious of cold. Neither is the act of sensorial knowledge a species of substantial change. When my hand gets cold, it does not become coldness in the sense of losing its essential form to take on another. What, then, does happen?

Let's call this "power" or ability that allows us to be put in the conscious presence of the properties of another being the "power of sensation." The power of sensation--the power that makes sensorial knowledge possible--is a power that can receive the form in a unique way, not in the way of ordinary physical change. Ordinarily, acquiring a form means changing in a physical way; physically becoming the thing or property in question. The modification to the quality of temperature that alters the form of my hand makes my hand physically cold. By contrast, in the case of the power of sensation, I receive the form in a **unique** way; I receive the form as a form of the object itself, not of me. I acquire the form of the object in its specificity without being it physically myself. In other words, in addition to the physical change that does occur, I become, in my sensorial power, the coldness of my glass without physically changing in the ordinary way. Quite shocking, but unavoidable.

Indeed, in a narrow sense, one can say this power is an immaterial power, because this change transcends ordinary material change. In the act of sensorial knowledge, I become in this immaterial mode of existence, the coldness of the glass. This of course does *not* mean that it is *purely* immaterial; it isn't because it necessarily depends on material being and change. An act of sensorial cognition, for instance, of being made aware of the coldness of my glass, cannot even be conceived without also considering material processes being present: even during the very act of the sensorial cognition.[81] The act of sensorial knowledge is further limited by the specificity of the thing being sensed.

This analysis, of course, applies to all the senses. I don't just hear, I hear something--not some general thing,[82] but some particular thing. Again, we are brought back to the truth that the senses are that through which we know everything.

---

[81] St. Thomas's *Commentary on Aristotle's D'Anima* is recommended as a starting point for those who would like a little more discussion on these issues.

[82] Even if it is a hard-to-pinpoint, weak sound, it is a *particular* hard-to-pinpoint, weak sound.

We have established this primacy of the senses in our knowledge, but we have also discussed several first principles that don't seem to come from the senses. Isn't the principle of contradiction an example of something that we know that does not come from the senses? After all, we have just shown that the senses put us in contact with things, but only this particular thing and that particular thing. Sensorial knowledge does not give us universals; the senses, of themselves, do not put us in contact with something that transcends any particular thing. Yet, the principle of contradiction is a principle that applies generally to all being.

Where does our knowledge of such things come from? Such knowledge must indeed come in some way from the senses, because the senses are the only means we have of contacting things. But how does abstract knowledge come through the senses? More generally, our knowledge is something other than sensorial knowledge; when we say something is true, we are not applying sensorial knowledge. We are using a higher knowledge wherein truth resides in us. Hence, sensorial knowledge comes first *for us*, but absolutely speaking, principles and other truths are higher and, in that sense, first. Even substance itself, which may seem so physical when viewed with our imagination, is not seen with the eyes (or any sense); it is "seen" with a higher power or ability.

Before we move to discuss this ability and how it occurs, let's briefly reflect on the examples used in bringing forth our new philosophical knowledge. Note that the concrete examples that we used all involve common everyday things. They do not involve anything from modern science; there were no atoms or genes or black holes discussed. This is necessary, not incidental. *We must move from what is more known to what is less known, not the reverse*. To use the results of modern scientific research would immediately put into some doubt the things we were saying, because the results of that research depend on a whole network of theory and experiments. Furthermore, they depend on those results being correctly interpreted. So, if we were to base our understanding on them--though our ingrained tendencies may indicate otherwise--we would be basing our understanding on much less direct and therefore less firm ground. Again, we have direct experience of apples and animals, not atoms and quarks. We will consider objects that are known only by modern (specialized) scientific methods in Chapters 6 and 7.

Chapter 4

What Is Truth?

*I*n the last chapter, we concluded that although all of our knowledge comes through the senses, not all knowledge is sensorial. Man must be endowed with another power in addition to the power of sensation. This power is the intellect. The intellect allows us to distinguish truth from falsehood. Truth is the core issue in discussing the nature of the human intellect. "Wait, slow down," some may say, "You're discussing truth in rather broad terms. Isn't scientific truth the only really reliable truth?" And, the scientifically educated may add "Hasn't the idea that we can come to any truth with certainty been refuted by Gödel's[83] theorem? Hasn't he shown that we cannot rigorously ***prove*** anything? Aren't we investigating a power that really is quite powerless in the end?" We already know the essence of the answer to the first question, but need to investigate the second. Let's look closely at the Gödel's theorem objection; it will lead us to further illuminate the former as well.

For those whose first reaction to the beliefs of my student Bill was to think that such thinking (philosophical idealism[84]) is rare, pay careful attention to what comes next. It can be used as a test to determine whether someone you know is a philosophical idealist or has such tendencies. Start by confronting the person

---

[83] Kurt Gödel (1906-1978) was a U.S. mathematician born in Czechoslovakia.
[84] Recall "idealists" think only ideas are real (or think ideas are the first thing we know, which in turn ends in the same thing).

with the above Gödel's theorem dilemma about truth. Many will likely say, "What's Gödel's theorem?"

It is a mathematical proof and is itself a key example of the mathematization of modern thinking. Gödel *mathematically* proved two key statements about systems of ideas, such as those that are made by specifying a group of starting assumptions (axioms or postulates) and laws. You remember from high school geometry that proofs were accomplished using given axioms. Facts of geometry were built by doing proofs; this is an example of a system of ideas. Laws governing behavior, such as the U.S. federal and state constitutions, can be thought of as a system of ideas. Gödel proved that within any system of ideas that is as at least as complicated as arithmetic,[85] there are always propositions that *cannot be proven true or false* within the system. What's more, Gödel also proved that **the very consistency of a system cannot even be proven within the system.**

So, no matter how carefully and how many things we include in our favorite system of ideas, the system itself might not even be self-consistent. That is, the system might be intrinsically contradictory, and we would not even *be able* to know it within the system. If it is contradictory then, of course, no proof within it can stand. So, it looks as if we cannot prove anything and thus *cannot really know*. Gödel's mathematics appears to leave no escape from this conclusion. This seems to undermine everything we said earlier. Now, one can reassert the test question. Does it really follow from Gödel's theorem that we cannot know? Why? Or why not? If someone answers yes to the first question, you will know he has strong philosophical idealist tendencies. If he answers no, but cannot explain why, he has some tendency toward philosophical idealism.

Gödel's theorem only causes philosophic problems for those with idealist tendencies. Why? First, note that Gödel's theorem is purely about a system of ideas.[86] Hence, to deduce from Gödel's theorem that somehow our knowledge is without

---

[85] In fact, the theorem is stronger; it requires only a "sufficiently large part of arithmetic."

[86] Actually, the ideas used here are a very particular type of idea technically called beings of reason (Latin *entia rationis*).

foundation is to assume that the foundation of what we know is in our head, i.e. in our ideas. This is the error of the philosophical idealists. Recall idealists think that we know only our ideas, so they have to try to prove everything from them. On the contrary, we've seen that we know *things* through the senses. *Our proof that something is true comes from conformity with reality, not from systems of ideas.* An idealist expects ideas to always contain their own proof, because ideas are all he thinks he knows.[87] Hence, when Gödel demonstrates that no system of ideas contains its own proof of consistency, he is left with the belief that he can never know anything with certainty. To try to shut oneself up inside one's mind is to try to cut oneself off from our source of knowledge. Further, as renowned philosopher Ralph McInerny says in his Gifford lectures: if a philosopher shuts himself inside of his own head,[88] the goal of philosophy becomes to go out of one's head.

Since Gödel's theorem is sufficiently well known and discussed in scientific circles, it is important and helpful to explore it in a little depth. I encourage you to do so in the box below.

Gödel's Theorem: The Two Key Points

Gödel's Theorem can serve as a springboard to understanding truth, and the higher power by which we attain it from our senses. It is especially revelatory of our modern approach to thinking, especially in its highly algorithmic and mathematical approach. The theorem and its consequences are very interesting, but so is the methodology of arriving at the theorem.

This theorem is proved by assigning unique numbers to propositions and expressions. To illustrate the general idea, consider how one turns a word into a unique number. This process is known as arithmetization or "Gödelization." One Gödelizes the

---

[87] There is a subtle point hidden here that pivots around what ideas are. The nature of ideas is extremely important. We will discuss these issues in this chapter.

[88] That is, refuses to acknowledge the source of our knowledge as from the senses.

word "idea" in the following way. First, take the prime numbers[89] beginning with 2 and use them to mark the places of the letters; thus, one could write, putting the letters that belong in the given place as an exponent: idea=2^i 3^d 5^e 7^a. Next, assign each letter of the alphabet the number of its position in the alphabet; so, a=1, b=2, c=3, d=4, e=5, g=6, h=7, i=8, etc. Using this, idea =$2^8 * 3^4 * 5^5 * 7^1$ = 362,880. So, 362,880 can be used to represent the word "idea."

Because each position of the word has been assigned a unique prime number and because each letter has a unique number assigned to it, every word has a unique number in such a scheme. Think of it as giving each word a social security number. Such linking of words with numbers allows verbal statements to be put on the same plane as statements about numbers. In this way, statements and propositions (in an algorithmic sense) can be transposed to the mathematical realm; this is half of the hard part of Gödel's work. The other half makes use of a statement superficially like the following:

"There is no proof of this statement."

If by "proof" one means "a way of knowing," the statement can be rewritten as:[90]

"There is no way of knowing that this statement is true."

Now, this is a contradiction,[91] and therefore just words without meaning. However, if by proof I mean a very narrow thing like,

---

[89] Prime numbers have no factors but themselves and 1. For example, 2, 3, 5, 7, 11, 13, 17 and 19 are primes.

[90] In this form, it is related to the "Liar's Paradox," where a man from Crete says, "All those from Crete are liars."

[91] First, I cannot know it true or false. If I know it true, the statement itself implies it is false. If I know it false, then the truth of the negated statement implies that I know it true. Well, maybe it can be true or false, but I can never know. But, if I cannot know the statement true, then it is true (that's what the statement says); this is a contradiction. Note the self-referential nature of the statement gives one the appearance that the statement is something more than a contradiction. In fact, it has, like all statements, the conceptual framework which includes the distinction between predicate and subject. It also is itself a group of words that can be referred back to as if it said something. So, in thinking about the statement, one has these three real concepts that are in themselves perfectly valid that one can grab onto. But, one is really only bouncing around between these three concepts and trying to mesh them together

"cannot be deduced within a system," or equivalently "cannot be proven within a system," where *system* means a set of axioms and rules, then, the statement becomes:

"As a statement within a system, there is no proof of this statement."

In this context, the statement is no longer a contradiction, for one can know it true outside the system. Notice that this statement, like the previous one, is self-referential. This aspect allows it to be combined with the Gödelization mentioned earlier. How? Well, if the statement can be made into a series of numbers connected by the rules of arithmetic, it becomes part of the arithmetic system and thus can be self referenced in the required way. (They must in some sense be on the same plane, while our view of the statement is outside the system.) Using the power of mathematics that becomes available when everything is expressed as a number, Gödel showed that there are statements within any system that are true but that cannot be proven true.

We might have guessed the truth of Gödel's theorem before its proof. Any system that is sufficiently complicated will have to point outside of itself, because of the oneness of reality;[92] that is, everything is related to everything else. Trying to close one part off from the rest will be a thankless task.

Gödel's theorem reveals more about our own psychological state (i.e., our patterns of thinking, and the types of things that attract our interest) than about the intellect itself or truth itself. However, if we find we have strayed off the main path, we should find the point where the side path left the main path, so that we may better understand how we went wrong. We can then prevent a similar mistake from happening again later down the path. Thus, we leave Gödel's Theorem aside till later in the chapter so that we

---

during the process of seeing that the statement itself is a contradiction and thus just nonsense. Here again, as we saw in Chapter 2, having to articulate an error as error already gives error more than it is. In this case, it gives it a bunch of words and concepts that make it appear to be something more than it is.

[92] We will discuss this later in this chapter when we discuss "being" more abstractly.

may get the fuller picture of the intellect and truth necessary to see better where we went astray and, most importantly, where the right path is.

We are back to our original question: How do we understand? What is this ability called the intellect that gives us access to truth? In the process of understanding how we understand, we will prepare the way to understand *being* from the perspective of *truth*.

What Is the *Sense* in Thinking?

Since sensorial knowledge is, in some sense, the source of *all* of our knowledge, let's first summarize what we know of sensorial knowledge. Sensorial knowledge starts with the "external"[93] senses (touch, sight, hearing, smelling, and tasting). The senses put you in direct contact with things. You have sensorial memories of these things that allow you to make these things present to yourself at will. In other words, the imagination allows you to bring forth images or phantasms at will. *By* these phantasms or images, you know these things. The imagination can also disassemble and rearrange the data and then reassemble it into a new "image."[94] So you may have seen Lassie on TV. Lassie is a particular brown and white collie. But, even if Lassie was the only dog you ever saw, you could still imagine a black collie. You could picture a solid black "Lassie," because you could extract the

---

[93] In a more full treatment, one could discuss, as done in a footnote in Chapter 3, explicitly the "internal" senses that coordinate and utilize the sensorial data. For example, the "common" internal sense takes information from all the external senses to make present to the individual all the sensed aspects of the thing in a unified way by way of a phantasm or image. The supplementary senses, such as the sense of acceleration from the inner ear, which we discussed in the previous chapter, belong in a category with the five external senses.

[94] Do not be misled by the word "image," which tends to imply a presentation of only the visual aspects of a certain thing. The sensorial memory includes information from *all* the senses (including the sounds, smells, etc. of the particular object). In drawing phantasms from our sense memory, we often leave behind these other properties, especially in our modern visually oriented culture (computers, TVs, and movies).

"color"[95] black from a previously seen black object, and "color" in Lassie with it. What's more, you can even imagine a sort of outline of a dog where the detail is extracted. This ability to take apart the various images and put them together in a different way is what we commonly think of when we talk of the imagination in everyday language. When we say "That little boy has quite an imagination," we mean precisely that he uses his imagination to extract various things from his sensorial memory that he then rearranges in ways not found or seldom found in reality. He may imagine, for example, a purple dog on a mountain of chocolate next to a unicorn; again, all of which he put together using pieces from sensorial data from real things in his experience.

Further, recall sensorial knowledge brings us in contact with a particular thing. Take again the example of picking up a glass of cold water. There we showed that one acquires the form of the coldness of the glass in a unique non-material way. I acquire it as the form of the coldness of the glass, not of me. When I touch the glass, I become,[96] by way of a phantasm synthesized by a unifying internal "sense," the coldness of the glass. Also, when I *recall* the coldness of the glass, I do so by way of a phantasm;[97] I am, in some way, once again in contact with that coldness. I

---

[95] Black, of course, is not a color but the absence of color. I here use the word "color" as one might in referring to a marker or crayon.

[96] If we use our imaginations instead of our intellect, we may think that we physically become the coldness of the glass when we touch it. This is obviously not the case. Another image that may come to mind to explain how we know is that of acquiring knowledge as one might pick up a rock and put it in a box. These are just so many more instances that should warn us against improper use of the imagination. In order for us to know the coldness of the glass, we must in some way, become it, otherwise we are saying it is separate from us, and we thus, could never know it, which is not the case. One may say the thing just becomes a part of me, but that part must be (for *me* to know it) the central part of me (not for example my hand or foot) where my knowledge occurs which I reserve *primarily* for the designation "I." Through the sensorial power, we, thus, have the capability that we've already labeled as partially immaterial, that of becoming more than we are by taking on things outside of ourselves. We will see that all knowledge has this property of allowing us to become more than we already are.

[97] The phantasm (of the thing under consideration) synthesized by the unifying sense puts one in contact with the thing with all of its specific accidental forms (quantities, qualities, and relations) received by the external senses.

become, in my sensorial power, the coldness of the glass again.[98]
Thus, the phantasm or image allows me to become the coldness of
the glass again. This makes it clear that an image *must* be that *by
which* we know the thing (in this case the coldness of the glass). If
a phantasm were *that which* we know, instead of that *by which* we
know things, then a phantasm would **not** put me in contact with the
coldness of the glass but with *itself.* I would know an intermediary
thing, an image, not the coldness of the glass itself. We are
compelled by the fact that we know *things first* to say that
phantasms are that *by which* we know things. To try to argue
otherwise would be to not put "first things first."

    If I unwisely chose **not** to put "first things first" by taking
the image as *that which* I know, I would trap myself inside my
head. I would become a philosophical idealist. My sensorial
knowledge would be knowledge only of images, not of the external
world. This point is crucial. It remains crucial as we come to
discuss ideas. We will elucidate it further after we talk a little about
ideas.

Ideas Are Not Images

    There is an analogy between images and ideas, as you may
have already surmised. But what are ideas? When I say I have an
idea of an animal, what do I mean? Do I mean I have an image of
an animal in my mind? It cannot mean that, because an image is of
a particular thing. An image of an animal is, for instance, an image
of your friend's dog; allow me to call him Fido. This is not the idea
of an animal; it is at best an "idea" of Fido in particular. However,
to call this image of Fido, the "idea" of Fido would be to use the
word "idea" as equivalent to the word "image." We would then
need another word for the concept we are discussing, because the
word "idea" would no longer be available for us.

    This brings us to two general points about technical
vocabulary. First, we'd like to stay close to Standard English word

---

[98] Of course, there are differences between actually being in contact with the
cold glass and recalling the experience. When one is actually sensing, the
phantasm is "simultaneous" with the external act of sensing, so, obviously, is not
prone to error of memory as one is in recalling the experience.

usage, so as to tap as much infra-scientific understanding as possible. As we've noted, all natural languages (such as English) are rich with words and expressions that carry meaning from infra-scientific understanding.[99] Second, we want to have a unique word to designate a unique concept, so as to make proper distinctions more easily.

What then does the word "idea" refer to? When I have an idea of an animal, I may have a hazy, vague image that continually varies in shape and size attending my concept of an animal, but it is **not** the image that is the thought. *Ideas are general; images are particular.* When I think about an animal, I, at one instant, picture a giraffe, at the next instant a lion, and later maybe even an image of a whole zoo of animals. The idea of an animal is not the images; they only attend and aid my concept "animal." The idea of an animal is a universal, not a particular; that is why I cannot handle it with an image or even many images. You may say, many images can be dissected and put together, as described above, to make an infinite number of images, thus one can always identify the concept "animal" with this set of images. But, to know this set of "possible"[100] animals is a set of animals means you have a general knowledge of what it means to be an animal. Furthermore, what if there is an animal that is of a completely different type, which cannot be pasted together from pieces of phantasms from real beings that you've seen so far? You would then not have included it as an animal and your definition would not be complete. For example, if you had only "seen" worms (this means the observer had not seen man either), a dog would not be "constructible" by your *imagination* (your use of phantasms). Yet, because we have

---

[99] In natural languages that mature under the influence of a high civilization, words also take meaning and evolve to accommodate post-scientific (after philosophical reflection and analysis) understanding. In such cases, one will find words that carry the full philosophical meaning already. For example, Latin and Greek are two such languages that stand out in this way. Of course, Latin was the major language of western civilization until relatively recently. The Romance languages evolved from it, and academics used Latin; for example, Isaac Newton's (1642-1727) major work, the *Principia,* was written in Latin; indeed, some Eastern schools in the US *still* use Latin in their graduation ceremonies.

[100] Assuming that you somehow know that pasted together "animals" that you've imagined are, in fact, possible.

an idea of an animal, we know an animal as an animal when we see it, even if we've never seen any of that type of animal before.

To further probe how we understand through ideas, let's just spend a little more time pursuing the idea of an animal. Again, we are not now primarily looking to come to conclusions about animals (we will do some of that in Chapter 5); we are primarily trying to understand better what an idea is as distinct from an image.

So, in this context, let's ask, "What is an animal?" Here we come to a harder question. Before we go into a little detail on this question, notice that we have indeed an idea of an animal, but it is a confused idea lacking in scientific[101] rigor. The question "What is an animal?" prompts us to develop our idea of an animal more completely. One thing we notice immediately is that animals have the capacity of self-movement.[102] By self-movement, we do not mean simply movement that occurs without any continued contact with another. This latter qualification would exclude, for example, the box I'm sliding across the room, but is not enough. We mean movement that *originates from within*. With the correct

---

[101] In this case, we are concerned with that science called currently called philosophy. It is also true that our current discussion of animals is non-rigorous with respect to the particularized science of biology (cf. Chapter 5). Recall that the statements that we make in this section depend only on common experience and thinking (the business of "philosophy"), not on detailed methodologies and specialized forms of experimentation (which involve inducing man-made conditions).

[102] This definition includes plants if movement is taken in the broad sense to include being "able to *extend* oneself from one place to another." We thus must use a restricted meaning of "movement"; we can qualify the type of movement we mean by specifying locomotion, that is, motion from place to place. As we've said, there is much more to do here, (e.g., more qualifications and reasoning to be done) before one can state the essence of an animal. Among the things left to consider are microscopic plants and animals, viruses, etc, and the classification problems they introduce. Philosophically, the important thing to note in such classification problems is that we first know about macroscopic plants and animals; we know there are seaweeds and grasses and zebras and lions. For example, we know a zebra is qualitatively different from grass. It is only after we know there are animals and plants that we come to the problems of specifying the essence properly enough to deal with borderline and anomalous cases. We will discuss animals in more detail in Chapters 5 and 7.

understanding of self-movement, there is no temptation to ascribe an animal type nature to things like a baseball.

For example, we can and do easily distinguish between a bird and a baseball, although both, at some moment, may be seen "flying" through the air. Both move, yet the ball's movement (unless acted on by something else (e.g. wind)) is completely given and initially determined by, for instance, the collision with the bat. If one were to try to establish a definition of "animal" based upon motion using images, it could not succeed in reaching the universal that is the idea of an animal. An image is particular, an idea is universal; there is a qualitative difference between the two. Try, for example, to define an animal as motion defined by the set of images fashioned by piecing together all images from real locomotion (motion from place to place like that of a baseball). Now, such a definition utilizing the imagination would now falsely classify baseballs (and things like them) as animals. Of course, one could then exclude certain specific circumstances such as those images associated with images of bat swinging. However, note the whole process of excluding and including of images makes use of one's already present understanding of the general idea of an animal. Hence, the process could continue and thereby one could get a more complete set of images, but the result after each iteration is not the general idea of an animal. It is just an incomplete but finely tuned functional equivalent, which was fashioned by a process that was, in turn, regulated by the *idea of an animal* already present in the mind of the man who fashioned it.

Hence, we see that the idea of an animal is a universal. In other words, the "idea" of an animal transcends images. Again, *ideas are universal.* Mathematics can bring home this point concisely. Think of a circle. Nominalists,[103] people who think ideas

---

[103] Nominalists basically confuse intellectual knowledge with sensorial knowledge. Among this group are Hobbes, Berkeley, Hume and in a narrow way Locke. However, Locke's overriding common sense and respect for reality (as well as some contact through for example Hooker with St. Thomas) make him contradict his foundational position that says that all of our knowledge is sensorial knowledge. Unfortunately, this leaves him in bad shape with regard to the consistency of his various positions. Locke notes that "brutes abstract not" but man does, and still proceeds to act as if he does think man has abstract (universal) ideas. Hobbes, Berkeley and Hume follow their initially chosen

are particular, would say one cannot think of a circle without thinking of this particular circle of this particular radius. However, this is not true. When we think of a circle, we usually do also have images of circles of various sizes and possibly colors attending our idea of a circle. Yet, we know that the idea of a circle is a general object. It is a set of points that are equidistant from one given point.[104]

Well, you may say a circle is thus just the set of all images obtained by varying the size of any one circle. So, the imagination can have a sort of equivalent class of this sort of mathematical entity. Nonetheless, this set, as in the case of the animal set of images, was fashioned by already knowing what a circle is. The imagination does not know the essence of a circle. Hence, how can sensorial knowledge tell that there is something special about this particular set of images that it forms? By itself, it cannot. Recall sensorial knowledge puts one in contact with the particular in the world. From these particulars, *one can imagine many particular circles, but one would have no way of knowing that this particular imagined circle has something in common with that particular imagined circle.* In short, there is a difference between *using* a thing (e.g. generating a list) and *knowing* a thing (e.g. *knowing* what the list is).[105] For example, in school, a student may learn something by rote, which means he does it without thinking about it. A small child may, for instance, recite a selection from Shakespeare completely accurately. The words may all come out clear and in order, but he may have no idea what they mean.

The universality of ideas is even more clearly present in the case of the law of contradiction (*"Something cannot be and not be at the same time and in the same manner"*) presented in the last chapter. As we observed, this idea cannot be "seen" in any way with the imagination.

Therefore, we see still again ideas are universals. Phantasms, on the other hand, are particular. The intellect gives us

---

foundational path and thus avoid contradiction in logic, but then run head long *against* reality by saying that we do not know universals.

[104] Here we use, of course, Euclidean geometry.

[105] With respect to classification, (the recognition that an individual thing is of one kind and another thing is not) this point can be stated as: "There is a radical difference between the *ability* to distinguish and *knowing* the distinction."

general knowledge, the senses particular knowledge. But, where does our intellect get its general knowledge? Where, for example, does the idea of a circle come from? One fact that we did not mention, which would have made even stronger the point that the idea of a circle is radically different from sensorial images universal, is that circles don't really exist in reality anywhere. Nowhere, if truth be told, does one see colorless, odorless, soundless, one-dimensional objects.[106] A true mathematical circle like we're discussing cannot even exist in reality; it can only exist as an idea in one's mind. We abstract the idea of a circle from real things. From the moment after the first time you saw the moon or the sun or a pie for example,[107] you had the sensorial data from which you could pull out (abstract) the idea of a circle. In the same way, we abstract all of our ideas. The "power" or ability that does this pulling from sensorial data is called the intellect.[108] The word "intellect" comes from two Latin words, *inter* and *legere,* so it means, "to read between or within."

Take another example to explore further. Consider "substance," that which exists of itself, not in another. The idea of substance, like the principle of contradiction, which is not at all subject to images, comes after we first sense any existing thing. It takes a particularly high type of "abstraction" (St. Thomas calls it separation) to pull out the idea of substance.[109] The intellect can act on the phantasm of Fido and draw out of it the idea of substance.

---

[106] A circle can be thought of as a line segment (one dimensional) that has been bent so as to link the two ends together and then manipulated into the right shape.

[107] We most likely, but not necessarily, did this with the aid of our parents drawing and pointing at circular shaped things.

[108] Philosophers distinguish two aspects in the human intellect: the *agent intellect* (in Latin, the *intellectus agens*), which draws what is essential (in various degrees) from the phantasm of the thing under consideration, and the *passive intellect* which then forms a *conscious* idea of the thing. The act of sensorial knowledge and intellectual knowledge are spontaneous, and we are *only* directly aware of the resultant act of the passive intellect which presents us with a general thing, the general idea of animal say, rather than the particular animal, say Fido.

[109] We have glimpsed the three levels of "abstraction" in our three examples of animal, circle, and substance respectively called physical, mathematical, and metaphysical. We will discuss them in Chapter 6.

A nagging question yet remains: The phantasm of the thing puts one in contact with the particular thing, so how does one get general from particular? The intellect must be of a totally different and higher nature than the sensorial power, for the intellect has the power to pull out what is only hidden in the sensorial contact with the object. What the intellect sees is not present in the phantasm *as* phantasm. When we observe Fido by our phantasms, the intellect acts. The intellect makes "visible" what is hidden to the sensorial power; it pulls out the *essence* of Fido from the phantasm. *Essence* is that which Fido primarily is. It will be helpful to expand on this later but, simply said, the essence is the answer to "What is Fido?" Of course, one does not abstract the essence in a clear, distinct way at first. The idea at first is vague and confused. It is only with further thought, experience[110] and effort that we can gradually make precise our idea of animal.

Human Knowing:
Sensorial and Intellectual Knowledge

We see intellectual knowledge is in many ways analogous to sensorial knowledge. Sensorial knowledge puts us in contact with particular things by phantasms. Intellectual knowledge puts us in contact with the universals in things by way of ideas abstracted from phantasms. Therefore, all of our knowledge (sensorial and intellectual) comes through the senses. As in the case of the phantasms, ideas are that *by which we know things* as opposed to *that which we know*. Again, one who forgets to put "first things first" in his thinking can assume that he knows only ideas (i.e. that ideas are *that which* he knows), and thereby become a philosophical idealist and lock himself up in his mind.

To emphasize the critical point that ideas and images are that *by which* we know, we will digress briefly to discuss the important concept of *signs* found in scholastic philosophy.[111] Ideas

---

[110] We learn most about a thing from the way it changes and the changes it causes.

[111] The "Scholastic" period refers to the era of intense and fruitful academic study that took place in the High Middle Ages.

and phantasms are *pure signs* as opposed to *instrumental signs*. Start with the concept of an *instrument*. A paintbrush is an instrument; it is that *by which* an artist paints his canvas. A "Construction Ahead" sign is an *instrumental sign*. The sign is *that which* we know primarily and only secondarily that *by which* we conclude that there are men working on the road ahead. Be careful here; we do not properly know the latter. We only have proper knowledge of the sign itself (we see it); we could be misinterpreting the meaning of the sign, or its meaning could be deliberately deceptive; we do not know. On the other hand, a pure sign is that which by its very nature exists to bring us into contact with something else. It is primarily that by which we know something else. We only know it exists by reflecting back on the act of knowing the thing. For example, in the example of the cold glass, I know the coldness of the glass when I pick it up; I do not know a phantasm. It is only by reflecting on the experience that I later realize that I must know this thing by a pure sign called a phantasm. Now, let's return to our probe of the intellect by comparison with sensorial knowledge.

In sensorial knowledge, I become, in my sensorial power, the coldness of the glass I pick up. This happened by me acquiring the form of the glass's coldness in an immaterial mode whereby I do not change in the ordinary physical way. I do not acquire the form as my form, but as the form of the coldness of the glass. Since the power of knowledge is a primary power and thus close to the core of our being, we are able to say that in a certain sense, by becoming the coldness of the glass in my sensorial power, *I* become it.

Not surprisingly, the intellect has an analogous aspect. From phantasms of Fido, I can abstract the essence of an animal and many other things. How does this happen? From phantasms of Fido, my intellect extracts various general things about Fido; for example, his "dogness" and "animalness." I do not abstract everything about Fido at once. But from observing Fido,[112] I can abstract enough to receive an idea of what Fido is, what the

---

[112] In actuality, of course, I don't observe just Fido. I observe other dogs and things and abstract general ideas from them as well that I can compare and contrast with what I know from Fido.

essence of Fido is. That is, I can acquire the substantial form of Fido. Remember that all material substances, like Fido, are something (substantial form), but potentially can become something else (matter). The substantial form of Fido of necessity includes his "dogness," the essence of being a dog. Yet, I don't physically become "dogness." In any case, I could not physically become the dogness of Fido, because even if my *matter* lost my *substantial form* and became the substantial form of the dog, it would be a particular dog not the *universal* idea of dogness. Remember normal physical change, the kind of change we see all day long, the kind we call in Standard English physical (or material) change, comes in two varieties: accidental or substantial change.

So, it is clear that intellectual knowledge, like sensorial knowledge, is not a physical change; it is a unique species of change. I acquire the substantial form of Fido as the substantial form of Fido, not of me. An idea in my mind puts me in contact with dogness. I receive Fido's dogness in an immaterial mode of existence. In other words, I, in my intellectual power, become dogness. Since my intellectual power, unlike my sensorial power, is *right* at the core of me, it is even more true than it was of my sensorial knowledge to say, "*I* become 'dogness.'" We emphasize this aspect of unity of knower and thing known for two reasons. It manifests the fact of experience that we *know things not ideas* and also manifest the immaterial nature of the act of knowledge.

The Human Intellect:
A Startling Discovery

Furthermore, unlike sensorial knowledge, there is no physical organ that acts during the process of apprehending "dogness." True, I initially need the phantasm generated by the material-bound sensorial powers, for the intellect abstracts the idea from the phantasm. However, the act of abstraction is only a precondition that allows the act of understanding to occur; it is not the act of understanding itself. Once the idea is in my intellectual memory, the intellect no longer needs--and indeed cannot use--the phantasm to accomplish its act of understanding. Hence, although in both sensorial and intellectual knowledge, the knower (myself) becomes the thing known (the "dogness" of Fido) in an immaterial way, only intellectual knowing is *purely* immaterial. It cannot have any part in matter, because ideas are general, not particular. Material being (i.e. *matter* and *form* composites), on the other hand, must be particular, because a *substantial form* is made specific by its union with *matter*. Hence, man's intellect is immaterial.

We will discuss the makeup of man more in Chapters 5 and 9. For now, note that the intellect is the chief power of me (of the substance which is me). We've already said that the intellect of itself operates independent of anything material, thus by necessity it must be a power of something immaterial. That is, *my substantial form*, that which makes my substance what it is, must be immaterial.

This seems incredible. Quite astounding. Right in the heart of my own being, which I experience from day to day and think I know so well, is immateriality. It is like "The Purloined Letter" of Edgar Allan Poe that was set in the middle of a well-traveled room where all could see, but none would suspect its importance or investigate its content. Philosophy is full of such surprises. Like the immateriality of the intellect, these surprises are thrust on us by reality; we can revolt and complain or we can do what Einstein did when his preconceived idea of cosmology ran against reality. When he found out that reality (as apparently manifested by experiments in the specialized science of physics)[113] did not square with his static theory of cosmology, he abandoned the theory.

---

[113] Einstein had introduced the cosmological constant into his theory of general relativity, so that he could fashion a model of the universe that was static. When he found that experiment disproved his static universe, he bravely discarded his belief in it. There is an interesting twist to the story. Unfortunately, along with discarding his belief in static universe, Einstein discarded (in principle) his "cosmological constant" that his equations almost "demand" the presence of. This constant now looks like it is needed to account for current experimental results, though they still bear out a non-static universe. His belief in a static universe was a consequence of a necessitarian tendency in his thinking that mostly came from his pantheistic belief system, but also came partly from the mind-set necessary for doing good theoretical (particularized modern science of) physics. We will discuss these issues more in Chapters 6 and 7.

You may say, "The arguments for the immateriality of the intellect are sound and irrefutable, but nonetheless *the intellect's immateriality itself* seems to run, in one way, headlong against reality." A man in a car accident who suffers a head injury may lose his ability to think (i.e. to use his intellect). If the intellect operates without *need (necessity)* of the material, how can this be? One does not even need this extreme example to see the problem. When you are sleeping, your reason is not active, at least not in the ordinary sense,[114] therefore bodily action does impact the activity of the immaterial intellect. Furthermore, we know by direct experience that when we think of something, we have in attendance vague images that we use as touch points for our thinking. As we've said, we have to free ourselves of *incorrect* dependence on images in some areas of thinking, and in other areas of thinking, we have to free ourselves of all *direct* dependence on images. Obviously, Aristotle and St. Thomas would see these objections as clearly as we do, because they do not depend on modern scientific knowledge, just on simple observation of life. What is the solution to the dilemma?

The source of the confusion is resolved when I realize that my sensorial powers and intellectual powers are not two separate things that exist in isolation. They are two powers of me. I am one thing, one substance. The *substantial form* of a man we call a human soul. Like any substance, I am a unity; I am a whole composed of parts and powers that work together as one. The *substantial form* informs the body, makes the body be a body--not a hunk of flesh. I am a soul animating body, not soul and body, as if either one makes any sense without the other. My powers of intellect and sense are accidents (qualities) of the one substance, me. So, since the soul works as one, we expect an interdependence between its sensorial and intellectual powers that, while not absolutely necessary, is necessary for my completeness, the oneness of me. In this normal mode of existence of body animated by soul, I expect phantasms to be very important in my intellectual

---

[114] It is true that some do get incredible ideas (e.g. the benzene ring in organic chemistry) while sleeping, so even here, reasoning is not completely turned off, indicating something of its immateriality. Nonetheless, most will acknowledge that while sleeping, your thinking ability is generally quite impaired.

life, and ideas to be very important in my sensorial life. Again, this interdependence does not change the fact of the pure immateriality of the intellect. The effect of the physical on the immaterial is simply a manifestation of their real unity; it's how the two work together. Consider a metaphor: compare my intellect's dependence on the body to a driver's dependence on a car.[115] A driver is a *man*, who as a man can move by himself with no absolute dependence on a car for movement; this is like the immateriality (being entirely free of direct dependence on matter) of the intellect. However, considered as a *driver of the car* (the intellect is the chief power of the soul), he will be impeded or completely disabled in his ability to travel if the car is damaged.[116]

Let's close our discussion of the immateriality of the intellect by stepping back from our more refined analysis. We could have glimpsed the immateriality of the intellect without the detailed analysis above.[117] For example, we have the idea of justice. Well, how long is justice, how much does it weigh, what color does it have? The same questions could be asked about an idea. In each case, we see the silliness of the questions. An idea has none of these properties. Justice has none of these properties. These are properties of material things. Hence, we have a capacity that can obtain and receive immaterial things, things that are radically different from physical things.

---

[115] Like all metaphors, this metaphor will have limitations, but it can help in elucidating the issue if it is used within its bounds. Specifically, in this metaphor, the car-plus-driver system is just an imitation substance. "Driver-plus-car" system is only united in the following sense: the designer, using various substances, made the car so that it could act as a car-driver system with the main function being to get people from one place to another. We will discuss such imitation substances later; we can call them pseudo-substances, because they consist of multiple real *substances* fashioned into a system to perform some function to *mimic* a single real substance.

[116] In summary, in this metaphor, the following relations obtain between the driver-car system and man (body as animated by soul). The driver ~ soul (i.e. substantial form of the body, whose chief power is the intellect), the car ~ man's body, the driver-car system ~ man (body and soul), and locomotion ~ use of the intellect.

[117] However, without detailed analysis, we would not be able to answer many other questions.

In a similar vein, I am constantly combining ideas. For instance, in thinking, "the apple is red," two ideas are made into one. "Apple" and "red" are two separate things in my mind that can be brought to one point; something impossible in the material world. Or again, note our capacity for self-awareness. When you have a notion, you can "see" yourself having that notion. You have the ability to reflect on the fact that you are thinking about justice. You are, in some way, present at the same place as your thought of justice. Moreover, you can even reflect that you are reflecting about your reflecting. You can thus be present at one point with an arbitrary number of thoughts. Again, this ability is a strictly immaterial ability, for material things exclude each other. A baseball cannot be in the same place as a baseball bat. From the self-reflection example, you can also see that in your reflecting on reflecting, you are able to, in a way, duplicate yourself without changing physically.

In Chapter 5, we will further investigate our makeup by comparing and contrasting man's intellect and the ways of knowing of animals and computers. For now, the concern of this chapter is to understand our intellect. What it does and what it knows. We've seen what it knows and does at a deep level, but we need still more depth to answer the question that really queries the depth of intelligibility and intellect: "What is truth?" We will be poised to discuss these issues at a deep level only when we've firmly understood and elucidated the foundational concepts and related vocabulary. Specifically, "essence" and "existence" need to be further understood. "Essence" and "existence" are, in turn, related to "being," which is the most primary concept of all. Let's move then back to fortify our understanding of these concepts, building on what we know.

The Primacy of Being

Upon seeing the phrase "existence precedes essence," a friend of mine commented that it was confusing because, to him, existence and essence were the same thing, so he said, "To me 'existence precedes essence' says 'the thing' precedes itself." Despite this statement, under questioning, he revealed that he had a somewhat clear, yet obviously only partially conscious understanding (infra-scientific understanding) of the meaning of each of the words. In other words, he did, at some level, know existence and essence to be distinct. Nevertheless, his first thought is the first thought of our infra-scientific experience. Existence and essence seem like the same thing.

Using the available infra-scientific platform, as one always should,[118] St. Thomas starts his work *On Being and Essence* in a somewhat similar vein by saying both existence and essence refer to being.[119]

"Being" is literally rich beyond words.[120] We can only hope, in an introductory book such as this, to briefly glimpse the depth that the concept carries. We've said a being is anything that "be s," anything that exercises the act of being. From this statement, we can resolve *being* into two concepts: "the act of being" (Latin *"esse"*) and "a being" (Latin *"ens"*). We have the verb "half" and the noun "half" of the concept "being." The verb half, "to be," *(esse)* is primary. *"Esse"* is the very act of existence: "to exist." The "to be" is overflowing with intelligibility;[121] it is the sun that blinds our vision if we look at it, but becomes the source of our ability to see things if we look at what it illumines. Even this analogy is quite imperfect, because, among other things, "to be"

---

[118] Indeed, one must start there to really build one's understanding.

[119] In St. Thomas's day, the Latin *"esse"* had two meanings: 1) existence 2) essence. The primary meaning, which is "to be," is what *"esse"* will mean for us.

[120] The intellectual perception of being is on such a different plane from our everyday thinking that Jacques Maritain says, "... it remains true that this intuition [of being] is, as far as we are concerned, an awakening from our dreams, a step quickly taken out of slumber and its starried streams. For man has many sleeps. Every morning, he wakes from animal slumber. He emerges from human slumber when intelligence is turned loose..." (Quoted from *Degrees of Knowledge,* chapter 1.)

[121] Its intelligibility is inexhaustible in itself, but not to us, not to our weak intellect. St. Cajetan (1469-1534) a great commentator on St. Thomas Aquinas and contemporary of Martin Luther (1483-1546) says "existence does not exist." By this he means that the concept we have of existence is not existence. It is so intelligible in and of itself that we can touch it directly only at the tip of our intellectual capacity every time we touch something in the world. Hence, the genesis of a danger of idealism, forgetting that existence is known first and considering only essences as real.

infuses all that is; it's not just reality's illuminator, because where "to be" isn't, nothing is. It is a sign that one is near something primary, when the best concepts one can use to describe the thing are less able to carry the meaning than the thing itself. What we know first will not be definable; it will be that which we use to define other things. Nothing comes before the "act of being." "To be" is primary; however, "to be" is to be something, so one is led to ask: *what* is? The general answer: "a being." This is the noun half of the concept "being," meaning anything that is. We will use the word "being" for the noun concept *(ens)* and "to be" for the verb concept of being *(esse)*.

It is largely this noun concept of being that interests us in this chapter, because here we are exploring *what we know of being.* Specifically, the question is: What is the relation of "things that are" ("beings") to what we know? The mind grasps existence first, but when it understands things, as we've said, it is not able to grasp existence itself, but only the *whatness* of the being. In some ways, the mind leaves the existence of the thing behind. Recall, in our intellect, we know universals, not particulars; in reality, all things are particular. Hence, because of the different kind of existence that the thing under consideration has in the mind, we do not know by our intellect alone whether the general thing under consideration really exists in the external world. For example, the idea by which we apprehend "black holes," does not, of itself, contain its existence in the real world. However, we always come back by a second act of the mind called "judgment" to determine whether something exists in reality and/or really is the way we conceive it.

In other words, we have to come back and make a judgment to determine whether the being: 1) actually exists, 2) could exist, or 3) is purely a "being of reason" of the mind and could not even possibly exist outside the mind. Unless it is clearly self-contradictory, the concept itself doesn't tell us this. I know Fido by my sensorial knowledge, thus I know Fido exists and hence that "dogness" exists. But, the idea of "dogness" in my mind does not contain the existence of the thing in its notion, just its possible existence (all dogs may have been wiped out in a plague since you last saw Fido, for example).

Of course, none of these arguments changes the fact that the intellect recognizes that "being" is. It knows that "there is an is"; indeed, it is the first thing we know. However, the intellect does not know of itself that this particular thing exists or did exist without referring back to sensorial knowledge. Nonetheless, once something has been verified as existing in sensorial knowledge, we can use our reason, the mind's ability to manipulate ideas, to prove that something else must exist or must have existed. For example, from this book you are reading, you conclude that an author exists or did exist.

What then, in the first act of the intellect, is apprehended by the idea of the thing? Or, in other words, if it is not the *particular* existence outside the mind that is presented to the intellect,[122] what then is presented to the intellect? It is the "whatness" of the thing in question. It presents us with what the being--say Fido--is. When we ask what Fido is, we seek to know the essence of Fido. In other words, "being" approached from the point of view of *intelligibility* to the **human** intellect brings the question: What is essence? To answer, we must keep in mind the distinction between the noun concept and the verb concept of "being," and we should note an important subdivision within the noun concept of being. Let's investigate this interesting subdivision that will help also us understand better the place of Gödel's theorem.

Real Being and Beings *of Reason*

The noun concept "being" (Latin *"ens"*), St. Thomas says, can itself be split into two halves: 1) beings existing or capable of existing in reality and 2) beings *only* capable of existing in the mind, or what we call "beings of reason."

In the first subcategory, "a being" means the whole range of substances: pigs, cats, flowers, atoms, trees…etc., as well as the properties that exist in them. Analogous to the way the imagination disassembles images to make new ones, the mind can "take apart" ideas and make new ones. Some of these "fictions of the mind" will be "beings of reason." Some will be real beings *(ens reale),*

---

[122] The intellect here is considered *as intellect,* that is, conceptually isolated from the sensorial power.

which exist or are capable of existing, and thus falling into this first subcategory of "being."

In the second subcategory, we have most of the arena of mathematics;[123] for example, take negative numbers. Have you ever seen "-2" people sitting around? Of course not, the entity "-2" is only a concept used in mathematics; taken as such,[124] it *cannot* exist outside the mind as conceived. Modern mathematics usually operates in a symbolic mode wherein one is thinking about and applying rules to abstract entities (symbols). In this mode, one finds "beings of reason" such as -2 and the square root of -1. However, it must be added that mathematics is *ultimately* about real being,[125] because its distinctive concepts are reductively real,[126] having been put together by analogy with or abstracted directly from the real.

---

[123] Foundational mathematical concepts like mathematical figures (such as a circle) or natural numbers are __not__ "beings of reason," because they are abstracted from real things and thus exist in them under the conditions of material things; e.g., they have color, temperature, smell, bumpiness, etc. However, because they cannot exist as they are in their mathematical purity, we will call them *preter-real*. We will discuss the extremely important subject of mathematics in Chapter 6.

[124] Still, "-2" is *reductively* real. One can think of "-2" not as a single entity (to be manipulated by certain rules) and thus on a par with "2" as mathematicians do, but as removing two items from a larger number of items. In this way, one sees it can be broken into an operation (subtraction) and a natural number "2," both of which come directly from the real. In other words, one can see the real being from which the concept "-2" was "constructed." Note that although "2" cannot exist outside the mind in its mathematical purity, it can exist *under the conditions* appropriate to material things. By contrast, take animal as an example of a real being *(ens reale),* in this case, a material being, in the full sense of the expression. The essence "animal," though it is a universal and thus cannot exist as universal, can exist as particularized. For example, instead of an indefinite length body and indefinite coloring included in the idea of an animal, Lassie has some definite length body with brown and white hair. "2," on the other hand, has *no* color or length, not even an indefinite one; in its mathematical purity, it deliberately excludes those. Again, that's why we call such mathematical objects *preter-real*.

[125] Even concepts like the limits of calculus, which give us integrals and derivatives, are taken from iterating concepts, such as addition, that are abstracted from sensible reality.

[126] Again, mathematical concepts can be looked at in two ways: 1) as taking you to the actual real objects or 2) as symbols in a formalism built to investigate

We also have concepts like "category." How could a category exist outside the mind? There also are the concepts of the "subject" and "predicate" of a sentence. Nowhere do you find an instance of a "predicate" outside the mind. The concept "nothing" is a "being of reason." It literally means the opposite of being, so we know by its definition the thing it signifies cannot exist. How could "nothing" exist? It is by definition nonexistence. Such concepts must find a place within philosophy, because, as we've emphasized, philosophy is about reality, so it must have a place for everything. Such concepts are called "beings of reason." They are "beings" because they exist, but they are "of reason" because they can exist *only* in the mind; they are purely mental beings fashioned from and used by reason.

In this second subcategory, it is most natural to speak of logic.[127] Logic separated from its connection with real things falls clearly in this subcategory. Logic is a tool we use to do science (i.e., it is a branch of philosophy (see Chapter 6)). I can say "If X, then Y" and talk about it without referencing any existing thing outside the mind. General propositions (a part of logic) also belong to this second subcategory. I can say X is Y without referring to anything real. You've never seen a proposition floating around, nor can it happen that a proposition exists outside the mind. It is a being of reason. It is here that we finally find a proper category for Gödel's statement; we will later return to Gödel's theorem as promised.

Beings of reason are necessary for us, but like all things, their proper import and role should be kept in mind. That we must make use of beings of reason is simply a sign of the weakness of human intellect. The human power of cognition is, St. Thomas says, "barely" an intellect. Yet, it is an intellect, and the distance

---

some particular arena. Philosophers call the first way or mode "first intention" and the second mode of conceiving "second intention." It is "second," because in it, one reflects on his act of knowing of something else. In short, the second intention is the concept about concept(s). Second intentions are the realm of logic. They are beings of reason in the most proper sense because they come from a natural operation "of reason" which is to think about its thought.

[127] In an analogical way, even the "beings of reason" of logic are remotely founded on the real. They are based on real relations found in things.

between having an intellect and not is infinite,[128] just as the distance between accepting a principle and not is infinite.[129] For example, if I take it as a principle that breathing clean air is always good for you, then I will have to disagree even with those who say that breathing dirty air (that is, not breathing clean air) is sometimes, though rarely, good for you.[130]

The first subcategory, real being, is the primary way of viewing "being" *in relation to human knowing*. Recall that because human beings abstract from sensorial knowledge, we leave behind the existence (the "to be"). We apprehend things apart from their actual existence in the external world, that is to say, apart from their act of being. [131] From the human perspective, "being" *is that which actually exists or can exist outside the mind*. How then is being related to what we understand? We have already seen the answer. By our intellect, we apprehend the thing itself in an immaterial mode of existence. Without physically changing or losing our own being we become, in our intellectual power, the thing apprehended. In some way, the being of the thing becomes

---

[128] It is infinite in the sense that even an infinite number of non-rational beings will not make a rational being.

[129] There is no way to get to a principle by putting together any number (even an infinite number) of fractions of the principle. You either have the principle or you do not. It is the same as saying there is no such thing as half a principle.

[130] This hinges on facts that healthy people must breathe air, and that there is *only* clean and not clean (dirty) air.

[131] Note that a limit of human knowing appears here. Human beings, in the first act of the intellect, must consider being in the mode of that which exists or can exists. Apropos to this, Jacques Maritain says: "A deep vice besets the philosophers of our day, whether they by neo Kantians, neo-positivists, idealists, Bergsonians, logisticians, pragmatists, neo-Spinozists or neo-mystics. It is the ancient error of the nominalists. In different forms, and with various degrees of awareness, they all blame knowledge-through-concepts for not being a supra-sensible intuition of the existing singular, ... They cannot forgive that knowledge for not opening directly upon existence as sensation does, but only onto essences, possibles. They cannot forgive it for its inability to reach actual existence except by turning to sense... But why this incurable nominalism? The reason is that while having a taste for the real indeed, they nevertheless have no sense of being. Being as such, loosed from the matter in which it is incorporated, being, with its pure objective necessities and its laws that prove no burden, its restraints which do not bind, its invisible evidence is for them only a word." (Quoted from *Degrees of Knowledge,* chapter 1.)

our being.[132] The being of the thing is what we know. Being is thus intelligible. Something that is rich in being will, thus, be more intelligible than something less rich in being. In other words, the degree that something is, is the degree to which it is intelligible. To use our metaphorical way of speaking, the closer something is to "nothing," the less it is understandable.

What Is the Essence?

We are now nearly ready to define "essence." First, to define something in or relating directly to the *first subcategory of "ens"*, i.e. of *being (ens) proper*, is not an exercise in logical consistency and correct grammar. It is an act of judgment whereby one identifies what properly belongs to the thing under investigation. We have identified something (in this case essence) at a confused level, and we now seek to properly lay out its true meaning. In this section, we are discussing being as presented to the intellect, being as intelligible. We call being as viewed under the aspect of intelligibility, *essence*. So, we come to a wide, loose, definition of essence. *Essence is what a thing is as intelligible.*[133] Well, if a part of something is not intelligible, then that "part" *is not*. In other words, using the equivalence of being and intelligibility, the definition of essence given here can be rephrased: *essence is that which is*. With this definition, any idea of

---

[132] Recall that something cannot be and not be at the same time and in the same manner. Hence, the type of being that a thing takes on, as we become it in knowing it, must be of a special type; this type of being is produced and sustained by the intellect and is called "esse intentional." It is a unique mode of being that frees the thing from its natural mode of existence, which is particular and circumscribed. The thing's new mode of existence (esse intentional) is one that opens the thing up to the understanding. It is a universal mode of being, not a particular. An idea's mode of being is "esse intentional," purely referential, surviving to bring knower and known into unity. In the thing, the mode of being is particular. In our mind, it is universal. Incidentally, our minds abstract from the sensible particular, so our minds, of necessity, leave the particular behind; however, a mind that obtained the idea of the thing in another way could understand the particular as well as the universal.

[133] Or, said another way, *essence* is what a thing is from the standpoint of intelligibility; essence is the being of the thing viewed from the standpoint of intelligibility.

real being (i.e. in this first subcategory) that we have corresponds to an essence. The idea of red, cold, dog, book, man and collie all correspond to essences of really existing things.

To further resolve our definition of essence, we recall *that which is* in the material world[134] is a composition of substantial "form" and "matter"; form is that which it is actually (act) and matter is that which it is capable of being (potential). In Chapter 3, we introduced the analogy between the substantial change and the making of a statue. We saw that the word "form" can be transposed from its limited meaning of shape in the statue analogy to meaning all that a thing actually is. The shape of a thing is often the first distinguishing aspect about a thing, but it is also one of the most superficial; one has to observe how the thing behaves to really probe what it actually is.[135] Because substantial form by itself does not constitute a material thing, I can talk about the form of a cat, without talking about this cat or that cat. I can have a cat here and a cat there and both will be cats; the difference is one here and one there and thus they can have different colors, shapes, sizes, length of hair, health... etc. The unity of the cat itself is a less full (therefore intrinsically less understandable) unity than that of an immaterial thing, because its unity consists in pieces; it is "broken up" by its extension (the first accident of material substances). The cat's tail is here and his leg is there; the same could be said about each of the parts of his being. The idea of substance, for example, has no extension, so its unity is more complete, therefore more intelligible. Furthermore, because extension is involved in material forms, I can differentiate one member of a species by simply putting the form in a different place, i.e. by informing different matter.

---

[134] The material world is the *only* world we know *directly*.

[135] Observing behavior means to watch the thing undergo accidental change. For example, to learn about a squirrel's substantial form, watch it "freeze" when you first approach and then bound from the ground onto a nearby tree and scurry up it partway and freeze again as you move closer. Watch it bounce around looking for food and gathering nuts. Or, in the case of an inanimate form like water, watch it flow down the stream, freeze when it gets cold, and evaporate when it falls on a molten rock from a volcano. When it's cold outside, see it condense from the air onto your car window or on the grass in the morning.

Recall that our intellect, by its very mode of operation, abstracts from the particular. It leaves behind the particular, so we cannot by our intellect see the principle that makes something individual. This problem is one of a pair of problems associated with our ability to understand corporeal (material) substances as individuals. The second is the "element of non-being" in the material world. Or, said more properly, the material world is not as rich in being as, say, our rational nature. Hence, it is less intelligible in itself than our rational (immaterial) nature, so we cannot expect as profound answers to our questions about material being as we can to questions about immaterial being.

Using the thoughts of the two preceding paragraphs, we can consider a material thing's essence (in the wide sense), *that which is*, in two different ways:

1) Intelligibility to us.
   a. As completed substance (form and matter)
   b. Substantial form
2) Intelligibility in and of itself, but not to us.
   a. The thing as this individual in its entire being. That which primarily exists. This is called suppositum in general or for rational nature (such as ours) a person.

We will elucidate the meaning of these two ways in the following paragraphs, starting with 2) and then returning to 1).

The second way of approaching essence stretches the definition beyond what is customary. One can speak of "individual essence," but usually philosophers reserve the name "nature" for the "individual" essence. One can, nonetheless, speak in loose terms about the individual nature as an essence. One can say Fido's essential nature is to run after little Joey. The individual nature is only known by us in the manner of signs given to us by our sensorial knowledge. In Fido, there must be a principle that makes Fido to be Fido, not Lassie. However, this principle is secondary to the primary principle of intelligibility that is Fido. Fido is a dog, first. Then, Fido is that dog that runs after Joey. His dogness comes before his "Fidoness." Our mind extracts from the phantasm of Fido, that which is primary from the standpoint of intelligibility; it leaves behind the "act of existing" and the specifics of the individual.[136] This brings us to the first way of viewing, essence in the proper sense.

In following this first way, we can immediately define the essence in the restricted sense. Essence in the restricted sense is "that because of which (or in virtue of which) a thing is primarily as intelligible." In other words, *the essence of a thing is what the thing is necessarily and primarily as the first principle of its intelligibility.*[137] We see that this, in turn, can be taken in two ways. In the "1a" way, we take substantial form and matter (not the specific matter, but the general idea). For example, a dog is dogness informing certain matter. But, I can consider matter in a general way; for example, in the way I consider flesh and bones in general without considering Fido's flesh and bones.

In the 1b way, we find the most restricted and *most proper sense of the word "essence."* In this final perspective, *essence is the form of the thing.* In the case of an accidental form (a form which must exist in another), it is clear that this definition captures that *which is as intelligible*; the form is that which is actual and implicitly refers one back to the substance as that in which it alone exists or is intelligible. In the case of a substantial form, the definition is also very appropriate, because the substantial form implies the matter, and hence does not leave any part of the thing out.

Examples are concrete, not abstract, so they are at the heart of philosophy, which is about knowledge of real, not abstract, things. Let's take one. What is the essence of Einstein? Einstein was a physicist; he was of German descent; he sometimes laughed and sometimes was serious.[138] We have an idea of Einstein; we know his essence. However, his essence is only known in a very confused way. We proceed to clarify and make distinct and accurate what we know of his essence. Well, we know right away that this list of things does not contain the essence of Einstein in the proper sense. Some of them are essential in the sense that he

---

[136] The individual man, the human person, because he has an immaterial substantial form, has his individuality in his substantial form in a way that other form-matter composites do not have.

[137] This definition is Jacques Maritain's.

[138] Note that all these things listed are essences (in the proper sense) of something, though not of Einstein.

must have them to still be himself. However, when we look for the proper essence, we look for that which is primary, for the intelligible root out of which these facts about Einstein sprout. The essence of Einstein in the proper sense is that he was a man. All other principles that specify Einstein as a *unique* man take their root in his being a man, a rational animal.[139] For example, because he has a rational nature he can think and be a physicist. Because he is a rational animal, he can laugh and cry.

Existence Precedes Essence

We can now close the discussion on existence and essence by pointing out that, in the process of elucidating the meaning of the word "essence," we have found that "existence precedes essence" in another sense. In Chapter 3, we discussed that one knows things exist, before he knows the proper essence of things. Now, we see that essence is to existence as matter is to form. Essence is "that which a thing is primarily as intelligible." However, in the order of existence, the act of being *(esse)* must suffuse the essence in the actually existing thing, otherwise it would not exist. Essence in the mind is only a possible, not an actually existing thing, but even there it received whatever being it has from an act of an existing thing. Remember: no being, no intelligibility. A comparison can be made to illustrate the point. "Form is the actuality of the thing, as matter is the potentiality of the thing," in proportionately the same way that "The existence is the actuality of the thing and the essence is the potentiality." As potentiality only makes sense with respect to something actual, essence only makes sense with respect to existence *(esse).*

---

[139] Again, as a man, he has a unique substantial form (specific essence or what we called an "individual nature"), but recall we are talking about the intelligibility directly accessible for the human mode of knowing, which is through abstraction. Still, his *unique* "essence" (that which makes Einstein, Einstein and not, say, Newton) is a final specification of the essence "man," thus requires the essence "man." The "as a man" starting phrase of the first sentence of this footnote reflects this truth.

The distinction between essence and existence and the priority of the existence over the essence is seen clearly in a statement like baseball great Yogi Berra's "It isn't over till *it's over*." Look again; it goes by fast. The first part of the sentence is the essence (or possible) and the second (italicized) part is the existence (act of being).[140] Because we conceive an essence in the purely referential (also called intentional) mode of existence, we can think of the game as over, even though it *is **not** yet actually over*. I attended a basketball game in which one team was behind by a seemingly insurmountable number of points; many of my group wanted to leave to avoid traffic because the game, they said, "was over." In fact, we stayed and the game went into triple overtime and the previously losing team won.

Truth

We finally can consider the question "What is truth?" We have seen that "to know" properly speaking is "to know things," not "to know ideas or abstractions." What we know of a thing is true when it corresponds to the way the thing really is. When we make the judgment that an apple is edible, what we say is true if, in fact, people can eat the apple and be nourished by it. In other words, edibleness must be a property of the apple for my statement to be true. Hence, truth is conformity of the mind with the thing under consideration. ***Truth is conformity of the mind with reality***. This meaning, like all in philosophy, has a depth that at first is not perceived. Moreover, once one perceives and understands completely at the new level, he sees still further depth. Mind you, the new understanding never undoes the old understanding; it fills it in where it is bare and extends it where it did not reach.

The first question then arises: What about the truth of propositions in logic, such as Gödel's theorem. Logical propositions are true only in an analogical sense. Their truth is only remotely founded in reality. In logical propositions, I fashion a world modeled after real being in my mind. These are the already-

---

[140] Note here again the appropriateness of St. Cajetan's statement that existence doesn't exist; that is, existence as an object of thought loses its "to be," and becomes an essence.

discussed "beings of reason." They exist only in my mind, and are subject only to laws drawn from different aspects of reality. For example, I might choose to impose an algorithm for determining how to respond to certain predicates and certain subjects. In any case, the truth of the proposition then is determined by agreement with the chosen rules. In this way, it is like the rules of a game such as chess. Rules of a game such as chess are freely chosen with certain things imposed as one fixes a certain framework. For example, in chess, once one picks a square 2-D grid of alternating black and white squares, one has significantly, although implicitly, restricted the rules of the game. In general, a move will be valid or true if it conforms to the rules imposed. Hence, in systems of ideas, like games, there is a large degree of artificiality imposed freely by the mind, yet the mind itself has obtained the rules from reality, but divested of the particular context in which they are normally found.

Thus, we see even more clearly why Gödel's theorem cannot call in to doubt our ability to acquire knowledge with certitude. Still, Gödel's theorem is interesting, of course, from the point of view of mathematics. It is also interesting because it reminds us that even in such artificial constructs of ideas, the interconnectedness of reality is not circumvented. How is truth connected with the interrelatedness of reality? What more can be said about truth's relation to being? These are questions that will complete our understanding of how we understand and lead us to ask questions, fascinating *particular* questions about animals, artificially intelligent beings, angels, and God. Do the last three exist? What are they? These are questions for the next chapter and beyond. First, we address the questions raised concerning truth, being, and interconnectedness. Being is the key, so focus on it.

"To Be" True

Since being is primary, we should not be surprised that it explains other things, but is not easily explained itself. Being has a depth that is so different from anything else we encounter, so I will take a moment to admonish us that we should not expect to understand it in one fell swoop; it will take time and meditation. Being should not be approached so much as a problem to be solved, but as an ocean to be explored. Again, being is not a problem to be solved like a crossword puzzle or chess move; it has not a problem aspect where algorithmic thinking or years of technical expertise might substitute for one's thinking. It requires primary effort from the mind as mind, not as finely-honed algorithmic computer or skilled processor of technical functions, or even as creator of elaborate beings of reason to model a complex system. It has a profound mystery aspect. Scholastic philosophers give a definite meaning to the word "mystery." "Mystery" here means a little bit of what it means in a detective novel, but this is only a very peripheral aspect of its meaning. *Mystery means an area of reality* **so intelligible** *that we can never understand it all.* In this very circumscribed sense, we say being should be approached as mystery.

A first effort at understanding "being" might lead one to try, in a problem-oriented fashion, to make it a genus or category. We'd make it the largest genus because everything has it. But wait, how do we go from one genus to the genus that contains it? We take away distinctions. For example, the genus "dog" is lower than the genus "mammal" which prescinds from the distinctions between dogs and cats and cows, and the genus "animal" higher up the list prescinds from the differences between dogs and worms. Hence, by the time one gets to the genus that includes every possible thing, all differences would be included in the genus, and the genus descriptor "being" would not have any positive content left. In other words, if "being" refers to a genus that includes everything, being would really be nothing. This is obviously an absurd conclusion. What, then, is to be done with "being"? Being is called a transcendental, because it overarches all and is in all things without being contained by any of them. Probing "being" by thinking about one of its principles will lead naturally to another of the transcendentals: truth.

Now, some principles come first and some come later. We often forget this in our scientifically driven culture. In the sciences, one often makes hypotheses and freely draws on principles that best suit the given problem. We then choose to call these primary. This methodology is even more prevalent in certain areas of mathematics. Because of the pervasiveness of this method, one sometimes forgets that some things are primary and some things are secondary. In other words, *behind these concepts that we choose to call primary for use in a specialized science, there are concepts that are primary in reality, not just by our choice.*

One example is the principle of contradiction. It is also more directly referred to as the principle of identity: "every being **is** *what it is.*" (Note, once again, the essence's (italics) dependence on real existence (bold)). This is not tautological. A tautology (for example, x=x) is from formal logic and hence is about beings of reason; as such, it is something devoid of real content. "x=x" is a being of reason made in analogy to the principle of identity; it is the vague shadow of the principle of identity in the world of beings of reason. It is not the principle of identity. The principle of identity (and its equivalent, the principle of contradiction) expresses something primary about "being." Every other statement about things will in some way rest on the principle of identity. It is a self-evident principle, because it is impossible to think its opposite. It expresses the interchangeability of being and intelligibility, which we have already discussed. Again, everything that is, to that degree is intelligible. This is key to all the sciences. It is implicitly assumed by all of them, including modern sciences. It is part of the science before the modern science. The interchangeability of being and intelligibility obviously has deep implications for our understanding of truth and being. Being is so rich that our mind must look at it from various aspects,[141] one at a time, to see it.

Truth is being as viewed from the standpoint of intelligibility. We will discuss the transcendentals further in Chapters 5 through 9. The transcendentals are: *being* (ens), *reality* or *thingness* (res), *unity* (unum), *identity as something apart* (aliquid), *truth* (verum), *goodness* (bonum). Beauty is the "splendor of all the transcendentals together."[142] Each of the transcendentals is interchangeable or, said another way, they are "being" looked at from various viewpoints. With these brief words, we only *begin* to cause one to *ask the questions* that will lead us

---

[141] For example, we've seen when we approach "being" *(ens)* from: 1) the standpoint of *intelligibility*, we get the *essence;* 2) the standpoint of existence, we get substance; 3) the standpoint of action, we get *act.*

[142] Said another way, beauty is the "goodness of truth."

deeper into our understanding of being. We will discuss these issues more especially in Chapter 8. We will say briefly something only about the transcendental oneness or *unity* (unum), because it relates to our topic of truth. A "being" *is* to the extent that *it is one*. The idea of *two* comes after the idea of *one* and implicitly includes it. Being is struck through with unity. Hence, we glimpse that "the degree to which something is one" is the degree "which it is"; therefore its unity expresses its intelligibility. That is, the more unified a thing is, the more understandable it is. With this background, let's now re-point our probe directly at our topic: being as intelligible, i.e., truth.

Because of the "convertibility" of being and truth, all things must be true. You may say, "On the contrary, it is obvious that all things are **not true** because all of us have false ideas at times." But, a "false idea" is a being of reason. For example, to say that the sun is a square green rock is false. But, it is composed of true things, for example: "the syntax of the sentence including the subject being assigned a predicate"; "green"; "sun"; and "square." What is false in the statement does not really exist; this is what we mean by false. The sun is not green.[143] All *things* are true insofar as they *are*.

But how can it be so? The great philosopher Plato (427-347 BC) taught that "all things are true" because what we really know are ideas, which he thought were archetypes given to us from eternity.[144] We know differently, so how can it be that all things are

---

[143] The apparent reality of falsehood is only an illusion created by the many real things in the statement that give it aspects of reality; one of which is not its false predication. As mentioned earlier, by the very articulation of an error, we in some way give it more than its due. Only what is true in an error can really be articulated. What is false is a negation, a being of reason, like "nothing." Beings of reason, as we've seen, are necessary for us because of our limited intellect.

[144] This belief makes Plato (Aristotle's teacher) the first philosophical idealist. However, this serious error and other errors that he makes are much less damaging than they are in modern philosophical idealist systems for two main reasons. First, Plato was the first in history to really see many philosophical truths, so his errors are more easily excused, for no pioneer should be expected to find everything. Second, Plato touches lightly on things that a lesser philosopher would have insisted on. This leads Maritain to say "But of Plato himself we may say that his false principles grew in an atmosphere too pure to allow them to yield their full fruit and poison the essence of this thought. St.

true? How can we conform our minds to things? After all, conformity with the mind is an act of the mind, not the thing, is it not?

St. Thomas gives a clue to the answer when he says "The mind's act of intellection itself constitutes and completes that relation of conformity which is the nature of all truth." (*sent.* I, 19,5). In other words, that the thing itself is intelligible means that *it* has a relation to the knowing mind. This means, as we've already seen, the inherent nature of any existing thing has an essential form that can be received into a knowing mind. Now, this relation is a potential relation, because we do not know the given thing all the time. Yet, for something to be potentially, it must be actually somewhere or it could never be. If all things have a permanent relation to a knowing mind, where then does this relation have its being? This being is the truth of the thing. All intelligibility implies a relation in the given being (a *property*) to an intellect.

Another principle of "being," the principle of sufficient reason, will elucidate the origin of this relation between a thing and an intellect. The **principle of sufficient reason** is: *"Everything must have its reason for being in itself or in another."*[145] If you say all things do not have a reason for being, then you deny the intelligibility of being and thus deny the basis for the sciences at their root. You may say this is not true; I can deny part without denying the whole. However, this denial is not like denying a part of a whole, as one's imagination leads one to believe. One may think, "I just deny that particular thing, not all truths." Well, this particular truth happens to be one on which all else depends. If there is nowhere a reason for things to exist, then the secondary things that spring from that existence would have no core reason either, so things would not be intelligible, but things are intelligible. We must acknowledge the fact that all things have a

---

Augustine was therefore able to extract from Plato's gold-mine the ore of truth." St. Augustine (354-430 AD) is a genius of towering stature who is universally considered one of the biggest single influences on our Western culture. He was Bishop of Hippo in North Africa.

[145] This principle is fundamentally the principle of causality (which is "nothing changes itself" and is discussed in Chapter 5) viewed from the standpoint of intelligibility.

reason for being. The principle of sufficient reason is self-evident, because its opposite is not thinkable.

From this principle, we see that there must be "a being" that contains its own reason for existence, for otherwise there would be no intelligibility, and there is intelligibility.[146] That is to say, there must be a "Being" that contains the whole ground of its intelligibility. Such a Being must be completely understandable, having no shadow of unintelligibility, for any lack of intelligibility indicates a "reason," a relationship to another, in the Being that is not explained by the Being. But, the Being we're discussing contains its reason for its "act of being" from which all other secondary reasons must emanate. Hence, such a being must be pure intelligibility, intelligibility in act. Now, intelligibility implies intelligibility to an intellect; we already noted this at the end of the last paragraph. If the Being is to contain the entire reason for its existence, then it must, by the reasoning just articulated for intelligibility, be pure intellection, intellect in pure act. Thus, we come to a Being that is pure intelligibility and pure act of intellection. This Being we call God.[147] We see that He is the perfect conformity of reality to itself, so He is most appropriately called Truth itself.[148] This section is not meant to explore the details of the proofs of God's existence; it is just a sketch of one such proof. The proofs of God's existence will be discussed in appropriate detail in Chapter 8, when we have more philosophical facility and depth.

---

[146] Even an infinite number of beings like ourselves, which do not contain their reason for the very act of their being *(esse)*, would leave all reasons without a reason at bottom, and thus unintelligible. That is, there would be no intelligibility, but things are intelligible, so this cannot be true. An argument such as this is called *"ratio ad absurdum,"* because, in such an argument, one shows a premise to be false by following it until one sees that it leads to an absurdity.

[147] Because intelligibility and being are interchangeable, God, who is pure intelligibility, is pure Being. Unlike any other being, He contains the reason for His existence. Hence, there is an infinite abyss between Him and any other being. It is the difference between uncreated being (Being *a se* (of itself)) and created being (being *per se* (by itself, but not of itself)).

[148] Only in Him are essence and existence one and the same. He is *who is*. The first part is the existence; the second part (italicized) is the essence.

We have come to Truth in its full meaning; it is still "conformity of the mind with reality," but in the end, that mind must be the mind of God. We have seen that the relation we call "truth" is not simply that of logical proposition; this is only a shadow of truth. Truth in things is their actual relation to the knowing mind of God and their potential relation to our mind. We will explore the rich field of "being" more in the chapters ahead.

Finally, as in Chapter 3, all that we've concluded in this chapter is independent of the results of specialized sciences (i.e. modern physics, chemistry, and biology—even less so of the soft sciences of psychology), for we did not use any results from them in formulating our conclusions. In fact, most of our statements came directly from thinking about common experience. If we had utilized instead, or in addition, conclusions from specialized sciences, the conclusions would have been less certain, because of the dependence of the results of the specialized sciences on an interconnected web of particular theories and experiments. As we will see, the conclusions of these sciences also are--by mode of practice--on a different plane of explanation than the philosophical level, which we seek in this book. As a result, we also know that what we've concluded will not be changed by future results of the specialized sciences.

However, the reader now may gently prod us by saying, "All this is well and good and true, but at some point I should see this applied to *particular* things in a more complete way, so that I can both understand better what has been uncovered, and see how all this fits with the modern *specialized* sciences." The next chapter moves us from uncovering the fundamentals to applying them to interesting particular cases, such as the making of animals in the lab. Meanwhile, we have to wait to explore the relation between the sciences, for that is the subject of Chapters 6 and 7.

A Word of Encouragement

There's no way around the real effort it takes to get one's arms around the deep points raised in the last two chapters. Philosophy requires intellectual muscles to be worked and habits to be established. Indeed, most do not even realize that they have the intellectual muscles that they are starting to use in this and the previous chapter. So, do not be discouraged that you do not understand it all quickly. In fact, it would be superhuman to absorb philosophy without much meditation on the important truths. Again, to most it's so new and so deep. Many search high and low to experience something new, even if it costs heavily in money, time, and effort. Whereas, the newness of these other activities dies, their depth is plumbed and no permanent benefit is obtained. In true understanding (philosophy), the more one knows, the more he sees he doesn't know, but would love to know, and every new understanding is a permanent gain.

As a result, unlike those other activities, here the return on one's effort is beyond price, for it is nothing less than finding meaning (understanding) in life. Jacques Maritain says in answering the question "What is the use of philosophy?":

Philosophy, taken in itself, is above utility. And for this very reason philosophy is of the utmost necessity for men. It reminds them of the supreme utility of those things which do not deal with means, but with ends. For men do not live only by bread, vitamins, and technological discoveries. They live by values and realities which are above time, and are worth being known for their own sake; they feed on that invisible food which sustains the life of the spirit, and which makes them aware, not of such or such means at the service of their life, but of their very reasons for living and suffering, and hoping.

This is also true of all the pure sciences in their full sense. Further, the understandings we are obtaining and will obtain, as we'll see clearly in later chapters, are essential in enjoying those other activities, because they reveal the real value and place of those activities.

Chapter 5

On Animals, Men and Robots

*W*e now have enough philosophical foundation to ask some pivotal questions. Does an animal think? What is an animal? What is a man? Will a robot ever be able to think? What is a robot? Are there any other thinking beings besides man and God?

Animals

Proceeding in order, it sure seems as if animals can think. One young student of mine told me how her cat could not get in the house one time and, without being trained to do so, jumped and rang the doorbell. I myself saw a documentary on public TV about a gorilla named Koko that responded to human hand motions (sign language) with its own hand motions. Such abilities left Koko's human researchers adamant that Koko knows sign language.

So, can an animal think? To answer this, we need to be clear about what we mean, and this always involves making distinctions. If by "thinking," we mean such activities as the above, then obviously an animal can think. However, is this really all we mean by thinking? We saw in the last chapter that man has an intellect that includes the capacity of abstracting general ideas from sensorial knowledge. If this is what we mean by "thinking," we--after careful analysis--may have to conclude that animals do not think. Thus, we would have to make a distinction between two ways of "thinking," an animal way and a human way. Let's first decide whether animals have an intellect.

Well, if animals have an intellect, they should have ideas, which, as we've seen, are universals. Recall when we have the idea of a thing, we know what its essence is, what is essential to the thing for the understanding, what the *form of the thing is*. Because of this fact, if animals have an intellect, they must, for example, have the *capacity* to do science. The fact that they do not do even rudimentary science is strong evidence against their having an intellect. By science here, I mean not just the modern sciences, which are highly developed sciences, but *any* directed effort to get at what is essential in a thing or things. What we mean by science here includes even rudimentary attempts to understand essences, like when a child asks why the sky is blue or why there are bad men. Not even the most rudimentary attempts to find out what is essential and what is not is found among animals in the wild.[149]

In truth, the fact that animals do not do science is just short of a proof of their lack of intellects. Here's why. Not exercising an ability indicates a block of some sort to the exercise of that ability. Now, such a block or impediment is either physical or not. If a physical impediment is involved, such as not having an opposable thumb (some animals do), it would not stop the development of the life of the intellect but only impede it, and we should see some evidence of it. For example, Stephen Hawking certainly has major physical impediments; he can barely move any part of his body. However, no one would deny that he is one of the most profound physicists in the world.

One might also consider the example of stroke victims; they have trouble communicating what they are thinking. Maybe, as Koko's trainer, Francine Patterson, suggests about some gorilla communication, some animals are in an analogous state. In other words, maybe gorillas, for example, have some lack in the brain that prevents their communicating what they're thinking. If this

---

[149] Following our inviolable rule of beginning with what is more known and proceeding to what is less known, we start by thinking of animals as we see them in the wild. By contrast, considering animals among men introduces effects that make the interpretation of their behavior less clear, because animal behavior is influenced in complicated ways by the human actions. In short, specialized science with its highly specialized techniques should only begin after the conversion of infra-scientific knowledge (improper knowledge) into proper knowledge.

block is a partial, as she seems to suggest, then we should be able to resolve the dilemma by observing *some* evidence of immateriality in the animals' thinking process; in particular, rudimentary attempts at science. Furthermore, if this "stroke" scenario were true, it would make animals rather absurd creatures because they would have an immaterial intellect, but in their natural state not be able to make much use of it throughout their short life; their chief power would be their most ineffective power. It would be similar to having a human race whose lives were lived from beginning to end as stroke victims![150]

Human stroke victims usually show signs of their continuing intelligence, and we also know that it's human nature to have an intellect. With animals, on the other hand, we see *no* signs of asking questions about the world. Yet, if we say animals have an "impediment" that is so severe that the intellect's presence can only be determined by specifically looking for signs of it with experiments proper to a specialized science, we have the absurd situation mentioned above that appears to be ruled out because of its irrationality. Nonetheless, we can check for the presence of the intellect, and we will discuss this fascinating topic shortly.

Is it a non-physical (immaterial) block? Well, immaterial things are simple, and so they cannot be divided or broken. Why? They have no extension; the first accident of a material thing is its extension (the fact that part of it is here and part there). Such a thing can, in principle, be broken into pieces. However, an immaterial thing has no parts outside of each other, no extension. Consider the mathematical entity of a triangle. As a mathematical entity defined as a three-sided (closed) figure, it is an idea, hence immaterial and thus simple. If I try to break or take away one of the sides, I will no longer have the idea of a triangle. I can either have the idea of a triangle or not; I cannot cut it in half.[151] An

---

[150] Of course, if the block ***completely*** prevents the animal's intellect from being expressed during its life, then we are no longer talking about an animal with an intellect, but some external intellect acting on the animal. Remember we are talking about species characteristics, not genetically defective individuals.

[151] Of course, in my imagination or in the physical world, the situation is different. I can, for example, take apart the sides of a triangle made of sticks, break one of the sticks in half and make a four-sided figure with the same perimeter as the triangle. And that's the point; this is the nature of the physical

immaterial thing cannot be broken. Hence, an immaterial block to the exercise of the intellect must be an act proper to the intellectual substance itself.[152] Only an act of will,[153] a decision to not do science, could provide such a block. Hence, it could be possible that all animals we've seen up till now have made a decision to not do science. This is a highly implausible explanation. Furthermore, it appears totally irrational and thus impossible (recall that the degree to which something is intelligible, is the degree to which it is). One can make a lot of decisions, but is a decision to not use one's intellect and therefore to make no more decisions really possible? It is suicide of the core of the person (an intellectual being) while remaining a person.

What's more, in the wild, animals perform none of the uniquely human actions that come from having an intellect. None are scientists, engineers, artists, musicians, teachers, comedians, priests, actors, doctors, lawyers, politicians, salesmen, linguists, or philosophers. Even in non-wild (experimental) settings, no animal becomes one of these in any real sense. One could extend the list just given quite a bit, but what is the point? All these uniquely human abilities derive from man's intellect.

But how can we verify that animals do not have an intellect? Further, even if animals don't do things like those listed above, they certainly do amazing things. Dr. Anne Russon of York University in Toronto says that:[154]

In my study [in Borneo], I found ex-captive orangutans doing many things they must have learned by imitating humans. They chopped firewood, washed laundry and

---

world. From the image, I could then proceed to abstract a new idea, that of a square.

[152] One might say that the intellect is completely barred from acting in the case of an animal, which is to say it is outside, not part of the animal. Thus, such a statement implicitly acknowledges the point at issue.

[153] Will is the appetitive power of the intellect. In the sensorial powers, the appetitive powers require the acquisition of sensorial knowledge; the animal sees something and "decides" whether it is good or not. A similar situation obtains in the intellectual powers. We will discuss this later in this chapter.

[154] Taken from the web at URL:
http://www.pbs.org/teachersource/scienceline/archives/jan99/jan99.shtm

dishes, weeded and swept camp paths, sawed logs, sharpened axe blades, hung up hammocks and rode in them, and siphoned fuel. One even tried to make a fire and almost succeeded; she tried every single trick she had seen camp cooks using daily. [Russon does not say using what instruments, possibly matches and kindling.] In all of these cases, orangutans did the jobs the same way humans did yet no one taught them--you'd have to be a fool to show a free-living orangutan how to make a fire or wield an axe --and these tools were even hidden from the orangutans. So we concluded that the only way they could have learned all of these skills was by watching humans.

In another place she says:

...But actually learning by imitation is an impressive mental accomplishment because it means learning new behavior just by watching, without practice. This is a very advanced ability because the imitator has to make a sort of 'mental video' of the model's behavior then use that video, and nothing else, to make new behavior...

They rarely use tools, but I've seen them build 'workseats' to make a job more comfortable, fashion leaf 'gloves' to protect their hands and make leaf 'hats' to protect them from rain...

Dr. Francine Patterson says:[155]

Learning the signs for Koko's most frequent requests - like "eat," "thirsty," and "drapes" - was fairly easy. And since Koko understands spoken English, I could ask her questions verbally, and she would answer with signs - hopefully ones I knew. But Koko knows over 1000 signs, and she often signs quickly and uses several signs in a row. And if I miss something, she will rarely repeat herself.

---

[155] Excerpt from *The Education of Koko* by Francine Patterson and Eugene Linden, Holt Rinehart Winston, 1981.

How can such things be explained? Well, we have all but eliminated intellectual power as the reason for this animal behavior. Let's eliminate it. We need to determine if animals have any ideas in the sense discussed in the last chapter. To do this, we need to think about how ideas manifest themselves. Language is obviously important in how the intellect manifests its knowledge to the world outside the mind. If I say "dog," you know what it means. How? You know what a dog is (*at least* in an undeveloped way), and second because you have learned to associate the sound and sight of the word "dog" with this idea of a dog.

So, when I say "I saw a dog," you recall the image of a dog and idea of a dog, and from that base, we can discuss and hone our knowledge of what a dog is. Some words, like "dog," are learned by direct association; for example, your mother may have pointed out a dog to you as a child. Second, some words like "North Pole," you may learn by being told that it's the point where the rotation axis of the earth intersects the northern[156] part of the earth. Much of our language is learned in this manner of words getting meaning from other words already known. This is what might be called the "dictionary way" of learning words. My three-year-old son, for example, did not know what a wallet was, and I defined it for him as "a small thing for keeping and carrying money and cards." Then, I pulled my wallet out of my back pocket, and he correctly identified it. Most words are probably learned by some complicated combination of these two ways: the direct association way and dictionary way.[157]

The crucial point comes from the dictionary way of learning, for it illustrates our capacity to learn words (symbols or instrumental signs) from other words (symbols), not by chain association, but by understanding the meaning of the words. Ideas are, after all, pure "meanings." If animals can transfer the meanings, they must have ideas. However, a chain association would not be a transfer of meaning. For example, if I were to bring

---

[156] The northern half might, in turn, be explained as the half of the earth that contains Europe (halves defined naturally by a plane perpendicular to the rotation axis).

[157] At first, for example, many learn the North Pole as a vague area pointed at on a globe, and only later is it the idea elucidated above.

my son to his bike and tell him that it was a "vehicle," i.e. identify his bike with the word (symbol) "vehicle," and then, in turn, identified the word "vehicle" with "device for anthropoid locomotion," he could identify his bike as the latter set of words without even knowing what the words meant; he could do this by mere signaling ability. Signaling in its narrowest meaning refers to response-to-stimulus type behavior. In the case of my son's bike, one could learn to associate a set of sounds together with an image of the bike; either one of the two sounds (say vehicle) would then trigger identification with the bike and the other sound ("device for anthropoid locomotion"). This involves a response to an object, not an understanding the meaning of the words. If someone could show evidence that animals can acquire such meanings, by showing that an animal can learn by the dictionary method, we would have to consider that the given animal has an intellect. It would be even more convincing if evidence were found that animals have ideas that are in principle ***not picturable*** (which means not directly referable to sensorial knowledge) such as the idea of an idea or the idea of God.[158] However, despite immense research efforts, no evidence of either variety has been found.[159] *Hence, we must conclude that animals do not have intellects.* This is no great surprise, given the strong arguments that we were able to adduce above without even considering animal research.

So, we ask again, how do we account for the marvelous behavior of animals such as those tabulated above, as well as of the sometimes seemingly near-human behavior of our pets? We have both intellectual knowledge and sensorial knowledge; perhaps an

---

[158] The profound meaning that a word contains prompted a philosopher at a conference I attended to say, "One word is worth a thousand pictures." This truth obtains because a word signifies a meaning, an idea. For example, no number of pictures could accurately describe what a black hole is. Its reverse, "One picture is worth a thousand words," obtains as one approaches purely sensorial knowledge.

[159] The late, great philosopher Mortimer Adler (1902-2001) widely known for his work on the *Great Book* series, *Encyclopedia Britannica* and innumerable other important contributions, studied the cognitive sciences for at least 45 years. His reasoning and conclusion that animals do not have intellectual knowledge is articulated very well in his book, *Intellect.* Also, renowned researcher into signs (semiotics), Thomas Sebeok, concludes that animals have no ability that should be labeled as uniquely human.

animal is a creature with only sensorial knowledge. Let's explore this possibility. We can then later discuss how sensorial knowledge is to be included in the definition of "animal."

Recall that sensorial knowledge is awareness of particulars by way of phantasms, and includes the capacity of imagination and memory. Such knowledge can account for all of the above behavior. Furthermore, if the behavior is of the stimulus-response type discussed above, one does not even need sensorial knowledge to be present.[160] You no doubt have experience with such mechanisms. The motion-activated lights that are very common outside suburban homes are one example. Much of the above behavior can be explained in this fashion. All can be explained by sensorial knowledge.

Let's look at some of the examples. The apes that "aped" the human activity mentioned above, such as wielding axes, did just what Dr. Russon suggests: they "ran the video back." A "video" is nothing but a series of images run in correct time sequence.[161] If apes have full sensorial knowledge, they can remember sequences of images (phantasms) and can "run them back." The cat that rang the doorbell had associated (by seeing) the physical act of the door opening with the pushing of the button. The cat needed to go in (for food or whatever) and its previous association--i.e. the sensorial knowledge "video" of the door opening--was triggered, and it mimicked the chain of actions visualized. Note in doing this, it does not have to be *aware* of the door or the bell. However, all evidence suggests that the cat is aware, that is has true sensorial knowledge, of the door and the doorbell; this distinguishes it sharply from a "robot" like the automatic light. The behavior is still amazing and involves an impressive array of complexity that moves from the acquisition of sensorial data to the processing of the information to the execution of the jump that made it able to ring the bell. Even more amazing is the awareness the animal has of particular things in great detail; for

---

[160] I myself have designed and built fairly complicated mechanisms that respond to stimuli and am very sure that those apparatus have no sensorial knowledge.

[161] Note the ape (and cat) do not *know* (intellectual sense) time, but the organisms are certainly complex enough to keep in original order a series of snapshots (phantasms), especially at the small number of frames per second needed.

example, noticing the bell. A lesser animal could not have done what that cat did.

Similarly, a cat could not accomplish the feats of the apes described above. The ability to learn and recall 1,000 signs, like Koko, shows quite an advanced sensorial knowledge. Bees communicate by flying in certain patterns, but these are not imposed from the outside, as are the signs given the gorillas. Yet, the ability to sign in the fashion seen is quite readily explained by animals having sensorial knowledge. To illustrate further how sensorial knowledge without intellect functions, consider how the orangutan uses foliage as a rain hat. A scenario follows. First, the orangutan watches rain fall to the ground and records how a leaf blocks rain from hitting him. At some later time, it rains while the orangutan is out in the open doing a task. The rain triggers the running of the previous "video." Next, the orangutan senses rain on its skin while out in the open, and imitates the "video" by placing the leaf in the appropriate place as indicated in the image. Note that the orangutan does not have to understand, for example, the general idea of an umbrella to do what it does.

In a similar way, one can account for the reported dolphin (porpoise) ability to identify circles of different colors. Say, for example, the animal was trained to pick a red circle from among other shapes, and in a later test it was able to pick the *circle* even when the circle was yellow. This is not the abstract ability that it appears. An animal that has recall of an image of the yellow colored circle prompted by a similar shaped red circle placed in front of it can simply compare the two particulars (the phantasm and the currently perceived one) and see that they have in common a shape. The animal does not have to understand anything about what it means to be a circle; it just compares two particulars. Indeed, if the animal's imagination had been active, it may have already colored a circle yellow, making the comparison near trivial.

Animals are amazing, but they are especially amazing when they are around human beings. Man and animal together raise animal to a higher level in some ways.[162] The "Clever Hans phenomenon" is a case in point. Of this horse that lived at the early part of the twentieth century, renowned semiotics expert Thomas Sebeok says:

> *Ever since the Byzantine Empire was ruled by Justinian (A.D. 483-565) there have been reports of clever animals, but none so captured the imagination of layman and scholar alike as that attributed to Clever Hans, the horse of Mr. von Osten.[163] Hans gave every evidence of being able to add and subtract, multiply and divide, read and spell; and he could solve problems of musical harmony. Hans communicated with his questioners by converting all answers into a number and tapping out that number with his foot.*

Some time ago, it was learned that the horse was responding to very subtle communications from its trainer and the audience, and none of the information was coming from the horse. The horse had learned to pick up on the slightest clue as to what was expected of it. Basically, sensorial knowledge can be very powerful in higher animals.[164]

Even this "Clever Hans" cuing does not exhaust sensorial knowledge's capacity. The power of sensorial knowledge is why some animal researches feel that their animals are human-like.[165]

---

[162] In technical language, these animals in the human environs are called "artifacts," because they are not animals as animals, but in some way animals as molded by men.

[163] I have a strong suspicion that this horse inspired the very old TV series about a "talking" horse, *Mr. Ed.*

[164] To get an idea of how powerful, consider the following. It is widely known that blind people develop their other senses (e.g. hearing and touch) to a much higher level than others. They are aware of hearing things that the rest of us would miss. Similarly, but at a qualitatively different level, animals, lacking an intellect, have to lean on their senses in a profound way that we can barely imagine. Hence, animals are aware of things through their senses that we would miss because our intellect's power allows us to be somewhat slothful in the use and development of our sensorial powers.

[165] In the documentary on Koko, one anecdote stands out as an example of how easy it is to read our abilities into animal abilities. Koko had "drawn" a picture,

We must just reiterate that sensorial knowledge coupled with the presence of human activity can give animals a wide range of interaction capabilities, but these do not mean that animals think in the sense of having intellectual capacities.

Hence, *the only plausible explanation is that animals are living things with sensorial knowledge.* Can creatures with sensorial knowledge be self-aware? Self-aware means knowing oneself as a thinking self; it means one knows that he knows (that he knows that he knows that he knows...one could go on indefinitely). Well, an animal knows things only by way of phantasms. Sensorial knowledge is only partially immaterial because it is particular and because it is necessarily bound to a material organ (for example, the eye in the sense of sight), yet it *is* partially immaterial. So maybe it can be self-aware; let's follow the reasoning through and see.

If an animal were to know that it knows, it would not only be aware of this cat, this grass, this tree, that star... but know all these diverse particulars as instances of a general thing called knowledge; in other words, it would have to be able to form the idea of sensorial knowledge. But ideas are general and purely immaterial, and we have said this creature does not have knowledge by ideas, only sensorial knowledge by phantasms. Hence, animals cannot be self-aware in this primary sense. But, this does not mean they cannot be aware of their physical body, and their pain and pleasure, and of all particulars about themselves.[166] They are. This awareness, in the highest animals, can "ape" self-awareness.

---

which looked like a random ink blot test of colors (to me, I vaguely recall it looked like a volcano). The trainers were excited by the picture, because Koko signed "stink gorilla more" and they thought it looked like flowers. (They say the word "stink" is what the gorilla uses for flowers.)

[166] Note another amazing capacity of higher animals: because they have an imagination, they can dream (be aware of imagined happenings while asleep).

Definition of Animal and Plant

We can now further refine our definition of animal. Aristotle, the great philosopher, was also a great biologist[167] who classified about 500 organisms.[168] He identified the four primary abilities of living things: [169] nutritive or vegetative capacity (growth and self-maintenance through assimilation of nutrients),[170] locomotive ability (ability to move from place to place), sensorial and intellectual knowledge. Sensorial knowledge and intellectual knowledge, as already mentioned, also have powers correlative to them, the appetitive powers; they are sensorial appetite and the intellectual appetite, called the will. Man has them all. Animals have sensorial knowledge (and thus, sensorial appetite), not intellectual knowledge. Animals also have vegetative abilities, for, of course, sensorial knowledge cannot occur without nutritive life, without the growth[171] in size and complexity and/or the ability to maintain itself. In order for an animal to be an organism (that is, organized)[172] or, said another way, to be a real unity and thus to be

---

[167] Charles Darwin (1809-82) says of Aristotle, "I had not the remotest notion what a wonderful man he was. Linnaeus and Cuvier have been my two great gods, though in very different ways, but they were mere schoolboys to old Aristotle." Quoted from *"The Relevance of Physics"* by S. Jaki, page 30, which says, Darwin's comment on reading William Ogle's translation of "the "The Parts of Animals." See F. Darwin, *"The Life and Letters of Charles Darwin,"* III (London, 1888), 252.

[168] St. Albert the Great (1200-1280), a student of Aristotle and the teacher of St. Thomas, was also a biologist of some note.

[169] Aristotle and St. Thomas give the name "soul" (Latin *anima*) to the substantial form of a living physical organism, because of its qualitative difference from the substantial form of inanimate things. This does not mean "plant" and *mere* "animal" do not obey the laws of the modern specialized science of physics; they must. Said a different way, the laws of physics must be such that physical life--including all the relations among parts that obtain in it--can exist as it does.

[170] Under this power is included the ability to reproduce.

[171] Growth is, of course, followed by decay.

[172] I am not here using organism in the technical way a biologist might, but in the infra-scientific sense where we give the broadest, deepest meaning, rather than the narrowest meaning. The specialized sciences give "precise" meanings by leaving aspects of reality behind. Recall that the word "precise" is related to the word "prescind," which means to detach or isolate.

a being (remember the transcendental "oneness" from Chapter 4), the vegetative principle and animal principle must work together in some way. How? The vegetative principle is subordinate to sensorial knowledge; sensorial knowledge contains the vegetative implicitly. It thus is a higher being (*is* more)[173] than the vegetative ability and in some way, in an animal, subsumes the being of the vegetative in itself. Before we analyze further what we mean by "animal," we have to find a place for the locomotive capacity.

In the last chapter, we started our discussion of animals by linking them to locomotion. Is it absolutely necessary start this way? No, we can also start from higher powers and move to the lower. Sensorial knowledge is higher (*is* more), because it is more intelligible than simple locomotion.[174] Similarly, the vegetative principle is higher than the capacity for locomotion. A simple way to see both of these truths is to note that locomotion--as we also saw in the last chapter--can occur without life. Now, the highest power in a thing is the one that contains and/or regulates the others, that's what it means to be highest. So, we can define an animal without regard to whether it has the ability to move or not, though we may later discover that self-locomotion is one of the properties that the essence then demands. Hence, philosophically[175] speaking, that is, from the point of view of what's essential to the understanding, **an animal**[176] *is a living organism with the capacity*

---

[173] Or to make the point clear, one might force the language and say, "has more *is*."

[174] Capacity of locomotion is simply the ability to move from here to there. Though we will see it is more complicated than it appears, it is nowhere near as rich in intelligibility as the ability to know by use of one's senses. Sensorial knowledge, recall, partially transcends ordinary material things.

[175] Recall again the difference between the philosophic mode of thinking and that of the specialized sciences; we will discuss this difference and its genesis in detail in the next chapter.

[176] We will use the word "animalae" for the technical category of classification that belongs to the specialized science of biology. The Standard English word "animal" will refer to the philosophical concept. This choice is made because philosophical concepts are refinements of our common experience and thus closer to our common use of words than are the specialized science concepts, which require technical and specialized experience and theories. In using different words, a clear distinction is made between the philosophical concept and the somewhat parallel biological concept. Hopefully the Latinization will help in remembering this distinction.

of sensorial knowledge. The capacity for locomotion is used by perhaps all[177] animals to put their sensorial knowledge to best use in food gathering, moving from danger, and in social communication. For an example of an animal with minimal locomotive abilities in its mature stage, St. Thomas points to a shellfish, like the clam which depends largely on sea motion. A clam has a sense of touch[178] and the ability to respond in a way compatible with sensorial knowledge, thus should be classified as an animal.

Furthermore, we can, philosophically, define ***a plant***[179] *as a living organism that has nutritive*[180] *and reproductive powers only.* The issue of the difference between biological classification and philosophical classification is an interesting subject but off our main path. [181] We may even wonder, "Why bring plants in?" The

---

[177] If one includes various stages of an animal's life, it seems all animals as defined above have the capacity for locomotion. Indeed, if an organism has sensorial knowledge (say minimally, touch), it must be, in some place(s), in very close contact with the environment and thus vulnerable. Therefore, it must have the ability to move in some way--for instance, closing an opeing--to avoid danger, or it would not survive as a species.

[178] Touch is the most primitive and fundamental of the senses, as we discussed in Chapter 3.

[179] Similar to above, we use the Latinized word "plantae" to label the biological concept and the Standard English word "plant" for the philosophical use.

[180] Note again, we use the infra-scientific meaning of the word, not that of the specialized science of biology. Biologists often use the word "nutritive" to mean the source of energy --which for plantae (plant as biologists define it) is photosynthesis (direct conversion of energy from the sun). Here we mean the ability of the organism to assimilate "compounds" from its environment and make them an intrinsic part of itself and thus grow and/or maintain itself.

[181] For example, one may ask what about the Bacteria and Archaea, Protista, Fungi, etc.? Which among them are animals? Which plants? These are questions that involve detailed knowledge of these organisms; such knowledge is not part of our infra-scientific knowledge (it requires a microscope and thus understanding the limitations and properties of a microscope, as well as experience in surveying this new microscopic environment). We repeat our slogan: always use infra-scientific experience first, as it is more known then proceed to incorporating the less known.

Note for now that one more possible group of living things comes to mind based on the three divisions above. Namely, what about an organism that has only nutritive powers and the ability to move? What category shall we put it in? Is it possible? For locomotion to be a survival advantage to the organism, it

main reason is to clearly elucidate the various life powers. Grass is a good example of purely vegetative life. A dog is an example of sentient (sensorial knowledge) life that does not have an intellect but includes the vegetative life as contained in the sensorial life. As we've seen, sensorial knowledge can only exist in an already growing and/or maintained organism.

Of course, sensorial knowledge can be more developed or less. We can go all the way down to the most unsophisticated animal that barely has sensorial awareness—for example *possibly* an amoeba, a protist, is only vaguely aware of vague aspects of the things it contacts, and thus would be the lowest of animals (other microbes such as a bacterium, for example, a *Vibrio cholerae* might not be animals at all). Take a higher animal[182] (maybe a slug), which has sensorial awareness of a very limited type.

---

must have the capability of sensing the presence of food. Further, such an organism, to be able to survive, must have the capacity to sense the presence of things dangerous to its existence (e.g. too high of an acid content or not enough food content). In other words, it must have at least a "mechanical" sense of touch, so that when it moves, it can avoid or minimize contact with things that are dangerous to it. Hence, such an organism, at least, analogically can be an animal. We can say even more. We can argue that it is necessary for the organism to have true sensorial knowledge, which requires an organism to be aware of something at some level, even if it be vague and blurry awareness. Indeed, if the organism only moves "mechanically" away from danger, one must, in a univocal classification, call it a plant. However, the unity of the organism demands that what one part is doing be, to some degree, controlled and regulated by a central part (as we'll later see). Regulation here is by interrelations between parts at the core of the organism (not initially imposed from without in the way of a robot or clock). In this way, the organism itself is participating in responding and causing the locomotion at its core. An organism is not a mechanism; its top level actions proceed from a real unity, not an artificial one. Again, an organism with a minimum level of unity relative to its locomotion requires a central core from which "decisions" to move proceed. This, in turn, allows us to say the organism is aware at some level. For the lowest sorts of self-moving creatures (e.g. single-celled organisms with flagella), one expects only the most rudimentary awareness; it would be an infinitesimal awareness barely worthy of the name that can only remotely be compared to that awareness we see in animals we routinely see in daily life. To recap: *if* the above dialectic argument connecting touch reaction to awareness is correct, then self-locomotion implies sensorial knowledge and hence, animal classification.

[182] In general, higher animals have more senses, both external (touch being the last remnant) and internal. The senses they have are also more highly developed.

Consider the possibility that it neither has an imagination (ability to manipulate images) nor the ability to recall sensorial images (sensorial memory). If this is the case, it is only aware of an accident of a given thing while it is sensing it; after that, it is no longer aware of it. On the other end of the scale of sensorial knowledge are the higher animals like monkeys. As we've seen, these animals can do incredible things. Yet, there is no reason to assume that sensorial knowledge can not be even further developed and so allow even more amazing feats. Monkeys can make rudimentary "tools" like "umbrellas" and "chairs." More advanced sensorial creatures might make spears and even start fires without understanding what a spear is or what fire is.

Man

The next level of life is *qualitatively and radically* different. Just as moving from plant to animal we make a discrete jump, so do we also when we move from animal to rational animal. Between the two cognitive types of life, sensorial and intellectual, there is a difference of kind, not degree. Man is a rational animal; he has an intellect, which means he has the ability to abstract the essence of a thing *from* his sensorial knowledge. Hence, sensorial knowledge is included in the intellectual, and, as stated, sensorial includes the vegetative. St. Thomas compares this nesting to the way that a square includes a triangle. Given the preceding understanding of the basic attributes of the living, we can investigate in more detail how the various parts and powers of man work together to form a being *(ens)*, a unity *(unum)*.

From the detailed discussion in Chapter 4, we found that man's substantial form, also called his *soul*, is immaterial; we discovered this by realizing that man's intellect is immaterial.[183] Recall that we know that the intellect is immaterial because it has ideas of things, that by which we know the essence of things. An idea is a universal thing, not a particular thing, whereas a material thing--which is a composition of form (act) and matter (potentiality)--is always a particular thing, not a general thing.

---

[183] As we saw, it would make no sense to say that a *purely* immaterial thing (the intellect) is a power of a material thing; it would be plain contradiction.

We used a driver-car system as a metaphor to help in our understanding of intellect's role in our substance. Still, we'd like to know more about how man, who, though he has an immaterial intellectual nature, can yet be subject to the material laws of physics. In answering, we start with the simpler case of how material laws function generically in animals.

Animals and Physical Laws

Recall every material substance (that which exists of itself, not in another) is composed of matter and (substantial) form. If I remove one, I cannot even conceive of the other; they are correlative causes. The matter is known as the material cause -- that out of which something is made. The form is known as the formal cause --that into which something is made. In an actually existing thing, the act of being *(esse)* of a substance is the form. Now, we've seen how the substantial form of an animal, like a dog, contains sensorial and vegetative powers. What about the physical (non-living) powers within these things? They are implicitly contained and presumed in the vegetative and thus in the sensorial powers. Hence, it seems that these two powers *should not* violate any physical laws. The goal of the modern specialized sciences is to understand the *laws* of material nature. This goal can be accomplished only because laws express an element of the universality in the behavior of physical things; after all, a physical law is nothing but an expression of what happens not in one case, but in a large group of cases. Indeed, one always seeks to find laws that, in their limited way, apply to all cases. Of course, at any given time, it may be that the laws are not general enough and need to be expanded to encompass broader arenas not yet sufficiently explored. Still, at present, it seems unlikely that the laws need such expansion to encompass use by plants and animals.

Man and Physical Laws

What then is man's relation to the physical laws? Since man is a being, he also has a proper order that obtains among his various powers and parts that gives those powers and parts an intrinsic unity. That is, there is an established relation between a man's different parts and powers. Now, there must be one power that orchestrates or regulates the others. Why? Consider a (renegade) power in the soul not under the direction of a primary or chief power; what is to stop that power from acting in a direction opposed to the primary power? Or more to the point, what is to make it work with the other powers? If we say this power alternates control with the first, then some third power must drive the alternation, which means this third power is the real primary power. If there is no subordination[184] either in the "renegade" power or in the "primary" power, then obviously the renegade power cannot be considered part of man, because we are saying that it does not take part in any of the unity (being) that is man. Hence, the degree that this power is not regulated by the prime power is the degree to which the organism man *is not*. The less essential to man the power is, of course, the less is the impact on the being of the man. To illustrate the role and necessity of the primary power, consider the metaphor of an orchestra. Without a conductor to decide what and when to play and to help keep the various parts of the orchestra acting together, there would be no orchestra.[185]

Now, the intellect is that chief power of man; it is the one that orchestrates the others. From the above discussion we see that the degree that the intellect does not orchestrate the other powers and parts of a man is the degree to which he diminishes in being. For example, everyone will recognize that a paralyzed man, while still a man, *is* less, for he has suffered a severe privation, having lost his ability to move on his own command.

---

[184] Subordination means literally "under order," so no subordination in a thing means no order in the thing.

[185] Of course, the original decision to play does not *have* to be the conductor's, but there has to be a first person to raise the idea to the group whether it be explicitly or implicitly. Again, as in the car-driver analogy of the last chapter, the orchestra does not have the unity of being (the ontological order) that a man or an animal has, because an orchestra is not a real substance but only an imitation substance. Hence, the orchestra metaphor, like all metaphors, must be only taken as far is it goes.

In the universal use of the phrase he is "out of his mind" to mean completely crazy and "unglued," we see another expression of the intellect's primacy.

The question arises as to how the powers exercise their control. The sensorial power and the vegetative powers work together in a complicated way, which makes very interesting study in a specialized science; work in this area is in a relatively young stage. We've discussed this interrelation some. However, the intellect's influence on the other powers is even more interesting and enlightening and is nearly ripe for philosophical picking.

How do the purely immaterial powers of the intellect and will mesh with the other powers of the soul (that are not purely immaterial)? The question needs a little more precision to elucidate why it's a question at all. A discussion of the will and then of specialized science will help us refine our question. We have seen that both sensorial and intellectual forms of cognition come with their own correlative appetitive powers. In the sense case, the evaluative power (an internal sense) "decides" whether a given sense experience represents good or ill for the organism (instincts). The appetitive power, in turn, causes the organism to feel revulsion or attraction respectively as the object presented by the phantasm(s) is good or bad for it.

Similarly, the appetitive power associated with the intellect is called the will. The will perceives what the intellect learns. Stop here for a moment and note that since the will utilizes the ideas (universals) of the intellect, it must be purely immaterial.

The will next recognizes the object under consideration as good or less good or not good at all (evil). In the first case, one is drawn in toward the object, the second less drawn, and in the third repulsed. The will is only drawn by what appears to it under the aspect of good, for that is its nature. The will, unlike the sensorial appetites, is not drawn inexorably by its apprehension of a particular good. Because no particular good binds the will to choose it, the will can always choose one thing over another.[186] We

---

[186] That man's will is free is also an undeniable datum of one's experience. If someone denies his own will is free, his denial proves itself vacuous. His act of denial requires that his act of denial be under influence of inexorable causes (usually such arguments mean causes that emanate from the material world). In

will discuss these issues--which are nothing other than the questions of moral choice--in more detail in Chapter 9. The important point here is that man is free to choose; his will is free.

How can this be reconciled with the specialized sciences, which demand causality in the material realm? In order to fully handle such questions, we need to define the various sciences and their relations and divisions; we will do this in the next chapter. We can say that the specialized sciences dealing with the material realm *do assume* strict causality in the sense that once the physical laws and initial conditions are known, one can predict what will happen. This assumption is necessary for them; it is not an extra.

So, two questions about man's soul appear: How does the immaterial power of the will regulate the material powers in man, and how can it do it without violating strict material causality? The intellectual powers contain and control the sensorial powers in the same way that the sensorial contains and controls the vegetative. See Figure 5-1 which shows a metaphor for the soul's powers that

---

short, if he has no free will, the act of denial is *not* his, for it properly belongs to the inexorable causes. So, according to his denial, *he* has not denied it. What's more, there is, according to his denial, really no "he," just a sea of causes. This is absurd, since the denier *knows* he himself exists.

Though you meet people who deny our free will, none really act like they believe this denial. They proceed through life as if they do have choice. They get upset when someone interferes with their freedom. They tell you why they choose this project over that one. They demand that people not shoot at them, and want laws passed to punish people for doing it. But, on what grounds should someone be stopped, if what they're doing is a result of compulsion, not choice? Why not say, "Do whatever you will do, for you must"? One can make an apparently nice closed universe that *appears* (recall Gödel's theorem says we cannot prove it is) consistent, and say there is no contradiction in saying there is no free will. However, such a facile thought, in the end, greatly misses the point at issue, which is not whether one can create "universes" in one's mind where everything works out as it did. For instance, in the last case, the issue is whether we really sanction the sort of moral, social, and political atmosphere that takes serious the proposition that we don't have a free choice.

As A.H. Compton (1892-1962) said, "It seems unfortunate that some modern philosophers have not forcibly called attention to the fact that one's ability to move his hand at will is much more directly and certainly known than are even the well-tested laws of Newton..." A.H. Compton was a renowned physicist who won the noble prize for his work on the effect named after him, the Compton Effect. He did not always follow the clarity of thought he showed here.

uses geometric figures[187] and figure 9-1, which shows a more literal metaphor of a train to illustrate the chain of command within the soul.

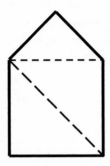

Figure 5-1: A pentagon, such as this one, has five sides. However, it in some way implicitly contains a square and a triangle; it potentially contains them. The short dashed line marks off a square from a triangle. The square, for its turn, implicitly contains two triangles marked off by the long dashed line.

The pentagon implicitly containing the square and the square implicitly containing the triangle is parallel to the intellect virtually containing the sensorial powers and the sensorial virtually containing the nutritive powers.

Take an example. Though a fireman has an intellectual power, when he gets burned, he pulls away automatically, because of his sensorial activity; but the good of saving the woman inside the burning building can override the appetitive "decision" of his sensorial power. He can proceed to use sensorial powers to judge which direction is the safest to go. The will controls the material power by its *immanent* powers, not as one body (a physical thing, a matter-form composite) acts on another, for it is not a body. Two bodies push each other, say by magnetic interaction of one on another and vice-versa. The intellect (and will) acts from within the various physical parts of man; it becomes part of their way of

---

[187] St. Thomas (in his rebuttal to the Islamic commentator, called by him "the Commentator," "Averroes"(1126-1198), who thought that there was only one intellect for all men) says, "...vegetative and sensitive are in the intellective as triangle and square are in the pentagon. For the square is indeed a figure specifically different from the triangle, but not from the triangle potentially in it ..." (p. 69 of *Aquinas Against the Averroists*—1993, edited and commentary by Ralph McInerny). For example, one can imagine drawing a diagonal in the square, thus "turning it" into two triangles.

behaving. After all, the soul is the form of the body; it is what makes the body to be a body, and the controlling power of that form is the intellect (and will).

One might say metaphorically, the intellect becomes a new law of the behavior of man's physical parts in the way that magnetic force is part of the law of behavior of a chip of iron. With this elucidation, it is clear that the action of the will *does* violate causality, but only if one confines causality to material causes proceeding from material things. However, it is also clear that the will does not move the bodies in a way that obviates the need for sensitive, vegetative, and even material powers (such as magnetism); on the contrary, each higher power presupposes and works through the lower. Hence, we do not have the ability to levitate; this would violate the physical powers, not make use of them and work through them. Immaterial "laws" augment the physical ones.

A real confusion may arise here about the meaning of immaterial causes, because of certain cultural assumptions that have been built into us. We saw in Chapter 2 that much of what we think we know is really belief, a level trust in authority, for example, our belief (improper knowledge) that the earth goes around the sun. We saw how we can verify this belief and bring it closer to or even into the realm of proper knowledge. However, it will be no surprise if some of our beliefs turn out to not be true; we expect some false beliefs (including implicit ones) to be uncovered, as we try to bring our improper knowledge into the sphere of proper knowledge. The existence of immaterial substances, like the human soul, is one example of this. We have become accustomed to thinking that immateriality does not exist or even is impossible or is supernatural. It is not supernatural.

We've seen the immaterial is a part of this universe of ours; it is already found in sensorial knowledge in an incomplete way. To clear away the potential confusion, we need to define the words "natural" and "supernatural." The *natural,* properly speaking, is anything that is a part of nature. God is the only thing that is completely above nature; so He is the only truly supernatural agent. In the last chapter, we glimpsed the split between nature and super-nature is the most radical split possible. We saw, on the one hand, natural things, those that have an essence which does not include their reason for being, that is, those things that do not include existence as necessary to their essence. On the other hand, we have God whose essence is His existence. We only see these concepts in a rudimentary way now, but we will bring them to light in Chapter 8. At this point, we only need to see that the immaterial is a part of the universe, not somehow exterior to it.

We are now left with a worry about how the specialized sciences can work at all. The answer is relativity simple. The immateriality of the human intellect really does not affect the modern specialized sciences because they are, after all, about causes that come from physical being. They have limited themselves to the study of changeable being or mobile being (what we also have called material being). When I do an experiment in physics, for example, I setup the apparatus with the conditions that I want (in physicist's language, I specify the initial conditions). I deliberately arrange the setup so that it is not influenced by external phenomena.[188] The external influences that I want to eliminate include anyone who might *want* (will) to come in and fiddle with the apparatus.

What happens if one does an experiment to look for the motion of atoms or electrons in the brain? Will the atoms and electrons move differently than they otherwise would have? Will we be able to see them do so? We know that the immaterial power does not grossly violate, but augments the physical laws. We now want to talk more specifically about *how* the immaterial activity comes into play. Again, we should not say these activities violate the laws of the physical being of man, because they are part of what man is. We do not say after all that the motion of a falling chip of iron violates the laws of its motion because it acts differently in the presence of a magnet; we just include the magnet's effect. We must learn to do a similar thing with the immaterial powers of the intellect. Now, this is all we can say using our infra-scientific data. To say more, we would have to do

---

[188] Of course, one cannot completely eliminate all external influences, so I just make their effect small enough so that the effect I wish to understand is large enough to be measured above the background external influences (called "noise" in physics).

# # #

detailed experiments and utilize theories and other experiments in the specialized sciences to gradually elucidate the answer.

We can, however, given the right assumptions and right understanding of the disclaimers involved, give an example of how it might work. In the specialized science of physics, two quantities (among others) are conserved: energy and linear momentum.[189] To set up our example, it is essential to understand the concept of conservation laws. It is fairly simple. For instance, energy is conserved. It changes into various forms but is never lost or created. As new aspects of material reality have been explored, physicists have always been able to account for loss of energy in one place by attributing it to gain in some other place. Now, here's our example.

Consider two electrons inside the brain[190] that need to move in a certain way (along with similar process in other places in the brain) to cause one's finger to move; the immaterial will moves these electrons apart in such a way that their net linear momentum is conserved. In the process, they are given more energy (they move faster), but, somewhere nearby, another pair of electrons that need to move in another way to execute the action are moved so that they conserve linear momentum and *lose* energy. In this way, we do not violate linear momentum conservation and only minimally and locally violate[191] energy conservation.[192] Could one

[189] Linear momentum of a body is, roughly, a measure of the body's tendency to continue in its linear motion. See Chapter 7 for more information on these physics concepts.

[190] It is by no means clear that the intellect only acts on the brain (however, this is a subject for biologists). It may have a larger scale of action. Certainly the soul informs the whole body, so the soul of necessity acts everywhere in the body.

[191] Recall, violation is not a good word to the extent it implies that immaterial action is out of place in the universe. We use the word to make the sentence structure less complicated. But, we simply mean it violates the conservation law of linear momentum as we originally conceived it in purely physical substances.

[192] Other effects that would appear outside the small region (such as the already laughably small gravity waves generated) would be cancelled within the region in a similar way. They cancel not so the will may hide its effects (its effects are evident to us when I move my finger), but to make its effects efficient in maximally using (this includes minimizing "stray" effects) the physical realm and minimally violating it. Again, the electrons are just an illustration of how the "intellect-physical interface" might work. Another example might be to think of the electric and other fields themselves getting modified in subtle ways. If

measure this violation? No, probably not, because to isolate the electron enough to determine the effect to be immaterial would be to remove it from the living man and thus to destroy the action of the immaterial.[193] Recall that the atoms (and electrons) in the man are subsumed under the being of the man.[194] Further, recall the immaterial intellect acts through the material. After all, these are all part of one universe, so the physics laws must mesh smoothly with the immaterial ones.

To look for immaterial effects in this way[195] misses the point. It is the same error as looking at an atom (or even an organ)

---

interactions between forces in modern physics are a good model, the way it really happens will be much more profound, i.e., even more integrated with the laws of physical nature.

[193] Modern physics is relevant in a secondary way here. Namely, given the necessity that the immaterial power, by mode of action, minimally violates physical laws so as to work with them not against them, the magnitude of the electrons' violation of energy conservation will be very small. Hence, the Heisenberg uncertainty principle (see Chapter 7) may "hide" the deviation in energy from measurement. Thus, if the point weren't already moot, another barrier to detection would likely arise. The Heisenberg uncertainty principle of quantum mechanics says that one cannot simultaneously measure to arbitrary precision the position and energy of a particle. We will discuss the uncertainty principle and related issues such as Bell's theorem in Chapter 6.

[194] We will discuss this "subsuming" in more detail in Chapter 10.

[195] Recall, our free will (specifically, we are interested in freedom from direct material dependence) is a *primary* datum of our experience. Hence, any "proofs" would really be less convincing, because they would implicitly depend in the end on the initial datum that we have a free will. We think, "Okay, do I have a material driven 'will?' I want ('will') to know." But, if your will is driven by material forces, the direction you (which, as we've seen, you've implicitly denied exists) proceed will not be towards finding the true answer to this question, because your will is not a "will" but part of blind material forces (they cannot be intelligently directed; you've denied a will). The very profound nature of this error makes it nearly unintelligible to discuss. It really only makes the little sense it makes when viewed in a land of "beings of reason," where propositions have their own existence. Recall, Gödel's theorem proved his important theorem in this land. *Primary* things are used, at least implicitly, in all the scientific conclusions and thus cannot be disproved by science. The intellect's ability to attain truth is another primary datum. To disprove the trustworthiness of the intellect is to disprove the science (a work of the intellect) that brought you that disproof.

in isolation from the organism, and trying to find life.[196] Life is the organism, which is a complex immanent organization of heterogeneous parts; it requires a relation among parts and so is not found in isolated parts. We already know the intellect is immaterial from its effects. To demand that it be subsumable into a narrow part is to strain an elephant through the kitchen sieve and expect it to remain an elephant.[197]

Man's Substantial Form

Can any more be said about man's substantial form without using any conclusions from the specialized sciences? Yes, let's probe further into the meaning of the substantial forms and immateriality.

In all simply material forms, when the form is taken out of the matter, the form is lost. For example, recall from Chapter 3, when I eat an apple, the form of the apple is lost once the apple is integrated into my body and thus becomes part of me, part of my substantial form. Similarly, when an animal dies, a nonliving form replaces the animal's substantial form, which is thus lost. What happens in the case of the death of a man?

------

[196] Remember also if one zooms in to a part, one can miss the forest for the trees. We saw this in Chapters 1 and 2 in the reductionist tendency to think of an atom in isolation from the man. If one zooms in on the atom, one can no longer see the vegetative; it is partly hidden in the atom's particular actions, but not in a way that can be seen. Even more so, examining a single atom for the presence of the intellect's action will be a thankless task.

Again, "Missing the forest for the trees" sums the above up. It is easy to miss the import of this common statement. It means that if one concentrates on an individual tree to the extent of thinking the forest as bunch of (isolated) trees, one will miss the real forest that is a very intricately balanced ecosystem, of which trees are the most prominent part because they are big (not necessarily the most interesting or important thing in it).

[197] Looking at a damaged organism (such as splitting brain hemispheres) to understand the organism as itself (not as parts) also misses the point. A pathological state only makes sense as pathology, that is, as damage relative to the normal state. Indeed, one has to know what the normal is before the pathology is identified as such. Of course, studying such pathologies is very interesting and can be revealing about how parts are in relation to each other.

Another shock awaits us around this corner. We have to brace ourselves again to remain steadfastly anchored to reality by following reason where it leads, not where we wish it to lead or where all the people who like us think it leads. Thus braced, let's proceed. To answer the question, it is important to understand the statement made earlier about where being (the act of being), the *esse,* proceeds from in a thing. That is, in an actually existing thing, the act of being *(esse)* of a substance is the *form.* It is the *form* that makes the thing to be what it is. Now, material forms are incidentally destructible, not destructible in and of themselves. Why? Because forms are immaterial, i.e. have no parts, there is no way to take them apart.

The first accident of a material thing is its extension (quantity): the fact that it is spread out in space. Because a cat has its tail there, its head over here, and its heart in the middle, it can be destroyed by separating its parts. An immaterial thing, like a *form* of a purely physical thing, has no such parts; it is simple. Of course, the substantial *form* of a purely physical thing cannot exist by itself. Why? To be purely physical means that the *form* has no proper act outside of the material. It means that it has no existence not bound up with its union with matter. Hence, a physical thing, such as a cat, is subject to degeneration and destruction by the break-up of its parts. Such *forms* only have an independent existence in our minds as our ideas.

By contrast, a purely immaterial substantial form like the human soul has, as we saw in Chapter 4, a life that is not bound up with matter. Hence, although one can destroy the part of the human soul that is bound up with matter--namely the body--one cannot destroy the immaterial substantial form itself.[198] Hence, the human soul is immortal.[199] It cannot die.

Wait. What of man's thinking? Didn't we say he couldn't think without his body? No, we said he could not think with a damaged body. We also said his body is a necessary part in the

---

[198] To speak in the *metaphoric* language of the imagination, the soul is a unity in "one place," and one cannot rip "a point" apart. It is evident from this fact that man's soul is a higher level of being than the material world, because it is more truly one, more truly unified, because its unity is not spread out.

[199] Of course, in principle, God could choose to annihilate it, but such reasoning is outside the domain of the natural.

sense that only with it is he completely himself. Once the soul is separated from matter, the mode of being of the soul is clearly different. The intellect no longer has access to phantasms, so it *cannot* gain knowledge. In general, it loses the contact with the material world that its nature is ordered towards. Its level of being is lowered. In this new mode, it obviously must work in a purely immaterial mode. Hence, the soul is not encumbered by a *damaged* body, but that is only because it has no body at all, and so has to work without it.

Call up our driver-car system metaphor. Here the driver was analogous to the soul; the car was the body; locomotion was the intellect and the driver-car system was the complete substance: "man." If the car completely broke down and was not fixable, the driver could then get out and walk. However, the driver-car system only exists in a sort of potential manner once this happens, and the man's walking will be a much less efficient way of locomotion. This is, metaphorically, how man is without the body. Like the walking man, the disembodied soul (substantial form) will be much inhibited but will have some freedom from not having the car. The walking man can walk down narrow alleys. The soul can think without any access to phantasms that are necessary when the substance, man, is complete (i.e. soul united to body (substantial form united to matter)). This purely spiritual mode also allows the soul to directly know itself. It will know general things by its ideas. However, because it does not have access to matter and phantasms, it will no longer directly know the particular things it knew before death, when it was united to the body. It will know them indirectly because the substantial form, by its nature, must maintain a (transcendental) relation to its matter. Through this relation it should know vaguely and confusedly what those things were. However, the soul will have to depend on illumination by God for direct clear knowledge of these things.

Shall we risk offending our cultural sensibilities further by thinking more on this topic? I think my readers are bold explorers. So, after we get our eyes adjusted to the strong light,[200] let's continue.

---

[200] By, for example, meditating on some of the thoughts in this and the previous chapters.

Animal and Human Zygotes

The indestructibility of the human soul can lead one to contemplate the origins of the human soul. Unlike the above, for this discussion, we must access some findings of the specialized science of biology. Because animal origins are simpler, let's start with higher animals that share a bodily nature similar to ours. When does animal life begin? At the moment of union of the sperm and egg when a zygote forms, we have a unique animal. It has everything it needs to become what it will be in its maturity. No one will deny that an animal zygote is living; but a living *what* is the question? Since it is a living thing, it is a unity. It is an organism, an organization or ordering of various parts, a relation among heterogeneous parts. Etienne Gilson[201] (1884-1978) says that a living being "is that order of all which has in itself the principle of its own change ... the living being is endowed with spontaneity, not only in its reactions, but a fortiori in its operations and its actions."[202]

To discuss the changes of the zygote, we need the principle of causality. The Principle of Causality is implicit in much of what we've said in the last three chapters. The ***Principle of Causality*** is *"Nothing changes itself."* A more profound way of stating the principle is that *"Something can act only so far as it is in act."* Change is reduction of potentiality to act. If "X" *heats* up water, "X" must be *hot.* If something changes itself that means it gives itself something that it doesn't have. This statement is equivalent to saying that something *is* and *is not* at the same time and in the same way. This is absurd. Hence, we see that the principle of causality is self-evident, its opposite cannot be thought. In philosophy, something that causes a change is called an *efficient cause.*

Therefore, if a zygote is not already an animal but *becomes* an animal, something outside of it must change it into an animal. Yet, there is no such cause available. The zygote is only in contact

---

[201] This renowned philosopher and historian must be ranked with Jacques Maritain as one of the best philosophers of the last two centuries.

[202] Gilson (p. 3) from *Aristotle to Darwin and Back Again.*

with its mother. Modern biology has shown that the biological role of the animal's mother is passive in the growth of the organism; the mother's body supplies food and proper environment. You may say the zygote itself supplies the efficient cause. Well, if this statement is not to violate the principle of causality, the zygote must really be two things, not one. However, if the zygote is two things, it is not an organism, not a living thing; we've already said this is precisely what it is. Hence, if the unity that is the zygote is not an animal already, it could not become one. The animal's life begins when the life of the zygote begins. Better said, the animal begins its life as a zygote. As a zygote, the animal must already be, in a hidden way, whatever it will become. It is the law of its own development. It thus has implicitly (e.g., in the DNA) those properties that it will, in its mature stage, have explicitly. For example, the zygote will exercise an efficient causality over its various parts to change those parts into arms and legs, etc.

The same reasoning applies to human zygotes, for man is a rational *animal*. Hence, the life of man begins as a zygote. But where does the human soul come from? At the moment the zygote is formed, it "calls" for the substantial form of a man. The physical (material) powers at work in the zygote cannot make an immaterial thing, for again something (a material thing) cannot give (immaterial thing) what it does not have. Hence, we must conclude that it is infused from the outside[203] at the moment the embryo (zygote)[204] comes to be.

Making Animals

Thought experiments are often helpful in physics; Einstein presented many of the ideas of the theory of relativity using thought experiments. One or two will be helpful here. Can one, in principle, make life in the laboratory? If so, what happens if one

---

[203] In Chapter 8, we'll see that the infusion must be a direct creation and infusion by God. In short, we will see that only God can create *ex nihilo,* from nothing. This direct action by God on the part of man reveals a unique status for man (and any other rational animal that may exist in the universe).

[204] In other words, a human zygote "calls for" the infusion by God, independent of how that zygote was brought to being.

makes an exact material duplicate of oneself? Finally, can I make an electro-mechanical equivalent of an animal or a man? That is, can a robot think?

Animals are completely bound to the material,[205] and thus it seems there is no reason, in principle, why they cannot be made. However, to make an animal, one has to understand the *process* of educing the form of the given animal from the potency of matter well enough to be able to do it. Remember, some first thing can only be changed into some second thing if the first has the potential to be that second. Wood has the potential to burn, water does not. So, in making an animal, one has to know the proper steps to follow in the lab. In short, man can be the efficient cause only if he understands the potentialities of the material he has to make the animal out of (material cause) and something of the form[206] of the animal he is trying to dispose the matter to become. Note that *making* is not *creating*; it is only, in some way, using what is already there, at least in an implicit way. Properly speaking, creation means to make from nothing *(ex nihilo).*[207] So, in principle, man can make animals, though not create them. Of course, there may be insurmountable technical issues or impediments in nature that prevent his making any animal or a particular animal.[208] Considering the present state of the science, I think it highly *likely* that man will make animals at some point.[209]

These same arguments apply with little change to man. The only difference between the animal and human case is that man

---

[205] No part or power of an animal exists of itself outside the material realm.

[206] The form is that which he is trying to bring to be; it is the formal cause. Recall "essence" (in the restricted sense) is the form. In Chapter 7, when we discuss evolution, it will become clear that what we are really doing here is making the proper material dispositions. Because of our limited ability to act (for example, we can move something from one point to another), we can only *directly* cause certain types of forms.

[207] Again, in Chapter 8, we will see only God can create in this sense.

[208] For example, Heisenberg's uncertainty principle implies one cannot measure the entire physical state of a thing with absolute precision.

[209] Of course, in cloning, one already has a rudimentary making of an animal. Here though, I speak of making one from "scratch." In the foreseeable future, it's nearly certain that only simple animals can be made in this latter way. However, there are likely potencies in matter that allow other types of animals than we know of. Scientists may even stumble on one of these.

cannot make[210] a human soul (it's immaterial). However, the infusion of the human soul is part of the "workings" of the universe.[211] Hence, man can, in principle, by his action (though not by *his* simply making), cause another man to come to be.[212]

Making a human body from scratch seems technically impossible. However, suppose it is possible. Suppose a future-day Frankenstein makes an identical copy of your body. I don't just mean your exterior appearance; I mean down to the atomic arrangement (to the extent the laws of quantum mechanics demand and allow). A soul would be infused at the moment the last critical atom was aligned correctly. He would start to think, but he would not be you. You are you. He would have his own substantial form, as everything that shares a material nature to any degree does. His intellect would have no ideas, because it would have just now for the first time come into existence and been able to extract them from phantasms. He would have many *sensorial* "memories."[213] He would be quite confused. It would be a horrible, nightmarish way to begin life.[214]

---

[210] Recall, no one but God can, for it must be *created* (from nothing) whole or not at all.

[211] In Chapters 7 and 8, we will note that God ordains all laws for the universe; in this unique case, He *directly* participates in the action of a law. As the pure act of being, He is behind and in all things.

[212] Of course, technical difficulties of the type described above have even a higher probability of interfering with this possibility.

[213] More precisely, initially he would have no phantasms. He would only have physical memories, impressions (species impressa) that would have to be, by vital action of his animal powers, specified as phantasms (species expressa). He would then be aware, by those phantasms, of various objects from your life, as he chose to call them up or as associations (from the initial physical state of the body) brought them up. They would *not* be memories of *his own life*, which would have just begun. Metaphorically, he would be looking at a scrapbook from someone else's life. His intellect would be blank until the phantasms were present. He would have no intellectual memories yet of his own, for his substantial form just came into existence. But, he would have many sensorial phantasms to abstract ideas from. Yet, not knowing *when* the memories occurred (and possibly not able to distinguish between memories of actual things and memories of imagined things), they would not have the cognitive content that they have for you.

[214] Chapter 9 on moral philosophy will discuss the crucial issues of what one should do and should not do and how those decisions should be made. Certainly, I hope the above discussion of the possibility of scientists causing men to come

Robots

Now, what if we decide to make a robot? Can I ever make him so he can think? No. This is clear from what we've said about the intellect. The intellect is immaterial and thus cannot be made. Recall "made" means to inform different *matter*. Alan Turing (1912-1954), a pioneering and brilliant computer theorist, devised a test to determine whether he had achieved artificial intelligence. It basically was a test to see whether you could make a device (robot) that could fool a human being, who is, say, behind a curtain, into thinking the device was human. Such a test is a very good way to tell how well one is doing in his making of *artificial* intelligence, but it cannot make one to think that he has made a rational mind. Recall life requires activity from within. Such a device has no immanent activity; so not only is it not a rational mind, it's not life. Just because I can make a painting that is an arbitrarily close facsimile of a man's face does not mean that the *painting* is actually a face. I can even make a 3-D equivalent, a sculpture, and get closer. Still, a perfect *replica*[215] of his face does not make it a man's face. Even if I make it move and fool many people who view it; *that fact* does not make it a man's face. Indeed, in making the painting or sculpture, I was never really trying to make it a man's face, just a good image.

Similarly, in making a robot, one is not making an exact reproduction; we've already discussed that in the last section. One is making a sort of *functional* replica, something that does the tasks I choose for it.

In the case of the sculpture, I wanted the head to *look like*, imitate, a man's head. For the robot, I want it to imitate, for example, human conversation of a certain type. For example, if I want to make the robot say "summer" in a sentence, I give it as many such sentences (and ways to create them) as I view to be necessary, and then associate it with as many sentences in ordinary

---

into being does not lead my reader to think that I sanction such offensive behavior.
[215] Here, replica obviously means, "*looking* just like it."

conversation as I can.[216] I do this until I am satisfied with how well it *appears* to respond. "Appearance" is what I'm after. By the very task the robot designer has put to himself, he has determined not to make a man, but something that imitates a man. He can, *in principle*, make the imitation do more and more until *maybe*, though highly unlikely, it even passes a Turing test. It is still not a rational animal. It's not even an animal. Why?

We know the answer. We've seen that "living" refers to organisms; heterogeneous parts ordered towards the whole and its immanent activities. Heterogeneous refers to the fact that one can take one part of an organism, and it will be much different than another. It also means any one part will *not* be made of that part. Every chunk of sugar that I scratch off a sugar cube is basically the same as the next and as the original cube. A sugar cube is homogeneous; the thing is composed of smaller parts of the same type. Your hand is not composed of smaller, differently shaped hands; it is composed of bone and skin and blood and veins and cartilage, etc. The *cells* that make up the top layer of skin are, in turn, *not* composed of skin cells. The organelles, say mitochondria, inside those cells are not composed of other mitochondria. One could go on. Yet, it's not the heterogeneity itself that makes life living. It's the order among the parts, the relation established among the parts. This ordering towards the whole is what makes the substantial form of the living qualitatively different from that of inanimate substantial forms.[217]

Such immanent (proceeding from within, not without) ordering of parts to make a whole is an instance of *final causality*. Each part makes no sense outside of the whole, because each part has as its reason for being that part in that place *only* in the whole. Case in point: the heart is to pump blood to the brain, organs, and limbs, etc. in order to nourish the body.[218] To examine the heart by

---

[216] This example is just to recall the method of such programming. Obviously, more sophisticated algorithms could and would be used (for example, "infant" programming), but the choice of programming does not effect the reasoning that follows.

[217] Again, this fact led Aristotle to give substantial forms of living things the special name "soul," which we currently reserve for the human substantial form.

[218] Similarly, in the blood, white blood cells "patrol" "looking" to destroy enemies of the "whole."

itself, with no reference to the organism (a hard thing to even think), would make it unintelligible. Relation is always between one thing and another. The relation of the part called the heart is towards the other parts, but most fundamentally to the whole animal. The parts of an organism have an end,[219] which is the whole. It is a mysterious cause, but we've learned not to discard something just because it's mysterious. Conformity with reality is our aim, not chopping it to fit into our heads.

The final cause can already be seen in the specialized field of physics, as we'll discuss in various ways in Chapters 6 through 9, in the rotation of the earth and at a deeper level in the laws of Newton, Einstein, Maxwell, and Heisenberg. It is simply the statement that things behave in some way the same everywhere and every-when.[220] They are ordered. In their domain, the laws of Newton and the rest are the same today as when Newton was alive. To the extent that they aren't, we're looking for better theories to capture the part we missed. Final causality is the ordination of the various parts of the universe to act always in the same way. Final causality is fundamentally the ordination, which implies, in the end, foreordination (the ordination is there before the reduction of potentiality to act) of potentiality to act.[221] For example, an electron in an electric field moves in a path determined beforehand by the quantitative law specified in Maxwell's equations. Indeed, in any given change, this specific thing can only become some things, not anything. There is an order. Note that to recognize order here does not mean to recognize it over there as well. Further, one does not have to have a perfect degree of order. As Gilson says, we do not have "to go into raptures about the wonderful adaptations of

---

[219] End, or completion in Greek is *"telos"* probably originally meaning "turning point." These are the roots of the word "teleology."

[220] The whole purpose of a law of physics is to capture those things that are invariant. A physicist doesn't mind if functions of time are included in his equation of a physical law. He does mind if the form of the equation itself is a function of time; that is, he does not want to have to erase his equation and replace it with another at every moment.

[221] The order, we will see in Chapters 7 and 8, is foreordained by God, who gives things the properties, relations and directedness that they have at the first instant the Universe exists (if it were to exist from eternity, it would be given them from eternity).

means to ends." The degree that there is order is the degree that there is final causality.[222]

Now, robots are imitations of this immanent order. We start off with the idea of making something that has its parts ordered one to another to make a whole. We, however, choose deliberately to do it using substances[223] already made. So we start with a metal rod to use as a camshaft to turn a wheel. A metal rod is not heterogeneous; it is homogeneous, "made" of other metal rods. Without heterogeneous parts, one does not have the complementarities to set up complex relations; for instance, the interior of the "part" cannot become part of the robot in an immanent sense. It remains exterior in this sense. Furthermore, the metal rod is clearly a separate substance that will be linked in this case by bolts, rivets, and cotter pins, and so remain a separate substance connected to other substances. One can, in some places, start with more complicated pieces of whole forged metal. But that does not change its substantial nature or its homogeneity. Shape was not the key issue for heterogeneity. The sugar cube pieces had different shapes as we knocked off different pieces, but fundamentally, each piece was the same as the whole.

One does order the parts towards making the robot (the whole), but it is an external ordering. You do not, so to speak, build its laws into it from the inside. The scientist can use nature to do this, because matter's potencies are such that if one activates the potencies in the correct manner (following a certain procedure to give form (activate these potencies) and order), the needed relations among parts and toward the whole obtain. However, remember, one is trying to make a functional replica, and thus not even trying to give form to these "internal" potencies.

It is clear from this that robots are not living things, but as we've said, imitations of living things. It is also clear, thus, that robots cannot have true sensorial knowledge. Sensorial knowledge requires that a "living whole" exist first. It means the whole is

---

[222] This is to say nothing against the purely *biological* concept of evolution, which is by far the best theory we have to explain biological life. Philosophical considerations will, however, lead us to make significant changes to the implicit *philosophical* aspects of the presentation of that theory.

[223] Recall, substance is something existing on its own (it's not a part except as artificially used).

aware. Without that "whole," there is nothing to be aware. We saw earlier that sensorial knowledge builds on vegetative (the lowest immanent whole, i.e. its actions coming to some degree from whole rather than externally).

Robots are made to imitate key vegetative, sensorial, and intellective capacities. They are, therefore--if the term is properly understood--*artificial, not real*, intelligences.

Other Forms of Intelligence

So, are there other forms of real intelligence? It's more than likely. There could, for example, be other rational animals in the universe; nothing seems to exclude that. They may even have much greater (or lesser) brain capacity than us and be physically very different from us. They may fly and see in the infrared. We don't know.[224]

Furthermore, there is another radically different form of intelligence that may have already occurred to the alert reader. We have discussed creatures that are fully material and partially material. Man is a sort of hybrid, a sort of amphibian that lives in the immaterial realm *and* the material realm. Is there a creature that is purely immaterial? Man gets his ideas by abstraction from sensorial knowledge. What about a creature that has his ideas innately, so he doesn't need to abstract them from the material world? Such a creature would be completely immaterial, and the lowest such creature would be as far above us as we are above the amoeba. Such creatures are called angels. The major creedal religions of the world (Judaism, Christianity, and Islam[225]) assert the existence of angels as revealed by God. We will see in Chapter 9 that there are strong philosophical reasons to assert their existence, but not a strict proof (yet?)--this is unlike the case of the

---

[224] The Drake equation is a way of making a wild guess at such likelihoods (it typically includes factors for rise of advanced civilization). Fr. Stanley Jaki has pointed out the need to include a factor for the probability of forming an Earth-Moon system in the Drake equation (since the effects of the moon on developments on earth are non-trivial).

[225] Islam is itself an offshoot of Christianity.

existence of God and of the immaterial nature of the human soul for which *there are* proofs.

Christianity has well-developed ideas of about angels that are quite fascinating. Some of the concepts are based solely on philosophical considerations. For example, an angel's nature is completely determined by its essence; one angel cannot be differentiated from another by matter, because they are not bound up with matter. Hence, each angel must be a species unto itself. Furthermore, the fewer ideas an angel has, the more insightful and probing is his knowledge, because he can "see" all things in fewer "views." Take a metaphor. If I had to look at a picture of a man's face in ten separated pieces, I would be less able to comprehend and analyze his facial features than a man who could see the face in one or two pieces. Angels are interesting in themselves, but they also can help us to understand ourselves. Indeed, understanding the idea of angels helped scholastic philosophers to better understand human nature.[226] In an analogous way that understanding animals gives us insight into our material side, understanding angels can give us insight into our core selves, which is our immaterial soul.

We have now quite an array of proper knowledge. For the most part, this knowledge has been obtained by analyzing our infra-scientific experience. However, for the first time in the book, we used conclusions from the specialized sciences. We did this only in the following cases: discussing tests for animal intelligence, discussing zygotes as the beginning of animal life, and in trying to offer models of how the intellective powers exercise their dominion over the material powers. Innumerable other issues will also depend on knowing the specialized sciences. As we've seen, this dependence will make their conclusions less certain than those conclusion made from only non-specialized experience and modes of thought. Nonetheless, philosophy has begun to call for the specialized sciences, which will have their own proper force and domain. What their considerable force is, what their scope and limitations are, and where they fit in with the proper knowledge we've developed is part of the task of the "science before science."

---

[226] For example, if Descartes had spent more time thinking about angels, he may not have been so prone to think our mind was like that of angels, knowing things by innate ideas rather than through abstraction from the sensorial knowledge.

We must begin this task by asking what each of the sciences is and how each interrelates to the others.

Chapter 6

Galileo versus St. Thomas?

*T*he reader might now ask, "Is it not true that the ideas and approach we've discussed in the last few chapters are the very things that prevented 'real' science from coming to be? Did not Aristotle's and St. Thomas's thinking actually prevent the birth of science until their demise by demonstrations of science coming from Galileo (1564-1642), Newton (1642-1727) and the rest?"

Renowned physicist Stephen Hawking says in his intriguing book, *A Brief History of Time,*

> *Galileo, perhaps more than any other single person, was responsible for the birth of modern science. His renowned conflict with the Catholic Church was central to his philosophy, for Galileo was the first to argue that man could hope to understand how the world works, and, moreover, that we could do this by observing the real world. [pg 179]*

Here we have quite a dilemma. We have seen that philosophy has led us to many important and undeniable truths. Are we to abandon those truths to retain modern science? Are we to abandon modern science to retain them? Obviously, we must do neither. Nonetheless, the issues involved are complex and the resolution of the dilemma can only be reached by looking more deeply at what modern science is and what philosophy is. Further, we have to make explicit our cultural beliefs as they relate to these questions, because much of the improper knowledge[227] that leads us to the above incompatible judgments comes from the cultural milieu in the fashion discussed in Chapter 2.

Hawking articulated these cultural *beliefs* very succinctly. Let's see if we can parse out some of these beliefs:

1) Modern science is radically different from any science that came before it.
2) Galileo was largely responsible for its birth.
3) Catholicism is at least in some ways, or at least was in Galileo's time, intrinsically opposed to modern science.
4) Galileo was the first to argue that man could hope to understand how the world works.
5) He was first to argue that we could understand it by observing it.

We will consider each of these in order of importance to our dilemma. The last four are somewhat historical (if one takes number 3 as only applying to Catholicism in the past). Though all have implications for how we view philosophy, they are--in various degrees--secondary to understanding our dilemma, which is whether the special sciences and philosophy are intrinsically opposed. On the other hand, the first item directly spurs us to consider the central topic of the relation between the science before science (philosophy) and modern science.

We can give a short answer to the dilemma almost immediately, for our philosophizing in the last few chapters has shown **no opposition** *between the two*. In fact, our philosophical investigations *themselves* started to ask for the specialized sciences. We began to need their conclusions; this is why the question of their conflict came up. Why, then, the apparent conflict, and why do so many see it differently? There are many reasons, which we will discuss. However, the most significant reason is that, in speaking about philosophy and modern science, many do not know what philosophy is and because of that ignorance, do not know what modern science is. The philosophically uninitiated may know philosophers and he may know scientists; he may even know modern science, but what

---

[227] Recall, improper knowledge is really a species of more or less well-founded belief.

exactly each field is and where each fits into the scheme of his knowledge is not something he thinks about. Aha, more infra-scientific knowledge ripe for harvesting and converting into the leaven of proper knowledge!

We know about many different forms of science. To find out how they all fit together, recall that in them, we all seek knowledge *(scientia)* of the world. The world of things is where our attention *should be* focused. The purpose of the mind is to know reality, to conform to reality, and to find and hold onto truth. This cannot be overemphasized. Nonetheless, it is *you or I* who knows. Our human intellect, as St. Thomas implies multiple times, is barely an intellect, so we can, for example, expect that more work and care must be taken to avoid falling into error. Further, if we are to justly classify our knowledge, we need to think more about human cognition, so that our classification will reflect the various areas of study that necessarily arise because of our modes of thinking about the world.

The Three Levels of Abstraction

We saw in previous chapters that we think by abstracting from sensorial images. We also glimpsed the ***three levels of such abstraction.***

Physica

At the *first* level, the human thinker abstracts the least; he leaves behind only particular matter, not general matter. Matter is left behind only to the degree that it is the principle of individuation. For example, he abstracts the idea of "redness," say from an apple. In so doing, he leaves behind the specific matter of the apple (as he must, because this is what abstraction means), but he keeps the general idea of matter that redness demands. I might, for example, when thinking about redness, refer to an imagined red plane whose edges fade off into blackness. In its definition, redness will have to include general matter. In short, this first level is the "world" of changeable being;[228] the study at this level, the study of changeable being is called physics (Latin *physica*, Greek φυσιχη). Be careful not to confuse this *wide* use of the term physics with the specialized science of physics. We will discuss their relation shortly. To circumvent confusion between the uses, we will use the Latin, *physica*, for this wide use of the word physics, which means the study of changeable being, anytime ambiguity might result.

Mathematica

The *second* level is the realm of mathematics (Latin *mathematica*, Greek μαθηματικὴν). Here, one leaves behind all of the sensible aspects of a thing and keeps only the quantitative. One removes the qualitative aspects of a thing and keeps only the quantitative, the first accident[229] of material substances. Here, by qualitative, I do not mean all qualitative aspects, for there are qualities "proper" to quantity, such as shape. I mean the primary qualities (the sensible ones, like color and all the other dynamic ones, like the appetitive powers). Of course, in picturing quantities in our imagination, one will tend to paint them black and white or some color, but this is not necessary to the quantitative itself. The circle that we mentioned in Chapter 4 is a good example. Though we may imagine a circle with primary qualities, as a mathematical entity, it is a one- dimensional, colorless, odorless, tasteless object that is neither hard nor soft.

What is quantity? It is extension. Recall we know the primary qualities of things directly through the various senses. However, quantity follows immediately. Further, we quickly grasp, by abstraction from the various senses, that quantity is primary in material things--in the sense that I can conceive quantity without quality (e.g., color), but not vice-versa--relative to the qualities through which we perceive it. However, it is not primary in the order that we know them, thus not primary to us; *never forget that we only know quantity through quality.* We see it when we look at anything, for example a table. We feel it when we run our hand

---

[228] Also called material being or mobile being. In any case, it is being that is composite of form and matter.
[229] See Chapter 3's discussions on change, including the list of the types of accidents.

across the table. We hear it when we note the difference of place of the sound's emanation when we put our glass down versus when we kick a leg of the table. What's the definition? As we've discussed, attempting to define something primary, such as quantity, will force one to use less known concepts to define something more known and thus not properly constitute a definition. However, we can describe it. *Quantity is the basis of quality*; I cannot have red without having a red surface (quantity). Indeed, quantity is to quality as (prime) matter is to form.[230] Lastly and very important, *quantity is that which has parts outside of each other*.

In other words, unlike qualities, I can put two pieces of a quantity together and get another quantity of the same type but twice as big and, in fact, I can get any quantity by assembling enough of one primary piece. For example, from enough 1 inch lengths, I can make as long a length as I want. However, this is not true of quality. Take for example, the quality of being a good mathematician. If I assemble a bunch of mediocre mathematicians, I will not have a great mathematician, a Gauss or a Leonhard Euler (1707-83). Indeed, even an infinite number of mediocre mathematicians will not make one of these.

Similarly, with the quality of temperature, if I want to boil water, I cannot do it by assembling *any* number of snowballs at zero degrees Celsius. Qualities do not have parts outside of each other so they cannot be assembled out of lesser pieces of the same type the way quantity can.

Qualities, in their turn, have the property that they can be *more or less whatever they already are*. They can be "more red" or "more hot" or "more hard." Quantity, such as number,[231] does not "have" a more or less in the strict sense. Seven cannot be "more seven" than it already is. A friend of mine used to say, "1+2=4 for large values of one and two and small values of 4." Of course, a given 2 cannot be more 2 than another. His joke illustrates the

---

[230] *When* we include shape and the like (which are truly qualities, though in common thinking we view them as mathematical), we see that quantity and quality are correlatives, like form and matter.
[231] There are many important distinctions to be made here. They will be discussed later in this chapter.

absurdity of attributing "more or less" (intensity) to *quantity*. On the other hand, a temperature can be higher or lower than another temperature. We can put this higher and lower on a scale and see it as a quantity, but this is not the quality; it is just the "more or less" aspect quantified. We can see this by noting that the same scale could be used for two radically different qualities; hence, by looking at the scale alone, we'd never know which quality was under consideration.

From the viewpoint of abstraction, one can say, quantity is the study of things that can be conceived without matter, but can only exist in matter. Recall mathematics is closely associated with the beings of reason. However, we stepped back from saying that mathematics is just about beings of reason. Why? Because some objects of mathematics can exist (though not in the condition that they are conceived as stripped of their material garb) and the others are reductively like this.[232] A circle, at least an approximate one, can exist in matter, under the conditions of the material; this is where we got it. However, we still must say that these beings are *not* real in the sense of being able to exist outside the mind in the purity that they do in the mind. Hence, Jacques Maritain uses the fine phrase, "*the mathematical preter-real*" to describe the world explored by the mathematician.

Metaphysica

The *third* level leaves behind all material aspects. The third level considers being as being. St. Thomas describes this level as a process of separation. In it one separates out that which can exist without matter. There are the purely immaterial things that must exist without matter, like God or the angels. And, there are the things that can exist in matter or without matter, such as the human soul, quality, potency, substance, causes, unity, and all the

---

[232] Recall, to see the reductive reality of the entities of mathematics, one must switch one's mode of thinking from second intention (symbols) to first intention (what the symbols represent). One can summarize as follows: Three arenas must be distinguished to be clear in thinking about mathematics: 1) quantity as it really exists under the condition of material things, 2) quantity as abstracted from the material (preter-real), and 3) quantity as symbolized and manipulated by algorithmic rules. The first two are real; the third are beings of reason (having entered into the realm of mental relations like logic).

transcendentals in their full meanings. The study of this arena is called metaphysics (Latin *metaphysica*) meaning "beyond *physica.*" It is first philosophy. It is the one from which all truly first principles get their formulation.

Looking from a different vantage point is also helpful. We may summarize the three degrees of abstraction by reference *to how conclusions are verified* within each mode of abstraction.

Degrees of Abstraction	How Conclusions are Verified
1st level	*Physica* - being resolved in the sensible
2nd level	*Mathematica* - being resolved in the imagination (use and manipulation of phantasms)
3rd level	*Metaphysica* - being resolved in the mind

The three levels can be represented as shown in Figure 6-1. The three finite width planes are the three levels of knowledge. Each of these regions or worlds of intelligibility is separate; one has no continuity with the other. This fact is represented by the separation between the planes. The finite width of each plane represents the divisions and distinctions within each field of abstraction.

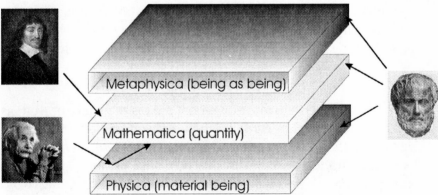

Figure 6-1: The three levels of "abstraction" are shown. The three planes represent the three fields of intelligibility within the world of mental (intentional) existence. Descartes is shown looking at *mathematica*, Einstein at p*hysica* as reflected in *mathematica,* and Aristotle at all three.

Recall that knowledge is that unique mode of union whereby the knower becomes the known without ceasing to be himself. In the non-entitative mode of being known as intentional being, the knower becomes the known; we've seen this mode must be strictly immaterial. Hence, we can name two "worlds": the world of intentional existence, where things exist in the special mode characteristic of knowledge, *and* the world outside the mind, where those things exist of themselves (entities) and from which the knower obtained the universal that he apprehends. In these terms, Figure 6-1 shows how the first universe is divided up into three sub-universes or fields of intelligibility.

In each level of abstraction, one apprehends being in fundamentally different aspects. In *physica,* one studies mutable or changeable being. In *mathematica,* one studies the being called quantity. In *metaphysica,* one studies being as being.

The Division of the Sciences

We are ready to classify the various sciences. Figure 6-2 shows the classification. The diagram is organized as follows. At the far left we have the full universe of sciences, or what we will call philosophy in the widest possible use of the term. This use of the word is fitting because philosophy, at bottom, is love of wisdom, and he who loves wisdom will exclude nothing from his purview. Philosophy (wide sense) immediately splits into three parts. Moving to the right on the diagram yields a three-fold split.

Pure Science

The top and the most important area is the study of truth as truth. These sciences study reality and, in various ways and degrees, succeed in *conforming our mind to reality.* Our discussions up to this point in this book fall in this top division, known as *the theoretical sciences.* I hesitate to use the word "theoretical" here for, in current usage, it implies a lack of certainty. When we talk of string theory or the theory of everything, we are talking about things that are by no means decided and may not even be decidable. Aristotle makes the distinction between dialectical[233] sciences (see methodological sciences) and sciences in the proper sense of the word, because

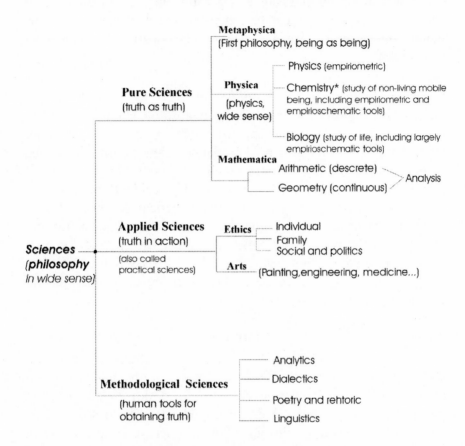

*Chemistry is usually discussed in reference to a particular environment. Thus, one can speak of the chemistry on the earth or on the Jovian moon, Io.

Figure 6-2: The division of the sciences is shown. The diagram proceeds from top to bottom beginning from arenas of most importance (in terms of containing the general principles in some way for the ones below it), except for the last categories in each branch which are not in any particular order. Note: this order is not necessarily the order in which our knowledge *proceeds*. For example, *we* must start with *physica* (i.e., what comes through our senses) to get to *metaphysica*.

---

[233] This use of the term *dialectic* is different from what is meant by Hegel, where an opinion breeds its opposite—although it seems that all such idealist concepts are closely related to dialectics in that they treat all beings as beings of reason.

"dialectical" sciences involve merely probable reasoning; they are not properly sciences.[234] Although "theoretical" is the term commonly used by philosophers for this group of sciences, to avoid the confusion, we can call them the *pure sciences*. Divisions within this group arise because of the degrees or levels of abstraction.

Metaphysica

The highest in the picture and in absolute status is the study of being as being (metaphysics). Aristotle says metaphysics "is not the same as any of the so-called particular sciences; for none of the other sciences attempt to study being as being in general, but cutting off some part of it they study the accidents of this part. This, for example, is what the mathematical sciences do."[235] Metaphysics is the overarching science, the one that unifies and explains all the rest. St. Thomas calls metaphysics "the common science" to distinguish it from all the specialized sciences, not just the modern specialized sciences, but even the next most general pure science, that of *physica.*

Physica

Physica (physics in the wide sense), because it deals with *mutable* being, is a restricted science. Now, *physica* can be divided up in many specialized sciences…the most developed ones are physics itself (especially in the restricted sense discussed below), chemistry, and biology. Physics *(Physica),* as we've already seen, is the study of changeable being generically. Chemistry is specified to the study of nonliving stable substances. Biology is the study of the living.[236] We must quickly jump to clarify here; these are not yet the modern sciences as they are *currently practiced*. The latter sciences work in the mode of "dialectics" that we will discuss shortly. The remarkable developments in these fields, as well as tremendous problems that attend them, arise because of a shift in

---

[234] St. Thomas, *Commentary on Metaphysics*, book 4, lesson 4, number 574.

[235] Aristotle, *Metaphysics,* book 4 chapter 1, 1003a23-26

[236] There are sciences such as the study of man, psychology, which straddles two levels: Metaphysics for man's immaterial intellect and will, and *physica* for the material aspect of man.

emphasis that we will also discuss then. I will use the word "modern"[237] to modify "specialized sciences" when I wish to refer to those particular aspects of the given science (e.g., physics) that are uniquely emphasized today.

Mathematica

The last member of the group, *mathematica,* is the study of universal quantity. One can leave behind the general science of extension and just consider the most obvious qualification of extension, which is its shape; this is the science of geometry which studies magnitude, i.e. continuum. It has all the qualities of shape and figure. One can make a further abstraction and leave behind the qualitative aspects of figure and just consider number. One can just consider the unit and what happens as one assembles these units; this is the science of arithmetic; it studies number, i.e., discrete quantity. Both these sciences are directly founded in the sensible. One can see ball-shaped things and cube-shaped things. One can count coins or marbles. Modern mathematicians have added the study called analysis that creates a bridge between these two branches. It consists of pure beings of reason (though reductively real), because, for example, nowhere do we see an infinite limit as is required, for example, in taking a derivative or an integral. Many other beings of reason have been and will be made and utilized, ever expanding our understanding of the mathematical realm of the preter-real.

The Applied Sciences

Below this group in the diagram and in importance are the sciences that study truth in action. Whereas the goal of the pure sciences is to conform one's mind to reality, the goal of these sciences is *to conform one's actions to reality*. They are called *the practical sciences* (or in analogy with the above, *applied sciences*), because by them we know which actions conform to reality and thus what we should do and how and why. As you may surmise, one can only be successful at these sciences to the degree that one

---

[237] Such a time conditioned word demands cautious treatment. For example, the word "modern" was first introduced by the medievals, for they were conscious of departing significantly from the technologies and the thinking of the past.

has been successful (even if it be inchoately) at the pure sciences.[238] This is why, for example, Aristotle did not have a cell phone; its development required advanced modern science. The pure sciences are higher than the practical sciences, for truth comes before action; otherwise one literally does not know what he is doing.

The highest practical science is ethics because it answers the question: what should we do and why? The other practical sciences, called the arts, are subordinate to them because one must first decide what he should do (this implicitly involves knowing why) at least in the broad sense, before he gets the detail of how. Of course, usually ethics will need to know the how before it can pass final judgment on whether an action should be done. We will discuss the subject of ethics (or morality) more in Chapter 9.

The arts, as noted in Figure 6-2, include not only things like painting and sculpting, but also things like electronics and medicine. To do these things properly--that is, so they meet the end decided on in ethical study--one must conform one's action to the reality. In other words, you must know the truth of these things or your circuit may smoke and your patient may die. During a test on electronics, one of my students hooked up an electrolytic capacitor[239] backwards and a giant spark drew my attention to him. A small splotch of his test paper was burnt away before the flame was extinguished. The student learned that one must understand and use an electrolytic capacitor the way that accords with the reality of its nature as an electrolytic capacitor if he wants it to perform as, or in this case even remain, a capacitor.

The Methodological Sciences

The bottom group of sciences studies the human ways of getting to truth. They are called the methods. They include, for example, logic, linguistics, and dialectics. Logic is the head of this

---

[238] For example, a carpenter who, from lived experience, understands something of the nature of different types of woods makes a better carpenter. Of course, at some point for a given activity, knowing more specifics and depth doesn't help that activity.

[239] A capacitor is an electronic device that stores charge. If water is like charge, then a capacitor is like a storage tank.

group. St. Thomas emphasizes that logic should be learned before the other sciences. This may seem strange, for logic, of itself, is among the least important sciences because its importance comes from its directedness to something outside of itself. To do logic with no content or purpose would be inane. It would be like using a hammer without nails or boards with no present or future intention of building.   Still, logic is the most important pedagogically, because all the other sciences depend on the correct use of logic.

Linguistics is important for its role in careful use of words, without which accumulated knowledge would easily go astray or, in the extreme, cease to be passed on at all. Pure dialectics, the study of the means used at arriving at probable conclusions, is technically a part of logic. Applied dialectics views all things from the standpoint of beings of reason *(ens rationis),* not of real being *(ens reale).* Although it has the same subject (all things) as metaphysics, its approach *(ens rationis)* distinguishes it from metaphysics *(ens reale).* Because of this approach, its conclusions are only probable. Only an approach that directly addresses things as they are can be demonstrative and give conclusions that have certainty. Nonetheless, in some parts of a science, because of the weakness of our minds, the dialectic approach is the only method available. Such applied dialectics properly belongs to the various particular sciences that utilize them. This is appropriate, because, although using beings of reason, dialectics still tries to speak of real being.[240]

We thus have three divisions of philosophy (wide sense): *the pure sciences, the applied sciences, and the methodological sciences.*

The above wide use of the word philosophy[241] is not how we've used the word in this book. The wide use was common up to the time of Descartes, who misused it by interpreting philosophy as one undifferentiated science. We are still suffering from this particular misuse; what's more, it is a key to unraveling our

---

[240] Forgetting this goal and confusing beings of reason with real being will lead to idealism. Dialectics is near the huge abyss of idealism; this is why so many moderns fall into it.

[241] It is still common in some areas to use the wide sense. For example, one gets a PhD, which means doctor of philosophy, in many subjects.

dilemma.   The wide use of the term "philosophy" remained common till the time of Christian Wolff (1670-1754) who changed it. We've used philosophy in a restricted sense that is commonly used today. We've used it to mean the first principles of all things. This, of course, does not move metaphysics from its place of primacy, nor move any of the positions. However, for the restricted use of the word, we only include the parts of each division whose formal object is being. So philosophy would consist only of the ontological sciences[242] of *metaphysica, physica, mathematica,* ethics, and logic. This leaves behind arithmetic and geometry (but not the universal science of quantity) and all the modern specialized sciences and all the arts as defined above. It is helpful to make this split, as we've seen. Indeed, we will continue to use the word "philosophy" in the restricted sense. Yet, it is also clear that the split, and hence use of the restricted use of the word, is one of convenience, not an absolute split, for wisdom is one.

Our primary interests in this chapter are the pure sciences. The remainder of the chapter will address only these. In particular, we can now explore the modern specialized sciences, and then answer our questions about Galileo and resolve the apparent conflict between the modern specialized sciences and philosophy.

What Are the
Modern Specialized Sciences?

Let's concentrate on the "hard"[243] modern (pure) sciences: physics, chemistry, and biology. They are called "hard" because of their highly developed state. Among these, physics is the best developed and the oldest. It is also the one that our dilemma centers on. Lastly, physics is my field, so I can shed the most light on it. Let's begin with it. What is the unique part of physics that is called modern physics?[244] It is a crucial *tool* of the science *physica.*

---

[242] Ontology refers to the study of being.

[243] Hard is used here as contrasted with soft, not easy.

[244] Please note this phrase is often used to mean the areas of physics that emerged in the last 100 or so years, particularly the fields of quantum mechanics and relativity. Our meaning is broader. Although, the last hundred years *is* the period when the full force of the "new" science reached the physicist's

It, by itself, can be called a science in an extended sense of the word, but *is* a part of *physica*. Even if we call modern physics in its typical mode a science, as I think we should, we will see that it cannot stand alone, because no proper knowledge of being (science in the strictest sense) can come from its methods alone. Nonetheless, because it does have such a unique methodology and power of accumulating empirical facts, and because it has learned much with some level of certainty (though far below that of *physica* proper), and, finally, because it does attain a certainty about things *at different order* (for example, a certainty about the quantitative relations that obtain among things under certain conditions), we should and *will* call it a science in an extended sense. Furthermore, the conclusions of modern physics, as modern physics, do not directly depend on the broader subject, *physica*. We must, however, always remember that the modern aspect (science or, more appropriately, sub-science) of physics, here called modern physics, is a tool of the broader subject of physics *(physica)*. We will see why as we explore further.

The modern science of physics, which is largely how physics is practiced today, is what Aristotle and St. Thomas call *a mixed science*. It is formally mathematical *(mathematica)* and materially physical *(physica)*. In this science, one tries to understand changeable being under the mode of quantity. It is the *study of changeable being as quantitative.* Figure 6-1 depicts this view of the mathematical through its "reflection off" the physical. In this figure and Figure 6-3, think of the personage shown as sighting along a flashlight aimed in the direction of the arrow. Einstein, for example, in his justly famous theory of (general and special) relativity, sees the physical real as reflected into the mathematical. Descartes looks only at mathematics, and Aristotle directs his light at all areas, though less at the mathematical than the others.

Figure 6-3 shows the three degrees of abstraction using a picture similar to one used by Jacques Maritain in his *Philosophy of Nature*. Here, Aristotle looks at the small middle sphere, which

---

consciousness in a profound way. Still, Einstein's relativity, Maxwell's theory, quantum mechanics, thermodynamics, and Newtonian physics all are key examples of this "new" (modern) science.

represents *mobile (changeable) being*. The top of this sphere is sensible being, being that can be directly apprehended by our senses. The middle of the sphere contains things that can be learned (from sensible data) in the order of *mobile being*. Aristotle probes the sphere of *mobile being* in the study called *physica*. Finally, his investigation penetrates through the sphere, refracting to reveal the large outer sphere representing *being as being*, the study of which is *metaphysica*. This is the arena of immaterial substances that we (and he first) learned must exist by studying mobile being, being tied to matter.

Descartes is shown looking at sensible being, but his "view" is reflected onto the *quantity* sphere that represents quantitative being, the domain of *mathematica*. This is the domain of the mathematical preter-real.

Einstein's "view" also ends in this sphere of the quantitative, but his view first dives into the heart of the *mobile being* sphere. He dives right into the heart of material being and then is refracted up to a *subset*, a smaller ball inside, of the *quantity* sphere. For example, in general relativity, he very accurately describes the behavior of bodies under the influence of only gravitational attraction. What kind of description is it? It is a *quantitative* description. It captures the measured quantitative relation among massive bodies under certain idealized conditions. Hence, general relativity is a clear example of the mixed science of modern physics, since bodies, which are material things (mobile being), are its subject, and equations (mathematics) are its mode of explanation. This science is also more generically called empiriological. We will explain "empiriological" in more depth shortly, but the obvious meaning is not so far off, the study of the empirical *(empirio)*, i.e., the sensible, in a *purely* logical way.

Modern physics *is* a study of sensible being, but *not* under an ontological (being- oriented) light, not looking for the purely intelligible explanation. Modern physics is the study of sensible being as sensible (observable) and as expressible mathematically. It is *empiriometric*. It is metrical because its mode of explanation is mathematical, so it must use measurement of quantities. The use of the word "metric" in the SI or metric system of measures can help one remember that it means "measure of a quantity"; "metric" particularly refers to length, but we use it in a more general sense.

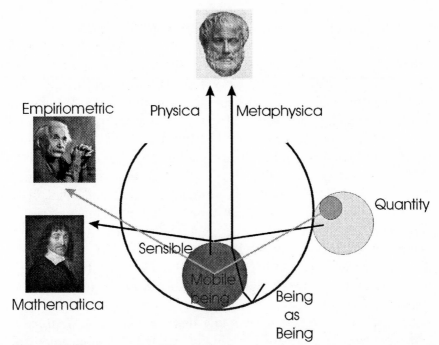

Figure 6-3: Aristotle is shown studying *physica* and through it *metaphysica*. Einstein is shown looking at the material world as reflected into a subset of the preter-real world of quantity; this is the mixed science that we call empiriometric. Descartes is shown looking only at the quantitative aspects of things in the science of *mathematica*.

Astronomy is given by St. Thomas as an example of a mixed science (empiriometric). The ancients looked at the planets and stars very carefully and tried to use mathematics (the epicycles of Ptolemy (second century AD) to describe and account, at the requisite level, for the motions.

Geometric optics, that is optics as existed until the modern empiriometric explosion (in particular, until the arrival of Maxwell's equations), is another example used before modern times. In it, one studies light travel using Euclidean geometry of lines. Thus, it is formally geometry and materially light travel.

To further understand what the modern sciences are, we must distinguish between the empiriological and the ontological approach. In this discussion, always keep in mind we are trying to understand mobile being (the first plane in Figure 6-1).

Empiriological versus Ontological

If I come across any material thing, say an insect, I can approach understanding it in two ways. The most fundamental and important approach is from the standpoint of ontology (also known as philosophical, in the restricted sense). In this approach, I want to know the essence of the insect. The question is what is it? More specifically, what is it primarily as intelligible?[245] The "what is it?" question is intrinsically linked with the question of *all* the four "causes" of Aristotle: material, formal, efficient and final. The causes imply the following questions. What it is made out of? What is it? What caused it to be what it is? What is its reason for being (which includes what it tends towards)? If I start in this direction, as we did in this book, it will not be long before I will need to adopt an empiriological approach as a tool to obtain the answers I seek.

In this book, we have found that we can reach *significant* and *certain* conclusions without detailed empiriological knowledge. In fact, we avoided it because its nature would only reduce the certainty of our conclusions. However, we reached a point where we needed to start specializing, and that specialization demanded the empiriological approach.

The empiriological approach either correlates measurements about our insect *or* categorizes our insect with respect to other insects. In this "or," we have a subdivision within the empiriological; the first is the *empiriometric;* the second is called *empirioschematic.*[246] Empirioschematic refers to a science (extended sense) that uses "schemas" (diagrams) or other symbolic references as its rule of explanation instead of mathematics. Because empirioschematic science stays entirely within the first level of abstraction, it is not properly a mixed science; yet it is composed of two different degrees within the first level, so we can call it mixed in an improper or less full sense.

In summary, both the ontological (or philosophical) and the empiriological have as their subject mobile being. Both start with

---

[245] Refer to Chapter 4 where we discussed essence in some detail.

[246] The term empiriological as well as these later two terms are J. Maritain's.

sensible being. After that, they diverge. The ontological *ascends* to the intelligible (the being of the sensible being), whereas the empiriological *descends* to the observable (the sensible of the sensible being). The empiriological starts in the sensible and develops beings of reason from it, which it then resolves and verifies back in the sensible. The empiriological starts in the observable, more particularly in *the measurable as such,* and ends there. Jacques Maritain, whose *Philosophy of Nature* and *Degrees of Knowledge* are "must read," says of empiriological knowledge, "Not of course that the mind no longer refers to being, for that is quite impossible: being always remains; but here it enters the service of the sensible, of the observable, and especially of the measurable. It [real being] becomes an unknown assuring the constancy of certain sensible determinations and measurements."[247] He then notes how this affects vocabulary. Not surprising. In the ontological, one seeks the essence, the *form* of the thing, but, in the empiriological, essence is replaced by a being of reason. The vocabulary of the two will manifest the radically different methods and goals.

With these distinctions made, we can discuss physics more completely.

Physics

Physics *(Physica)* is the generic study of mutable being. Physics, however, as it is practiced today, does almost no deliberate ontological science. It is *nearly* all what we have called modern physics (empiriometric science).

Physics, as practiced today, is not all empiriometric. Sometimes a subfield of physics uses an empirioschematic mode in its formative stages. In solving any given problem, it seldom uses the empirioschematic as its main mode, but sometimes it is forced to. Consider, for example, Steven Weinberg's memory of his years in graduate school.[248] He recalled[249] that the particle physics he

---

[247] J. Maritain, *Philosophy of Nature,* p. 75.
[248] Last time I looked, physicists typically get a bachelor's degree in physics, followed by a PhD that takes on the average around 6.5 years. Then they spend

learned was so many disparate facts that reminded him more of zoology than physics. When he was in graduate school, there were an ever-increasing number of particles being found and *no* mathematical or even simple schematic theory to unify that complex data. As the empiriometric method supplied measurements and quantitative analysis began to suggest a theory, the empirioschematic aspect was gradually eliminated, until the remaining minimal schema totally served beautiful mathematics. More specifically, it was proposed that the hundreds of "seen" particles were composed of quarks[250] with certain properties, and the quark and its properties were quickly subsumed into mathematical equations (having a beautiful property of gauge invariance).

A similar route was followed in Mendeleev and Mosley's discovery of the periodic table of the elements. An even more purely empirioschematic method is found in astronomy. Namely, galaxies and stars were first classified by qualities like shape and color (as opposed to measured features) before a properly empiriometric study of these objects was obtained. For a physicist today, to be reduced to the condition of using only the empirioschematic is his worst sort of nightmare. Indeed, he seeks and worries until he is able to bring it under empiriometric control. He wants to incorporate all measurements into the already known laws and/or find the appropriate enlargement of those known laws. His final goal is that all possible measurements will be correlated in one beautifully self-consistent mathematical system. This is the final theory Weinberg wishes for in his *Dreams of a Final Theory*. When a segment of empirical reality is successfully described by a theory, the physicist has reason to believe he has made progress

---

about six in so-called post-doctoral positions. These are typical numbers; there are large variations about this mean.

[249] I saw this in a taped interview on CNN (1/23/02).

[250] There are now thought to be six types or flavors of quarks (called: up, down, charm, strange, top, and bottom) and six leptons (electron, muon, tau, and their neutrinos) and their twelve anti-particles. In addition, there are thought to be only a small number of other "particles": photons, W+ and W- boson, and Z boson and gluons. Currently unverified theories suggest there are many more particles; string theory, for example, introduces a whole set of paired particles "due to" a property called supersymmetry.

toward such a "final" theory. On the side of very large things (planets and stars), Einstein did this with gravity. On the side of the very small (subatomic), Glasgow, Weinberg, and Salam did this for particle physics in their electro-weak theory. As the name implies, it united electricity, magnetism, and the weak nuclear force, which is responsible for beta decay of radioactive isotopes.

Physics: Waves and Light

To get a better idea *how and what* these quantitative theories reveal, let's follow typical modern physics methodology for a pivotal experiment, the so-called double slit experiment in the study of light. It will help us understand how two of the most renowned modern scientists could make the following startling comments about reality in the realm of light. Einstein said,[251]

All the fifty years of conscious brooding have brought me no closer to the answer to the question, "What are light quanta [photons]?" Of course today every rascal thinks he knows the answer, but he is deluding himself.

And, Richard Feynman told the following story:[252]

It was a wonderful world my father told me about. You might wonder what he got out of it all. I went to MIT. I went to Princeton. I came home, and he said, "Now you've got a science education. I have always wanted to know something that I have never understood; and so, my son, I want you to explain it to me." I said yes. He said, "I understand that they say that light is emitted from an atom when it goes from one state to another, from an excited state to a state of lower energy. I said, "That's right."

[251] Quoted in I. J. R. Aitchison and Hey *Gauge Theories in Particle Physics* 2nd edition, p. 83. Adam Hilger, IOP publishing Ltd., 1989. Quoted as by Einstein in 1951.
[252] Ibid. referenced from R. P. Feynman, *The Physics Teacher*, Vol. 7, No. 6, Sept. 1969.

"And light is a kind of particle, photon, I think they call it." "Yes." "So if the photon comes out of the atom when it goes from the excited to the lower state, the photon must have been in the atom in the excited state." I said, "Well, no." He said, "Well, how do you look at it so you can think of a particle photon coming out without it having been in there in the excited state?" I thought a few minutes, and I said, "I'm sorry; I don't know. I can't explain it to you." He was very disappointed after all these years and years of trying to teach me something, that it came out with such poor results.

When we see a double slit pattern produced from light passing through two closely spaced slots (slits) onto a screen as shown in Figure 6-4, we recall that we have seen the same essential pattern already in our experience (colors and other qualities are different, but there is a shape that is the same). We've seen water waves interfere when throwing two rocks in the right proximity of each other into a lake (see Figure 6-5).

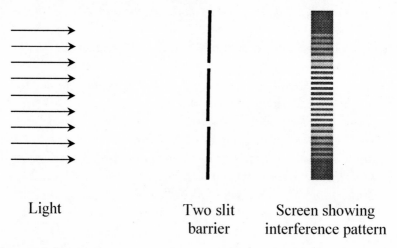

Light   Two slit   Screen showing
                       barrier   interference pattern

Figure 6-4: Diagram of double "slit" experiment with light.

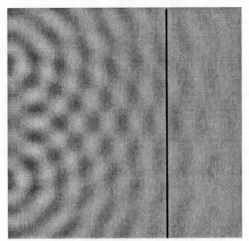

Figure 6-5: Double "slit" experiment with water. Here we are looking at only two dimensions, so we have "points" instead of "slits." Note the waves emanating from each of two point-sources, where, for instance, a rock is dropped. The line represents the location of an imaginary screen.

For example, at one point in time along the line, one could record the height of the waves indicating bright for high waves and dark for low ones. On such a line, one would see a pattern of light and dark, indicating a pattern of high waves and low waves. When the crest of a wave from one source happens to arrive at a point on the screen at the same time as a crest of the other, the waves reinforce; one thus gets a maximally high wave, which we can mark as a bright spot. When a trough and crest arrive at the same time, they cancel; one thus gets a zero height wave, which we mark as a dark spot.

We then use this fact to say there are light *waves*. This reasoning contains a *jump* in logic, because two identical patterns can be caused in many different ways. For example, a dark circle in concrete can be caused by a narrow deep groove in the concrete or by a black line painted on the surface of the concrete or by a shadow. Yet we have to say there is a certain simplicity and allurement about following the assumption that the pattern indicates some similarity of causes. Still, its force is *only* a force of *probability,* not of certainty.

Okay, we say at this point that we have a hypothesis that can be tested. But how can we test it? Can we use the ontological approach directly? By comparison with the dark circle on the concrete, we might think we can.

The question "What is the dark circle?" may be answered at the most general level with a directly ontological approach. We can touch the ground and feel the difference between the dark part of the concrete and the lighter part. We can move our eyes closer to get a better view. We can change the lighting. If we feel and see a slight circular groove where the dark circle is, we have a general answer to our question about the nature of the dark circle. However, if it takes a magnifying glass, we are already one step removed from our senses. We have to verify the magnifying glass does not change what we're seeing...a fairly easy task at the level of this problem,[253] and this can be verified at the sensorial level, for it typically magnifies features that we can already see at some resolution.

If we have to proceed to a microscope, the task of convincing is harder, and finally if we have to use an electron microscope, a thick layer of theory is imposed between the CRT screen that is showing the image and the actual shape of the thing. Indeed, to use an electron microscope, one has to coat the specimen with a material that conducts electricity; this introduces another layer of theory and potential of distortion of the object's shape. After much work, one obtains increasing certainty that the shape he sees under the microscope is correct at a level of precision. However, because of the nature of the interposed theory- -not to mention the physical manipulation of the object--many other attributes of the thing are obscured or completely left behind. For example, the color is lost. The point is not that one cannot recover these aspects by a different investigation directed specifically at them using different samples of the dark circle. The other aspects may *or* may not be recoverable by us. The key point is that these sorts of analyses isolate only *some* aspects of the thing and those only with a degree of probability, not a certainty.

It is a constant occupational risk of the scientist to forget both these limitations. Because he has focused on one aspect (in our case, the shape) and has done many experiments and read about others that mesh well with his proper knowledge of the thing under consideration, he develops a "gut" feel for what makes sense and what doesn't in this area. The constancy of his sharp focus, the

---

[253] Lenses are known to introduce distortion of shape and color that are very important to understand and eliminate to the degree possible (and needed) in experimental science.

fact that he seldom draws back to live in the larger view (outside of the aspects he is concerned with), and his well-developed intuitive ability to hone in on the right answer in this limited regime can make him forget that the science he deals with is both narrow and probable, not complete and certain. He will remember these two points, especially the latter--as I have on occasion--when he misreads a physical situation and for a while is confounded by what is happening in his experiment. To emerge from his consternation, he may examine foundational issues that lead him to see a new level of complexity that enlarges and completes what he instinctively thought was large enough and complete enough already.

What about the double slit? The double slit experiment is not amenable to the direct ontological approach, because it does not help to look more closely or feel or listen more attentively; nothing we can do with our senses directly avails any further information than the pattern already seen. We must proceed to a method that introduces a qualitatively new level of ontological uncertainty.[254] However, because we will be dealing with matter stripped of many of its physical attributes, we can penetrate the quantitative interrelation among things with some depth. We will use an empiriometric approach.[255]

Having analyzed water waves in detail, we know that, at some level of approximation, the wave equation applies to their amplitude.[256] The wave equation describes at some approximate

---

[254] If it helps the reader, he may consider each layer of instrument and theory as a new level removed from reality. The fact is that theory and experiment are interwoven in modern physics so that any one experiment tests the whole theory. Some parts of the theory are considered untouchable while others are more mutable. However, when a significant result is found, the whole theory may undergo what Kuhn calls a paradigm shift (as with the advent of general relativity with respect to Newtonian gravity). Key quantitative aspects are saved, but the ontological aspects, the truly explanatory parts, are fundamentally modified. However, this volatility may be tamed by making the proper distinctions that we discuss herein.

[255] Before entering the purely empiriometric mode, we could do more pattern matching by throwing three rocks and comparing with three slit pattern.

[256] The one-dimensional wave equation is: $\dfrac{\partial^2 A}{\partial x^2} = \dfrac{1}{v^2}\dfrac{\partial^2 A}{\partial t^2}$. Here the amplitude of the wave is A, and v is the speed of the wave.

level the motion of water waves. We can now use this fact to check whether the light also follows this equation in some way. Here we see several aspects of the empiriometric method.

First, the water wave that we *can see* has become a sort of metaphor or model for the light that we *cannot see*. Already this is a substitution, at least temporarily, of a being of reason (the idealized water wave) for the real essence of the light. Yet it goes further; we use the metaphor as a starting point to begin a mathematical correlation of measured aspects of the light's interaction with other things. Here we seek the quantitative aspects of light; more exactly, the form we seek is no longer the form of light as it is, but as it manifests itself *quantitatively* in its many relations or interactions with other things. We seek a mathematical form, or, as it is still called, a mathematical *form*ulation of the theory.

Second, we have the approximate character of the measurements and the mathematics. Even as quantitative correlations, the measurements we make and the equations we assign to those measurements will only be verified at an approximate level. In other words, even the equations we pick can only have a more or less probable correspondence to the measurements. Hence, two levels of uncertainty emerge, one in the ontological and one in the quantitative. Unlike the ontological, the quantitative uncertainty can be resolved (usually relatively quickly and to some deep level) within the theory, and any more general theory must reduce to the appropriate approximate theory.[257] This is no surprise because the theory is an empiriometric theory; it can deal with empiriometric problems, not ontological problems. It will be no surprise then that ontological explanations can change quickly and drastically, but quantitative aspects, although they change, they gradually evolve with stages that can be discerned. On the other hand, the change in what one may believe is ontological explanation is fundamental, like from the absolute time of Newton to the relative time of Einstein, or the absolute motion

---

[257] For example, in the study of the motion of water, the full hydrodynamic equations must reduce to the wave equation under the right conditions and measurement uncertainties.

of Aristotle to the relative motion of Orseme, Buridan,[258] and Galileo. It is like the paradigm shift described by philosopher of science Thomas Kuhn (1922-1996).

We will discuss how to deal with the ontological interpretation of empiriometric theories later. For now, we should emphasize that the ontological approach is deliberately excluded in the empiriometric approach, so we should not try to directly translate their results into essence of things. The procedure must be much more indirect. Because of this, most of the time, the degree of certainty of ontological conclusions reached via the empiriometric science is *much* lower than that of the quantitative conclusions we come to via it. It is important then to realize when one is in the empiriometric regime to correctly gauge the certainty. But, even more, if one does not realize he is doing empiriometric science, he may--as has happened more often than not in the past[259]--take empiriometric constructs directly as ontological explanations. Thereby we not only ignore the inherent uncertainty in most ontological conclusions drawn from the empiriometric, but we do not even do any of the ontological work necessary to reach conclusions that minimize that uncertainty. Thus, as "paradigm shifts" manifest, we have to keep radically changing our minds about the reality manifested by our mathematics. The clear danger is that, after so many steps in apparently random directions, we begin to despair of reaching ontological reality. This relates directly to our Galileo question.

Back to light and the wave equation. Once armed with the wave equation,[260] we can calculate what should happen in the water wave case in detail. We can then see if we can assign a

---

[258] These latter two are physicists from the Middle Ages who we will discuss in the next chapter.

[259] The phenomenon of mistaking mathematical description (beings of reason) for reality is well documented by Stanley Jaki in *The Relevance of Physics*. He also documents the general problem of reducing reality to any one of its varied types. Being, as we say in Chapter 4, is multi-layered, not univocal but analogous.

[260] We have introduced an approximate hydrodynamic equation, called the wave equation. We could also have introduced certain approximate quantitative aspects of waves, such as the principle of superposition that allows point sources to be summed to create a wave front.

length and a frequency to light in such a way that we can account for the patterns of the double slit experiment. If we can do this in some non-contradictory fashion, we will assume that our mathematical description has some validity. The more we verify this attribution in various settings, the more we will come to identify light as a wave.

We will use the wave equation along with the correspondence between the measured quantity and equation variables to determine how light should behave and see if it does. We will naturally want to know what *waves* in light. We call the thing that *waves* an electromagnetic field (an electric field and magnetic field). We will want these concepts to be related to something in our immediate sensible experience. Making this connection will lead to an increasing number of layers between us and the thing to be known. We will associate the mysterious label "electric field" with that mysterious thing called electric charge (commonly known as static electricity),[261] which is in turn caused by rubbing certain objects together. The electric field will be the amount of force caused per unit charge, where force, in turn, relates to other empiriometrically defined objects, especially the empiriometric quantity known as mass.[262] We will create a web of interconnected concepts in this way and will become gradually more certain that the wave theory of light is correct in the sense of fitting into a sweeping theory that gives valid predictions over a large range of phenomena. However, the number of beings of reason between the full ontological reality and us will have been increased with the sophistication of the theory.

---

[261] Note that calling something a name and getting used to using it in the empiriometric scheme does not mean we understand what it is the way we understand, say, that a man is a rational animal. This definition captures the essence of man, all things to do with man from his ability to solve problems and write symphonies to his having a heart and hands are implicitly explained in that definition.

[262] In theories of physics that incorporate quantum mechanics, as we believe they must, the concept of mass becomes even more distant from any simple ontological interpretation. Quantitatively, of course, it must (the procedures of empiriometric science will demand it) reduce to the quantity measured on larger scales. As mass (or any empiriometric concept) becomes further incorporated into a larger web of theory, it moves further from ontological understanding.

Once again, even if we convince ourselves beyond doubt of the correctness of quantitative relations (equations)[263] at a particular level, this doesn't mean we have explained the reality. If anyone doubts this fact, consider the following. Although the success of the wave theory of light (partially elucidated above) is remarkable and has attained a high degree of quantitative certainty, if one then concludes that light *is* a spread out thing called a wave, trouble accompanies such a jump of logic. A separate approach from the quantum mechanical side will lead with the same force to the conclusion that light is a localized thing called a particle (photon). It cannot *be* both spread out and localized at the same time and in the same way, which is what a simple-minded ontological interpretation of the empiriometric results demands.[264]

No such problems would obtain if we remember that empiriometric science is formally mathematical and material physical. The fully ontological is thus usually fairly hidden in the empiriometric.

Considering Einstein's deep understanding of modern (empiriometric) physics, his remark that he did not know what a photon is--which for him is tantamount to not knowing what light is--reveals the non-intelligibility (non-being or non-ontological) oriented nature of the empiriometric. The conversation between Feynman and his father is even clearer. It shows the lack of ontological knowledge in Feynman's deep empiriometric knowledge. He could not explain to his father what an atom was

---

[263] We encounter another difficulty and that has to do with the fact that many equations can describe the same data, because of the approximate character of all data. Every measurement is an approximation. We can get more and more accurate measurements and convince ourselves more, but there will always be other equations than the one we pick which will equally well describe the data. Physicists use many methods to develop more certainty about a given theory, but none is a crucial experiment in an absolute sense, only a relative sense. One can rule out certain theories with crucial experiments, but one cannot rule out all theories. Simplicity is a guide that scientists often use with great success. The simplicity of a theory is part of what I'll call a "beauty test" that all physical theories must pass. (Note that this test is still a part of the empiriometric approach.) As a result of the working of the method, the science does progress, and we obtain more certainty about the quantitative theory (at some level) itself, though not often its ultimate meaning.

[264] We will discuss such issues in the next chapter.

and what light was. Just knowing the equations and their interpretive scheme--which together reveal quantitative interrelations between things--does not reveal the reality, the essence of the things. Why? At the simplest level, the reason is that one equation can describe two totally different physical situations.

An example from physics can bring the point home. Take the very successful and beautiful electro-weak theory, which has to do with nuclear forces, forces relevant on the scale of the size of the nucleus of the atom. It is formulated in terms of a system of equations that were first, and still are, used to describe superconductivity.[265] Superconductivity is the phenomenon whereby certain materials take on zero electrical resistance and other fascinating properties.

Another example is seen in Kip Thorne's popularized book, *Black Holes and Time Warps:*[266]

> *What is the real, genuine truth? Is space-time really flat, as the above paragraphs suggest, or is it really curved? To a physicist [empiriometric scientist] like me this is an uninteresting question because it has no physical consequences. Both viewpoints, curved space-time and flat, give precisely the same predictions for any measurements performed with perfect rulers and clocks, and also (it turns out) the same predictions for any measurements performed with any kind of physical apparatus whatsoever.*

We will discuss general relativity, my sub-field, and what it has to say about time and space in the next chapter. For now, note not just modern [empiriological] physics' inability to decide directly about

---

[265] More specifically, P. W. Anderson (1963) first noticed that a gauge theory associated with superconductors could get mass by certain mathematical manipulations. This was identical to the case of "giving mass" to a photon in complex scalar field. Glashow, Salam, and Weinberg used this Higg's "mechanism" in their electro-weak theory, a particular type of gauge theory (called non-Abelian), to explain (in the empiriometric sense) the mass of the intermediate bosons.

[266] See page 400 of Thorne's book.

ontological questions, but also its lack of interest in those questions.

Again, one equation can describe the quantitative aspects[267] of two qualitatively different things.[268] For example, light and water waves are both describable by the "wave" equation. Although one cannot, with logical certainty, identify what the cause of a phenomenon is from a mathematical relation, one can form negative conclusions from the mathematical statement. Specifically, any cause that is not consistent with the required quantitative results is ruled out. Remembering these two things will save a physicist a lot of headaches. No, this is not strong enough. Don't just remember; keep them in mind. We will see more reasons why later.

Does this mean that one can *never* learn any reality from empiriometric science? No. We do learn abstract quantitative relations (even though they may be approximate). Further, though they may not be always able to give us ontological content, sometimes they do. St. Thomas points out that empiriometric sciences "treat it [the thing under consideration] not insofar as it is a mathematical, but insofar as it is a physical thing."[269] He uses the example of astronomical evidences for the spherical shape of the earth. Specifically, St. Thomas says that "...this [the round earth] is demonstrated by astronomy from the figure of the lunar

---

[267] These "quantitative aspects" include things that are not properly quantitative accidents, but degrees of the qualities of the thing. As an example, we mentioned earlier that more hot and less hot is measured by degrees of temperature.

[268] As a further illustration of the effect, consider that two physical phenomena can have the same data sets that describe some aspect of each of them and, yet, be totally different physically. For example, consider plotting the speed versus time plot for my drive from my home to LSU to teach. One day the data (and the equation obtained from the correctly fitted curve) plotted could be the same as the plot (and fitted equation) of the number of cars per day produced by GM in 1996. The fact that the experiment is not reproducible should not worry the reader, as it should if we were trying to develop a physical theory. We are only trying to point out the lack of one to one correspondence between two similar sets of data and the physical things that are behind each data set. In our example, it is clear that the same physical mechanisms were not behind these two radically different actions. The data leave out all but the quantitative interrelations.

[269] Commentary on Aristotle's Physics Book II, lect. 3 para 164.

eclipse..."[270] This ontological conclusion (round earth) from a minimally empiriometric observation is, because *minimally* empiriometric, not far removed from direct sensible evidence.[271] At this relatively direct level, one can often make these sorts of ontological gains about the thing itself in empiriometric science. Indeed, in some cases, these conclusions are so close to sense experience that they can be verified, in principle by direct sense observation. For instance, the earth's approximate spherical shape can be verified by sense experience by continually looking back at the earth from a spacecraft from launch to orbit and through one orbit. Conclusions so minimally empiriometric as to be subject to later *direct* verification by the unaided senses are clearly on the edge, not in the heart, of the empiriometric science. When one really has a developed empiriometric theory, there are many layers between the observer and reality, as well as a whole network of interconnecting concepts, no one of which, as we've noted, can be easily separated from the rest. Such interconnectedness is, moreover, the sign of a good theory. In the thick of the empiriometric science, we do not expect as much chance of explicitly ontological gains. Still, we find them here also.

As the empiriometric scientist constantly returns to the less abstract ideas of *physica* to understand what the equations mean, he will make explanations that will involve beings of reason *(ens rationis)*, but remember real being *(ens real)* is always present, as the remote or proximate foundation, and is responsible for the stable relationships he sees. Nonetheless, sometimes even in the rarified world of beings of reason that is empiriometric science, a real being will be so clearly present in the quantitative relations as to demand notice. Usually, this "being" is first seen as a convenient schema and is only acknowledged as a real being after crucial

---

[270] Ibid., lect. 3 para 165.

[271] The eminent philosopher William Wallace, in his book *The Modeling of Nature* (published in 1996), discusses how arguments from dialectic science (he uses the shape of the earth as an example) can sometimes be reformulated, by careful thinking, into demonstrative arguments. His book is recommended as well for the broad history of science he includes, as well as his description of various logical elements. He has a deep understanding of Aristotle.

experiments,[272] whose purpose is to answer the question at some level. We've discussed some of the beings found by modern physics; they include: atoms, electrons, protons, neutrons, and quarks. Though we've never seen (or sensed in any way) any of these beings and in principle *cannot*, we must say that their existence in varying degrees has a high degree of certainty. I would say the list is pretty much in order of decreasing certainty. Yet, one would be ill-advised to assert that any of these are *mere* beings of reason; that is, that they have no real existence outside the mind. Then, what are they? What, for example, is an electron? Now, that is a different question. We first know *that* something is and only in a confused way know what it is. We, of course, have much purely *empiriometric* knowledge "about"[273] electrons; we know they have "spin," "charge" (of a certain amount), and that they obey electro-weak theory, etc. These are mathematical empirical concepts and not easily reduced for the understanding itself. We can only give metaphors for them; spin is indeed *like* the spin of a top, but is by *no* means the same. So, what is an electron? With the empiriometric method, we do not even know, in one sense, if it is small (a particle) or big (a wave).[274] We only know in the most vague form what it is really (ontologically), and in most cases, it is vagueness with a low probability of truth.

---

[272] Such experiments are not crucial in the sense of logically compelling, but in the sense of providing a highly probable argument.

[273] The empiriometric knowledge does not always allow us to identify when something is *about* a particular thing or *about* the thing and the system together or sometimes even about averages, which excludes the individual as individual.

[274] Feynman tells the story of the great modern physicist John Wheeler calling him in the middle of the night to tell him of his latest thought. He had discovered why all electrons have exactly identical properties. He knew why electrons are "identical." There was, he said, only one electron! Feynman convinced him otherwise. But, this is the constant danger of empiriometric science and tells how often it can completely miss the individual, let alone the properties of that individual. John Wheeler has been academic father to many well-known physicists including, in a short list, Demetrios Christodoulou, Richard Feynman, Kip Thorne, and James York. He is my academic "grandfather" because Demetrios Christodoulou was my advisor as a graduate student at Princeton. If John Wheeler had done nothing else but influence students in the way he did, his contribution to physics would already be hard to overestimate, but he did much more.

Note that we have left much behind in our empiriometric search. Since we are only correlating quantities, it should be no surprise that we cannot go very far by utilizing only the empiriometric method. In this method, qualities only appear as quantitative, i.e. as measured quantities. In fact, it is surprising that the empiriometric method is able to do as much as it does without conscious ontological effort. How much more can we learn, say about an electron, by trying to extract ontological knowledge from the empiriometric output discussed above? This work of trying to establish the ontological ground of the empiriometric results is little done and will be discussed in Chapter 7. Why has so little been done? It requires two very hard things: a deep understanding of the foundational part of *physica* (science of mobile being), such as discussed in the previous chapters, as well as of empiriometric (modern) physics. In particular, it requires understanding the issues correctly. It requires understanding what empiriometric science is. If one stays in the empiriometric, he can forget what we've seen; the empiriometric presupposes the foundational part of physics *(physica)*. Doing the aforementioned work presupposes explicit knowledge of most of the first six chapters of this book.

Kant's Attempt to Ground Modern Physics: Kant's "Gödel's Theorem"

Obviously, people *do* care to learn about reality; that's what physics is about. What do they do? When someone does have the courage to approach the task, it is usually in the pattern set by Immanuel Kant. Kant[275] set the pattern by (inadvertently) taking the empiriometric as the whole of *physica.* He wanted, as mentioned earlier, Newton's mechanics to have a certainty it did not have. He wanted the dialectical "science" to have a demonstrative value that only *physica* (philosophy of mobile being) itself, *not its tool, empiriometric physics* had. He proceeded to make the empiriometric the ground of all philosophy. In so

---

[275] Not knowing the empiriometric science (modern physics as it was in his time, particularly as advanced by Newton) in any real way (cf. Chapter 3, ~footnote 57) also damaged his ability to assess it correctly.

doing, he inadvertently stood the way we think on its head. He became a Cartesian (follower of Descartes) because he thus put beings of reason (or at least things acting like beings of reason) as the first things that we know. In other words, this is equivalent to saying that we know our ideas first. It gives him no ability to back up and see that beings of reason themselves are founded on the real.

Again, let's chant, by now an important mantra, he did not put "first things first." We know "there is an is." Things exist. We know this by our sensorial knowledge. As a result of starting in the wrong place, he became an idealist. In so doing, he came to the inevitable conclusion that we cannot know the thing itself. He basically proved Gödel's theorem 150 years before Gödel.[276] In our terms, he showed that if one takes beings of reason as all of reality, one can never prove anything, even what one believes about the beings of reason. He showed that Newtonian physics (indeed, all empiriometric (modern) physics) couldn't stand alone. It can *do* its job alone but it cannot stand alone as knowledge, for it cannot prove its own foundations. Even more, if it takes itself too seriously, it can in fact undermine its own foundations.

Physicists do not show any tendencies, while they're doing their physics, to be philosophical idealists. Physicists want to know about the real world. If nothing else, the experimental side of physics constantly reminds them that they are in contact with something that is not themselves. Just when we physicists think it must be this way, experiment shows it is another even more astonishing way. However, physicists *do* tend to forget what has been left behind in the very rarified process of empiriometric science.[277] Steven Weinberg[278] fell into this, at least in the use of imprecise expression, when he described modern science as using

---

[276] Kant actually does not go all the way, because he talks about a thing in itself but he says you cannot know it. He illogically, but sensibly, holds onto "the thing" that has no place in his philosophical system.

[277] Pierre Duhem (1861-1916), the renowned physicist (e.g. the Gibbs-Duhem equation) and unmatched historian of medieval science, wrote on this topic in his landmark, *The Aim and Structure of Physical Theory*. It is a must-read. He describes very accurately and completely the empiriometric science, in its most rarified mathematical form (but not its only form).

[278] He said this in the same CNN interview (1/23/02) mentioned earlier.

the same processes as when you pick up a rock and learn about it by looking at it and feeling it.

It is very easy to forget the nature of empiriometric knowledge. Once one has made the abstractions and substitutions described above, one can become enamored with the beauty and the integrity of that description of that part of reality that one has brought out. The modern physicist can then easily take what he knows (including, to compound matters, all the unsifted empiriometric forms) as all of reality. How? It is easy to forget the parts of the world that one has deliberately left behind. The powerful quantitative predictive ability that is intrinsic to the empiriometric method is quite useful, if not always (though very often) for practical things, for increasing the depth and breadth of the empiriometric theory itself. As one becomes accustomed to *only* taking from reality those things useful in empiriometric analysis, one becomes less and less conscious that he is leaving something behind. It becomes natural to ignore, even to forget, what's left behind. It is then all too easy to start to think that one has everything in the empiriometric construct. The world ruled by this kind of thinking is somewhat foreign to the average non-physicist. So, let's take a metaphor.

Take chess. Chess is just a game and is not about the real world, so in this respect, it is not similar to modern physics. However, if one considers that chess is about rules that must be related to real-world properties in some way (otherwise it could not be played) and modern physics is about mathematical equations that arise from some real being(s) in the world, then a parallel with modern physics appears. Consider the following fictional story.

An elite group of men forms some 400 years ago. They are elite, not by status, but by education and ability in chess. They are able to play chess with expertise and finesse. They have become so good that it is no challenge, and hence no fun, for them to play those outside their circle. They eat drink and sleep the various intricacies of chess. They see and relish all the fascinating ins and outs of the game. But it doesn't stop here; soon this group manages to establish a tradition of chess playing that survives into successive generations and finally into our own time. We approach one of these people about ordinary aspects of life, such as the way a rock falls or the ripples in a stream. They have not paid attention to such things and were taught and believe these things unimportant and even uninteresting. You are at first amazed that they did not know of or care about these things. But you are more intrigued when you push the chess traditionalist to explain the phenomena of a rock falling downward, and he explains that following an expanded law of the pawn, which must move one square at a time forward, the rock must move downward at the given pace. To your astonishment, he finds the explanation completely satisfactory and exhaustive.

Of course, knowing that I am a scientist myself, you will see that the point is not to say scientists are naïve of the real world, but that they are, by long personal habit and ingrained tradition, accustomed to the narrow, but highly fruitful and useful empiriometric thought pattern. This can, if not dealt with appropriate care, lock them out of accessing the larger realities.[279]

If one still has trouble believing or understanding such complete habituation, consider the following example. During a discussion about the philosophical idea of change, a good friend of mine and a first-rate scientist said that I am trying to establish the "time derivative."[280]   I do not in any way want to poke fun or belittle my friend. When I approached philosophy for the first time many years ago, I had the same sorts of tendencies and approaches. The "intuition of being" that Maritain and Gilson describe as so hard to obtain and maintain was for me invisible. My friend's response just reveals the modern physics mindset, and because of the success of modern physics, part of our cultural mindset.

Of course, all professions have their own mindsets and habits that must, in varying degrees, be checked at the door when leaving the office, but here we are talking about physicists. We discuss it to help us better understand the very powerful nature of

---

[279] In fact, this metaphor is even more relevant when it comes to thinking about the artificial intelligence question discussed in the last chapter. Those who are most active in making "artificial intelligences" usually think the complex algorithmic manipulation (the finite, but complex, rules of chess (i.e. a system of beings of reason) lend themselves to just such algorithms) required to play chess encapsulate the essence of thinking. If that is what thinking is in its fullest meaning, and we've seen it is not, then artificially intelligent things do think.

[280] For example, speed is the time derivative of distance traveled, x, and it is written dx/dt, where t is time.

the empiriometric science and its *limitations*. The fact is that the time derivative is a mathematical expression of the fact of change. Change is prior (in time as well as principle) to "time derivative." We know change without a concept of a derivative or the putting of time on a spatial picture that is required for the concept of time derivative. To try to understand the fundamental broad idea of change by such narrow instruments as derivative can only end in the reality of change being completely missed. This is the danger; we can pull the ground out in the name of the floor. This is why we must keep in mind the limitations of the empiriometric science.

Want one more example? Another friend of mine, who is absorbed in modern physics, thought that gravitational and electric fields are real *immaterial* things. It is clearly contradictory to claim that the *material* world's most elemental parts are *immaterial*; his statement is obviously not true. However, it is in fact quite true that the mathematical entities that are used to describe the phenomenon of the gravitational field are immaterial, as are all purely mathematical entities. It is equally true that we cannot see the gravitational field with our eyes directly. This feature of Newtonian gravity in fact caused some of the biggest objections to his theory when it was first introduced; they called his gravity an occult quality, because they wanted to include only things directly in the imagination after a mechanical model. These confusions again arise from a use of the empiriometric in a directly ontological way.[281] These are the fruits of an empiriometric science closed on itself. Such thinking can end, like Kant's work, in unintentional proofs of Gödel's theorem.

As with Gödel's theorem, empiriometric science makes heavy use of mathematics. Recall that modern (empiriometric) physics is formally mathematical. It is, in turn, because mathematics is *about* the real (it is abstracted from the real) that empiriometric science is so powerful. Indeed, this is the reason for what Eugene Wigner called "the unreasonable effectiveness of mathematics."

---

[281] Newton understood this fact much better than his critics. In fact, William Wallace holds that Newton's methods were, in the main, Aristotelian, implying that he understood something of the nature of *physica,* not just of the empiriometric science.

Here it is worth pausing to note that it is only because of our philosophical efforts in this and previous chapters that we are able to now understand what the physicist views as a mystical thing. Wisdom has just this character. We lose none of our wonder; wonder is only increased as we see the integrity of the world and as we come to grips with the vast horizons that have been within our reach all along. The unreasonable effectiveness of mathematics now becomes reasonable effectiveness, but is even more awe-inspiring. Philosophy has wiped clean the smudged glass of our understanding of physics and allowed us to see that the mathematics of physics manifests the powerfully unified reality behind it.

Yet, in modern physics, the very power of mathematics is also the source of strength of the illusion that one *only* needs the empiriometric method.

Mathematics

The power of mathematics is what makes modern physics successful *and* vulnerable. St. Thomas recognized the importance of mathematics to us by saying that of all the pure sciences, *it is the most connatural to man*. He means that mathematics is the level of abstraction most resonant with our natural powers. In its natural state, man's intellect, as we've seen, has immaterial ideas, but they are constantly attended by images that can become crutches that keep it from rising to philosophical level, let alone the highest level, the metaphysical level. Working with mathematics is thus an easy mode for man's nature, for in it one uses ideas, but one can resolve them in the images that his nature is constantly tempted to use for support anyway. In short, our minds are true intellects, but barely intellects, so they are more comfortable at the lower levels of thinking than the higher. Well, this makes the study of material things--whose first accident (property) we've seen is quantity--very agreeable to study by us. The less the thing is, the closer it is to this first accident of quantity (which is *like* the potentiality (matter) of the thing), so the more we can study it empiriometrically. The less it is (the less being it has) the more it can be described in *purely* quantitative terms that radiate, in some sense, its unity and intelligibility. Of course, choosing to study something because it is little will mean that we will expand ourselves little. It is the problem of our weak intellect that we can only approach easily that which is close to nothing, and that higher things only come with much effort.

Here then is the success and the vulnerability of modern physics. The success is that one can empiriometrically understand purely material things at a very deep level. The vulnerability is that one may mistake mathematics as the *only* type and mode of explanation and proof. If one is good at something, he will more easily learn a lot in that area and can thus easily become very comfortable thinking only in those modes. Then, by seldom thinking outside his area of strength, he can forget that the areas that he is not good in are **not** by that fact unimportant or, as he may even come to think, not sensible or useful in anyway. Descartes fell into the trap and from there into philosophical idealism. Descartes said, "The true method is to seek for reasonable evidence and the norm of such evidence is to be found in the science of mathematics."[282]

If one does take mathematics as the only mode of explanation (which is what happens by default to those involved in modern physics who do not consciously examine their thinking) what happens? First, as with Descartes, they become, at least implicitly, philosophical idealists. Then Gödel's theorem can lead them to doubt truth of any kind. Absurdly, the craving for *purely* mathematical certainty will end in complete uncertainty. Now, philosophical idealism, especially among scientists,[283] tends to be only a theoretical thing. No one can really forget that he knows the things around him. However, what you *think* will sooner or later catch up to what you *do* in some way.

Second, mathematics alone is a small world. Of the four causes we've seen in the world, only two obtain in the preter-real world of mathematics (the second layer in Figure 6-1): the material and formal cause. Material cause is only present in an analogous

---

[282] Descartes, *Discours de la Méthode*, 2e partie

[283] The philosophical idealism of a physicist usually has its biggest impact on those outside the physics community as physicists implicitly or explicitly (unintentionally or intentionally) teach it.

sense. For example, I can make three by taking three ones. Three is "potentially" divisible into parts. In that sense, the unit ("1") is material with respect to the larger numbers. The formal cause is only cause that is fully present in the preter-real world of mathematics. There are forms in mathematics. It of course is a very narrow type of form, quantity.

There are no efficient causes. Within mathematics itself, there is no agent that can make something turn into something else or change in any way. This means that there is no motion in mathematics. Wait, flag down, how can you say that? Physics uses mathematics for motion all the time, even at the freshman level. The answer turns on a subtle point. There is no motion *in* mathematics, but one can *use* mathematics to discuss motion. Here is where confusion between empiriometric and ontological starts for most physics students, so let's look at this more closely.

Young physics students are taught to draw a standard x-y graph like that shown in Figures 6-6a, b. On the vertical axis, one puts the distance from some point, say your home, and on the horizontal axis, one puts time. Figure 6-6a shows someone staying at the same point 5 miles away from your home for some time. Figure 6-6b shows someone moving at constant speed from that point to your home. We can now write simple equations (given in the figures) for these two motions.

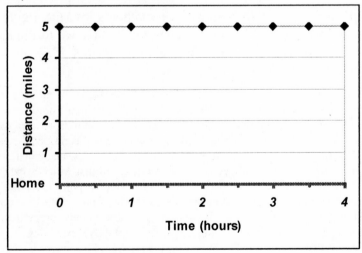

Figure 6-6a: Plot of a person staying 5 miles away from your home for 4 hours. Note that the line exists all at once, unlike the person who only exists at

one place at a time. The equation for this line is distance=5 miles.   The diamonds indicate some data points taken to make the line.

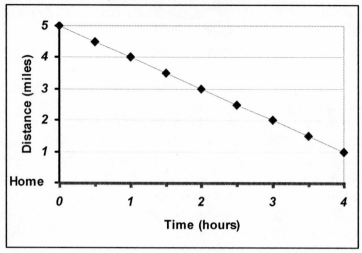

Figure 6-6b: Plot of a person starting from a point 5 miles away moving at a uniform speed of 1mile per hour *toward* your home. The equation for this line is: distance=-speed*time+5miles.

We have just *used* mathematics to describe motion. In so doing, we have not introduced motion into mathematics. Look at the figures; do you see motion? The only motion was in the making of the figures, but that is not the mathematics, just the process of expressing the mathematics. The mathematics (the figure or the equations) is fixed; it does not change.[284] Once we formulate them, they are forever the same. *We* can change our ideas or lose our

---

[284] Another way to think about this follows. Think of a point "moving" on a two-dimensional plane toward a line. Is the (zero-dimensional) point moving? No. One cannot ascribe motion to the point *itself*. First, a point is, as a friend of mine said, "an idealization of nothing." Like all mathematical concepts, the point is an idealization that cannot exist outside the mind in its mathematical purity. Further, the concept's only content is in reference to that which is external to it, e.g. the line and the plane. More importantly, since a point has no dimension, there is nothing to change; it has no parts outside of one another, so one cannot add or subtract to its "being." If we try to give it accidents (properties) that can change, we do so either by implicitly (or explicitly) extending it (think for example if we paint it red). Obviously, then it would no longer be a point. It is thus clear that when we think of a point moving along a plane, it is really only our own choice of a point on the plane that is moving, not any point itself. However, we can and do, for simplicity of speech, say that we move the point.

interest in these equations and graphs, but those mathematical constructs do not change because we do so. Mathematics is already touching eternity in some way; this is another reason why those from Pythagoras to Descartes were tempted to make it the rule of all.[285] So, how can changeless mathematics describe change? Only by leaving the change behind. This is what is dangerous about the figures: time is turned into a spatial variable, which does not change of itself the way time does. Time is treated as if all moments existed at once in the same way that space does. It is as if the driver is a one-dimensional thing that exists both at point A and your home at the same time. We will discuss this more in the next chapter. For now, note the implications of the above. Namely, due to inadequate philosophical awareness, modern physics (the study of *changeable* being as quantitative) itself has been a vehicle, at some level, for the return of the Parmenides' error that change does not exist.

Last, there is no final cause in mathematics. Recall that final causality is fundamentally the ordination of potentiality to act. For a given agent (thing causing a change) and patient (the thing undergoing change), the change that occurs is ordered to occur in a predetermined (foreordained) way. Applying a flame (agent of action) to dry wood [286] will always cause the wood to burn, not to freeze. In mathematics, there is no change, so there is no final cause. Final causality is what establishes something as good or bad.[287] For instance, the final cause of a leg in an animal is so that it can move. By moving, it can maintain its existence by removing itself from danger and by finding food and water. In short, the leg is *ordered* toward locomotion of the animal for its existence. It is for this reason we say that it is *good* for a cat to have four limbs. Because there is no final causality in mathematics, there is no good in mathematics itself. We can and do, however, say an area of mathematics is beautiful, but this is only our recognition of the *formal* and *material* (qualified sense) aspects present in the

---

[285] Aristotle thus explains Plato's view of natural numbers as eternal. We obtain them from the physical world, but the relations that obtain among them are always true.

[286] We assume standard environmental conditions with no impediments.

[287] The lesser the being, the more radically dependent is its final causality, and hence goodness, on higher beings.

system,[288] not the final causes. Because the modern mathematician chooses large parts of the order in a particular area, and because he is ordering it in a certain way and in fact has a reason for ordering in that way, mathematics can have a high level, but *external,* final causality. For example, if a mathematician wants the sum of the angles of a triangle to be 3 * 90 = 270 degrees instead of 2 * 90 = 180 degrees so that he can make a certain theorem work, he can pick a certain triangle on a non-Euclidean two surface (the surface of a sphere) to accomplish this. In doing this he is imposing a reason, final cause, on the otherwise bare formal mathematical "facts."

Hence, we can refer to final causes only when we somehow attach the non-mathematical arena. In modern physics, we say that Maxwell's equations are beautiful not because of the equations alone, but because of the order in the physical realm that they manifest. In other cases, we use mathematics as a tool, in which case we say it is good when it works and bad when it does not; this is our imposition of things outside of the second level of abstraction (mathematics) to pick what we like within it.

Because mathematicians impose the good (if at all) from the outside, if one takes the mathematical as the only valid mode of thinking, moral relativism must result. One will miss real final causality[289] altogether and hence the concept of intrinsic good and bad. Because we are human, we will still recognize the good at some level; however, the good will tend to mean something imposed from the outside as done in the mathematical realm. We will thus think the good is our choice, which is an oxymoron, since the good is the appetite of the intellect, the appetite that results from recognizing *something* as good or bad. The moral realm is the subject of Chapter 9.

---

[288] In particular, the forms of mathematics have definiteness, symmetry, and order, though not the active *ordering* (verb) within the system that is final causality.

[289] Furthermore, mathematics in its most abstract form has a homogeneity that can make one less sensitive to things like organisms. An organism's final cause rests on the unity of diverse parts ordered toward their continued existence; for a mind that only allows for homogeneity, such a final cause becomes unintelligible.

The choice aspect of mathematical work also can cause problems in the arena of formal causality. Forgetting that the primitive forms of mathematics (including number) are accidents of substances, not substances themselves, can lead one to think that mathematical essences are identical to essences of real substances. Since in mathematics, the things we define are often governed by what we choose to study, such an error can lead to the idea that there are no essences, but only how we choose to classify things. Like one engineer said to me (in the days before MS Windows), "It is like on a Macintosh computer, you can put whatever you want in whatever folder you want." A hardened habit of working exclusively with mathematics may make one think that a robin or a rose does not have its own proper essence, but only what one assigns it. My engineer friend could put a rose and a robin in the same folder labeled "red," but everyone can recognize that though such a grouping may have its use, it does not identify anything *essential* to a robin or a rose. In the non-precise,[290] non-rarified real physical world, we know they are different things and, at some level, we know what they are. For example, recalling our discussions of the last chapter, we know in a clear way that one is an animal and the other a plant and what difference that entails.

There are still other pitfalls of the habit of mathematics in the modern mindset. Among them, there are *three key modes of thought* that, when not kept in their proper place, are traps for the mind. The modes are serial and algorithmic thinking, and thinking that uses being of reason.

Serial Thinking

In the simplest of the mathematical sciences, arithmetic, we have numbers that come one after another with each step between any one and the next qualitatively the same; in all cases, we just

---

[290] The word "precision" comes from the Latin word *praecisio,* meaning *to cut off.* Cutting off is what we do in mathematics and physics all the time. We chop numbers and ideas so as to have simpler calculations and equations. Arithmetic, for example, is simpler than geometry because we have left behind the continuous. Mathematics itself leaves behind, cuts off, all the physical real except quantity. The more we cut off, the less prone we are to error in what is left.

add the unit to get the next value. When habituated, this series, and ones like it, can lead one to act, and soon believe, as if all steps are equally the same. Such belief can impede one from recognizing a step along one's way that might be of a completely different order than the ones proceeding it, many though they may be. For example, someone in such a state of mind might argue that the intellect can be made in the way that an automobile is. The assembly workers put it together one piece at a time. He might say the intellect started with the most miniscule of abstractions and gradually became what it is in us today. Such an argument implicitly assumes that all steps are exactly like the steps in making something. We have seen that this is not true. Immaterial things do not have matter (potentiality); that's what the word means. They are not composites of form and matter; they are pure form. Immaterial things do not have the potentiality (matter) to be other than they are; hence one cannot *make* them, they must be *created*. Many miss this fact because of ingrained serial thinking.

Algorithmic Thinking

Algorithmic thinking is common in fields related to mathematics. Because of the non-changing nature of mathematics, one can easily make procedures (algorithms) that, simply by executing a (possibly long) series of simple commands, can produce complex results. Unfortunately, this ability to do powerful things by rote can make the mind turn off. For example, when I learned logic in school, I learned it as a set of truth tables. I was taught that "if X, then Y" statements are false only if X is true and Y is false (so "if something false, then something else false" is true!); it was logic used purely as algorithm, with no connection with the ontological. It was completely locked within the world of beings of reason, and of course, even those were not discussed. The great philosopher and student of Jacques Maritain, Yves Simon (1903-1961) points out that he was taught long division in this fashion; it was just a set of manipulations that spit out the useful answer. Such rote activity can lead one to completely miss the real life of the mind, which is in understanding, not rote carrying out of rules. The metaphor of chess previously discussed is apropos here.

Beings of Reason

Lastly, exclusive use of beings of reason in empiriometric science and in mathematics can make one insensitive to real being. Case in point: I was recently in a conversation with someone of considerable scientific training who thought that the fact that dark and light are *not* two opposing *entities* must be demonstrated by modern science. A mind trained in the use of beings of reason tends to assign all concepts equal reality (or unreality). One tends to assign a sort of symmetry that does not exist. One cannot really take dark as an entity and light as the absence of dark; it's only our heavy use of beings of reason that can make the illusion seem plausible. In fact, dark is our word for the absence of light. We only know it because when we close our eyes, we see nothing. Light is what enables use to see things. Our eyes respond to light. When we say the sky is dark, we are noting that there is not much light. We do not sense dark. Dark is nothing; it is a being of reason that our weak intellect uses to express a particular absence, the absence of light. Because a man born blind does not know of light, he does not know dark, contrary to what someone might be tempted to think.

Modern Physics: Summary

We've now seen that empiriometric science and the mathematics that it uses can and have caused many pitfalls in thinking. They are also responsible for most of the rather large increase in our knowledge of the physical world. We have appropriately qualified what the nature of that knowledge is. With those qualifications, the scope and depth of the achievements of empiriometric science is by no means as all sweeping as some popularizers of science might have one believe. Still, just because someone has overestimated the import of something does not mean it is not very important. Indeed, in addition to the vast amount of empiriometric knowledge we've gained and the ontological knowledge that we've turned into proper knowledge (a small portion, at least at this point), we have a vast amount of ontological knowledge that is hidden underneath the empiriometric waiting to be mined from the field of improper knowledge[291] to the field of proper ontological knowledge.

Chemistry and Biology

The remaining two "hard" sciences recede in various degrees from the empiriometric and start adopting more empirioschematic methods. As long as one is only analyzing things as they appear stripped nearly bare down to the quantitative, one can do better with lesser beings, because they are closer to "pure matter" and hence extension (quantity), the first accident of material being. Recall that mathematics is the study of quantity. However, as one moves toward biology, through chemistry, from relatively stripped physical systems to complex inorganic systems to complex carbon-based systems to life itself, the empiriometric method becomes more and more complex and less and less effective. To study life, one cannot effectively use mathematics for various reasons (for one, it tends to depend on homogeneity). Though, with time, biology will incorporate more of the empiriometric, it will naturally be ruled by the properly empirioschematic (as opposed to schemas that are regulated by mathematics). The properly empirioschematic is not a mixed science in the proper sense, because it does not leave the first level of abstraction, *physica*. It is, like the empiriometric, a tool of *physica*. It is regulated within *physica* itself; however, the philosophical (ontological) concepts that it borrows from *physica* are translated for the purpose of the empirical schema, and in this way, the philosophical concepts lose proper ontological content. We will discuss this some in the next chapter. In general, the same advantages and pitfalls apply to these parts of *physica* as they did in modern physics.

---

[291] Improper knowledge, recall, is a species of belief or opinion; in this case it comes from the dialectic method.

Galileo

Finally, we can discuss the issues raised by the Galileo case. From the complexity and length of our discussions on physics, one may surmise the ease with which one could get tied in controversies based on misunderstanding. Once one factors in all the pitfalls that come with empiriometric science and human nature's propensity to fight, one may view such controversies as inevitable. In any case, the controversy did happen. We have to sort out what it means for our pursuit of wisdom, philosophy.

We start with item one on the first page of this chapter. Is modern science radically different from the science that came before it? Well, yes and no.

Yes, because no science before Newton really had an empiriometric theory in the *full* sense. Before him, parts of reality were described with various equations. It is only with Newton's theory of gravity that we have all the elements of a full empiriometric theory where one large segment of reality is brought under a predictive empiriometric umbrella. It encompassed not just this object on the earth, but all known objects on earth, the earth itself, and objects in the sky, including the distant planets, and it even--unlike the Greeks--considered *locomotion* mathematically. However, this watershed event was not, as it is often painted, a sudden thing but the culmination, by a man of great genius, of a gradual evolution that moved steadily forward from the Middle Ages.[292] Which brings us to the "no" half of the response.

No, because we've seen that St. Thomas and Aristotle knew about and used all the areas of science *including* the empiriological ones.[293] Why then did they and their followers get the reputation of not knowing the modern sciences (by this we mainly mean empiriometric physics, the first developed of such sciences)? The reason is four-fold. First, many of the promoters of the modern sciences did not understand the empiriological nature of the modern sciences and treated those sciences as pure *physica,* thereby confusing the real with the schemas and mathematical

---

[292] We'll glimpse this in the next chapter.

[293] Although, it was left to others, as we'll see, to use the method and for the first time apply it to dynamics (motion) in a serious way.

symbols. This, in turn, caused them to treat those who remembered and respected *real* changeable being (which is what *physica* studies) with, to say the least, less than adequate respect. Unfortunately, this cause still operates today.[294]

Second, there are reasons related to what fields they choose. Aristotle's scientific (in our narrow usage) interest was in biology, and he was not as interested in mathematics, which is the formal part of empiriometric physics. Aristotle's main interest was in philosophy (wide sense). St. Thomas's fields were theology, and of course philosophy. Both still made important contributions to physics *(physica)*.[295] However, Aristotle, because of his interest in biology and because of his theology (received from his culture, not his thought), made fundamental mistakes with respect to the science of mechanics. Among other things, he taught, contrary to experience (for which medieval commentators did not fail to take him to task), that heavy objects fall faster than light ones and that air keeps an object moving once it is released. (These issues are related to the concept of inertia, discussed in the next chapter.) St. Thomas softened some of the problems with Aristotelian physics (wide sense)[296] by not giving them the sort of absolute weight that Aristotle apparently gave them. However, he did not correct Aristotle's false mechanics. That said, one can hardly blame Aristotle or St. Thomas for not learning *everything* single-handedly. Aristotle, by establishing true philosophy for the first time, must be considered one of the great geniuses of all time.

---

[294] These tendencies to minimize the real were, and still are, often accompanied by a narrow pragmatism that, a priori, excludes any consideration of truth for its own sake.

[295] Aristotle, for example, proposed four "elements" (air, water, fire, and earth) as fundamental elements of all material things, precursors to the roughly 115 known elements. St. Thomas first formulated the fundamental groundwork that inertia could rest on. For both Aristotle and St. Thomas, their historical situation and the limits imposed by their own particular focus kept them from going further and in many instances, along with other reasons, caused them to say things that we now know are not true.

[296] Recall once again that *physica,* like all science, builds from the ground up. So the foundational parts are not affected by erroneous statements relating to such things as whether the earth goes around the sun or whether heavy objects fall faster than lighter ones. This is not to minimize these errors but only to put them in their proper place and context.

St. Thomas himself is probably the only mere man whose genius may surpass that of Aristotle, for he was able to understand him with some small fraction of his writings and to both clearly expose the roots of metaphysics and extend its reach and roots in sweeping and clear ways.[297] Both men's achievements, when they are seen in their full glory (and we've only glimpsed them), are much beyond ordinary comprehension. In the Middle Ages, St. Thomas was not alone; there were many followers of Aristotle. For example, Theodoric of Freiberg (c. 1245- after 1310), a Dominican trained in Thomism, made a calculation of the rainbow using fairly accurate refraction measurements that stands as an early, though partial, triumph of more fully empiriometric methodology.[298] How then did such rancor arise between Aristotelian philosophy and science?

Well, the third part of the reason is the rote, not living Thomism (philosophy of St. Thomas) that set in--because of the Black Plague (which killed as much as half of Europe) and other causes in Europe. But this does not completely explain it, for Thomism was, in some quarters, living, vibrant, and contributing to the advance of the sciences. We must factor in the ugly part of human nature. Someone must take advantage of the above nuclei to begin condensing the potential confusions and animosity into actual confusion and animosity.

Here we reach item three. We must discuss a deep-seated prejudice in the modern mindset. I've been warned by some to not talk of this topic in an unnuanced fashion. I've been told this will shut the reader down. I disagree. I consider my readers, as always, seeking the truth and wanting it in the least garbled form that it can be given. My reader, I hold, will subject thoughts to suitable scrutiny to determine their verity; this is what philosophy is about. So, what is this hidden prejudice? It's anti-Catholicism.

Before asking for a defense of this charge, you may reach further back and ask, "Why bring this up?" Because one's beliefs

---

[297] Because of this, his writings are sometimes compared to the spellbinding beauty of the cathedrals prevalent in his day.

[298] Of course, it was not only those explicitly trained in the philosophy of Aristotle who contributed to scientific progress. As we will see the culture of the time, Catholicism, had Aristotle in its bones; it was in the improper knowledge that was in some confused way "in the air" in such a culture.

(improper knowledge), as we saw in Chapter 2, are intimately linked with who one decides to trust and who to distrust. As we saw, one cannot verify (by carefully reasoned thinking and/or observation) everything personally. So, as a practical matter, one trusts the statements of others. If one has drawn false conclusions about a particular group, one must rectify that error quickly, or his ability to draw correct conclusions and make proper decisions will be severely compromised. Part of philosophy is to find reliable sources. To get one's sources straight is a sound reason to bring up anything. Yet, the reason for bringing up the charge goes even further than this. Catholicism is not just a group; it is the single greatest force in the development of our current Western culture. Universities, hospitals, law, music, medicine, respect for the human person... as well as worship all spring from or, at least, through it. If it is wrong about science, we need to know it. In general, if the basic "cult" of a culture is correct, one will have less trouble finding truth. It will be "in the air." To the degree that what is in the cult is true is the degree to which truth can flourish. By the same reasoning, a false cult will cause damage.

Now, the charge. Hawking claims the Catholic Church is or was intrinsically opposed to science. If we can show this false, then we have ground for our charge of prejudice (pre-judging) and also an explanation, partial though it be, for the Enlightment's rejection[299] of all things medieval, including the philosophy of St. Thomas.

On the face of it, we should already see the absurdity of the claim that Catholicism was inimical to science. Hawking uses Galileo as a fulcrum.[300] Galileo was himself a devout Catholic,

---

[299] The rejection has an ironic side, for many of the proponents of the Enlightenment sought to leap over the Middle Ages to antiquity, but unwittingly took an anchor from what they had inherited from the Middle Ages. We'll see part of that anchor shortly.

[300] A funny reversal of roles took place in Galileo's confrontation with the Church. He correctly argued that the Catholic position (clearly articulated by St. Augustine) was that an interpretation of the Bible should be corrected if proven wrong by some other means, for example by science. The Church authorities (some like Cardinal Bellarmine were conscious of Galileo's point as well) in their turn were right in saying that Galileo had not proved the earth went around the sun. That proof did not come for another 200 years when the measurement of parallax of the stars and the pendulum precession was observed. Galileo had

whose daughter was in a convent. Does the beautiful flower of modern science grow in the only part of garden that is poisoned? Modern science developed in the heart of the Catholic Church, not in Egypt or China or in Japan or undiscovered North or South America or anywhere else.[301] We and everyone else have obtained science from this culture that grew out of "the poisoned" garden, which turns out, after all to be the well-kept one. Such cultures, of course, include all the non-Catholic Christian denominations and all the secular break-offs from Catholic practice. They all accept in varying degrees a cult handed them by their fathers. What elements of this cult are relevant for science?

Three things are absolutely essential for science, including modern sciences. One must understand that:

a. The world exists independent of us and is orderly.[302]
b. *We* can understand it.
c. We should have no aversion to observing and working with nature (in particular to do experiments).

One of the most quoted verses of the Bible in the Catholic Middle Ages[303] was: God "has ordered all things in measure, number and weight."[304] As for items "b" and "c" above, Catholicism has

---

scientific insight that allowed him to see past the lack of proof…something that probably few others were capable of. But others could be forgiven if they did not take him at his word. Indeed, he held other views that were completely erroneous, such as his view on the cause of the tides. Unfortunately, he also had the tendency, which we discussed earlier, to take empiriometric science for ontological proof. Despite these and other deficits, Galileo, of course, should not have been treated the way he was, having to abjure his belief in the sun-centered system and being confined (although it was to the plush estate of a friend). A complex topic like the Galileo case cannot be elucidated briefly, so please consider this discussion, though completely accurate, only a sketch of the situation.

[301] In his *Science and Creation*, Stanley Jaki has documented the fact that in every other culture, science has been "still born."

[302] We will discuss in Chapter 7 the importance of a related tenet that the world is not necessary.

[303] See, for example, Stanley Jaki's, *The Origin of Science and the Science of Its Origin*. During the Middle Ages, as you probably know, the Catholic Church was the dominant force in Europe at all levels.

[304] Wisdom of Solomon 11:21. When Einstein said that science depends on the belief that there is an external world independent of us, he was both

always emphasized the dignity of the human person, which it attributes especially to man's ability to reason and understand starting from nature; its sacramental system manifests its belief in the necessity of the physical for man. The historians R.R. Palmer and J. Colton make the comparison with the culture of Islam, for example, that finally decided it was not okay to analyze the world in rational terms. Use of reason and its effectiveness in understanding this world were ultimately against the cult(ure), for according to Islam,[305] God is sovereign in a sense that excludes secondary causes; according to that culture, God's activity is completely inscrutable to man.[306] Palmer and Colton say:

> *If any historical generalization may be made safely, it may be safely said that any society that believes reason to threaten its foundations will suppress reason. Thomas's doctrine ... gave freedom to thinkers to go on thinking. Here Latin Christendom [Catholicism][307] may be contrasted with the Muslim world. It was ruled, in about the time of Thomas Aquinas, that ... the Gate was closed. Arabic thought, so brilliant for several centuries, went into decline.[308]*

The renowned historian Lynn White says of the Christian monks,

---

acknowledging and passing on (for he also received it initially from his cultural milieu) an undeniable truth.

[305] Islam succeeded in particular areas related to natural science *(physica)*, such as mathematics and medicine, because it had some elements of the necessary cult, but never gave birth to modern science because of its severe lack in these elements, and ultimately because its theology at its deepest level rejected them.

[306] It is thus no surprise to find Steven Weinberg noting the problem that his friend and co-Nobel Prize laureate, Abdus Salam encountered in Islam. According to Weinberg (CNN interview), although Salam considered himself a devote Muslim, Salam was considered a heretic by most Muslims and not allowed in his native Pakistan; he frequently complained about how the modern sciences were forbidden in Islamic schools.

[307] And again this is not just St. Thomas; Christianity itself defends reason and its domain.

[308] Palmer and Colton, *A History of the Modern World*, page 38.

...for the first time the practical and the theoretical were embodied in the same individuals. In Antiquity learned men did not work and the workers were not learned...the monk was the first intellectual to get dirt under his fingernails...in his very person he destroyed the old artificial barrier between the empirical and the speculative... and thus helped create a social atmosphere favorable to scientific and technological development. It is no accident therefore that ...the friar[s] were eminent and ardent in experiment.[309]

This attitude is no surprise given the Christians' emphasis on Genesis, which states that God created the world and said, "It is good."[310] In fact, we can give well-known examples of White's statement by remembering two priests, Mendel (a monk) and more recently Lemaitre, who each substantially advanced modern science. The renowned physicist Pierre Duhem set out to discover the roots of science and, to his own great surprise (because of the widespread belief, even then, in the academic cult that no science could come from Catholicism), found that science's roots are in the Middle Ages. He wrote a definitive ten-volume series documenting this fact. Modern historian, Richard C. Dales, in his short book *The Scientific Achievement of the Middle Ages*, says it succinctly: "It [modern science] is the child of medieval science."[311]

This diversion was necessary to establish that Catholicism is not inimical to science and that one should exercise caution in assessing information that one gets from our modern cult(ure) about the ubiquitous force of Catholicism, at least in the area of science.

We've thus shown all the points listed on the initial page of this chapter to be false, except possibly item 2. That statement, in its given context, is somewhat misleading. Let's clarify it. Galileo must be given much credit for the birth that happened with Isaac Newton. However, we must remember that what Newton said of

---

[309] Lynn White, *The Dynamo and the Virgin Reconsidered*, page 65.
[310] The Christian belief in the incarnation, the belief God took on human flesh (i.e. entered the world), emphatically underlines the Genesis statement.
[311] Cf. page 176 of Dale's book.

himself is also true of Galileo; if he saw further, it was because he stood on the shoulders of giants. Newton and Galileo had many predecessors in starting the empiriometric on its current fast track.

We've cleared the intellectual air of the *apparent* fight between Aristotle and St. Thomas on the one hand, and Galileo and Newton on the other, showing that they cannot really fight because, at a simple level, one is the foundation and supporting structure, the other an upper floor (with a view) of the same building. Yet, it still remains to clarify by example what the relation between the empiriological and the ontological is.

How to Properly
View the Empiriometric

Again, mathematics and measurement together are the keys to modern physics. The empiriometric is the key element in the modern sciences. In order to better understand what the empiriological science tells us and what its limits are, it's best now to turn to commonly discussed areas of modern science. In particular, in these fascinating areas, we will address some specific and potentially fatal (to thought) problems that arise because of misinterpreting the empiriological for the directly ontological.

Chapter 7

From the Big Bang
and Time Travel
to Evolution

*T*here are many interesting ontological problems that arise from modern science because of its empiriological nature. In this chapter, we will discuss the ones that I've seen, in my more than 20 years as a scientist, cause the most confusion and even, in some cases, cause fundamental doubt about nature and man's intellectual capacity to understand himself and nature. There are six such topics: **Inertia**. **Time** and **Space**: What about forward and backward time travel? **The Big Bang Theory**: Is Euclidean geometry real? Can time begin? **Quantum Mechanics**: Is there action at a distance (infinitely fast motion)? Are things there when we don't look at them? Are there an infinite number of universes? and **Evolution**.

Note that, in this chapter, we will explore cutting-edge research into real causes (ontology), and thus need to make research postulates, which will put us in a more speculative realm than we have been in up to now.

Inertia

Many trained in the modern sciences think that the existence of inertia[312] means that motion does not need a cause.[313]

---

[312] As we'll see, inertia is the tendency of a body to remain in its state of rest or uniform motion unless acted on by an outside force.
[313] Many think inertia proves that something can move (change) itself.

The empiriometric science seems to lead naturally to such an interpretation. Indeed, they often say rest and motion are just two states of being (act) not really fundamentally different; motion and rest, they say, are purely relative.[314] In short, they think that motion and rest are *essentially* indistinguishable; one man's rest is another's motion. They then conclude that because Aristotle and St. Thomas did not know about inertia that they were ignorant of an important fact that undermines much of their thinking. Of course, by now we see this is triply wrong. First, allowing no absolute distinction between motion and rest, that is the *ontological identification of motion with rest*, is, at bottom, either the error of Parmenides that change does not exist *or* the error of Heraclitus that *only* change exists (cf. Chapter 3). Second, we've demonstrated, or seen through first principles, the fundamentals of *physica* without any access to the particular sciences, so further investigation cannot overturn those fundamentals, but will indeed *depend* on them. Thirdly, the above is yet another example of using the empiriometric (modern thinking on inertia) *directly* as an explanation of the real, instead of remembering that the empiriometric is formally mathematical.

So, let's begin with inertia to unwind the truth and see the philosophical fundamentals at work. In the process, we will also uncover the rudimentary history of the concept of inertia. The history will, in turn, take us back to the importance, for science and philosophy, of having a culture that includes the beliefs and understandings discussed in the previous chapter, in particular the non-necessary character of the universe.

Inertia is the first really successful discovery of physics *(physica)* beyond the fundamental principles that we discussed in the first chapters. Those general principles are the underpinning and certain part of *physica*, but they themselves beg for increased understanding and specificity that can only come from more observation and thinking.[315] Inertia became successful by first

---

[314] We will discuss the relativity of motion in the next section.

[315] In the direction of metaphysics, one separates out what is restrictive in the material, one looks at being as being (considering what is common to all things), so the specifics will not be needed, although mediation on the specific character of things is always helpful in the metaphysical appreciation of contingent being.

being an ontological solution to the problem of local motion and then expanded that success through empiriometric study. All theories in modern physics need guiding notions. The ontological notion of inertia was a guiding notion of what was to mature into Newtonian physics. Without that first insight, we would not have the physics of Galileo or Newton. Currently inertia is thought of purely in empiriometric terms,[316] so we will need to recover what the ontological idea of inertia is. Both the ontological and empiriological are important, as they are intertwined, but let's begin, where we are today, with the empiriometric and let it lead us back to the ontological notion. History will be our first guide to the ontology of inertia, but it will take us only so far. From there, we will develop, to the degree we can here, a viable philosophical (ontological) notion of inertia.

What is inertia? We will answer first with only minimal philosophical interpretation of empiriometric science. Inertia is the tendency of a body to remain in its state of rest or uniform motion unless acted on by an outside force. More particularly, in "classical mechanics," we now distinguish two pieces of inertia; they are called conservation of energy and linear momentum, meaning neither is *ever* lost or gained.[317] I identify momentum as the principal piece, because it is the vector law (one law for each of the three spatial directions);[318] it determines that an object moving in any one direction will continue in its state of motion (or rest, if initially at rest). Energy conservation is a scalar law, so it alone

---

However, staying in the domain of physics *(physica)*, one must increase understanding by obtaining greater specifics.

[316] St. Thomas says that explaining through mathematics is through a "remote cause." From St. Thomas, *I Posterior Analytics* Lecture 25, n6.

[317] Angular momentum is a third conservation law related to inertia. In the simple case of idealized point particles (remember we are doing empiriometric physics here), only central forces are definable, and angular momentum follows necessarily from conservation of linear momentum. In particles with structure or other symmetry breaking proprieties, one hypothesizes a field to carry away the lost momentum so as to keep the conservation of angular momentum intact, for one wants to think of the "underlying space" as rotationally symmetric (in fact, tries to keep it locally Euclidean, which includes rotational symmetry) unless one is forced to do otherwise by a "crucial" experiment.

[318] These are the directions everyone is familiar with: up/down, left/right, back/front.

would *not* guarantee that, for instance, an object traveling along a north-going road might not suddenly veer off onto the grass and begin circling a billboard, keeping its speed (e.g., as read on the speedometer) constant.[319] Without energy conservation, on the other hand, there would be no law telling how the tendency to continue "forward" (momentum) should split between various bodies in a collision.[320] If you shoot one pool ball into another, what constrains the first ball to stop and transfer its speed unchanged to the second one? What, for instance, keeps the first from coming back at you with twice the speed, and the second from moving off at thrice the speed?[321] After all, momentum is still conserved in that case. It is energy conservation that fixes how the momentum divides between the bodies.

So, what more do we need? Well, note the equivocal use of the word "constrain." We've used the word in a way that suggests that we've explained how it happens the way it does. In fact, the mathematics cannot force a ball to behave a certain way. We know the mathematics just more or less accurately presents (and predicts) our measurements of the balls' behaviors. We do not mean we've found the cause. As long as we realize that we were simply making use of the language of empiriometric (modern) physics, we will not be confused by the way it's said. We will know what it means. However, if we do not keep the narrowness of that language in mind, we can--and many do--get confused.

---

[319] The kinetic energy of a body is given, in Newtonian mechanics, as: ½ mass speed^2, so constant speed means constant kinetic energy.

[320] It is interesting to look at what freedom is in the empiriometric scheme. Take a simple two-body collision of, say, two pool balls. The equations of conservation of linear momentum and energy are, respectively:
m v1 + M v2 = m v1p + M v2p, and ½ m v1^n + ½ M v2^n = ½ m v1p^n + ½ M v2p^n . Here n=2. Also m, M are masses of body one and two respectively. Also, v1, v2 and v1p, v2p are the speeds of body one and two before and after the collision, respectively. Assume the second body starts at rest and the first moves towards it at velocity, v. One can then show that for n=3, 4, 5 (probably out as high as one wants), there are no real solutions of the two simultaneous equations for collisions with M/m above a certain amount.

[321] As above, the momentum is mass (m) times speed (v); hence, the first ball would have momentum1=-2mv and the second would have momentum2=3mv, so that the total momentum would still be "m*v" in the direction of original motion, yielding unchanged total momentum.

So, what *causes* the above behavior of colliding bodies? That's an ontological question of *physica*. We need to look more deeply. What makes the ball keep going? What does it mean "to keep going?" Here, we are not concerned so much with explaining the particulars of the motions as with explaining the fact of the motions.

We need to go back to our definition of motion of Chapter 3. Motion is the *process* of reducing something (called a patient) from potentiality to act by means of some agent. Specify to our case of local motion. If I pick up a baseball and throw it, the ball starts here and ends there. Now, the ball is not everywhere at once. It is actually here. It is potentially somewhere else. How does something that is only potentially somewhere else get somewhere else? Something else (an agent), for instance, you, moves it; such an agent is called an efficient cause. That's all well and good, except for one thing: when you let go, the ball keeps moving. What causes the motion after you let go? Such is the problem in a nutshell. At this point, history can help illuminate the problem's answer, and manifest both the importance of one's cultural milieu (as we discussed at the end of the last chapter) and the role of empiriometric science. So, let's pick up the historical thread here.

Aristotle confronted projectile motion; he argued that it was air that acts as a mover of some sort, once the projectile is released. Aristotle also confronts the problem of the motion of the planets; what is his solution there? He takes them to be run by special separated intelligent beings and to have matter of a totally different type than that on earth. Why these solutions to the two problems of projectile motion and planetary behavior? They tend to contradict Aristotle's own dictum to start from the senses. As we'll see below, medieval commentators gave examples from "everyday" observation that refute his theory of projectile motion. And, his theory of planetary motion seems to go beyond the data very quickly as well as miss the similarity to the problem of projectile motion. There must be other influences at work on Aristotle. Almost certainly, the most important such influence is Aristotle's environment. Aristotle lived in a pagan culture, which historically-- to the degree that it becomes a thinking culture--always tends toward eternalism, the belief that the world always was and always will move through endless cycles. Stanley Jaki shows that this belief in the Great Year, which involves the idea that history (forever) repeats itself, even to the extent of the same people coming back doing the same things, is a major reason for the failure of science to take root in non-Catholic[322] seeded cultures. Because of these cultural beliefs, Aristotle, despite his deep wisdom, fell prey to the view that the world has an absolute necessity[323] that it does not have, and thus fell sometimes into an a priori approach when it came to the specialized study of nature. Apparently, even an Aristotle is not enough to overcome such a cultural mindset. Again, we cannot blame Aristotle for not discovering everything.

It is no surprise then that the person who made the deepest criticism of Aristotle's mechanics (dynamics) was part of the Catholic culture,[324] John Philoponus of Alexandria (c. 490 – 570 A.D).[325] Stanley Jaki says:

> *Aristotle's theory of motion did not lack critics in classical antiquity, but none of them was as incisive as Philoponus....*
>
> *Against ... [the] claim that all celestial bodies were moved by angels, Philoponus ...[says,] in view of the*

---

[322] The Catholic culture also includes, by definition (as well as by presence of ancestral and religious Jews themselves), heavy Jewish influence, because Catholicism is itself an essentially Jewish Church, having a Jewish founder (including initially all Jewish followers), as well as respecting that Jewish heritage.

[323] Aristotle *seems* to have thought that the universe *must* have always existed (i.e., not only that it did always exist but must). Although, as St. Thomas points out, holding this belief (which makes the world *necessarily* co-eternal with God) is contrary to Aristotle's own earlier (in principle, not time) statements about the natural world. In fact, the universe has a relative necessity, but only God, as we've glimpsed in Chapter 4 and will see clearly in Chapter 8, has an absolute necessity.

[324] The Catholic culture, of course, had its own problems. For example, it had yet to take to heart the lesson that *it taught* about interpreting the Bible. That is, the Bible was always to be taken as trustworthy, including its factual and historical content, but yet it *was not* a science text. St. Augustine articulated in an enduring fashion the Catholic principle that if an interpretation of the Bible contradicts something proven true by other means, then that interpretation must be modified.

[325] Despite Philoponus' criticism of Aristotle, Jaki says he declares, time and again, Aristotle to be the prince of physicists.

omnipotence of the Creator, 'could the sun, moon and the stars be not given by God, their Creator, a certain kinetic force (kinetike dunamis) in the same way as heavy and light things were given their trend to move...?'

...such a question struck as much at the roots of Aristotelian cosmology as did Philoponus' insistence that the stars were not made of the ether but of ordinary mater (fire); that they differed in colour....[326]

By emphasizing the freedom of God with respect to the creation *(ex nihilo)* of the world, one is guarded against thinking that the world has an *intrinsic* necessity[327] and thus against looking to *a priori* thought to divulge nature's secrets. By this emphasis, one is thrust back with greater force to Aristotle's dictum that, for us, all things come through the senses. One cannot *just* abstract top-level principles and then think he can deduce the universe as it is; the particulars are not contained in the abstract. For physics *(physica)*, this means much experiment, at least in the wide sense of observation, is an indispensable part of science.

In the high Middle Ages,[328] John Buridan of Paris (before 1300-1358) attacked Aristotle's contention that air keeps an object in motion.[329] He said take the case of a

... hoop and mill wheel,[330] if you should say that the surrounding air moves so great a weight circularly after a

---

[326] *Science and Creation*, pp. 186-187.

[327] Of course, the universe is, as we've seen, self-consistent and hangs together in a very tight way with universal laws; this follows from its being (i.e., intelligibility or rationality). We will discuss the universe more in a later section of this chapter.

[328] The high Middle Ages reinvented this idea, under the influence of the rebuilt and re-emerging Catholic culture, before having access to Philoponus's work.

[329] Like nearly all the scholars in the Middle Ages, Buridan took Aristotle as the place to start in science. St. Thomas's canonization (just 50 years after his death) helped insure respect for Aristotle would continue.

[330] In his text, one page before this quoted section, Buridan argues that the mill wheel would continue forever if there were no forces of resistance to slow it down and eventually stop it. He goes on to say that, "...it would not be necessary to posit intelligences to move the heavenly bodies." He argues God gave them an impetus that they would always retain, because of lack of resistance (now called friction).

man ceases to move it, I would object. Because if you should take a rag and wipe the contiguous air away from the wheel, you will not stop the wheel in this way... If the air which I set in motion when I throw a stone can move the stone, why will it be that if I blow the air at you as swiftly as I can without the stone you can hardly feel it?

Therefore... the mover impresses on the moved thing not only motion, but along with it a certain impetus or some force or other quality—not the kind of force we usually mean by that name--which impetus has the nature of moving that thing on which it is impressed, just as a magnet impresses on iron a certain force moving the iron to the magnet. And the more swift the motion the more intense the impetus will be. And this impetus in a rock or arrow is continually diminished by the resistance contrary to itself until it is no longer able to move the projectile.[331]

He further demonstrates impetus theory and explains the air's role in local motion. He says:

One who wishes to jump a long distance drops back a way in order to run faster, so that by running he might acquire an impetus which would carry him a longer distance in the jump. Whence the person so running and jumping does not feel the air moving him, but rather feels the air in front strongly resisting him.[332]

Buridan even indicates that the impetus is proportional to the mass and the speed of the object. Amazing. This is the concept of conservation of momentum discussed above, though without the connection with detailed experiment and without the equations. These are two big minuses, but note this is occurring in the early 1300s!

---

[331] *Questions on the Heavens and the World* Book II Question 2 by John Buridan in *The Scientific Achievements of the Middle Ages,* Dales, pp. 120-121 from Marshal Clagett's *The Science of Mechanics in the Middle* Ages (1959) pp. 552-556, 570. Maier, Clagett and Grant have compiled and used Pierre Duhem's massive works. They are secondary sources to the primary of Duhem.
[332] Quoted in *Savior of Science,* S. Jaki, p. 52.

We need to back up a little to complete the ontological picture as seen in the Middle Ages.

If we left the impression that St. Thomas did not contribute to mechanics,[333] we will correct that impression here. Pierre Duhem notes that in St. Thomas,[334]

> *For the first time we have seen human reason distinguish two elements in a heavy body: the motive force, that is in modern terms, the weight; and the moved thing, the corpus quantum or as we [Newtonians] say today the mass. For the first time, we have seen the notion of mass being introduced in mechanics and being introduced as equivalent to what remains in a body when one has suppressed all forms in order to leave only prime matter quantified by its determined dimensions...St. Thomas...came to distinguish three notions in a falling body: the weight, the mass, and the resistance of the medium...*[335]

Buridan and St. Thomas are not alone; there is a substantial subset of medieval academia involved,[336] working in various areas

---

[333] Further note, Aquinas says motions of the planets and stars are "produced either by the motion of the object seen or by the motion of the observer... it makes no difference which is moving."(II De Caelo, lecture 11, n2 and lecture 12, n4). Indeed, in empiriometric science, it makes no difference; this is the basis for the Galilean relativity principle.

[334] He is commenting on St. Thomas's *Commentary on Aristotle's Physics* Book 4, lecture 12 n535.

[335] *Medieval Cosmology*, by Pierre Duhem, edited and translated by Roger Ariew. University of Chicago Press, 1987, p. 379.

[336] Robert Grosseteste (c.1168-1253) did experiments (not yet of course with modern rigor) and was keen on using mathematics; he is known for his work on understanding the rainbow. Thomas of Bradwardine (c.1295-1349) at Merton College Oxford introduced the distinction between mean velocity (x/t) and instantaneous velocity (dx/dt). Bradwardine had an enthusiasm for empiriometric physics that started a whole school called the Merton school (his successors include: William Heytesbury, Richard Swineshead, and John Dumbleton) that was *extremely* influential throughout Europe. Among other things, they were known for the Merton mean speed theorem, by which they proved the correct formula for free fall distance was given by $s=1/2\ a\ t^2$. Interestingly, both Brawdarine and Grosseteste at some point in their lives were

of physics, and they are the legs on which Copernicus and Galileo will stand.

Now, recall that empiriometric science hides as much as, or more than, it reveals of the underlying realities, so we have to be very careful in coming to conclusions about the physical causes. We must be equally careful in noting the much lower degree of certainty of those conclusions, especially relative to the complete certainty of first principles and immediate sensorial data and the conclusions that are proximate to them. Never forget this fact. It is why we started in the first chapters by *not* using the results of the specialized science; we used only reasoning from our common experience of that which is immediately accessible to the intellect and senses.

With these caveats, we can now formulate the ontological import of inertia. We can say that any body has the potentiality to receive and, when it has it, give, a quality called impetus. This quality is not a proper accident (an accident springing from the essence of the substance(s)), but a *mere* accident (one that is not caused by the substance of the thing concerned). For instance, the particular temperature of a drinking glass is a *mere* accident of it. The glass can be hot, cold, or room temperature and still remain a glass; there is some range in temperature for which the glass is still a drinking glass. The temperature in that range is a mere accident-- not again meaning that it is random, but meaning that it inheres in a substance and the particular temperature does not spring from the essence of a drinking glass.

Archbishops of Canterbury.   Nicole Orseme (<1348-1382) and Giovanni di Casali (c. 1350) independently developed use of 2-D graphs. Orseme described all change using these graphs in particular local motion, including calculating area (integrating) under velocity curve to get distance. Orseme's arguments for the sun-centered and moving earth were widely known: he said, for example, that "...not only is the earth so moved diurnally, but with it the water and the air, as was said, in such a way that the water and the lower air are moved differently than they are by winds and other causes. It is like this situation: If [sic] air were enclosed in a moving ship, it would seem to the person situated in this air that it was not moved." (p. 133, Dales.) Buridan, for example, was not convinced that the earth rotated, because an arrow shot up into the air came back to the same point, which it would not if it was rotating (indeed this is a small, thus hard to measure, effect).

Once a body[337] has received a certain impetus, it begins to move. The *measure of a body's resistance to the action of the impetus* is called its (inertial) **mass**. The larger the mass of a body at rest (rest mass), the less a given degree of impetus is able to make it move. We *measure the "amount of motion"* by its *speed*. The **momentum** is *a measure of the intensity of the impetus* (in each of the three directions) of a given body. Given a body with particular mass and momentum, one still needs a measure of the body's ability to, during collision, acting as agent on another body, give its impetus away and, acting as patient, receive impetus from the other body.

We approach this measure indirectly. As we've already indicated, conservation of energy is related to how the impetus "splits" after a collision, i.e., after the action and reaction of one body on another. Indeed, we need to introduce another quality; we will call it **dynamis** and call its (measured) intensity **energy**. Again, these two qualities, dynamis and impetus, are obviously intimately related. Dynamis appears to be a higher, more general quality; for instance, it has the ability to cause either **heat or impetus** (and thus locomotion) in a body.

The dynamis associated with the locomotion of a body with a given impetus, we call *kinetic dynamis* and its measure *kinetic energy*. Upon colliding with other bodies, kinetic dynamis causes some heat, caloric dynamis, and some impetus. How much of each is determined by the particulars of the bodies involved. The kinetic dynamis can only be received as heat under particular dispositions of the colliding bodies; these conditions are (practically) always present to some degree. Specifically, in bodies with surfaces that don't rebound like an ideal spring (elastically), but act a little like clay and stay deformed, the dynamis generates the quality of heat (caloric dynamis) in the ball, which is related to random motion of

---

[337] Here we use "body" to mean any type of material thing that has the properties so described. In other words, we are not making a judgment on whether other types of form-matter composites (the most general definition of the word "body") exist. In short, it is not necessary, a priori, that that all types of matter have the correlatives of resistance to changes in local motion and the ability to receive impetus.

the parts of the ball (a kind of randomly directed impetus distributed among the parts (atoms)).

The total "amount of dynamis," energy, is conserved in all changes. Kinetic dynamis can, for example, be converted to caloric dynamis, measured by heat content, but the total dynamis always remains unchanged. In collisions that involve only changes in impetus, called elastic collisions, the kinetic dynamis remains kinetic dynamis, and thus kinetic dynamis and impetus are separately conserved.[338] This means the sum of the intensities of the kinetic dynamis of the bodies is unaltered by the collision, and the same is true (taking into account direction) for the impetus. This is expressed in the two separate conservation laws of their respective measures, energy and momentum. For two body collisions in a line (one-dimensional), the resulting two equations tell how the speed divides after the collision.[339]

With this ontological depth, the empiriometric surface will no longer lead us to absurd conclusions such as trying to identify (uniform) motion and rest as somehow fundamentally the same thing.

Again this is *only* a likely[340] ontological explanation, not a certain one, because of the nature of our knowledge in this arena, which is by way of correlated measurements mediated by mathematics. Furthermore, it cannot be complete because we still must--among many other things,[341]--take into account the special relativistic laws, which substantially modify the Newtonian ones above. In special relativity, we see an example of the empiriometric moving one further from the ontological. In it, instead of energy conservation, we have a generalized "mass" conservation; one uses the concept of mass-energy, where the two

---

[338] In the case of elastic collisions, the mass and the energy are the only quantities needed to describe the collision; from those two, one can calculate the kinetic energy, i.e., the amount of kinetic dynamis.

[339] Take a simple case of a body of mass, m, moving at speed, v, towards a second one of mass, M. For an elastic collision, the Newtonian energy and momentum conservation laws yield: speed of second = 2v/(1+alpha) and speed of first = (1-alpha)v/(1+alpha) where alpha = M/m.

[340] We may want to just call it a research postulate.

[341] For example, we should take account of Newton's definition of force and his law of gravity.

are interchangeable. Empiriometrically, energy is now generalized to include in some sense the motion (momentum) of the body. Thus, one no longer makes a distinction between the motion of the body and a property of the body itself. Now, we would go far wrong if we took this for a reason to do the same with our ontological analysis. A body moving (the process of traversing from one place with respect to local bodies to another) is not the same as a property of the body. To identify them ontologically would be absurd. Instead, we should think through what the new empiriometric expression of conservation of mass can say to us about the underlying realities. To do this would take us off the main path,[342] so we will not. However, we will examine other aspects of special relativity.

Relativity: Time and Space

With special relativity, empiriometric theory enters its full glory. As Maritain says, through relativity and quantum mechanics, Einstein[343] and Heisenberg (and the rest) liberated (modern) physics from philosophy. By this he did *not* mean that philosophy is not important, but that the tendency of many to demand that modern physics (empiriometric science) retain ontological notions had/has caused some problems; relativity, for the first time, really left completely behind some of the key ontological notions. The most prominent thing that it left behind is the ontological (real) distinction between time and space. Special relativity completely mixed space and time. Let's discuss three intimately related things: time, space, and relative motion. For empiriometric physics, the latter is the first historically and in principle.

---

[342] We'd need to include everything that special relativity tells us, including its modified forces and tensor analysis. Some of the effects will turn out to be just the effect of viewing something as it moves, which is a somewhat odd posture to adopt to study something. Even the empiriometric theory of relativity recognizes the precedence of the rest frame of the object, that is, the frame in which the object is not moving.

[343] As with Galileo and Newton's work, it was not just Einstein. Maxwell, Poincare, Lorentz, Minkowski, and many others played essential roles.

Relativity of Motion

Galileo and indeed, as mentioned, St. Thomas recognized the *relativity* of the *perception* of motion;[344] nonetheless, it is called Galilean relativity. Newton's grand work, the *Principia*, which he fashioned utilizing the dynamics and astronomy developed the previous four to five hundred years, discusses the relativity of *perception* of motion. However, in Newton's system, though motion could appear to be relative, it was in fact absolute. Newton's empiriometric system held back from going all the way. Newton wanted to do physics *(physica)*, not *just* empiriometric physics, following the example of his predecessors (he also used many Aristotelian methods--cf. for example *The Modeling of Nature* by William Wallace). His system was nonetheless largely empiriometric, making heavy use of explanation at the mathematical level.   His hypothesis that time and space of themselves are absolute is an empiriometric hypothesis.[345] It must be so, because, as we'll see, time and space have no ontological meaning "of themselves," that is separated from matter.

But first, we continue with our discussion of Galilean relativity. If one takes the relativity of perception of motion not just as the basis for an empiriometric theory but also the basis for ontological understanding, one encounters severe trouble. This mistake is easy to make if one is habituated by constantly making use of relativity in empiriometric theory. Habit wears a track that it is hard to see beyond. In fact, those with a scientific background may even now question whether it is so impossible to have relative motion. Let's analyze the problem in detail.

Remember that motion is the *process* of the reduction of potentiality to act. Imagine a universe with only two bodies, two identical pool balls (A and B), in it. If one imagines a physical

---

[344] That is, when one is in the closed cabin of a ship, one cannot tell the difference between being tied at port in calm water and sailing at high speed on smooth water. Recall, we earlier used the example of a closed compartment on a train.

[345] *Principia*, Vol. 1 *The Motion of Bodies*, Motte's translation (from Latin original) revised by Cajori. p. 6. I think that this hypothesis was an easy way to preserve the *physica* fact that motion cannot be absolutely relative, and preserve it in a simple way.

observer of arbitrarily small size and mass[346] sitting on ball A, ball B will either appear to be at rest or in motion. If it appears in motion, how does the observer decide whether B or A (and himself) is in motion? An empiriometric physicist would say it makes no difference, for we are only interested in finding the mathematically succinct understanding of the measurements that our observer can do.

By contrast, the broad physicist (dedicated to *physica*) would note that something couldn't move unless something reduces it from potentiality to act. In short, using our above ontological analysis of inertia, one is asking: "In what way is the impetus actually divided? In what way is the quality responsible for the motion divided between the two balls?" We can apply the fundamentals of *physica* and the available empiriometric science to put forward a convincing answer (not a proof). Specifically, utilizing the empiriometric concept of center of mass, one can say that the impetus is equally divided. To understand this more completely, we need to better understand local motion.

Locomotion means change of place. Place is one of the categories of accidental being, which we discussed in Chapter 3. The (common) place of a body is its relation to the immediately surrounding material things (i.e., the things nearest to it--contacting it). In the idealized case of just two balls, one can only reference one with respect to the other.[347] Note, only by establishing a measure of place can we quantify it. We must be careful, because, as we've seen, a systematization of measurements is not the final explanation we seek. We seek the real objects of which we measure certain aspects. How does the observer decide when an object is in motion? In this case, there are no other objects, so he must judge by the motion of the other ball. Given the mass and relative speed of each, he can deduce where they would originate if they had started as one joined body with a certain amount of dynamis available for conversion to impetus (say an explosion in

---

[346] In fact, we want to impose all conditions necessary to insure that our hypothetical observer does not significantly influence the experiment.

[347] In a realistic (not idealized) analysis, we'd note that space has things in it (something is extended, not nothing); it is not just emptiness, and thus we can specify the place by the "fields" or whatever things are contacting the surface of each ball.

which an original body divides into our two pool balls). When together, because there are by definition no other "bodies" in the universe, this is the point of rest, from which motion should be measured before and after the collision.

This analysis will lead one to the correct conclusions given the right understanding of how the impetus divides. However, we have neglected to consider everything. We have looked from the "angel eye" point of view[348] that our material observer does not have. We cannot tell how fast the other moves unless we somehow measure it. To measure it, we must in some way be able to sense the balls; for example, we need the equivalent of light. We also may find that bodies have a predisposition to attract each other (gravity). There may be many other things and properties, and they can have very complex interrelations that may not be easily unwound from an empiriometric theory. Let's try to take both light and "pool balls" into account. This is what led Einstein to special relativity.

Special relativity is, in important respects, more empiriometric than Newtonian mechanics because it takes literally both the Galilean relativity of motion and the mixing of time and space.[349] Further, Einstein's method of considering how actual measurements are done, as well as how to correlate the measurements mathematically, is fully empiriometric (it respects the empiriometric method, which wants to find mathematical "explanation" of the physically measured). Newton never asked how measurements of a clock's hands in one frame of reference (say on a passing train) could be correlated with measurements of the same clock viewed in another frame (say someone standing next to the tracks).

Consider, for example, a clock by a train track that audibly says the time every second. If an observer listens to this clock from a just departing supersonic train, first he will hear the time in the same way as someone on the ground. As he picks up speed, it will take longer for the newer "times" to reach him. "Time" will appear

---

[348] "Angel eye" means the view of an immaterial being not bound by matter.
[349] In the empiriometric explanation, the mixing of space and time is a consequence of the finite speed of light and the equivalence of all inertial reference frames.

to slow down. When he passes the speed of sound, he will catch up to "times" emitted before he left and time will appear to go backwards. This example is only meant to give *some* insight into the difference between the empiriometric correlation of measurements and ontological realities.

Again, Einstein recognized the power of such *empiriometric* correlation of measurements. Indeed, it is this method that led Einstein to his conclusion that time and space should be mixed. On the ontological side of the ledger, Einstein's requirement that one consider how measurements are actually done caused him to maintain the reality of the connection between time, space, and matter, which is ontologically much better than Newton's absolute space and time.[350] In short, in taking time and space as dependent on material things, Einstein is less empiriometric in his outlook than Newton. All empiriometric science ties up the ontological entities in beings of reason so as to coordinate the measurements. In so doing, it is very hard (if not impossible) to take the being of reasons, "the qualities" and "substances," used by the theory and determine what constellation and interactions of real ontological qualities and substances are truly causing the measurements (including all the valid predictions of the theory) to be as they are.

Up to this point, we've attempted to bring forward an ontological understanding behind the empiriometric physics for two related cases, inertia and relative motion. It is beyond an introductory level to do this for every other case. We don't even know to what extent such a process can be done with present knowledge.[351] So, we will instead take a less lofty but still very interesting goal of trying to find and/or unwind severe problems that arise in these other areas. We begin with the Special Relativity.

---

[350] As Steven Hawking rightly observes, "St. Augustine points out that time is created with the universe."

[351] In fact, it may be that certain things can only be known by us in the hidden way of the empiriometric.

Forward Time Travel (Special Relativity)

Special relativity successfully predicts, among other things, that *time slows down* when one moves. For example, in the famous twin paradox,[352] one twin takes off in a spaceship going near the speed of light. Let's say he wants to see the relatively recently discovered three planets orbiting the star Upsilon[353] in the Andromeda constellation.[354] Upsilon is visible to the naked eye; Figure 7-1 will give you an idea of its location in the sky.

This star and (hence) its planets (named "b," "c," and "d") are about 50 light years away.[355] If the traveling-twin is able to travel at .9806 times the speed of light, it will only take him, according to *his* local time, 10 years to go to the planet and 10 years to come back. Hence, when he returns only 20 years have passed for him, but the stay-at-home-twin is now about 102 years older.[356] All the people he knew will be either dead or very old. The traveling-twin has traveled forward in time to the earth's future. How do we understand this? Is it even possible? Yes, remember the prediction of measured values through mathematical methods is central to the empiriometric science. It is *very* good at prediction; that is what it's designed for. What it is not designed for is telling you what's really (ontologically) happening. If asked what is happening, the empiriometric scientist will start talking about the mixing of space and time and the space-time continuum. He, being human, before being an empiriometric scientist, will probably attempt to explain beyond the empiriometric science.

---

[352] We will not be directly considering the paradox aspect here.

[353] See *The Astrophysical Journal*, 526:916-927, 1999 December 1.

[354] The Andromeda constellation is composed, like all constellations, of stars that visually look like they belong together when viewed in the night sky from earth. However, we know by now that correlating observations is not the same as knowing. The Andromeda galaxy, for example, which can easily be seen in the same field with Upsilon, is 2 million light years away.

[355] This means it takes 50 years for light to travel there. A light year is the *distance* light travels in one year.

[356] The round trip is 100 light years and he is traveling at .9806 times the speed of light; one need only divide. The equation of time dilation is: $T_{Travel} = \sqrt{1 - \beta^2}\, T_{StayHome}$, where β is the speed of the traveler given as a fraction of the speed of light.

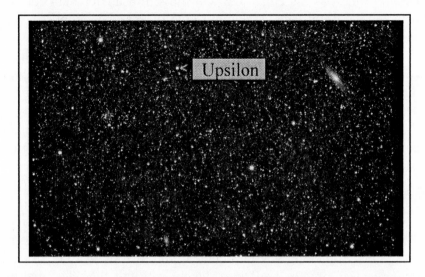

Figure 7-1: The traveling-twin's destination is the star named Upsilon in the Andromeda constellation. It is visible with the naked eye. The light reaching our eyes left 50 years ago, so we are seeing what happened there 50 years ago. Note the Andromeda galaxy, which is also visible without a telescope, on the right top side of the picture. (Photo credited to Till Credner and Sven Kohle.)

After all, this is what physics *(physica)* is about. However, the transition to philosophical explanation will most likely be an unconscious act and will thus be philosophy that appears to be most consonant with the empiriometric. He will use concepts that are used in the empiriometric, because they are consonant and because he knows them so well. The explanation will thus tend to be highly mechanistic because it meshes well with mathematics. The explanation will, in general, neglect the other categories of accidents discussed in Chapter 3: quality, relations, action, receptivity, etc., in favor of the first accident of material substances, *quantity*.

To better understand what's left out of consideration in an empiriometric theory, let's find a truly ontological explanation of the predictions of the empiriometric theory of special relativity. Remember, the *specific* answers we will give are somewhat tentative and incomplete,[357] but will show how an apparent conflict between the ontological and empiriometric may be, as must be the case, resolved.

Special relativity, in its purely empiriometric form, assigns equal value to all reference frames, but we can, without changing the mathematics or predictions, determine one frame to be a preferred frame. There is an analogy to this in general relativity in the big bang cosmology discussed in a later section; there the preferred frame is the one at rest with respect to the cosmological background radiation.[358] For definiteness, let's use a frame that is at "rest with respect to the universe."[359] Again, special relativity allows this choice, because any frame can be picked as my favorite and predictions about all events from that frame will be correct. There just won't be any dynamical (empiriometric) reason for my pick; indeed, picking any particular frame in some way breaks the dynamical symmetry built into the theory, and thus destroys the economy of the empiriometric theory as empiriometric. Why would we do this? We *don't* do it to improve the theory *as empiriometric*—that would make no sense. Indeed, by definition, our choice doesn't change any of the predictions of the theory. We are not even trying to do empiriometric science. We only do it to move beyond the empiriometric in an effort to understand the underlying physical causes manifested by the empiriometric. Remember the world is not just quantity.

---

[357] It is necessarily incomplete because we are just speaking of special relativity in isolation from the rest of physics. Indeed, even if we included the other branches, our current knowledge of nature is incomplete. It is tentative because, as discussed in the previous chapter, the empiriometric does not necessarily point to a logically unique underlying reality; one equation can represent many different situations. Lastly, it is tentative because the complex network of interconnecting concepts that characterizes a developed empiriometric theory makes it hard to determine what factors are relevant for uncovering the real substances and accidents whose interactions manifest themselves in the empiriometric theory.

[358] It happens in other instances as well; for example, in asymptotic limit of far away from a black hole, where one finds "flat space" (special relativity). One can reference all time to this faraway rest frame.

[359] Here we are using averages and many other concepts as intermediaries to get to what we finally mean by "rest with respect to the universe." In particular, I have in mind the center of mass frame.

Thus, as a hypothesis about the physical causes, we now interpret relativity to mean that time actually slows down when one is moving relative to this frame. How in *particular* this happens[360] is a separate question that demands much investigation,[361] and is beyond our scope here. Nevertheless, let's discuss in *general* how time slowing down (called time dilation) might occur.

First: What is time? Again, we want to know the meaning as it really is; we are not asking how to measure it, but *what it is*. **Time** is the measure of motion; it is numbered motion. Motion is only possible because material things are composites of form (actuality) and matter (potentiality). Material things are something, but potentially can be many other things. Because of this, they can change. Without the element of potentiality (matter), one could not have change and hence no measure of change, time. Hence, absolute time *of itself* (in the sense of it existing independent of the rest of the universe (matter)) makes no sense ontologically. With the correct definition of time, we can now understand the situation of our twins. Understanding the twins will work backwards and give concreteness to the definition.

Assume the stay-at-home-twin is at rest with respect to our globally preferred reference frame.[362] From the empiriometric theory of special relativity, we know less time passes for the traveling-twin than stay-at-home-twin. Events (changes) are occurring at a slower rate for the traveling-twin. The stay-at-

---

[360] One must have time dilation and length contraction relative to the first frame *such that the transformation equations of special relativity* (that tell one how time and space appear relative to a moving frame) are preserved. Time dilation is the most immediately interesting because it can lead to an accumulated effect that can be seen in the proper (rest) frame of the things involved (such as the twins considered above). Still, length contraction is also interesting, because given time dilation, without length contraction, the speed of light could not be the same in every frame, and the empiriometric theory, backed up by impressive experimental evidence, says that it is. Hence, we must admit a length contraction along with a time dilation. Kennedy-Thorndike found in their experiment in 1932 that these two assumptions are necessary and sufficient to account for the interferometric data.

[361] It's tied up with what light is, how we detect it, and what we use to measure time and distance.

[362] In a rarified case, just take the earth and the planet (not moving with respect to the earth) as constituting the whole universe.

home's body is receiving one set of pacing of events and the traveling-twin is experiencing less. The travel-twin can have fewer conversations, less total number of breaths, and in general, less activity of all kinds. But, you may say, the body, like all material things, has its own motion independent of the rest of the universe. Well, that's partially true. One's body is "taking input"[363] from the outside world and is then modifying its condition to keep pace. For example, if it gets cold near me, I will gradually begin to feel cold and my body will start to shiver, responding to the changed environment by trying to reestablish the heat activity needed to maintain the body. Furthermore, if one puts certain simple animals in colder environments, one can slow down their growth rate (make them age slower) relative to ones at room temperature. In fact, even the aging of human embryos can be slowed to a virtual standstill by cooling. In short, your age is regulated by your place through the bodies immediately surrounding you, and they, in turn, are in constant relation with the bodies near them.

To see how this applies to our twins, do the following thought experiment. Let both twins have their own light pulsing watches. The watches send out a powerful pulse of light, one every day. We've already indicated what each will see, if he looks at his own watch; traveling-twin will see 20 years (7,300 days or watch pulses), stay-at-home will see 102 years (37,230 days). Using special relativity, one can also readily calculate how many light pulses from the traveling-twin reach the stay-at-home-twin during each of the two phases of the traveling-twin's voyage. The stay-at-home-twin sees, during the first phase, 3,650 pulses from the other twin in the first 101 years; in the last year, he sees 3,650 pulses. By contrast, the traveling-twin, looking at the stay-at-home's watch, sees 365 pulses during the first phase and 36,865 pulses during the return phase. Now, do such pulses set the pace for time for each twin? Obviously not; we see from above that the traveler receives the faster rate of pulses and thus should age faster. This contradicts the prediction that the stay-at-home-twin ages faster, i.e. that time moves faster for the stay-at-home-twin, who is in "the rest frame of

---

[363] Philosophically, we say substantial and accidental changes occur near one's body that in turn result in accidental changes to the body.

the universe." Thus, we have an unexpected and somewhat odd asymmetry between the two twins that remains unaccounted for.[364]

What causes it? We've allowed no other "bodies" but our two planets with various things on them, our two twins, and a spaceship with various things in it. Now, what can cause the different rate of motions? It cannot be the things on the planets or on the spaceship themselves, because we've assumed that those things are also "moving at the same rate" (rate of time flow) as the respective planet or spaceship. Something else must be causing the rate of motion difference between the two twins. We are at a point that often happens in many fields including modern (empiriometric) physics; we have an effect that cannot be explained by known entities, so we postulate new entities.

In the case of empiriometric physics, we sometimes postulate a new real being[365] or at least a new being of reason to account for the effect. Here, the task we've set ourselves to is to move beyond the empiriometric twin paradox and look explicitly and only for real causes, not beings of reason. To explain the effects we see, we postulate the existence of a material being that permeates the entire universe and is at rest in the universe frame. This new material being will have to be of a totally new type. It will not be the mechanical ether postulated by nineteenth century scientists (again using empiriometric concepts in the way

[364] Within the empiriometric theory of special relativity, this is the cause of the paradox. The question is asked, "How, if all uniformly-moving frames are equivalent (as the empiriometric theory says), can there be this difference?" The answer is that the stay-at-home twin is the only one who doesn't feel an acceleration, and thus the equivalence of frames only applies to him and his frame, not the traveling-twin, who must accelerate upon leaving and decelerate upon returning. Of course, this description doesn't answer the ontological question of what causes the time to slow down for the traveling-twin. Further probing of the empiriometric theory will only get an answer like, "The generalized distance given by the metric is shorter for the traveling-twin." The metric, in its simplest terms, is just a Pythagorean theorem that expresses the measured correlations in terms of time and space. The standard Pythagorean theorem is: (total distance)^2 = (hypotenuse)^2 =$x^2 + y^2$, and for special relativity one gets ("distance")^2 = (time)^2 − (position)^2 . Note that "distance" in this latter case is an empiriometrically-generalized concept of distance.

[365] For example, to account for lost momentum, the existence of the neutrino was postulated and later the evidence mounted more for it.

previously discussed). It must have all the generic accidents that changeable being *must* have (cf. list in Chapter 3), but it need not have the specific properties we associate with ordinary things of our experience, such as apples and trees, just as electrons and quarks do not have those properties. However, unlike those, it does not necessarily have mass--i.e., the ability to acquire impetus--or similar things that we are accustomed to assigning in the empiriometric scheme. Indeed, it cannot have those things to the degree they manifest themselves as contrary to the empiriometric results.

In *some* ways, the non-mechanical ether we're discussing is parallel to what Einstein tried to do in his theory of relativity, where he wanted to impose boundary conditions so that no inertia would exist as a body moved far from all mass. His reasoning was that without bodies to reference to, inertia didn't have a cause; he was considering the so-called Mach's principle.[366] So he postulated a change in (i.e., imposed a condition on) the empiriometric beings of reason used in general relativity. He used empiriometric reasoning to solve what is mostly an ontological problem.

In this way, our work is radically different from his, because we are consciously considering a fully ontological explanation and trying to avoid changing the empiriometric results; we are using those results to understand the reality that manifests them. He tried to make the empiriometric conform to the ontological. This mistake could have cost him many dead ends, but in the empiriometric scheme, one never knows until he explores. Sometimes, as we'll see, aspects of the ontological can be

---

[366] Basically, he wanted "ponderable bodies," (by which he seemed to mean bodies that can be conceived in the imagination (i.e. can be pictured in simple way, like a pool ball)) to establish all effects of gravity and mechanics. This principle was enunciated earlier by Ernst Mach (1838-1916) (hence, called Mach's principle). The Kerr solution of Einstein's equations is an example of a case where no "ponderable" body is present but the black hole itself, yet one can define a rotation. If one includes "non-ponderable" bodies such as is indicated in the empiriometric system by the presence of a gravitation field, one can have motion with respect to it. Indeed, fields must be descriptions of qualities (something that causes activity) of something. Later, Einstein reputed his connection with Mach's ideas.

transformed into beings of reason that can be very useful in the empiriometric.[367]

But, how does this non-mechanical ether help us understand time slowing down? Note that because our ether is material, it has extension (the first category of accident in Aristotle's list). It thus has the potential to be divided and thus can have many parts. The various parts of it then can interact with all the things in the universe and can change (in principle drastically) how things behave. Those things moving with respect to it will interact differently with it than those at rest. Hence, we can say that things moving throughout the ether experience a reduced rate of motion in a way specified by special relativity. We could postulate that the ether somehow intrinsically sets a timing scale[368] for things it is in contact with. Things moving through it, for example, may be less coupled to it and thus less able to experience the pace set by it. Or maybe the ether just impedes the motion of things that are in local motion through its parts. For example, the "electric field"--

---

[367] The next section will discuss how physicist and priest Fr. Lemaitre sidestepped this issue and discovered the big bang cosmology using Einstein's general theory of relativity.

[368] For example, in the big bang cosmology, there is a universal expansion at every point in the universe; perhaps this is the motion that sets the scale for the other motions in the universe. Take, for example, the daily rotation of the earth, which causes an apparent rising and setting of the sun. This rising and setting regulates motions on the earth. For example, when the sun sets, it's known that winds are kicked up; this, in turn, causes other effects. Some animals go to sleep and others hibernate. We are triggered to turn on lights, which in turn causes bugs to swarm near our windows, and on and on. Evolution was/is certainly driven to go on this cycle. Similarly, the tides (and all their effects on marine and land life) are caused by the relative motion between the moon and the earth.

Of course, parallel considerations apply to the seasons. Such primary motions are regulatory of the other motions on the earth. If all such motion stopped, motion on earth would be radically different. Indeed, the reason we use day and night as a standard of measure of time is because of its primacy in regard to regulating motions on earth. In a similar fashion, the big bang expansion regulates the motions of the constituents of the universe. At first, the universe is so dense that molecules, atoms, not even protons or neutrons can exist. At some point the expansion causes motion to be such that they can be formed. Further on, stars and galaxies, etc. form. The expansion regulates the time. In this vein, one can view the non-mechanical ether discussed above. In fact, order among motions in just this manner is *necessary* for the universe to be a uni-verse (one world).

remember, "electric field" is still an empiriometric term that we've not shined ontological light on it yet--may travel in the ether from one atom to the next in different ways such as to make the special relativistic equations true. In short, interaction with our ether would be the cause of the observed effects of special relativity.[369]

---

[369] In fact, solutions to Einstein's equations that look like special relativity far from all mass (material in the modern sense) do intrinsically specify a preferred frame similar to the one we're discussing; it is called the center of mass frame, and the gravity field might be thought of as a sort of ether. Unlike our ether, the gravity field is an empiriometric device and it has "energy," in the empiriometric sense of contributing to the curvature of space-time.

To begin to see how our ontological interpretation fits with the empiriometric theory of special relativity, note the two postulates of special relativity. *First*, all inertial (uniformly moving) frames are the same, meaning experiments done in any such frame will come out exactly as in any other and all things viewed from that frame will "look" the same as in any other inertial frame. *Second*, the measured speed of light will be the same in all frames. In understanding these principles, the relativity of simultaneity is of prime importance. In particular, these principles demand that two separated events (say ticks of separated clocks) that are simultaneous in one inertial frame will not appear simultaneous in another inertial frame (moving with respect to the first). No matter what those in the second frame do, as far as measurements are concerned, they will always conclude that the events are not simultaneous. To see how this can mesh with our ontological explanation, consider the following metaphor.

Imagine a time in the far future where there is daily use of near light speed interstate travel in the US; imagine, then, the trouble of those investigating crimes and asking observers to catalog what they saw. Those on the ground could see two planes take off simultaneously and those in a fast jet would see one leave before the other. Cataloging events by what occurred in one's own frame would create a bewildering array of facts about the same sequence of events. Suppose further a law is passed, in a manner similar to the time zone laws that specify what time one should use at each place in the country. The law would say that all observers should reference according to simultaneity on the ground. This law would make those moving relative to the ground use clocks in their own frame that don't look synchronized to them. It would be a great burden to them, but they could do it, and far from violating special relativity theory's predictive content, they would use it all the time. They would, however, violate the empiriometric theory's spirit and frustrate its goal, which is simplicity in manifesting the measured quantity's interrelations. However, there is something preferred (for those affected by this law, those living in a particular area on the earth) about the ground frame; it is where nearly everything is and happens. For the most part, people only leave it to come back to it. Further, special relativity itself, recognizes, as it must even empiriometrically, the rest frame of an object

While on the topic of ether, does the transmission of a "force" (still empiriometric) such as gravity require such a medium? This question brings us back to Einstein and to Mach's principle, and hence general relativity, which is our next topic.

Before we leave the topic of time *dilation*, we should reemphasize that our non-mechanical ether is much different than Einstein's and those of the nineteenth century. The men of that period postulated the mechanical ether as a part of their empiriometric scheme (unwittingly)[370] and later found *quite correctly* that it is of *no* use in that scheme; it only added unnecessary clutter. Einstein's special relativity is very beautiful when viewed in its proper context. It expresses the quantitative relations that obtain among the measured quantities associated with various terms in an elegant and concise set of equations and highly coordinated beings of reason.[371] However, when one wants to understand the real behind the mathematical, the real that is responsible for the quantitative and measured aspects that are correlated in the empiriometric theory, one needs to consider the real in its fullness, including all the categories of changeable being. The ontological rethinking of the empiriometric, such as we discussed above, would probably not affect the empiriometric scheme, but, in general, it may. In such a case, one *may* be led by

---

as preferred; it makes much more sense to look at something when its still. The first thing we try to do when we're really interested in seeing something is to keep it from moving as much as possible.

The ontological solution we propose is parallel to the convenient preferred frame above, except, the reason for the choice of frame is not convenience in the ontological case, but the requirement that the time dilation have a cause. We pick out the frame in which everything is happening, just as in the case above. But also, this frame is the rest frame of the non-mechanical ether (not like the nineteenth century ether which could affect the speed of light, it was created in direct mimic of the way waves travel in water or air). Our ether is what drives the movement of things; as such, it is the preferred physical frame. Again, we violate the spirit of the empiriometric theory, but only to get at what the quantitative theory is pointing to, i.e. what is really going on physically.

[370] They were not conscious of the empiriometric character of their work and that it left out all categories but those amenable to empiriometric science.

[371] Weight and length, for example, refer back to some standards, which serve as a nominal definition of those quantities.

further empiriometric work to conclude that different ontological explanations apply.

Therefore, although it is convenient *in the empiriometric theory* to work in a way that is not deliberately ontological, one cannot expect theories obtained in this way to be ontological, that is, to explain what really is as it is. For instance, it is convenient in special relativity to treat all inertial frames as identical. However, if one then concludes that this implies an **ontological** (real) condition that all frames are identical, he will quickly run into radically irrational statements like time and space can be converted into each other (by just moving at a different uniform rate) in reality, not just in their mathematical description.

Why can time and space not be mixed? The answer was already discussed in Chapter 6. There we showed that the very act of making time one axis of an x-y plot, which is spatial by its nature, leaves behind the essential aspect of time. Let's look again at this issue with our newly-acquired knowledge and habits. We've seen that time is a measure of motion. Space is the object obtained by leaving behind the matter between bodies.[372] Space thus leaves motion behind. Time and space are thus completely distinct ontologically.[373] Again, this fact should **not** stop us from considering such concepts as time and space as we do in special relativity; we must just be cognizant of what we leave behind and what beings of reasons we are using.

Lastly, we must constantly recall the limits of our human nature. *We can only understand things through abstraction from sensorial data*; hence, *some* knowledge of the physical real may be always hidden from us under empiriometric disguise. A purely immaterial being such as one of the "angels"[374] discussed at the

---

[372] For example, the bases of two glasses sitting on a table can be thought of as being in an x-y grid with air and table and all other material left behind. One also represents the glass base, say by a circle, thus leaving all but one approximate aspect of its shape behind. We will discuss "space" in more detail in the next section of this chapter.

[373] Again, this does not mean that they can exist without matter; we've seen both require matter for their existence outside the mind.

[374] Our use of angels here is a thought experiment parallel to the tradition of the great (James Clerk) Maxwell's "demon." See, for example, the Princeton Series in Physics volume by that name. Maxwell's "demon," so called because of the

end of Chapter 5 would know what is in motion and what is not, and what motion regulates some things to age (move forward in time) more slowly than others.[375] Just because our empiriometric methods do not immediately reveal the real, we cannot abandon the real, for physics *(physica)* is about conforming our minds to *real* being (being that exists outside the mind).

Time Travel (General Relativity)

General relativity predicts one can go forward *and* backward in time. Is this possible? It also predicts that "space" is not Euclidean (the geometry we learn as a child). What does that mean ontologically?

General relativity unites special relativity and gravitational force in one empiriometric theory.[376] It includes special relativity

---

mischievous result he shows possible, is a hypothetical being that Maxwell used to illustrate the statistical nature of the second law of thermodynamics. In analogy to the demon of Maxwell's thought experiments, we will name the protagonist of our thought experiments after the greatest philosopher of the last several centuries, Jacques Maritain: Maritain's angel.

[375] Said another way, time can be seen most clearly by immaterial beings, such as angels, because they can understand the motions from the inside. We, on the other hand, have to look from the outside. We must make measurements and define standards of measure that are themselves subject to change and only known through change, and thus it is very hard for us to separate out the absolute under the relative, which is our goal (even in empiriometric science this is true; Einstein once bemoaned that his special theory of relativity was being interpreted as relativism and said that he regretted not calling it the theory of invariance (which is indeed really what makes it what it is)). It may be that there is no frame from which any physical being will measure all things in such a way that they measure exactly the way they are; in other words, we may not be able to pick out one frame that looks, to our measurements, like all it corresponds to "now." This, of course, does not mean there is no "now." "Now" is the sum total of what exists at this moment whether I measure it or not; my inability to find a coordination of places (a frame) from which my measurements look nice cannot militate against the reality of the sum total of what exists at this moment (or the next). To make this clear, let's use Maritain's angel (cf. above footnote); he could verify (i.e. would know) all the things (for concreteness say there are 10^{120} substances existing in a certain state in the material universe) that exist at this instant.

[376] It reduces to Newtonian and Galilean mechanics in the appropriate limit. Another important empiriometric tool in Einstein's development of general relativity is the principle of covariance.

by way of what is called the equivalence principle. Everything nearby an object that falls only under the force of gravity is said to be *locally* in an inertial (a reference frame that feels no linear forces) frame. If you jump off of a high dive, once in the air, you feel no forces acting on you except the wind caused by your local motion through the air (a non-gravity force). This means that if you jump off a diving board with a ball (assuming you minimize air resistance by using a small, heavy ball and by "balling" yourself up), when you let go of the ball, it will appear to be subject to no forces, and thus will follow you into the pool, staying near the point of your body from which you released it. All such inertial (free of externally acting forces including "gravity"[377]) frames are said to be approximately equivalent in a much weaker sense now; this is called the principle of equivalence.

Such brief statements cannot give a real taste of the grandeur of general relativity. General relativity is more beautiful in its order, unity, and intelligibility (as an empiriometric theory) than any theory that came before it, with the possible exception of Maxwell's equations[378] which were not understood completely until special relativity.

Euclidean and Non-Euclidean Geometry

Let's deal with the question of what space is first, and then move on to time travel. We've seen that space is what one gets when one leaves behind all material being accidents but quantity. This is called signed matter.[379] We can call this mathematical space. It is clearly Euclidean. When we leave behind all material properties, we are only left with three-dimensional Euclidean space, often pictured by three perpendicular axes, which represent the three directions of common experience left/right, backwards/forwards and up/down.

---

[377] This includes what Newtonians call pseudo-forces.

[378] Maxwell's equations inspired Einstein.

[379] This is what distinguishes two identical material things from each other. Let's assume, as it's usually stated, that electrons are all identical, that is that all have the same form actuating their prime matter. In other words, it's only their quantitative separation--one being here, the other there--that individuates them.

Now, if we want to incorporate, by beings of reason, the effects of physical things into our concept of space, we can make a concept that we can call "physical space." As long as we remember this is part of an empiriometric theory and is a construct that cannot exist outside the mind, we can use it and even advance in understanding of quantitative relations among measured things. This is the genius of Einstein. He took seriously the empiriometric nature of physical space and did not let ontological considerations stop him from making the boldest assertions concerning the physical space. He let the space-time continuum be the primary concept.[380] In so doing, he came up with equations that were self-consistent to an extent matched by no other theory, even today. The number of degrees of freedom is minimal in general relativity; it only has those that one can verify by measurement, such as choice of labeling of events. In the process, he used a geometry introduced by Gauss. It is non-Euclidean in many ways. Two parallel lines in this geometry *can* meet. The distance between two points can be zero (this is already true in special relativity).[381]

But the non-Euclidean geometry is not abstracted from the world. It does not exist in the world (outside the mind) in a directly ontological way. Euclidean geometry does.[382] We abstract Euclidean geometry from the physical world, and then piece together the non-Euclidean geometries.[383] If anyone doubts the importance of this fact, let him recall that Gödel demonstrated that

---

[380] In this being of reason, time is added to the three space dimensions, as is done in special relativity, to give a four-dimensional space.

[381] In teaching relativity, I constantly remind my students of the fact that special relativity cannot be pictured (not accessible to the imagination, i.e. sensorial knowledge) but only to thinking (intellectual knowledge).

[382] Although it does not exist by itself, it exists in the things from which we abstract it.

[383] Kant's position that we can know only Euclidean geometry is radically different than our position. Kant places "knowledge" of Euclidean geometry in the primary structure of the intellect. If this were true, our minds of their nature, as he says, could never apprehend anything but Euclidean geometry. Such a conjecture is easily seen to be wrong if one backs up from philosophical idealism to see the reality. Even given one did not do that, Gauss' introduction of non-Euclidean geometry should have woken them out of the absurdity of philosophical idealism. The fact that it didn't suggests other forces are at work besides pursuit of truth.

the proof of the self-consistency of a system must come from *outside* the system. Indeed, all non-Euclidean geometries are proven self-consistent only by reference to Euclidean geometry,[384] which we know, in turn, by direct abstraction from the physical.[385] Take the concrete case of the use manifolds in general relativity. A manifold is nothing but a mathematical construct that near each point is close to "Euclidean" geometry.[386]

It is just this sort of thinking that has to be done each time we try to understand the ontological implications of an empiriometric theory.

Backwards Time Travel

To further explore this process of unwinding the real underneath the empiriometric, we now tackle the question of backwards time travel. We will use the example given in Kip Thorne's fascinating book, *Black Holes and Time Warps*. Here is the scenario. We will describe it making liberal use of the empiriometric language.

In his book, Thorne imagines that someone manages to make a wormhole that allows one to take a shortcut "through the

---

[384] Consider the layman's tutorials on these non-Euclidean geometries; it is not an accident, but a necessity, that all such tutorials use Euclidean geometry as the starting point of explication.

[385] Things as they are in the real world must be consistent; remember the principle of contradiction: Something cannot be and not be at the same time and in the same way (or recall the positive version called the principle of identity: whatever is, is). Don't let the idealist tendencies of our culture fool you. This principle is a principle of being before it is a principle in logic. The logical principle is only the shadow the ontological (being) principle casts on the beings of reason of propositions. Recall also that the mode of being of the objects in our mind is different from the mode of being in reality; this is what makes error in the mind possible. In my mind, I can form propositions that are not true. In reality, whatever is, is. There is a parallel to a false proposition in things that are not what they *should* be. Yet, whatever in the being is not as it should be *is not*. It is a privation, not positive being, so it is *only* parallel, not the same as the case of the proposition.

[386] In general relativity, this "Euclidean" geometry is really a generalization of Euclidean known as Minkowski (special relativity) geometry; it is constructed by generalizing the Pythagorean theorem of Euclidean geometry. Again, its proof of consistency rests on Euclidean geometry's consistency, which we know directly because it comes from reality, not construction in our mind.

universe" to an otherwise distant place. Such a shortcut is like a hole made by a worm through a dirt mound; the animal enters through one opening on one side of the mound and exits on the other, and thus avoids having to go all the way around. Suppose such wormholes are present in the (empiriometric) space-time.

Thorne then puts one end of the wormhole in a spaceship (parked in his backyard) that his wife will take to a faraway place. Before she takes off, he puts the other end of the wormhole in his study. He then puts his hand through his end of the hole so that they may hold hands during her journey; through the hole, the distance to her is always only less than, say, a foot inside the wormhole.

The spaceship takes off near the speed of light, (she is thus like the traveling twin). **Looking through the hole**, *Thorne sees his wife and their held hands for let's say one hour. At that time, hearing a loud noise outside, he looks past her through one of the spacecraft windows to his lawn, and sees she has landed in their backyard. At the same instant, he sees* **through the study window in the back of his house** *that there is nothing in his backyard. In other words, through the hole it looks like she's landed, but through the study it looks like she has not! He releases her hand and gets up and walks to his backyard to find no spaceship; remember the trip takes much longer according to the reckoning of the stay-at-home.*

After many years, he ages noticeably and she finally does land; he quickly enters the ship and sees his younger self on the other side of the wormhole. He climbs through the wormhole, and voila! He is next to his younger self in the past.

This is what the empiriometric theory implies. Well, not quite. We need to mention a major caveat: we do not even know if the empiriometric theory allows such wormholes. Actually, all current information (to which Thorne himself made major contributions) requires, for empiriometric matter of the type we know, no such wormholes will be stable; they will either not form or very quickly self-destruct. But suppose the empiriometric theory did or does allow it.

How do we interpret it? Can we really go back in time? Of course not. What is past is past. It is no more. You used to be a little boy or girl. Now, you are an adult, no longer a little child.[387] What *is not* is not accessible in anyway. It is our empiriometric method that, right at the start, puts time and space on the same footing that leads us to believe otherwise. Does this mean such investigations into wormholes are useless? No, I don't think so. Remember, we are dealing with an empiriometric theory; although the direct ontological interpretation may be completely wrong, there may be a way to interpret the predictions in an ontologically consistent way. If so, the empiriometric theory may describe a real effect, but in a misleading way. By now, we come to expect the latter.

Hence, let's look at some options for interpretation. Words can easily lead to miscommunications. For instance, if we mean by the past something that *appears* to be the past, we already know we can go into the past in the sense of seeing the effects caused by past events. A suntan, for example, is an effect of having been sunning on vacation last week. In a very direct way, we see the past every time we look up at the stars. If the sun, for example, popped out of existence, we would not know about it for eight minutes, because that is how long it would take for the last rays emitted just before the sun vanished to reach us. Said another way, we are seeing the state of the sun as it was eight minutes ago. This is a sort of "going into the past" where we can watch it but cannot participate in it, because it is not really the past, but just the effects of the past.

We can now analyze the time travel scenario described above to find where some of the ontological problems come in. Note, it's the time travel aspect itself, rather than the relative motion between Thorne and his wife, that we are interested in. Because the ontological predictions of the empiriometric theory are ontologically impossible, the empiriometric theory fails in a way. One can always argue, however, that it is not an ontological theory; so it's only a partial failure or no failure at all if there is a way to interpret the predictions in a different way that is indeed possible. However, if the theory fails to have such an interpretation, then we

---

[387] When, some time ago, I brought this point up to friend who is also a physicist, he said, with a look of understanding, "I never thought of that before." One cannot easily overestimate how ingrained the empiriometric can become in one's thinking.

must adjust the theory itself, which may be as simple as recognizing a limited domain of some variables or the like,[388] or as complex and difficult as developing a new empiriometric theory that includes general relativity in appropriate limits. Recall the empiriometric theory is meant to give predictions of measured values; that's its mode of confirmation and self-correction.

Let's look again at the time travel scenario described above to see if there is a possible ontological interpretation, that is, a scenario that can really happen.

Things seem fine at the beginning of the trip and when Thorne and his wife agree that great distance separates them.[389] However, once she lands, for example, problems appear. Is she in the backyard or not when Thorne sees her land through the hole? She is not, because Thorne can not only see the yard through the study window, he can walk out there. Hence, one must conclude that what Thorne sees in the hole at that time is only an appearance of the future. Similarly, when he walks into the spaceship and views the hole, what he sees in the hole is *only* an appearance of the past. There is no problem with the last statement, but the one before implies that one is seeing into the future, seeing something that does not exist because the future (which consists of a landed spaceship in his backyard does not exist at that moment). In a world without free will, maybe one could argue that there is some kind of precursor wave that cannot be altered, because in such a world, all things would be determined by material causes. However, in the real world, there is free will as we've discussed in Chapters 4 and 5; hence, such a precursor wave cannot be known and propagated by physical causes. What's more, we do not expect general relativity to take into account free will; it is, after all, an

---

[388] There should be clear reasons for such restrictions *within* the empiriometric theory, so as not to damage its cohesiveness.

[389] In fact, already at this point, one may wonder if there are ontological problems related to having a distance "shortcut" like that of a wormhole; however, we have chosen to ignore this aspect and only focus on our time travel question. This choice does not negate its importance, for one would like to understand the whole of general relativity, as much as possible, from an ontological perspective. Yet, such a task is very complex and time-consuming, a research project in itself and thus, beyond the scope of our investigations in this book.

empiriometric theory that describes material being under certain conditions. We deliberately excluded free will interference in the construction of the theory (and all empiriometric theories). We left it out, so we shouldn't be surprised that we don't find it.

To get around the issue of free will, Thorne wisely considered, in his physics papers, only inanimate objects. Maybe in this case, because of the arguments in the last paragraph, we can find a possible ontological interpretation. To make plain that we are not considering the interference of free will, let's take Thorne and his wife to be two balls (a blue and a pink respectively). Initially, they are resting against each other in the wormhole, such that the blue ball is on the house side of the hole and the pink one is on the spaceship side. After one hour, blue "sees," through the wormhole, the spaceship landing. However, he does not see it landing when he looks out the study window. Many years later by blue's reckoning (in the house), just before the spaceship actually lands in the lawn, there is an explosion, sending the blue ball across the study, through the window, over the back lawn, into the landing spaceship, and finally into the spaceship-end of the wormhole where it hits its younger self.

In this scenario, there *does seem* to be at least one possible ontological interpretation here. When blue "sees" the pink ball's ship land through the wormhole, he is seeing a "precursor wave" generated by some odd physics which gives a preview of what will happen (the equations "know" after all). It's not showing what's actually happening in the spaceship; it's giving a sort of 3-D *real* (because interactive) movie of what will happen. Blue's view into the wormhole is like a viewing port that reveals by reenacting (pre-enacting) the future, but it is not the future. It's similar to a scientist who puts his equations into a computer and displays what the position of, say, the earth is two years from now; the display is not the real earth, but it can accurately show its characteristics. Indeed, there is now astronomy software that can do this with the position of the stars in the sky many years in the future.

Also, when the blue ball flies into the hole, it cannot hit the blue ball in its past and make it move, since the past is gone. On top of that, empiriometrically, the blue ball did not move until the explosion, yet it moved long before the explosion when its older self hit it. Of course, it cannot move and not move, even in the mathematics. This is a violation of the consistency of the theory itself. Thorne addresses this latter (empiriometric) problem by saying that only self-consistent solutions are allowed. Let's change our scenario to make it consistent and then see what happens.

Through the wormhole Blue "sees" the entire trip of the pink ball up till just after it appears to land. A few moments after the apparent landing, the blue ball rockets away from the hole quickly and moves into orbit around the earth. After many years, Blue's orbit decays, and it reenters the atmosphere to land at the same time that Pink's spaceship lands. Blue's trajectory sends it into the spaceship and then its wormhole entrance. The wormhole entrance in the spaceship is still playing an old movie. It's giving a 3-D real movie presentation of what happened on the earth, starting from when Blue saw Pink's apparent landing through the wormhole. When Blue enters the wormhole, it bounces out apparently off its past self. In the "movie," the past Blue recoils (into orbit) just as it really did moments after the apparent landing. What did Blue bounce off of, since it's obviously not his past self, which no longer exists? Further, how does one account for the motion of the ball in the past if not by the impossible idea that it was caused by the future (i.e. things that do not exist yet)? Suppose that both the future "movie" and past "movie" are physical beings and their interaction with the balls causes the motion seen. In that case, they (the objects in the holes) are really present physical things, not the past or future things that they look and behave like but are not. In fact, they do not even have to be actual, but different, balls; the effects just have to be the same. Still, the latter is the simplest explanation, and thus should be the starting hypothesis.

The power of the empiriometric to mathematically "explain" and thereby predict the measured quantitative interrelations is hard to overestimate. Nonetheless, as we've intoned to the extent of a mantra, the predictions of the empiriometric theory, and the theory itself, hide as much (usually much more) than they reveal about the ontological nature of the beings that manifest themselves in the empiriometric theory. Hence, this scenario may, for reasons that we did not consider here, be impossible as well. Of course, the scenario is highly unlikely since, as we've already mentioned, wormholes are currently thought to be impossible (because unstable) in general relativity itself.[390] Still, the discussion above is important for many reasons. First, it serves to illustrate that in interpreting an empiriometric theory's physical consequences, the theory's predictions should be taken seriously, but so must ontology; otherwise, one can quickly end in absurdities. In the process of illustrating this, it gives us another example of the method of finding a reasonable interpretation. Furthermore, it helps one understand that the correct ontological interpretation of empiriometric theory will *hardly ever* be what the empiriometric theory suggests on its face.

Einstein's theory has other predictions; we now will explore those that relate to answering two questions.

Big Bang Theory

Is there a beginning to the universe? Is there a universe? We'll come back to the first question. Kant, as silly as it sounds on its face, called the existence of the universe into question. Remember the admonition of Aristotle and St. Thomas: Little errors in the beginning eventually lead to big ones. Einstein, by way of empiriometric thinking about gravity and mechanics, gave the first empiriometric theory that could describe in some way the universe as a whole. In conceiving general relativity and his subsequent cosmological solution, he brought back the consideration of the universe that Kant had excluded by taking Newtonian empiriometric physics as necessary. To regain the universe is obviously a major gain. Kant had implied that the universe was an impossible concept! The main reason that Einstein's theory could take the universe seriously is because, as we've seen, it did not take time and space as existing independent of matter. The universe was once again considered as a whole. Recognition of the universe is imperative for physics *(physica)*, since all material being can, in principle, affect each other.[391]

---

[390] But even if they were possible, it is probable that general relativity is been taken beyond its useful empiriometric bounds when one uses it to discuss wormholes.

[391] In fact, in the next chapter, we will see that one can even say that prime matter (potentiality) is God's way of making a radically *inter*dependent world.

Stanley Jaki's book, *There is a Universe,* is recommended for bringing out the philosophical issues involved in the controversy and clarifying, once and for all, that there *is* a universe. The universe is: all things taken together, considered in their unity-- one world. We'll use this definition later. Let's briefly turn to the empiriometric study of the universe.

What is the big bang theory? It's a theory based on a solution to Einstein's field equations of general relativity found by Fr. Lemaitre[392] and later Friedmann. By using this solution, many branches of physics were able to come together to give the consistent picture of our universe that we call the big bang theory. Specifically, the empiriometric theory of the big bang predicts the following history.

First, the universe is in a very hot, dense state in which no particles (such as atoms, molecules, nor even protons or neutrons) found in objects of our common experience can exist. Gradually, as things cool down, one can find stable protons and electrons. Light cannot travel very far at this point, because it is deflected by un-neutralized charged particles such as electrons and protons. Neutral atoms then form and allow light to travel much further. Also, as the primordial hot ball of material gradually expands, the light from the hot fireball cools (red shifts); we still "see" this remnant "light" called the cosmic background radiation. It is now only a few degrees above absolute zero (-459.67 F). At some point, enough gas (mostly hydrogen) condenses to form stars. From the stars, heavy elements like iron are formed. If a star is heavy enough, it will eventually supernova (implode) and release heavy elements that will later be the material that will form into planets. The big bang theory is very heavily confirmed by observation. It is a well-established (lots of experimental verification and checking of its mathematical integrity) empiriometric theory.

So, now the question: what does the theory predict if we keep asking what happened at earlier and earlier times? At earlier

---

[392]   In 1933, after Fr. Georges Lemaitre detailed his big bang theory, Einstein stood up, applauded, and said, "This is the most beautiful and satisfactory explanation of creation to which I have ever listened."
This quote is widely published: see for example: http://en.wikipedia.org/wiki/Georges_Lema%EEtre.

and earlier times, the universe is smaller and hotter. Finally, it predicts that if we go back approximately 15 billion years (a number now known to some accuracy), there is a mathematical singularity. At that time, the universe is all in one point. What are we to make of this? What is really (ontologically) happening? First, we note we are here making the assumption[393] that general relativity theory is valid near the singularity. If we make this assumption, the empiriometric theory, on the face of it, forces us to conclude that this is the beginning of the universe. Why? A singularity is a place where all mathematics breaks down. Since mathematics is our mode of explanation in the empiriometric method, one's ability to explain is cut off. Hence, if we think that the empiriometric theory is "what *is*," then we will conclude from the fact that explanation comes to a beginning at this instant, so does the universe. Indeed, at this point, the empiriometric theory appears to predict that time and space begin. Of course, we know that real being, not the beings of reason of an empiriometric theory, is the final object of our thought. We will thus not be forced to that conclusion.

Let's step outside the empiriometric and look at the whole picture. If one means by the beginning of the universe that the universe just came into existence, i.e., that it was created *ex nihilo* ("from" nothing), then the beginning of the universe can in no way be proved.

Why so? To answer, we must be clear that to determine if the universe will go out of existence or if it began in existence at some point is obviously a question of "being," of ontology, and thus not approachable by empiriometric science.[394] We also need to understand philosophically what the universe is. The universe is

---

[393] Empiriometrically, this assumption is now in question because of current advances in cosmology and has always been open to question because of our lack of knowledge of exactly how to incorporate quantum mechanics into such circumstances.

[394] If, on the other hand, one means, for example, by "end of the universe," the so-called heat death where all the pieces of material being are so spread out that they interact less and less, then we are not speaking about the universe going out of existence, but just its spreading out. The matter (potentiality) is still there as can be seen by a thought experiment of an immaterial being moving several pieces of matter together to make, say, a molecule.

the sum total of all things. It is, like all being, one. To the extent something is one, is the extent that it is. Recall from Chapter 4 that "unity" or "oneness" is one of the transcendentals. It is one of the concepts that our weak intellect "divides" "being" up into.[395] In Chapter 4, we saw that being and unity are interchangeable, as are all the transcendentals.

How do *we* get the concept of one? [396] We saw in Chapter 3 that the first thing we know is that "there is an is." We know being (to be). Next, we note that this being is not that being (the concept of division). Then we come to the concept of one, after which comes the concept of multitude, which later resolves into the natural numbers.[397]

Now, we see in the universe many different parts, but we also see that they are all interrelated. Interrelation among parts is nothing else but a unity. Now, we must explore what we know about the universe in order to see what we can say about its existence in the past and future. We know that the material universe[398] is a multitude of form-matter composites. Remember everything in the material (changeable) universe is a composite of form (actuality) and matter (potentiality). We've already pointed out that change is characteristic of the material world. In change, forms are lost and others educed. However, the potentiality (the matter) is preserved. In this sense, even the death of the animal is not an absolute ceasing of existence, for though the form of the animal ceases to exist actually, it still exists potentially. The remains of the animal are a collection of inanimate substances that have the potential to be subsumed by a plant and eventually be

---

[395] Take a metaphor (remembering all the limitations of the imagination). Because of the weakness of our intellect, the concept of being is too big for us, and thus we must look at it from multiple points of view. The transcendentals are those varied points of view.

[396] In thinking through the following, keep in mind that we are not God, so the order of our comprehension of things does necessarily indicate the order of things in and of themselves.

[397] Philosophically, that is, ontologically as preter-real entities, number is discrete quantity and magnitude is continuous quantity.

[398] We need not consider the purely immaterial parts of the universe, because we've already seen that they cannot perish; they have no parts to come apart. We must judge the universe's beginning (or not) by learning what we can about its material part.

again in another of the same type of animal. In short, among such changeable (material) beings, we recognize that there are potentialities that always remain even when we cannot actualize them at the moment.[399] In philosophical language, we say that matter (prime matter)[400] is neither destroyed nor created. Hence, the universe cannot be said to have a beginning or an end based on its own nature. However, this does not--as we will see in the next chapter-- exclude God, the Being that is the source of all being (both the verb (the "to be" or act of being) form and the noun form) from having at one point created the universe.[401] It's just that we *cannot* deduce a beginning of time with certainty from the material world.

Nonetheless, as we've seen in special and general relativity, we should take predictions of empiriological theories with some seriousness (balanced by ontological sobriety). The big bang theory indicates (not proves) that something special is happening near the point of the infinitely dense fireball (the singularity). Hence, whether the singularity turns out to be really singular[402] or not, the big bang theory does lend support, not proof, to the idea that the universe came into existence at that point by an act of creation of God.

Quantum Mechanics

Because of the lack of a unified empiriometric theory (the so called "theory of everything" for which string theory is a leading candidate), theoretical physics is divided into two separate camps: gravity and everything else. Many will know that gravity, which is described by Einstein's theory of general relativity discussed above, is the one force that we have not been able to

---

[399] Take a simple example: Water can always be boiled even if I don't have a way to do it at the moment.
[400] Recall that the philosophical term "matter" is fundamentally different from the modern physics use of the term, which always includes reference to mass and energy.
[401] This, of course, includes matter, and with it, time and space.
[402] Good empiriometric theories try to avoid the singularities, because of their attending infinities, so it is highly likely that the singularity will be dealt with.

incorporate into empiriometric theory in a unified way.[403] All other forces are unified to some degree by a quantum mechanics which is intimately related to particle physics because the realm of very small particles is where most of its discoveries, as well as applications, are to be found. Let's move to this second camp and discuss several related ontological problems encountered in trying to understand the empiriometric theory of quantum mechanics.

First, the Copenhagen interpretation of quantum mechanics says that objects have no properties of themselves, but claims that properties exist only in conjunction with measuring devices and not until measured (observed). One may now quickly recognize this as yet another example of taking an empiriometric theory as giving the real directly. In particular, one notes the implicit belief that measurements, which are readings taken from a sensor and processed to appear as digits on a computer screen (which are, in turn, interpreted by an interconnected web of empiriometric theory) are the arbitrator of what is real. Stanley Jaki has been in the forefront in trying to rally physicists and others to see that the inability to make exact measurements does not equate to the inability for something to exist in a definite state or change in a definite way.

Yet, major debates continue to rage on this issue inside and outside the physics community. It is what led Einstein to turn in dismay at his friend A. Pais and say, *Do you really believe that the world is not there when you're not looking at it?*[404] Einstein rightly observed that such beliefs undermine science at its core--attacking item (a) at the end of the last chapter. Physicist David Mermin[405] (in 1989) affirms his belief that the moon is not there when one is not observing it. How can this be? Two key empiriometric results

---

[403] Note the desire for a unified theory is an implicit recognition of the universe. It's an implicit recognition of the unity and hence existence of the universe.

[404] See, for example, the *Philosophical Consequences of Quantum Theory,* 1989, edited by Cushing and McMullin, p. 49.

[405] In the *Philosophical Consequences of Quantum Theory,* page 50, Mermin says, responding to Einstein's quote, "We now know that the moon is demonstrably not there when nobody looks." Seems hard to believe. Reminds one of a child who covers his head and thinks he is no longer visible, because he cannot see. Yet, it remains true that otherwise highly intelligent people say such things when sound philosophy is absent.

have contributed. The first, Heisenberg's uncertainty principle, is widely known and discussed by the public, but the second, though less widely known, is the one that is pivotal for the issues involved. It is called Bell's theorem. It seems to lend credence to what the uncertainty principle and the whole empiriometric system of quantum mechanics say if taken at face value. Because of this, *some have called Bell's theorem the greatest discovery of all of science.* Starting with Heisenberg, we'll work our way back to Bell.

Heisenberg's Uncertainty Principle

Heisenberg's uncertainty principle says that the more exact one's measurement of the position of an elementary particle is, the less certain one is of its momentum. Absolute certainty of its position implies no knowledge of its momentum. One measurement affects knowledge of the other. This principle comes from the wave nature *of the theory* of quantum mechanics. The mathematical formalism of quantum mechanics is very similar to that of water waves discussed in the last chapter, although it obeys a slightly different equation.[406] When a water wave goes through a small hole (relative to the wavelength of the water), it spreads out, implying that you won't know where it will be in the future. However, by passing it through the hole you have now momentarily localized it. By contrast, if it goes through a large hole, it does not spread out much. Hence, one's knowledge of where it will be in the future is very high, but as a result of the large aperture, one does not know where it is now very accurately. In water waves, there is nothing amazing about this. Similarly, when you apply the same mathematical description to something else, it should be no surprise that similar analysis follows.

In quantum mechanics, some physicists use this description for an electron and light to argue that an electron is no place until you measure it. This is easily rebutted, for just because something cannot be measured exactly doesn't mean that it doesn't exist exactly. However, Bell's theorem came along in 1964, and claimed

---

[406] The equation, called the Schrodinger equation, is the basic equation of quantum mechanics, which is remarkable because of its linearity. Relativistic quantum mechanics and quantum field theory extend this theory.

to prove otherwise. Because of this theorem's *apparent* success in verifying a part of quantum mechanics as directly ontology, completely irrational assertions were given new life. In short, taking the entire empiriometric theory of quantum mechanics at face ontological value became commonplace. For example, particles were said to literally, with no qualifications, pop out of *nothing* and fall back into *nothing* as long as you couldn't see it happen.[407] In other words, being was said to come from non-being, something from nothing. One book on the subject noted that such things attack our very sanity, but it claimed that experimental results leave us no choice! In order to help people trapped in the labyrinth of these statements, we will expose some of the issues that lead to such serious attacks on reason.

Bell's Theorem and the EPR Paradox

At this point, you may note that Bell's theorem is parallel to Gödel's theorem in the following way. If one thinks all he knows is his ideas, not things (by ideas), he can via Gödel's theorem come to doubt all truth. Similarly, if one thinks all he knows is the empiriometric (and thereby forgets the basis for the empiriometric), he can then, via Bell's theorem, doubt being itself, and hence the whole arena of things which he proposes to study.

Many use Bell's theorem to claim that we must give up on the reality of things[408] (when we're not looking at them) and/or acknowledge that action at a distance occurs. To really see what is happening, we have to explain the experiment involved in some detail. This is related to the so-called EPR (Einstein-Podolsky-Rosen)[409] paradox.

---

[407] Warner Heisenberg (1901-1976), one of the great (empiriometric) physicists of the last century (20th) even said, "The invalidity of the law of causality is definitely proved by quantum mechanics." *Zeitschrift fur Physik* 43 (1927): 197, quoted from *Miracles and Physics*, by S. Jaki. Remember, to claim causality in an ontological sense is invalid is to say that something can change itself; in other words, that something can both be and not be at the same time and in the same way.

[408] After all, if things are only there when we look, they're really just a part of us. Of course, as we'll see, this is just implicit philosophical idealism coming home to roost as explicit idealism.

[409] It's named after the three men who first articulated the paradox.

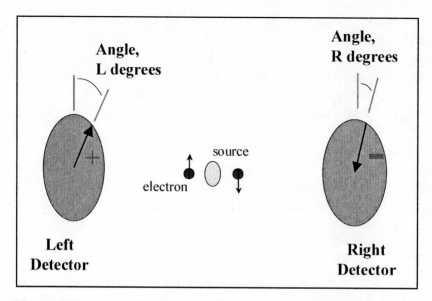

Figure 7-2: Setup for EPR experiment includes two detectors shown so as to allow seeing the angles that are set on each detector. Electrons are shown moving toward the detectors. The left (right) detector is set at L (R) degrees from the vertical.

     The left detector is shown indicating (by the black arrow on the detector) that the last electron that registered yielded a "+" spin component, i.e. along the direction in which the angle ray points.

First, I'll lay out the experiment and then describe Bell's conclusions from it. Two correlated electrons are emitted from, say, a nucleus of a particular atom,[410] and they move in opposite directions. By correlated, I mean that the two electrons' spins are entangled quantum mechanically. This means that certain mathematical relationships obtain between the measured values of the spin of each electron. The experimental setup is shown in Figure 7-2. On the right and left, symmetrically placed around the atoms (nuclei) that emit the correlated electrons, are two detectors. The right (left) detector can be set at some angle R (L) with respect to some vertical axis defined as "up," i.e. the vertical will be

---

[410] We assume here some general meaning to the idea of an atom, electron, and nucleus; we recall that even these things have their reality hidden as well as revealed by the empiriometric, and we have not done the work of sorting out the ontological content from the empiriometric science.

considered zero degrees; this is a mere convention that we choose for convenience.

When set at a given angle, an electron striking a detector yields a binary value, which we call spin up (+) or spin down (-), depending on whether the electron goes, respectively, along the direction in which the angle ray points or away from it.[411] The value of the spin at any one angle is called the spin component at that angle. Quantum mechanics predicts that after a series of nuclear emission events, each of the resulting pairs of spin measurements has a probability of $\text{Cos}^2 [(L-R)/2]$ of being anti-aligned (i.e., one electron + and its pair -), where, note, L-R is the *difference* between the two angles. For example, if L-R = 60 degrees, then there is $\text{Cos}^2 (30) = .75 = 75\%$ probability of the two measurement results being anti-aligned. To see the problem, take the following scenario:

1) With L=0 degrees and R=60 degrees, take 10 data runs, i.e., wait for 10 nuclear emission events. This experiment results in 10 electrons impinging on each detector and, hence, 10 outputs from each detector indicating whether an electron was measured to be up (+) or down (-).

2) Now say that *instead* of the above, we did the experiment by taking 10 data runs L=0 degrees and R=120 degrees.

3) Fill the data into the corresponding parts of the table below. We, of course, pick data in such a way as to be in agreement with the predictions of quantum mechanics.

4) A certain empiriometric law (the conservation of angular momentum) will fix the remainder of L=R=0 degrees, L=R=60 degrees and L=R=120 degrees portion of the table (that is when the angles, L and R, are the same). In other words, "+" on one detector implies "-" on the other and vice-versa. Since this portion of the table was not obtained by experiment, we shade it.

	LEFT DETECTOR										RIGHT DETECTOR										
L	1	2	3	4	5	6	7	8	9	10	1	2	3	4	5	6	7	8	9	10	R
0	+	-	+	-	+	-	+	-	+	-	-	+	-	+	-	+	-	+	-	+	0
60	-	+	-	-	+	-	+	-	+	-	+	-	+	+	-	+	-	+	-	+	60
120	-	+	-	-	+	-	-	+	-	+	+	-	+	+	-	+	+	-	+	-	120

Now, if we look at the various portions of the table, we see that they are correlated, as they should be, approximately according to $\cos^2[(L-R)/2]$. Specifically, L=0 degrees and R=60 degrees are anti-aligned about 70% of the time, which is as close as one can get to the predicted 75% with just 10 runs. Similarly, for L=0 degrees, R=120 degrees, there is 30% anti-alignment, compared to the predicted 25%.

So, what's the dilemma? Note that the quantum mechanical prediction of the correlation, which is $\cos^2[(L-R)/2]$, does not depend, at all, on the absolute angle of either detector; it *just* depends on the difference. On the other hand, if we look at our chart, we see that, for example, comparing L=60 degrees and R=120 degrees gives us only 60% anti-alignment where we needed 75% (i.e., should be 70 or 80%) by the prediction $\cos^2(60/2)$.

Someone who knows about statistics may object that all statistics imply some variation, and with this small a sample, one can expect a lot of variation from the predicted value. True in general. However, try to make the situation better by manipulating the "+" and "-" signs in the table. You cannot; it is imposed on you by the fact that each angle must give on the average ½ +'s and ½ -'s and the correlation between measurements of all the various angle combinations must be given by the $\cos^2[(L-R)/2]$ rule. One cannot satisfy the correlation for all angles simultaneously. So, how can the electrons, which are in principle separated by great distance when they're measured, "know" what angle to correlate to? They cannot be initially set to do what they do, because we've seen that the correlation would not then be what is observed to be. This is the idea of Bell's theorem. There are general proofs of it.

One nice proof of Bell's theorem is given in the appendix of an introductory quantum mechanics text by Rae.[412] In this proof, he shows that if one assumes that the result of each measurement depends only on a mathematical description that includes only what's happening *near the electron being measured,* not the faraway one, the resulting correlations will not agree with experiment. Specifically, he says assume that the outcome of each measurement at any angle is only[413] a function of a random variable,[414] say "λ," associated with each pair; then he proves that the predictions of quantum mechanics, which are the ones found in experiment, cannot be true. Thus, each electron seems as if it must be *dependent* on the state of the disconnected other.

Indeed, many conclude there must be action at a distance, meaning instantaneous action of one body on another. Others, trying to avoid conceding action at a distance, conclude that things do not exist until they are observed, making the entire universe a fiction of the mind...idealism. The dangers of taking the empiriometric tool for all of physics *(physica)* cannot be made clearer than by this latter conclusion.

What about action at a distance? Is it so bad? Most physicists instinctively reject such things. Can you see why? Action at a distance means communication between two separated places in *no* time; this means that something is in some sense acting directly at a place that it is not; it is somehow able to go outside the material universe and avoid having to go through it. There is an apparent contradiction in a purely material agent that acts in an apparently immaterial way, that is, by bypassing the key aspect of matter, which is its extension.

We can further verify this thinking. Action at a distance in this context means that the measurement of one electron (agent) changes the state of the other electron (patient). Remember time is the measure of material change. Where there is no time, there is no material change. Hence, action at a distance cannot be material

---

[412] *Quantum Mechanics* by Alastair M. Rae, Institute of Physics Publishing, 1992.

[413] In particular, this means it is not a function of the distant electron's state at the time of the interaction.

[414] Such an argument is, as Rae says, easily generalizable to more than one variable.

change. It must be immaterial. It is thus of necessity outside the material world. No wonder Einstein referred to the belief in action at a distance as "spooky." Now, electrons and measuring devices are *inanimate* objects; they have no organization directed toward immanent action, not even the minimal nutritive, let alone the one's characteristic of animals or men. Hence, we are left with only angels as part of (immaterial) nature that could be responsible for such effects.[415] However, one should not jump to assume the existence and action of beings without some necessity, and we will see that in this quantum case there is none.

Bell's Theorem: What Does It Really Mean?

The first empiriometric *sign* (not proof) we have of the fact that quantum mechanics does not imply action at a distance is the proof by Philippe Eberhard that within quantum mechanics there cannot be communication of *information* faster than the speed of light. In other words, quantum mechanics does not violate the letter of the law of (empiriometric) special relativity. The second sign comes from the statistical nature of quantum mechanics.

Quantum mechanics is a statistical theory. The use of statistics is an admission of lack of knowledge. We only use statistics when we do not know (by choice or in fact) the details of a particular phenomenon under consideration. In so doing, we leave out specifics and settle for averages. For example, in a coin toss, we say that there is a probability of one in two that it will be heads. In saying this, we are relating very little about the individual coin toss. We are relating something about a large group of coin tosses. This allows us to be unconcerned with the details of each toss, which are very complicated.[416] Hence, it would be a great error to conclude that because we have an element of randomness in our description that the flipping of our coin is *intrinsically*

---

[415] St. Thomas and St. Albert the Great talk about the terminus of a motion being instantaneous, not action at a distance.

[416] Yet, in principle, if we use a machine instead of a hand to do the tossing, the result of the toss is completely predictable on a one toss at a time basis. We would use the principles of Newtonian physics coupled with wind resistance and a few other effects.

random. This is to forget that we have deliberately left these details out.

Further, in taking averages as one does in statistics, it is easy to come to other conclusions that take root in the failure to remember what you've included and what you've not included in your theory. Consider the case of a man who drowned in a lake with an average depth of two inches. Each member of a group of non-swimmers who walked across this lake could be told that his chance of drowning is very small. For anyone who actually does drown, such a statement will have no importance. Specifics, not generalities, are in the end what reality is about. When we describe a group of things under consideration by statistics, we are admitting our deficit of knowledge about those things, and yet making use of that knowledge to say what little we can about them.

Since quantum mechanics makes use of statistics, we expect the individual to be largely left out of the account. Hence, concluding that there is action at a distance, which means one electron of a *given pair* is acting on the other of the *same pair* instantaneously,[417] from quantum mechanics seems untenable.

To resolve these issues, we now look more closely at the experiment and the proof. In the experiment, note that in our forming of the dilemma, we implicitly assumed that we could *measure* the spin state of one electron at *two* different angles without one measurement affecting the outcome of the other. The uncertainty principle testifies that we are allowed no such ability. The whole standard interpretation of Bell's theorem hinges on the possibility of making measurements involving at least three different angles, which, in turn, means one must consider the measurements at two angles for one electron *simultaneously*. Recall that the measurements above were taken by changing the angle (R) of detection of the right detector from 60 degrees to 120 degrees, but the measurement at each angle was taken as if the experimenter had not done the other (see steps one and two in the above numbered scenario). We did the first experiment with R=60

---

[417] Of course, ontologically one can imagine action at a distance between opposite members of different pairs as well. However, this is not what the (empiriometric) quantum mechanics predicts; it says that the individual pairs are in an entangled state.

degrees and then we said what happens if we did not do it, but did do R=120 degrees. Indeed, we can say that one of these two experiments is really simply a hypothetical experiment, because we are in some sense refusing to allow that both actually occurred. Yet, in our analysis, we considered the data as if the experiments were *both really done;* thus, we implicitly assumed in our reasoning that it would yield the same result if both were really done on the same electron. This is a leap of logic; it leaps over the implicit assumption that one measurement would not affect the other.

In short, as long as we respect our *inability* to *measure* two *different* spin components of the *same* electron (not a statistical electron) *without* one measurement interfering with the result of the other, the conclusion will not follow; that is, we will not be forced to assume action at a distance.

In the proof given in Rae, (which is similar to Bell's) because of the clarity of his presentation, the case is clear. In his proof, he twice assigns[418] *measured* values at two different angles to one electron.[419] The measured values purport to be independent of each other, one not affected by the other. This is a fine assumption as long as one is trying to prove that one cannot simultaneously know to arbitrary accuracy, by measurement, the value of two different spin components of one electron.[420] If this is the case, the proof goes through flawlessly. That is, one ends up either concluding that such simultaneous exact knowledge by measurement cannot occur or that there is action at a distance; we

---

[418] See top of page 234 in Rae's previously cited book.

[419] In Rae's book, each electron measurement is associated with one value of the hidden variable, λ, which can be thought of as a label for each given pair of electrons. One could assume that the measured spin is a bounded smooth function of the hidden variable and thus will be repeated after enough runs, so that one can in principle avoid having to measure the same one twice. One could further assume that there is a way (statistically or otherwise) of determining which electron pairs belong together. However, neither assumption is by any means forced on you. Indeed, each pair (and setup) can be completely unique in that sense; each is already unique at least to the extent that each pair succeeds another in coming out of the source, and they come out of different nuclei.

[420] Again, one cannot know what the result of two measurements at different angles on the same electron would be. The first measurement would destroy the reading that the second would have given if done first.

choose the former, which squares with Heisenberg's uncertainty principle. Of course, one's inability to simultaneously measure two aspects of a thing exactly does not mean that the aspects cannot exist simultaneously, so there is no real contradiction in this case.

As long as one does not consider the above (philosophical) distinction, he will fail to spot the import. Stanley Jaki points to the problem beginning in EPR's original 1934 paper where they say:

> *If, without in any way disturbing a system, we can predict with certainty (i.e. with probability equal to one) the value of a physical quantity, then there exists an element of physical reality corresponding to this physical quantity.*[421]

Can we come up with an empiriometric theory to serve as a counterexample *just* to show that such correlations as predicted by quantum mechanics can indeed occur without action at a distance? Before continuing, I should mention that the answer to this specific question was inserted after completing my draft of the book. Why? After completion of this chapter, I discovered, through contact with a physicist in England, another physicist, Thomas Brody.[422] He gave examples of mathematical systems that give Bell-like outputs,[423] but yet are completely "classical," having no faster-

---

[421] Quoted in Stanley Jaki's *Determinism and Reality*. Jaki says, "To prevent any misunderstanding, Einstein and his colleagues let the passage appear in italics." First, it is not true that just because one has a single measured quantity that this corresponds to a single element of reality; it is possible that many elements came together to make the measurement what it is. While, given this emendation, it is logically clear, as EPR implies, that the condition is a sufficient condition, not a necessary condition, the heavy emphasis on the possibility of exact measurement in acknowledging the reality of a thing is misplaced. Indeed, the most usual way of learning of existence of something involves no exact measurement.

[422] In my final review of this book for publication, about one and a half years after completing the manuscript, I now note that I have found a couple other physicists who also recognize these issues. They are Willem De Muynck and Luigi Accardi (actually a quantum probability expert), who even recently wrote a program (available on the Web) which he used to simulate the EPR experiment on separated computers, thus showing EPR does not prove violation of action at a distance.

[423] They are systems that violate the so-called Bell's inequalities.

than-light travel. One can find these interesting examples in the appendix at the end of this book.

Can we go a step further? Can we come up with an empiriometric theory that manifests explicitly that all the predictions of quantum mechanics can indeed occur without action at a distance?[424] I doubt this is possible, but it may be;[425] one must remember the *limits* of our knowledge and of mathematics, which is the form of explanation of empiriometric physics. Mathematics leaves many things behind. In this case, the most important thing it leaves behind is the potentiality of matter;[426] everything in a mathematical description is actual in a real sense. Given initial conditions, we can graph the solution to an equation in N-dimensional space, and there it sits whole and complete. On the other hand, the physical world, as we saw in Chapter 3, is both potential (matter) and actual (form).

Thus, in trying to describe the physical with *only* mathematical concepts with no other concepts to serve as intermediaries for the potential, we will have trouble (i.e. many pitfalls) in dealing with the ontological aspects in EPR-like experiments. In other cases, where our measurements give us more direct unencumbered access to reality--especially, for example, where direct sensorial contact comes into play--we have many intermediates to use in giving content and context to the

---

[424] We may even be willing to put up with faster-than-light speeds as long as it's not infinite. Of course, hidden fields that one cannot measure directly and that travel faster than light in some way and that avoid detection can also be postulated without violating, by definition, any empiriometric theory, because empiriometric theories deal only with what is measurable by us at least indirectly. Still, it is also clear we should not postulate things without a pressing reason.

[425] It certainly seems that one should be able to come up with an empiriometric theory that describes the behavior, and when correctly understood ontologically (this is the rub), has no action at a distance. Such an empiriometric theory's simplest interpretation probably will imply that there is (are) an action-at-a-distance variable(s), i.e., variables whose values are assigned simultaneously across arbitrary distances. The trick would be to have the theory be able to be the manifestation of the ontological underpinning that avoids the action-at-a-distance conclusion.

[426] Recall that the potentiality of mathematical concepts (for example, the continuum in geometry) is of a different order.

mathematical variables and equations. Through the intermediaries and the beings of reason that unite them in the theory, we can introduce the potentiality of matter indirectly (i.e. through its actual effects), and thus describe even very complicated changes (the process of potentiality being reduced to act).

Quantum Mechanics: How to Interpret It?

All this ties to a final problem in quantum mechanics called the measurement problem. It is partly an empiriometric problem; we will not address that portion of the problem. Indeed, we will only cover the measurement problem in a general way. We know such problems stem from misinterpretations of the meaning of the empiriometric.

The problem (in its ontological formulation) is: how should one interpret a measurement in quantum mechanics? What happens? We can conclude from the above analysis that what happens in a measurement is simply the following. We get a measured value (as distinct from actual value) relating to some aspect of our objects of study. Take the electrons in the experiment discussed above; measurement of one of the electrons gives its "measure state" described by quantum mechanics. By measure *state*, we mean a state that is classified by our empiriometric theory. Once we know what the state with respect to a given angle is, we can use our statistical knowledge about how things in that "measure state" respond to predict further measurements on that electron. Further, by using quantum mechanics, we also instantly know that the other electron will be in an exactly complementary "measure state" with respect to the given angle; this "fixes" probabilities for measurement at all angles. The electron pairs carry their correlation from their emission from a common nucleus, but we are ignorant as to the specifics of that process and how it relates to the results of our measurements because of the limitations under which our science works.[427] This limitation, in turn, springs from

---

[427] Fr. Benedict Ashley points out that John of St. Thomas, Jean Poinsot, one of the great commentators on St. Thomas, proves the reality of minimal parts and their "imperfect" extension. As one gets closer to these minimal parts, it is not unreasonable to expect these considerations to *also* come into play.

the dependency of our understanding on material accessible to the senses.

Quantum Mechanics:
Is There Infinite Number of Universes?

If the absurd conclusions of the above-mentioned examples do not convince the reader of the need for ontological sobriety in one's interpretation of the empiriometric, this one will. The many (infinite) worlds interpretation of quantum mechanics was created to solve the measurement problem in quantum mechanics. The theory says, believe it or not, that each time a measurement is made the universe splits into a number of universes, corresponding to the number of possible options open to the measurement. According to the theory, if there are infinite possibilities, infinite universes result from that measurement. When it says "other universes," it means the whole universe, you and me included, but each just has a different set of actually occurring events--ones which could have occurred in our universe but didn't. From the point of view of reality, there are, of course, a whole host of completely irrational things in this theory. We will concentrate on one aspect only because of its general importance, not its particular importance, to various many world theories.[428]

Can one have an infinite number of anything? No, because reality is definite (it is whatever it is), the infinite is indefinite (nonspecific). If I have an infinite number of horses and then someone gives me one more, how many horses do I have? Still infinite. One cannot both have that last horse and not, but this is what is implied by saying I have an infinite number of horses. Hence, it is absurd to talk of infinite number of actually existing things.[429] When someone speaks of an infinite number of things, he is not describing something. He is describing the absence of

---

[428] Some may argue that even though standard quantum mechanics is infinite dimensional (Hilbert Space), thus demanding infinite number of universes, someone may come up with a finite dimensional version. Still, many universe theories, in general, tend to lean on infinite possibilities being realized.

[429] Georg Cantor's infinite "numbers" are not numbers in a real sense; they are only so by analogy in the properties he gives them. They are examples of beings of reason, which cannot exist in the real world.

something, the absence of a bound. What's more, this is why physicists always avoid infinities whenever they possibly can; they view it as somewhat of a defeat when they cannot avoid it. The infinite cannot serve the empiriometric science, because that science is constantly trying to capture, not avoid, the specificity of reality. Again, this is only one of the multiple reasons that can be arrayed against the many worlds interpretation.

Having discussed the major issues in modern physics, we now move to biology.

Evolution

Evolution is very controversial and high profile in the public arena. There are two factions that keep the stage: those who have a religious perspective and those who have an anti-religious perspective. Let's unwind the ontological from the empiriological to shed light with little heat. We first need a few words about the special nature of biology.

Empirioschematic Science

Evolution, being part of the study of life, uses the *empirioschematic* approach rather than the empiriometric one.[430] To that extent, it will thus not be mathematical in its mode of explanation; instead it will build "beings of reason" in a world *parallel to, not the same as,* the ontological. The problems in interpretation of the theory will then stem from the difference between those beings of reason and reality. Like the empiriometric, the empirioschematic will rely on experiment. Further, like the empiriometric, it is only interested in material causality, only in the material universe. Why? Because of the material world's predictability (including the repeatability of experiments), it is amenable to the empiriometric and empirioschematic in a direct way. Predictability (repeatability) arises because when all the

---

[430] Recall that the empiriological sciences are tools of *physica*. That is, they are tools for us to use to understand the essence of things, to understand what things are. In the empirioschematic, one sets up schema to explain ones array of facts. An example of a schema that is used in the empirioschematic is an evolutionary tree illustrating animal mutations.

material causes are known and put into play in the same way, the same outcome can be expected.[431] With many samples of the same type, one can thus take averages and get a stable answer. In general, the answer will be a mix of various effects from various real beings, yet the empirioschematic will take the average *as* the real being. The being of reason of the average quality will replace real being in the empirioschematic. Note that any immaterial effects will be implicitly included in the schema, but not recognized as different, as long as those immaterial effects tend in a direction or have repeatability consonant with the material effects under study. Again, the empirioschematic approach will *only* recognize the being of reason that is a composite of all the effects that are represented in the average. It will try to incorporate more and more of reality into its schema, adding beings of reason only as needed. Its goal is to include everything. This universal goal is shared by the empiriometric approach.

Wait though. How can either empiriological approach include everything? We've seen, for instance, there may be real immaterial things, which, because they aren't material (thus no extension), cannot, of themselves, be correlated mathematically or expressed in a material schema. At bottom, the answer is that the empiriological approach cannot include everything. Nonetheless, things of a radically different nature may be present in reality. So, the real question is, how will they manifest themselves in the empiriological sciences? How would any effects of the immaterial that are not consonant with the material causes or initial conditions of unknown cause manifest themselves? It would appear as chance, which is also called probability or randomness. Chance is a mechanism that can and should be used both in the empiriometric and the empirioschematic. It is inevitable that anything that is radically outside the *schema*tic will appear in any schema as a sort of irrationality. Chance is that irrationality. Chance means there is no reason, i.e. it is *ir*-rational. We will discuss chance more later.

In general, we see that the empirioschematic--as with the empiriometric, though to a lower degree and/or with less clarity--

---

[431] This is unlike immaterial beings, where, for example, if one sets up the same material situation, a man (who we know has a free will) could change his mind and do something completely different.

manifests something of the underlying real being, while simultaneously hiding it in various degrees in other ways. There is much more to say on the subject of the empirioschematic, but we have a sufficient understanding now to examine the theory of evolution's content.

We will assume, as we've done with the empiriometric theories earlier in this chapter, that evolution is valid in its empirioschematic sense. In other words, we assume that the empiriometric and empirioschematic scientists have done their job correctly. Let's see what we can say ontologically.

What Does Evolution Really Mean?

First, evolution, in its broadest outline, states that the world "began"[432] and gradually more and more complex substances developed. Atoms, stars, galaxies, and finally at some point, our own star and solar system. Later, at some place on the earth, among the rocks and water and gas in the atmosphere, the first simplest forms of proteins appeared and eventually simple life, followed by more complex life forms. Eventually they developed into animals and plants (philosophical terms)[433] of all types. Gradually, they developed into more complex plants and animals. Finally, man developed. In the process, some things survived, and others, such as the dinosaurs, did not.

The first thing to note is simple. Each phase introduces new things. A rock is different from an atom, a plant (that which has nutritive life) from a rock, and an animal (that which has sensorial knowledge) from a plant. In philosophical terms, different actual beings (substances with new forms) appear as time progresses. Time is just the measure of change.

So, the question arises, where are these new beings coming from? There are only two possible answers. The first possible answer is: they are there already in matter, in a hidden way, from the beginning. Take for example, a proton flying around in space and electron flying around in space. If they are slowed down and

---

[432] To simplify points in the discussion, let's make the assumption that God created the universe at the moment of "time zero" in the big bang empiriometric theory.

[433] Confer Chapter 5.

brought together in the right way, say by an electric field, they will form a hydrogen atom.[434] Yet, an electron and a proton are two substances with different forms (actualities) that are again each different from the form of hydrogen; from where does this third form come? The electric field (again, we have not determined its ontological underpinnings, so are speaking in loose intuitive terms) seems to be commensurate with the electron and protons. In fact, the definition of the electric field and the definitions of the proton and electron are inextricably bound together in modern physics.[435] It is thus reasonable to see the electric field, the electron and proton as each being, in complementary ways, in act and potency so that each activates different potencies in the others, giving rise to the requisite new form (actuality) in a way that is hidden by the empiriometric entanglement of the various objects involved.[436]

Such an explanation is sufficient for hydrogen production and even more complex substantial changes, including those of carbon ("organic") chemistry, because electricity, heat, and other inanimate qualities are commensurate with these sorts of changes.[437]

However, when one speaks about crossing the line from advanced organic (carbon) chemistry to life, it becomes indefensible. There is nothing in the material universe in act in a remote way like the nutritive life.[438] Nothing existing before

---

[434] Now, as previously stated, we only know in the vaguest way what these objects are, but let's proceed in the fashion of this chapter to discuss only at the most general level and take such examples as only a means to illustrate the general principle.

[435] Like all empiriometric physics, all parts of theory are interwoven together, and each depends on the other. Definitions are modified and created to better fit together as the theory progresses in its accounting of measurement. The degree of the interweaving is dependent on how far advanced the particular area of physics is; electricity and magnetism is one of the most advanced.

[436] E.g., the electron, proton, electric field, and/or whatever else might be acting, but not given explicit form in the empiriometric theory.

[437] As we'll see in the next chapter, the motion (change) of all things, as well as their being, proceeds from God. We call this the general action of God in the universe.

[438] This makes evolutionary processes absolutely distinct from the development of the animal embryo we considered in Chapter 5. Take a zebra; its offspring get their form from their parents, for the parent zebras have "zebra-ness" in act.

nutritive life sustains itself by *immanent* action (action from the whole)[439] directed toward preservation of the whole like even the simplest nutritive life. In the inanimate world, there is no whole (substance) with an organization of heterogeneous parts ordered toward the growth, maintenance and reproduction of others of its kind; that's why we call it inanimate.[440] So, what causes the changes? Remember the principle of causality: nothing can change itself. Something can act only insofar as it is in act. There must be an outside agent. Now, it's not that new being is created in the proper sense, because then the material universe would not yet be created, and it is. Hence, we need several qualifications on what we mean by "outside agent." Do we mean outside the material universe? Not quite. We mean a little less than that, for we *must* say that matter has the potential to become living things, because *they* are here. So, our real question is, "What activated the life potentiality towards which the universe moves (in varying degrees in various parts) as it cools from the big bang up to formation of amino acids and beyond?"

We are *forced* to consider a second less general (because it deals only with life) *action of God* that does not appear until life can appear.[441] In other words, after many years of inanimate evolution described above, in some part of the universe, the matter there is brought to a point where it is disposed for what Maritain calls the *superforming action of God*. At the point where matter is brought to the point of calling for the first life form, God's general

---

[439] I pointed out to someone that the mere replication of a molecule does not prove that something is living and gave the example of a copy machine, which he then *refused* to admit was *not alive!*

[440] Although some have used the term Gaia to label the activity of the earth viewed as an entire ecosystem; this is clearly a metaphoric use of the term "life." No one who thinks deeply about the issues involved can think that an ecosystem is alive. It is the living things in it that are alive and give it any appearance of life that then warrants a poetic description such as Gaia. Obviously, neither is a crystal is alive; it is not composed of heterogeneous parts and doesn't grow or reproduce by immanent action of the whole.

[441] We have not yet proved enough about God to say that such actions are possible by God. Nonetheless, the reader will note that, from Chapter 4's proof that God is pure intelligibility and hence pure Being, it is certainly an eminently reasonable assumption. We will put the possibility of such things on sound irrefutable ground in the next chapter.

superforming action "automatically"[442] brings the first life form into being.[443]

Let me emphasize that this action is, in a real sense, ingrained in the matter at the creation, because the potencies of matter were there at that first moment and thereby always referenced the material universe implicitly to the actual forms of the superforming action of God. In other words, the order (final causality) existed from the beginning. Hence, in no way is God's superforming action an interference of God in creation; it is God who bound Himself to make this action necessary (in a relative way) right from His initial giving of being to the universe. Indeed, one could say God "interfered"[444] if God were to cease the activity of His (general) primary or secondary motions. [445] For example, if

---

[442] To appreciate further the "automatic" nature of this action, note that if a scientist were to bring material in the laboratory to the point of the previously mentioned ultimate disposition to receive the form of the first life form, the new life form would come into being just as surely then as it did in the past.

[443] Of course, the empiriometric sciences of modern physics and chemistry will incorporate the appropriate "laws" into a system of mathematics that implicitly includes the accidents of the beings of animals and plants that are amenable to being expressed mathematically. If those aspects aren't included yet, they will gradually be incorporated as more is learned about how to give such a unified empiriometric explanation. However, as we've said, it will not always be clear which parts are potential and which are actual, or how much of the mathematical description belongs to this being versus that being, and how much is a conglomeration of qualities lumped into one "being of reason" of the empiriometric system. Case in point: some of the parts in an empiriometric system may be actual only in living things, but may, nonetheless, come from analyses of the nonliving. How? Animal and plant life are present potentially in every thing in the universe, and that potentiality could show up as an actually measured effect of some experiment because such potentialities imply certain restrictions and specificities on the present actualities. Said another way, the inanimate must be able to be the instruments of life. The result relevant for the empiriometric scientist (and the test of his success) is his theory's ability to make successful predictions across a wide range of phenomena and its beauty (related to its mathematical and structural unity).

[444] And even here only in the crudest sense.

[445] Other examples include: God introducing forms not already potentially present in the matter of the universe or any other activity that goes against the order (final causality) established at the creation. The latter could be translated into the empiriometric world and given the following parallel formulation: Any action of God that "violates" the laws of physics, chemistry or biology is "interference." Such "interference" would not have its reason in the being of the

God were to cease providing a free body's continuation in uniform motion (impetus), that would be interference; concretely, picture a free-rolling bowling ball that instantly comes to a complete stop right before hitting the pins at the end of the lane.

So, we have a new life form. As the environment acts on this new simple life form, it is enabled to make minute changes and modifications that result in the actualizations of potentials that are now only realizable because of the presence of the new form (the first life form).[446] This may only happen to one or a small portion of these first simple forms; the remaining members may change in a direction towards stabilization of the new form, enabling it to exist for a many epochs. The strain(s) of the new life form that is oriented towards evolution changes over many generations (multiplications) gradually becomes more differentiated from the original population.[447] At some point, a member (or members) of the strain(s) reaches a point where it is in a disposition to receive a completely new (not before actualized) form, that of a second (ontological) species.[448] The superforming action of God "automatically" brings the new form into being. This process continues, and the branches of the evolutionary tree form and spread out, with stable species serving as the platforms from which new ones come.

At some point in earth's history, the evolutionary process produces a sort of overdeveloped animal that is almost, *in its*

---

universe in any way; that reason would reside in God and hence would not, in the final reckoning, be interference.

[446] Of course, this could happen at several places at once. We are describing what appears to be the most probable case, as well as the simplest one to describe without losing the primary principles involved.

[447] The empirioschematic concept of "natural selection" would be interpreted, for example, *first*, as the action of the environment changing genetic material. For evolutionary processes, the changes in the genetic material are constrained by the potentialities, and somewhat controlled by the form, of the matter-form composite (which is the essence of the given animal). Take the main instance of constraint: the genetic material of a sperm and an egg can only vary within certain limits and still be able to come together to yield a living embryo. *Second*, in our example, only a small number of offspring will be able to survive environmental conditions at a given time; this is a form of survival of the fittest.

[448] We use "species" here in the philosophical, not biological sense.

sensorial power,[449] the equal of man. By overdeveloped, we mean that it has power beyond what is needed for its suitable survival as an animal; moreover, in a crude metaphor, we could say it is like an appliance that has so many bells and whistles that they have become a detriment to its proper use. Concretely, it's like a moped with a motor the size of a small car. Empirioschematic biologists call this overdeveloped creature "primitive man." Philosophically, we will refer to it as "penultimate-man," because the state of its sensorial knowledge is just short of ready to "call" for an intellect. We know from Chapter 5 that penultimate-man can be a purely sensorial creature, and still be able to start fires and make spears, for sensorial knowledge is real knowledge of particulars. Animals much less than penultimate-man can do amazing things. Yet, between penultimate-man and man, there is an infinite abyss: the difference between not having and having the ability to abstract ideas, the difference between having and not having an intellect. As we saw in Chapter 5, a unique action of God is required to bring into being the soul (the immaterial substantial form of the man, whose chief power is the intellect) of the first man.

Such a transition from a material universe devoid of intelligence, to "material"[450] that can know in the full sense is *the* most important transition of that universe. It marks a transitional event of a unique and profound type. At the transition point, something is about to join the universe that is *infinitely* greater than the entire mere material universe. To be fitting, such a transition should be attended with appropriate sharp markings. There is already a unique material change marking the transition, because it is at the moment the sensorial knowledge becomes able to sustain intellectual activity that the human soul is "called."[451] This happened with none of the previous material transitions. In short,

---

[449] We are using the philosophical terms discussed in Chapters 3, 4, 5, and 6. We mean the partially immaterial power of sensorial knowledge. We are **not** referring to keen external sensorial ability like extended frequency range in hearing or extra sensitivity to low light and/or sound levels.

[450] Here we use only a figure of speech. Remember that the substantial form of a man is purely immaterial. Nevertheless, it is necessarily, for its proper identity, associated with a body.

[451] Recall, an increase in sensorial knowledge abilities involves actualizing potentialities (matter) in the penultimate-man.

motions. Mine has some other specific set.[456] The two sets, taken as they are, not as averaged, are very different. However, because the effects we are typically interested in are not affected by the differences, we ignore the differences. This does not therefore make them nonexistent. And again, consider the following. If I put a bunch of differently-colored disc-shaped blocks in a Plexiglas case and then start shaking them up and down and back and forth, and note that gradually a string of blocks forms. Did this happen by chance? No, the blocks obviously have some sort of mutual attraction, in this case magnetic, that enable them to stick to each other upon contact and stick hard enough to be not jolted by the motion. The choice of motion up and down and to and fro motion was particular. First, it changed directions now and then. A uniform motion would not have had the same effect. The *particular* set of the back and forth motions had an effect as well, though I may not be interested in it. It formed the chain in a certain way and at a certain speed. Again, chance exists purely from our perspective confined to a given system.

One last point about relative chance. Relative chance, the intersecting of two independent lines of causality within the universe, *cannot cause* a real being. In the case of chance causing a new being, that which in the end makes a new being "to be", i.e., the efficient cause, *must* (by definition) *remain outside the universe*. In the case of the formation of water by a spark introduced into H_2 and O_2 gas, the cause of the new being is implicitly contained in the system, so this is not chance. The fact that the spark happened could be the result of chance,[457] but that is not the cause of the new being, only the condition for the action of that particular cause. Because it is only a condition, not the strict cause, one can only say in an improper sense that the water is *caused* by chance. Hence, turning the logic around, if we find a

---

[456] Even assuming that each of our rooms is the same size, shape, and temperature and contains the same number and type of atoms, the atoms in each room would still differ in particular velocities and positions and states of their nuclei and many other things. Each would be a very definite *particular* set of beings in certain states of actuality and potentiality that call for an explanation like anything else.

[457] To find why this happened, we have to look outside the system to find, say, the student who is doing the experiment as part of a chemistry lab requirement.

two transitions must occur simultaneously, a material transition and direct creation of the human soul by God.

To illustrate, let's postulate a not unlikely scenario. To make the material transition fitting to the significance of the transition, and more importantly of the dignity of the new creature (man), we can *postulate* a particular penultimate-man falls asleep and while he's asleep the activity of a natural factors (e.g. cosmic rays and natural ground radioactivity, which intensity and type was set by God, say in the beginning, to be such as it is at any particular moment) and the direct activity of God refashions not only the sensorial knowledge of the creature (He concurrently lets the purely animal soul fall back into potency and infuses the human soul), but also his physical appearance. The change in physical (external) appearance serves to manifest[452] the radical and complete internal change that is wrought by God's action of infusion of the first human soul. The creature that then awakes is the first man.

The scenario I lay out above may not be the best possible one, but it's meant to give one a clear sense of the key issues involved.

Chance

Someone immersed in the sciences may still ask questions: Where is the role of chance in the above explanation? Or, are you saying that chance is totally an artifact of the empirioschematic? If so, this does not fit with the facts (reality) used in the empirioschematic. Answering these questions requires further illumination of the meaning of the empirioschematic and empiriometric approaches.

Recall that these tools of *physica* (which, recall, includes biology) explain everything in terms of mathematics and schema. These tools, as we've seen, avoid "being" because real being *(ens reale)* is not their mode of explanation. Chance will appear in them as a means of explanation for three reasons: 1) when there are being or modes of being in the universe that cannot be represented in the empiriological modes of explanation, 2) when there are

---

[452] It will also, no doubt, serve the changed material needs of the new creature, for having intellectually capacities affects how one will use his body.

entities that can be incorporated but have not yet been, and finally, 3) when the causes are outside the universe, that is there is no cause in the universe for the seen effect. Obviously, each of these three things appears in any given empiriological framework as imposed from outside and thus appears irrational; they appear as chance. Of the three, the last has not been discussed at all. It is chance in the true sense of the word. We will define it shortly. But first, we want to avoid chance as an explanation. Why?

Well, chance is the absence of an explanation. Proposing chance as an explanation is the refusal to give an explanation. We've already seen that statistics are used when we don't know or want to ignore some aspect of reality. In general, it's the admission that we don't know something. When I say "That happened by chance," I am really saying that I don't know why that happened.

To go further, we need a philosophic definition of chance. Chance is the intersection of two independent lines of causality. If an asteroid is set on a path by an explosion somewhere far from our solar system that *ends by intersecting* the path of the earth, which was independently set on its path by another event,[453] one calls it chance. In the empiriometric system of Newtonian physics, it can be thought of as initial conditions on the equations of motion. Take a simpler but, in principle, equivalent case. Think of two balls on a pool table. They will only hit if given certain velocities and certain starting positions; they will *not* hit each other for every set of initial velocities and starting positions. If they hit, the fact that they hit is what we call chance in the true sense. In such a case there is no cause in the system (pool table plus balls). There is no being in the system that can be considered responsible for the collision. Hence, it appears as an irrational element. Even in this case, however, as one can readily see from the principle of causality, there must be a cause. In the case of our pool ball, someone shot one ball at the other. In the case of the asteroid, God set the initial conditions. Hence, even in the most extreme possible ontological case, chance is a relative term. Absolute chance is a complete irrationality: being coming from non-being.

Hence, think of the explanation of life as arising from chance. What does that mean? The content given advocates is that, given enough time, anything will happen, not true. The initial conditions are specific conditions; they all possible conditions, they are just one set of conditions empiriometric science, one has a set of "laws"; given the la the initial conditions, what can happen is completely determ the empiriometric laws and initial conditions together already implicitly contain the description of the appearance then they will never be there.[454] We constantly forget means to say "probable."

In the popular debates about evolution, nearly ev argues as if the issue is *what is the probability that life will* They do not seem to notice the most important point: Prob implies possibility. The whole enterprise of evolutionary s depends on the fact that we already know that it is possible t are here, because we are.[455] This, in turn, means that the univ such that we can be. This finally means that "that which is" universe, the real being in the universe, is of a very profound Like all being, it is shot through with intelligibility and uni beauty. Intelligence is evidenced in all the being of the un even the simplest. Being is revealed in every corner of acti the universe. It is on the back of the "is" of the universe th "what is not in the universe" of relative chance is based. Ag our coin analogy, I cannot talk about flipping a coin witho reality of the coin, and the myriad other substances that mal flip possible.

Consider the room where I am typing this book; it is f atoms bouncing around. The room where you are reading the is equally full of atoms. It is common to hear one say that ther atoms moving around at random in the room. Yet, the a meaning of the statement is not the one most give it. Your contains some specific set of atoms with some specific s

---

[453] Say both of the asteroid collision with the earth was physically determined to happen from the moment of the big bang.

[454] Of course, empiriological science will remedy that situation to make it so true; that is what it's about.

[455] Some have elevated this into an *empiriological* law called the "anthr principle."

real being, we know it was not, in the strict sense, caused by chance. One last question may now come to mind.

Cannot a monkey given a computer and keyboard write a Shakespeare play, say *Hamlet,* if given enough time? *Hamlet,* no doubt has a real unity to it, so doesn't this disprove the statement above? No. An untrained monkey can type forever and it will *never* create *Hamlet.* A man standing next to the monkey who watches over it could, however, do so without ever touching the computer! He just sits and waits and reads everything the monkey types until eons and eons pass, and finally the monkey types a long sequence, a book-length sequence of obscure objects (which we call letters[458] and spaces) that the man recognizes as *Hamlet.* The man is the real cause of the existence of the play. He wrote the play by watching the monkey; without the man, or some intelligent being, to serve as the filter, one can never say that *Hamlet* was typed.[459] The man has simply found an extremely inefficient way to type *Hamlet.*

So, we see whatever elements of chance are in the universe are secondary to the being of the universe, and even those elements, in the end, must have their reason for being directly in God or another immaterial being (angels) outside the material universe.

Conclusion

In the above evolution section, we've made extensive use of statements about God that we have not proved. Indeed, it is

---

[458] Of course, the structure of the letters and the way they lay on the page is introduced by the experimenter who made the computer and set up the experiment. We know the letters as the English alphabet, but recall that they only have meaning relative to an intelligent being.

[459] Letters and words are instrumental signs. They are something of themselves first; they are, for example, dark ink lines with certain curvatures and sizes on white paper. We then assign them meaning *in addition* to what they *are.* The instrumental value of a word exists only relative to a being with an intellect not in the system itself. With no intellectual discernment to give the sign value, they are just so many things placed next to each other. They, of course, remain what they are, for example, ink on a page. However, the real order as marks on paper that they do have (independent of sign value) already existed implicitly from the beginning of the experiment (in our case, in the computer).

becoming clear that to grow in wisdom, it will be essential for us to understand and learn more about God. He will be the subject of our next chapter. Before beginning the new chapter, we need to short-circuit any possible misinterpretations of this current chapter by underlining some key points in it.

We have looked at a wide range of the results of modern science illustrating the irrationality that can enter science if one neglects the real by forgetting the nature of the empiriological methods used so extensively in modern science. In the process, we have seen possible ontological interpretations of the empiriological. Seeing something of the reality behind the empiriometric and empirioschematic in a more clear way is very interesting, pointing as it does to new facets of reality that modern science brings to light. However, the particular interpretations, though they are important, are not the most important aspect of this chapter. Indeed, the interpretations could all be wrong and the general point would remain. The general point is that empiriological science cannot undermine the philosophical proofs made in Chapters 3, 4, and 5, and any other proofs that precede, in principle, the aspects of physics *(physica)* that we discuss here. Why? Because these first parts of *physica* are not based on the specialized sciences. They are proved before we start them. We must keep first things first.

A second general point arises from the first: Empiriological (empiriometric and empirioschematic) science needs to be at the service of physics *(physica)* and, as we'll see in the next chapter, of *metaphysica.* Hence, all those who base their philosophy on modern (empiriological) science will end in absurdities. What's more, since they are starting from the wrong place, one should be wary of all their conclusions; in general, their statements will have value, if any, only within the empiriological framework.[460]

Philosophers, for their part, must recognize that it is the specialized sciences (though they be nearly purely empiriological

---

[460] The principle of falsifiablity of Karl Popper, for example, is not the starting point it purports to be. How, for example, can one falsify the principle of falsifiablity? On the other hand, within the empiriological sciences, it has some value in setting guideposts.

as they are today)[461] that fertilize philosophy and flesh out its insights and deepen them. It is those sciences that provide the raw material to expand the base beyond the fundamentals so one can approach the goal of understanding the whole landscape of reality both more broadly and deeply. This work of using the inchoate expressions of the empiriological to extract the ontological underneath is little done, at least correctly using the proper *physica* foundation. As a result, in virtually all areas of specialized sciences, the work modeled in this chapter still remains to be done.

We have discussed *physica* in some detail now. However, as we observed in Chapter 6 (cf. Figure 6-2), *physica* is not the top-level science. *metaphysica* is. The highest part of this science is the study of God. We now consider Him, whom we have identified as Truth Himself.

---

[461] This is true in the case of the very developed specialized sciences of modern physics, chemistry, and biology. More care needs to be taken when empiriological science is used in other realms where its methodology is less consonant with the subject.

Chapter 8

The GOD Chapter

"*I*t seems that God does not exist…. it is superfluous to suppose that what can be accounted for by a few principles has been produced by many.[462] But it seems that everything we see in the world can be accounted for by other principles, supposing God did not exist. For all natural things can be reduced to one principle, which is nature; and all voluntary things can be reduced to one principle, which is human reason, or will. Therefore there is no need to suppose God's existence."

Such is the second objection to God's existence in St. Thomas's masterwork, his *Summa Theologica*.[463]

---

[462] We see here a use of what is now called Occam's Razor. Science texts, scientists, and others constantly attribute this axiom to Occam (Ockham). It is curious that William of Ockham (1285-1349), who lived after St. Thomas (1225-1274) (and, of course, after Aristotle (384-322 BC) who also used the axiom), is credited with this axiom. The odd nature of this attribution is accentuated when one considers that Ockham was a nominalist and an occasionalist (i.e., believed that secondary causes were an illusion, not real; he thinks God continually works miracles to make the world look like it is). Nominalism makes science a useless enterprise, because it denies that things have an essence; in short, the question "What is it?" has no meaning for them. This belief undermines empiriometric science as well, because without essences, even the quantitative relations that we give can only be figments of our minds, not reflective of reality.

[463] The question of God's existence is addressed at the beginning of the *Summa*, but the *Summa* is a theological work and it assumes one already knows philosophy, so the arguments given there are summary ones.

A modern objection is given by Carl Sagan in his forward to Stephen Hawking's *A Brief History of Time*. Sagan says that he finds, "At least so far: a universe with no edge in space, no beginning or end in time, and nothing for a creator to do."[464] By now, we quickly recognize his misinterpretation of the empiriometric, but underneath that error we see essentially the same objection as made above the better part of a millennium ago. The repetition of the same argument centuries later is no wonder; such questions are much larger (more general) than the modern sciences, and as such, have been around much longer and indeed have been accessible to man from his first thoughts about himself and the world. Such questions do not need modern science for their formulation or, as we'll see, for their answer; both the question and answer depend upon things that come, in principle, before modern science. Modern science can and does, however, fill out and deepen one's understanding of the principles involved.

St. Thomas, after the first paragraph above, continues in answer to the objections against the existence of God,[465] "On the contrary, It is said in the person of God: *I am Who am* (Exod. iii. 14)." He then goes on to give five ways to demonstrate God's existence. Each leads to a deeper understanding of God. The first way is, as he says, the most manifest to us.

The First Way

We *cannot* deny that there is change in the world. Since everything we know comes to us through the senses, everything we know comes to us through change. Touching my water glass gives me a sensation of cold because my hand and the glass both change. Change is not confined to the action on our senses. It is all around. The sun "rises and sets," I age and you age, some die and some are born, rain and snow come down, the wind blows and then is calm, some stars steadily emit light and neutrinos, others supernova, and on and on. We saw in Chapter 3 that change is so apparently

---

[464] Page x.

[465] St. Thomas's *Summa Theologica* is organized as follows: a question is asked, objections are given, followed by a general answer, and finally followed by responses to individual objections as needed.

ubiquitous that Heraclitus thought that *everything* was change. Some moderns have adopted a "process" thinking in which Heraclitus' belief is resurrected. They justify or initiate their belief by reference to empiriometric science, especially quantum mechanics. While we know they make a serious mistake in interpreting the empiriometric science as directly revealing real being *(ens reale),* they are correct in noting that change occurs at the level of the very small as well as the very large.

Remember change (or motion)[466] is "the process of reducing something from potentiality to act." Now, this means, as we saw in Chapter 5, that nothing can change itself. If something were to change itself, it would be both in act and in potency with respect to the same thing; it would both be and not be at the same time and in the same way. Recall, the principle that "nothing changes itself" is called *the principle of causality.* A separate changer (something that changes something else--St. Thomas calls this a mover) must change something that changes (moves). In this proof, we are interested in looking at the effect, which is motion (change). All the things that we know *directly*[467] are in this funny state of changing. Again, since nothing can change itself, one thing (a changer) must change another. This creates the possibility of a complicated net of changes, one acting in turn, or together on another. Although very interesting in its own right, for the proof, it makes no difference what the *detailed* structure of the causal interconnections is.[468] The overall structure is what is important.

At first glance, there *appear* to be three possibilities for that structure: the chain of movers (changers) goes 1) on to infinity or 2) in a circle, or 3) has a beginning (not necessarily in time but in cause). In fact, the first two are **not** *real* possibilities. Take the

---

[466] St. Thomas uses the word "motion" in a general sense here to mean all change.

[467] The immaterial activity of our intellect (and thus our immaterial substantial form) is known only through first apprehending changeable being.

[468] This is another example of how general and certain conclusions can be obtained without *using* in its premises **or** *giving* its conclusion detailed knowledge of things. The temptation to think particulars are needed is more likely in the study of the specialized sciences, while the temptation to think the general gives the particulars a priori is common among those who study the general science of philosophy (wide sense).

infinite chain first. The metaphor of a chain hanging from the sky suggests itself. How can we explain how it hangs from the sky simply by adding links of the chain? Saying that we have an infinite number of links only pushes the problem farther and farther from sight (without bound).[469] One cannot explain something by avoiding it. Similarly, consider the case of a lawyer prosecuting a suspect. If he presents a large number of bad (incomplete or fallacious) arguments, he will not have, as a result, a better case. In fact, even an infinite number of bad arguments don't amount to a good argument.[470] We must admit that in explaining the existence of change, an infinite number of changers and changed things don't bring us any closer to accounting for the existence of change.

Similarly, changed things acting in "a circle" don't either. If one thing changes the next, which in turn changes the next, and then acts back on the first, one has accounted for the change of each thing, but not for the change as it occurs in the whole; recall, we are considering the three interacting objects as the entire universe. In other words, the whole is changing, and it cannot, any more than anything else, change itself.[471]

---

[469] For those with empiriometric or other mathematical backgrounds, it may help to start considering the difference between the following two series: $\sum_{n=0}^{\infty} \frac{1}{2^n} = 2$, $\sum_{n=0}^{\infty} n = \infty$ Our problem is like, the second, a series of integers (of the same sign), which will never converge (and, as an aside to our point, therefore have no hope of giving a finite sum), because each step is just like the one before it. Let me emphasize, however, what is at issue is not a complex mathematical truth, but a philosophical truth that this can serve only as an initial step to reach.

[470] The scholar of the medieval period, C.S. Lewis, once noted that moderns are habituated to a "fatal serialism" in their thinking from their constant use of numbers. By this he means that our minds tend to not recognize steps that are qualitatively different. We called this habit "serial thinking" in Chapter 6.

[471] To bring the point home, take an analogy of a simple oscillator. (Physicists (empiriometric) call the simplest such oscillator a harmonic oscillator.) Specifically, consider an oscillator that consists of two balls connected by a spring. Say they have been set into a one-dimensional back and forth oscillatory motion. Consider the motion from the instant when the balls are stopped, and the spring is maximally compressed. As the spring pushes them apart, the balls are given impetus (linear momentum) while the spring is in compression. At some point, the spring goes into expansion mode where it acts against the impetus of the balls, draining the impetus until the balls stop, and then the spring pulls the balls back, increasing the impetus in the opposite direction. Note that we have

Hence, one is left with only one choice; there must be a first mover. The first mover is that which is at the bottom of every change, the cause of all change. Now, if the first mover is to be truly first, it must be immutable (unchangeable), for if it were changeable, at some point it would change (that's what changeable means) and would itself then require a mover (changer) to change it. To not be changeable means having no potency, no potential to be other than it is; hence the first mover must be pure act. Therefore, we *must* admit the existence of a being that is immutable (unchangeable); it must be *pure* Act, *pure* Being, with no shadow of non-being. This being everyone recognizes as God.

The Second Way

The second proof starts from the efficient cause rather than its effect, which is motion. Recall, the efficient cause is what brings about the effect. A baseball, on earth, flies over home plate only because someone (or something) throws it. In space, a meteor changes its velocity only when something (an efficient cause, for example gravity or hitting another meteor) causes it to change.[472] The book in front of you is only here because someone (me) first had the idea to write it, and someone published it and brought it to the store or vendor that you bought it from. Everything that *happens* proceeds from a cause; this is undeniable. As above, we don't know the details a priori of the causal structure in the universe, but we know that every change has a cause. In the

---

not accounted for the motion of the oscillator, by this account. We need to know what causes the impetus, and what causes the spring to push and pull on the balls. In the empiriometric language, one could say (if one is careful to remember that using empiriometric language greatly attenuates what one can say and that what is said must be taken very narrowly) that we've given the laws but not explained what "enforces," causes, those laws.

[472] Similarly, for those with deeply scientific (empiriometric) thinking habits, we can talk in terms of modern physics to facilitate reaching the truth we're getting at here. A body departs from its gravitationally determined path (called a geodesic) only by another cause, e.g., being hit by another object. Please remember to use such descriptions as crutches to be dropped as quickly as possible, so that one can work with the realities directly instead of in terms of mathematical concepts and their associated experiments.

previous chapter, we discussed the fact that modern physics cannot and does not give any exception to this fact. It is a fact of being. Nothing can be the efficient cause of itself, for then--as St. Thomas says--it would be prior to itself. Nothing can give what it does not have; that is, nothing can be and not be in the same respect at the same time. Now, the arguments made in the first proof about the chain of causality follow through in exactly the same way here. Even an infinite number of causes would leave all causes as intermediate, leaving them no cause; thus, they could not be acting, and thus the causes that we see acting and their effects would not exist. But, we do have the effects. Hence, we must come to a Cause that is Uncaused that is ultimately responsible for all the causes we see operating. There must be an Uncaused Cause.

The Third Way

The second way was centered on the agents of efficient causality. The third way *starts* from the material cause, the potentiality of changeable things. It does *not* center on it like the second does around efficient; it only starts from it. From the material world, we recognize that things can happen the way they did, but they could have happened a different way as well. That is, the third proof proceeds from the possibility and its correlative, necessity, in things. We will use St. Thomas's own words for this proof because of his clarity. Further, this passage makes no use of outdated metaphors. In particular, some passages in St. Thomas make use of metaphors from ancient--now disproved--physical theories. These metaphors in no way take away from the core of his arguments, which are on a different plane, yet they can cause considerable confusion to a modern reader. We will discuss metaphor and the philosophical concept of analogy after finishing our discussion of this proof.

For now, we need only use our good sense and the concepts and habits we've learned and built so far in the book. St. Thomas tells us, in his usual lucid fashion, that:

> *The third way is taken from possibility and necessity, and runs thus. We find in nature things that are possible to be*

and not to be, since they are found to be generated, and to corrupt, and consequently, they are possible to be and not to be. But it is impossible for these always to exist, for that which is possible not to be at sometime is not. Therefore, if everything is possible not to be, then at one time there could have been nothing in existence. Now if this were true, even now there would be nothing in existence, because that which does not exist only begins to exist by something already existing. Therefore, if at one time nothing was in existence, it would have been impossible for anything to have begun to exist; and thus even now nothing would be in existence--which is absurd. Therefore, not all beings are merely possible, but there must exist something the existence of which is necessary. But every necessary thing either has its necessity caused by another, or not. Now it is impossible [see first proof] to go on to infinity in necessary things which have their necessity caused by another, as has been already proved in regard to efficient causes. Therefore we cannot but postulate the existence of some being having of itself its own necessity, and not receiving it from another, but rather causing in others their necessity. This all men speak of as God.

This argument is particularly compelling to those with a mathematical mindset. Why this is so is clear from what we said in Chapter 6. Namely, motion, efficient cause, and final cause are not to be found in mathematics; however, mathematics does contain formal causality and some aspects of material (potential) causes. We thus expect this third proof[473] will have an extra attraction to the mathematically inclined and trained.

In fact, empiriometric scientists make similar arguments, confining themselves, as the chess traditionalists of the last chapter, to their domain of familiarity and habituation. The tendency among empiriometric scientists is to think that a final

---

[473] One would also expect the next (fourth) proof, which is from formal cause, to be attractive to the mathematically adept; however, that proof requires philosophic depth and lucidity that sometimes makes it harder than the others.

(empiriometric) theory will explain everything. By a "final" theory, they often mean one that can be no other way than it is; they seek a theory that is completely necessary.[474] Note that reasoning exactly parallel to that of the third proof[475] is at work. The human mind in quest of truth naturally seeks the bottom of things. If one stays in the empiriometric realm, a final theory is the best one can do. However, if one steps out of the narrow world of beings of reason of the empiriometric, one will be not far from the third (and fourth) proof. On the other hand, if one continues to seek the "bottom" of things in beings of reason *(ens rationis)*, he eventually must confront two insurmountable obstacles.

First, Gödel's theorems will not only forbid him from proving that the theory is the *only* possible one, the theorems will forbid him from proving that things within it are true, and, what's more, it will forbid him from even claiming that the theory is self-consistent. Still, none of this is meant to squash the empiriometric efforts to find a "theory of everything." To do that would be to deny the very goal that empiriometric science, in itself, strives for.[476] Such a goal, kept at the right perspective, is a worthy one.

Secondly, he must eventually see that the empiriometric, as beautiful as it may be, does not make something exist. Hawking comes close to saying it in the following passage:

> *Even if there is only one possible unified theory, it is just a set of rules and equations. What is it that breathes fire into the equations and makes a universe for them to describe? The usual approach of science of constructing a mathematical model cannot answer the questions of why there should be a universe for the model to describe. Why does the universe go to all the bother of existing? Is the*

---

[474] Einstein phrased this idea in a more open way, when he said that his only goal in physics was to determine if God had a choice in His creation of the world.

[475] Also, some of the reasoning of the fourth proof is at work.

[476] In reference to the broader science of *physica* (study of changeable being as changeable being not as quantitative), its goal is to act as an instrument to aid in finding what things are. The empiriometric of itself naturally strives to synthesize all quantitative measurements into a simple mathematically expressed system.

unified theory so compelling that it brings about its own
existence? Or does it need a creator, and, if so, does he
have any other effect on the universe? And who created
him?[477]

He correctly notes part[478] of the nature of the
empiriometric, yet he still makes the completely untenable
statement that perhaps the "theory [is] so compelling" that it
creates itself. That is to say, he implies that the universe could
come from nothing. This is clearly absurd. Such is the power of
empiriometric habits over one's mind. This is not to denigrate or
belittle Hawking, but only to point out an occupational hazard. I
think it is very common for modern scientists interested in the
broader world to fall into this hazard.

Twenty-some years ago when I first started to think
seriously about these proofs, one rebuttal to St. Thomas's
arguments that entered my head was: perhaps it's just the nature of
nothing to turn into something.[479] Again, this is obviously
nonsense, because nothing is the absence of being, the absence of
anything; once one begins talking about a nature (or essence), one
is talking about a nature of something. I only was able to entertain
the idea because of my extensive training and immersion in the
empiriometric,[480] which, as we've said, works extensively with
beings of reason *(ens rationis)* and leads one to think of them as if
they were real being and often the only real being.

---

[477] Cf. *A Brief History of Time,* pg 174.

[478] He doesn't note, for example, the fact that quantity is not everything, but only
an extraction (abstraction) from the sensible things of part of their reality.

[479] This brings us back to the "nothingness of the atom" paradox discussed in the
early chapters. Recall that part of the resolution of that dilemma was the
recognition that what physicists call vacuum (nothing) is not really nothing in
the philosophical and common use of the word; the concept of a vacuum is a
being of reason, useful in the empiriometric science.

[480] One must also factor in one's age. Philosophy is a study best suited for one
who has attained a certain age so that he will have enough experience and
knowledge and skills to justly appreciate the scope of wisdom and the limits of
certain modes of knowing.

On Analogy and Metaphor

In order to better understand the next proof, we return to the crucial question of the difference between analogy and metaphor. Metaphors can aid a mind in seeing the right relationship between things, but they are not explanations, so they **cannot** be proof or disproof. We should stop and give an explanation of metaphors and analogy. In common language, people often think of them as more or less the same. Analogy, in St. Thomas, is fundamentally different than metaphor. An example of a metaphor is: *St. Thomas's mind flies to the answer like an eagle to the top of a mountain.* The eagle and the mountain obviously have no real relation to the thinking of St. Thomas; they are strictly parallel relationships, alike only in that there is a similarity between the relationship of the bird to the top of the mountain with the mind and the final resolution of a problem.

By contrast, an analogy is a real relationship. For example, St. Thomas uses the example of the use of the word "healthy." We talk of both healthy urine and healthy medicine. Both these uses are analogical uses, because they are between equivocal and univocal use of the word. A univocal ("one voice") word is one that has one sharply- defined meaning, such as the word "univocal" itself. An equivocal (same voice) word is one that has two meanings that are completely unconnected. For example, the word "box" can mean, "fight with the fists" or "a crate." These two meanings are not related; they just happen to have the same word as a designator. By contrast, one says urine is healthy and medicine is healthy in a way that is neither equivocal nor univocal. Each of these uses refers to a third more primary use of the word *healthy:* "A doctor says his patient is healthy." Medicine is only said to be healthy to the degree it aids the patient in becoming healthy; urine is said to be healthy only to the degree it indicates that the patient is healthy. The first is a cause of health, the second, in general, a result of health. Both tell something about the medicine and the urine[481] in relation to a given human patient.

---

[481] Empiriologically, both could be written in chemical formulas.

Analogy is a proportion of "being." Our statement from Chapter 4: "The degree something is intelligible is the degree it is" is a statement of proportion or analogy in our confined use of the word. Or again, take the example of substance and accident. Recall a substance is that which primarily exists; it is that which exists per se and not in another, and an accident is that which exists in a substance. Substance is being and accident is being in a secondary and analogous way. In general, one can deduce something about the nature of a cause from an effect. From the effects created by the sun, we can deduce the existence of the sun, and hence something about it. This is exactly what we are doing in the proofs of God's existence. The fourth way depends on the analogy of being.

The Fourth Way

The fourth way starts from the fact that among things some are more or less intelligible (true),[482] beautiful, unified (one), good, and the like. In short, things manifest diverse levels of these modes of being. These modes of being that we've called, in Chapter 4 and 6, transcendentals[483] are unique; they do not properly belong exclusively to the essence of any given thing or group of things, but to all things that we know. Can one say that it is of the nature of this thing to be intelligible and of that thing to not be? No, of *any* two given things, one can only say that this is less intelligible than that, similarly, with the other transcendentals. These transcendentals are shared by all things; moreover, none of the things that we have direct knowledge of has any of the transcendentals as perfections free from any lack. To be concrete, consider the case of goodness.

Since we've not spent time discussing goodness as a transcendental, it may not be clear why goodness is convertible with being in the same way intelligibility and unity are. We will discuss goodness in more detail in Chapter 9, but for now note that evil, its "opposite," is really just a privation. Because of our constant use of beings of reason in our empiriometric-oriented

---

[482] Recall, "truth" is being looked at from the standpoint of intelligibility.

[483] For more on the transcendentals, Maritain's excellent book, *A Preface to Metaphysics,* is recommended.

culture, we may think, like we did with light,[484] that one can say "evil is the absence of good" *or* "good is the absence of evil," treating them as beings on equal footing. In fact, all that we call evil is a privation of a good, a lack of something that should be there. Case in point: blindness and deafness are the lack of sight and hearing respectively. If not for the actual existence of animals with sight, there would be no such evil, no such privation as blindness possible. Indeed, because of the privative "nature"[485] of evil, the less something is, the less evil it *can* be; there is less order, so less ability for it to be in disorder, less to distort, less privation that can occur. Note that saying something is less good doesn't necessarily mean its evil; an atom is less good than a man, but this doesn't make an atom evil. So, to *the degree something is good* is *the degree to which it is* and vice-versa.

We see in the world various degrees of goodness.[486] Yet, nothing in our natural experience is pure goodness, having all goodness. Now, a being either has its goodness from itself or from another. But things that are lacking in some good, things that only share in goodness, things that are not perfect goodness itself do not contain their reason for goodness in themselves. For a thing to contain the reason for its goodness, it must be goodness itself, that is, essentially all good; its essence must be goodness. Any lack implies a reference to another, a comparison to something outside of itself, which is nothing but a reason (a cause) in another. Hence, it must have the reason (cause) for its goodness in another. Hence, we must come to a being that is pure Goodness. By identical arguments, this being must also be pure Being, pure Intelligibility, purely One, having every perfection. Hence, there must be a Supreme Being, God.

One may object at this point. Is not something fatally wrong with this argument because, by it, cannot I also say that God must be supremely white, hard, tall, and heavy? No. The above argument only works for the transcendentals, not for these latter

---

[484] See Chapter 6.
[485] Note, evil is not truly a "nature," but a privation of nature.
[486] Recall that this proof has already been given at the end of Chapter 4. There we used intelligibility; in that form the proof is more commensurate with training and education of those in the empiriometric and mathematical sciences.

types of qualities or any other generic beings, although for them a related line of argument reveals something about them as well. Let's look more closely.

Remember, the transcendentals, the modes of (or perspectives on) being, are truly unique. Being is intelligibility, but our limited intellect can only understand it by viewing it from various perspectives. As we said in Chapter 4, being is sun that will hurt our eyes if we look at it directly, but if we look at things, we recognize that the sun is that by which we see everything. This metaphor limps severely, for unlike the sun, being doesn't just allow us to see; being infuses everything. It is through their act of being, their "to be *(esse)*," that things *are*. Without "being" nothing is. As such, these various perspectives on being, the transcendentals, cannot be put in a genus, even the largest most inclusive genus. We saw in Chapter 4 that attempting the latter would make them literally nothing.

On the other hand, whiteness, hardness, and any other such qualities belong to a given genus rather than being a mode of being[487] *and* can only exist *in* certain substances.[488] For instance, a

---

[487] Remember that goodness is convertible with being; hence, it is not an accident (property), but infuses all things and makes them to be what they are.

[488] In particular, a thought that may occur in the mathematically habituated mind is the following: Given many bars of different lengths, must we really conclude that there is a bar of supreme length that is the cause of all various lengths of the bars? No. While there obviously must be a bar (or bars) of maximal length in the set, that fact does not mean that it is the cause of the length of the others, because the bars are not themselves "length." The bars are beings (things) with different lengths; further, length is a univocal concept--it only exists at one level of being. To try to find another more complete being of "length" by simply finding a longer object does not advance the thing any in the realm of the *level* at which it is; it is simply more of the same. Hence, although one must locate a (cause) reason for length, locating a particular being of infinite length (were that feat possible) would no more help account for length than the bars of finite length. Where then is the cause of length? One must locate the formal cause, the essence of "what length is" in the Ultimate Cause of all being (after, of course, the proof (using transcendentals) is completed and we know of His existence). In God, length must exist in a different and superior way to its material existence. Recall that even our idea of length is, in a narrower sense, superior to the actual length found in things (from which we abstracted it), for our idea of length includes all lengths implicitly in it.

fence can be white, but an electron cannot be, and whiteness only exists *in* other things, not of itself.

The transcendentals encompass all "being"; they transcend all categories and genera. Further, the analogy or proportion of being of the transcendentals that we see in all things means that some *are* more than others. A man *is* something much more than an electron; or, said in a forced phrase, he has more being. Being (and all the transcendentals) obviously admits a pure existence, and as such, can account for all other things, which it implicitly contains; by contrast, that which is a generic way of being cannot account even for itself, even in a pure state. Still less can a quality such as whiteness even account for its own existence, because it must exist in another. Hence, although the above qualities (whiteness, etc.) and indeed any ways of beings that fall into genera are not analogical, they nonetheless must exist in the Supreme Being in some eminent manner, because they are *particular ways of being* that also must have their final reason (cause) for being. They must exist as "ideas," or what Platonists called archetypes,[489] in God.

This proof centers on the evident fact of formal causality in its full ontological meaning, that is the analogy of being, and this implicitly includes the essences and accidents of all things. We saw that both the formal cause (the actuality ("to be" of things)) needs an ultimate formal cause and, in the same way, the essences of things need to participate in that Existence to account for their

---

Similar, though not identical, considerations apply to the essence of the bar, its bar-ness. While bar-ness can admit the pure state of perfect "bar-ness," having a perfect bar still leaves us with the question of the formal cause of bar-ness, the cause of the essence bar-ness.

A parallel in mathematics may be helpful. Remember we can use a mathematical analogy, because we make no use of motion, efficient causality, or final causality per se in this proof. If I want to explain why a triangle has angles that add up to 180 degrees and not some other value, I can refer to the essence of a triangle, which is a three-sided figure. However, this essence makes implicit reference to something larger that alone can explain this essence (within the confines of my metaphor that, in the end, must fail as an explanation because of Gödel's theorems), the axioms of Euclidean geometry.

[489] St. Thomas here puts an important truth of Plato's thought in its proper context. It is as if a jewel of Plato's thought is finally put in its proper setting in the King's crown.

existence. Hence, the Ultimate Formal Cause contains its own reason for being, and as a result, all possible perfections.

In short, we see that all lesser beings, i.e. all other beings, manifest God's perfection in various ways, by some participation in it. The truth, goodness, unity, beauty, and very existence of all things are participations in Truth, Goodness, Unity, Beauty, and Being Himself.

The Fifth Way

The last way starts from the order that we see in the universe. We've discussed it some already. I throw a rock in a pond; I see that it behaves in a certain way. I know that if, under the same conditions, I want the similar effect, all I must do is make a similar throw. Similarly, order is all around us in the high-tech world. Computers, like the one I am typing this book on, depend upon the deep order in the universe. Physicists' theories are the revelation of the deep and broad quantitative orderliness in the physical world. Maxwell's equations, the Einstein Equations of general relativity and the equations of the electro-weak theory are all manifestations of an underlying order. Another example: if I take a flask with hydrogen and oxygen gas in it and provide a spark, I will get water every time. Or again, if I take gasoline and provide a spark in a cylinder of a car, I will get a violent explosion; the fact that my car functions at all is because of this order. Like the beginning points of the other proofs, (change, efficient causality, possibility and necessity, the more and less in things), the order in the world is undeniable. Again, we do not have to say that all is order. We just have to note there is some order. That's all we'll need for this way to God's existence.

We can make our discussion of the order more general and clear by using the more fundamental concepts of act and potency. The order we see is nothing but the order of potency toward act. The gasoline is potentially violently burnable; the spark provides the heat needed to actualize that potentiality. Potentiality exists only in reference to an actuality. That is, as we've said, there is an ordination of potentiality to act. Ordination comes from the word "order." Such an ordination is what we called final causality, the fact of agents acting toward an end, not that the object has a considered purpose, but only that it acts toward a specific end. We will return to the absence of purpose in these agents, for one's mind naturally wonders at this absence. Again, a spark in gasoline always acts toward the end of combustion in the given circumstances (constellation of causes). Once one has ordination, one has order and vice-versa. Now ordination implies fore-ordination.

Now, things cannot act for an end unless there is an intelligence guiding them. Why? Things cannot be foreordained-- that is, ordained before they happen--unless somewhere they are ordained to happen. They cannot be foreordained in the things themselves, because then they would be causing themselves, giving something they don't have. The foreordination cannot exist in a physical state somewhere, for that would only compound the dilemma, by adding another unaccounted foreordination. It must exist in an immaterial way in the mind of another being, an intellect. If this intellect is itself subject to an end outside of itself, then it too will require a cause outside of itself for its tendency (its intention) or the foreordination implied by its acting for an end outside of itself. We must finally come to a Transcendent Being who is pure intellection directing and providing the foreordinations of all things, but not subject to the causality of an end. He must be pure intellection. Pure Intellect.

The Five Proofs in Retrospect

So, we see that God is Pure Act, the Uncaused Cause, the Necessary Being, the Supreme Being, and Pure Intellect. Each proof is sufficient to prove the existence of God, yet they gradually deepen our understanding.

The first proof leads us to being Himself, Pure Act, with no shadow of potentiality, who causes all motion and who causes all being, because for a change to happen, something that potentially is becomes something that actually is. God provides the act of being, the "to be" of all things. Being Himself is the source of all being.

In pointing to the Uncaused aspect of God, the second proof clears up the often-asked question "Who made God?" There is a story told about a priest from the early part of the twentieth century who lost his belief in God's existence when asked that question. The story rings hollow. Priests of that era were required to understand the proofs of St. Thomas; he would have known the absurdity of the question. God has no Cause; if He did, He would not be God.[490] With both of these proofs, we begin to see clearly the metaphysical truth that essence and existence are separate in all things but God.

The third proof highlights the necessity of God's existence. All other essences are not necessary; that is why they require God for their existence. Even an angel (cf. Chapter 5) requires a cause, because an angel's essence is not his existence; it doesn't contain the reason for its existence. Although it does not have matter and form, it still has an essence that can be or not be, and in this extended sense, it is potential; it is potential with respect to its very existence. It gets its being, its "to be" from God. God preserves all things in existence.[491]

---

[490] Neither can God cause Himself--as the Dutch philosopher Spinoza (1632-1677) incorrectly thought--for that would mean, as we've seen, He must precede Himself.

[491] Some try to prove (or point to) God's existence by applying probability calculations to existing things. Given the use of probability arguments by multiple factions, it's helpful to clear up some of these issues by more particular analysis. Two points are important to keep in mind: The beginning of all existence proofs is some existent thing(s), and probability assumes being, not proves it (see Chapter 7).

We've seen relative chance is, in a sense, the absence of being. We first come to being, so being is our starting point. Take the case of someone who finds sticks in a field that appear to make the letters of a sentence, apparently saying "Two paces, big rock." Since these things are just lying next to each other, their level of order (being) is very low. Yet, they have a real nature that requires that they be lying in some arrangement, so there is a level of being there; we know that. What of the instrumental sign? What of the apparent message? Is someone sending a message or not? Answer: That depends wholly on whether someone actually *intended* that particular organization of sticks to convey a message. If no one did, no matter how improbable it might appear, the sticks do not convey a message. Of course, one may not know whether someone did intend this or not. Adopting this viewpoint, one could then say, "Well, the closer these sticks are cut and arranged such that they clearly form the letters and

The fourth and fifth proofs bring home the point that all that is good, true, intelligent, and intelligible have their source in God. In short, the proofs show that all things move and have their being in God and are guided by His infinite[492] intelligence. We see that all things must come in existence by the power of God. Hence, even if the universe were infinite in duration, the universe would still be created in the sense of being brought forward from nothingness by God. Remember God does not create *in* time, God *creates* time, because time is the measure of motion. From our perspective, there are two actions of God: His creative action and His preservative action; from His perspective they are identical. God holds all things in being. If he removed his preserving providence from anything, it would cease from existence.

---

sentence, the more complex the sentence and the more intricate what it says, the less likely that it is an accident." By "accident," he means that no one directly intended this message. As the sentence and other aspects of the apparent communication get more complex, one approaches a near certainty that it is a message. One might say, "Cannot one in the last analysis always say it was God who left the message?" No. The same rules apply to that case as well, because, although all things have a reason in or from God, it's possible that the reason for the given arrangement of sticks is required for some other purpose; God would know this would appear to give this message, but he would also know that men could figure out whether it was a message or not by means of likelihood. In all such cases, the appropriateness of the message for the circumstance, and the probability that it happened by accident help give one some feel for whether intention was involved or not. Of course, if at some point, enough factors converge, it may become clear beyond reasonable doubt that intention is involved.

In any case, it is clear from the above that to attempt to prove God's existence by use of relative chance sidesteps the real proofs (often for fear of having to encounter metaphysics) in favor of looking for instrumental signs (messages) that may or may not be there.

[492] "Infinite" here is used differently than it is used in reference to matter. In the latter case, it means all the potentiality of a particular thing is "used up." Material things are perfected by their form, which in turn limits them. In reference to God, infinity means formally, in actuality (not referencing potentiality), God has every perfection.

God and the Universe

We can now see clearly many things about God's relation to the universe. In addition to what we've already mentioned, we now see that God can indeed carry out all the actions that we ascribed to Him in the preceding chapter to explain various physical facts as embodied in modern empiriological theories.

Recall that (prime) matter[493] is the potentiality in the physical universe. The physical universe, the material world, is unity of the form-matter composites, which we've discussed throughout this book. In short, matter is God's way of creating a radically interconnected, interdependent world. Any particular part can, in principle, be whatever another part can be or is. Each part of it can, in principle, affect any other part. Man's and the angels' part in the universe will be discussed later in this chapter.

We now also see clearly that the universe is not God; it is not necessary. We rule out pantheism and with it all the false starts it has caused science. In short, even the entire universe itself is contingent, being a unity of contingent things, all of which, including that unity, do exist, but could well have not. The universe is not Pure Act; it is like the system of the harmonic oscillator that we mentioned earlier. As good as the universe may be, it is not Goodness. Neither is it Pure Intelligibility or Unity or Intellect. Indeed, we have seen in earlier chapters that man is, in a significant way, greater than the entire universe, because he can contain the entire universe in his mind.

Lastly, Einstein's query about whether God could have made a different universe is answered by the fifth proof. It shows that God has no end outside of Himself. So, He has no compulsion. Why then did He create? Agents as agents act to give actuality to the potentiality. In general, we see that the nature of being (goodness) is to be diffusive of itself. The nature of goodness is to give of itself. A good man is recognized by his magnanimity; his largess is such that he gives and gives and it diminishes him but little. Perfect Goodness is changed not at all by it. So, this is why God creates: because that's the way Goodness is. This truth does

---

[493] Again, this is the philosophical use of the term "matter," not the use found in modern (empiriometric) physics.

not come from an exercise in reasoning, but an act of seeing by the intellect; it is something we see to be true. Goodness is diffusive of itself.

God's Essence *Is* Existence: He Is Who Is

There are two unfinished issues related to the proofs of God's existence. First, God's essence must be His existence, because if it were not, then it would be possible for Him to not exist, and this is contrary to what we've already shown. Hence, the most appropriate thing we can say about Him is the following. God is He who *Is*.

Second, why can't there be more than one God? We've already seen that God is pure act, so this means He can have no composition at all, for this would involve potentiality. He certainly cannot be individuated by matter like material things are; recall, this cat is different from that cat not because of a different essence but because of the particular matter it's joined to in each cat. This is potentiality in a radical sense and so in no way can be attributed to God. God is purely immaterial (not material),[494] which is the same as saying He cannot change. Immaterial things, which are pure forms,[495] can only be distinguished by their essence, and God's essence is simply His Supreme Being, His existence. Now, if there were two Gods, for them to be different and thus really two, one would have to have something the other did not. This would mean the one would lack something and it would not thus truly be God. Therefore, when one says there can be more than one God, he is saying something absurd, because it's intrinsically impossible.

It is instructive to recall that an *accident* is that which exists in another; a *substance* is that which exists by itself, *per se,* not in

---

[494] This means, among other things, that God is not in a place, inside a black hole or outside one. Nor does He have, or exist in, physical dimensions like the imagination (technical term) lends one to believe and like science fiction stories such as the imaginative one by Edwin Abbot (*Flatland: A Romance of Many Dimensions*) seem to urge.

[495] No correlative matter.

another. This latter does not however mean that it is its own existence. *Only* God is His own existence; He is *a se*.

A Backwards "Proof"

Even when one is not thinking of these proofs, one comes to them in a confused manner. Renowned physicist John Wheeler asks in the standard textbook *Gravitation*,[496] why does the universe fly?[497] He means the same thing Hawking meant above: Why does it exist? These two great physicists have come upon the fact that real existence is not contained in any concept in the mind. The existence of the thing is not in the idea of it.

This brings us to the "proof" of the existence of God by St. Anselm. He argued that the existence of God is self-evident. He said this is true because God is the Supreme Being, that which nothing greater can be conceived. He argues that the Supreme Being cannot be truly supreme unless it exists in reality as well as in thought.[498]

He argues as follows. Compare a being that exists in my mind but not in reality with a being that exists both in my mind and in reality. The former is not that which nothing greater can be conceived, because I can always add that it exists in reality. Hence, to say God does not exist is *self-evidently wrong*. This argument has a certain force that nearly everyone who hears it acclaims. However, *it cannot hold up to scrutiny*. Its basic argument starts from an idea in the mind and proceeds to existence. We know that we cannot start in the mind to obtain existence. We must start from

---

[496] By Misner, Thorne, and Wheeler.

[497] More specifically, on page 1208, he says, "Not one of those equations will put on wings, take off or fly. Yet the universe 'flies.'" Then he goes on to look for the answer in an essence, not existence. In particular, he looks to find its necessity or formal cause (in empiriometric fashion) in mathematical principles. He says, "Some principle uniquely right and uniquely simple must, when one knows it, be so compelling that…"

[498] Kant, who did not have any education in the real thought of St. Thomas and Aristotle (as one might have concluded by this point), thought all proofs of God's existence reduced to Anselm's argument. This is also not surprising considering Kant's (at bottom) philosophical idealism and the idealist nature of the Anselm arguments.

things that we know exist in the external world through our sensorial knowledge: things like we used in each of the above proofs. In each case, we started with real things. This is not to say we only used the phantasms that present those things to us, and did not think about those things. No. It is only to say we started with things that we know exist. Hence, in its given form, St. Anselm's argument can only prove that when we *think about God,* we must think of Him as not capable of not existing. Where then does its power and obvious force come from?

Part of the reason the proof has force is that it is indeed true that, in itself, God's existence is self-evident. But it is only so if one knows God's essence itself.[499] We have no such knowledge, so God's existence is not self-evident to us, and, hence, if it's to be known, it must be proved. We prove His existence from things that we know exist, proceeding from effects to the Cause. Thus, we only know the Cause in a very incomplete way. Indeed, because of the weakness of our intellect and our resulting indirect approach to God, we cannot give a definition of God. We know Him by what He causes.[500]

---

[499] Note the definition Anselm gives of "Supreme Being" is an iterative one that avoids definition by implicit reference to the world.

[500] St. Thomas says in this regard, "Accordingly, in the present life it is absolutely impossible to know the essence of immaterial substances, not only by natural knowledge but also by revelation; for, as Dionysius says, the light of divine revelation comes to us adapted to our condition. Thus even though revelation elevates us to know something of which we should otherwise be ignorant, it does not elevate us to know in any other way than through sensible things. Thus Dionysius says: 'It is impossible for the divine light to illumine us from above unless it be hidden within the covering of many sacred veils.' Now knowledge by way of the sensible is inadequate to enable us to know the essences of immaterial substances. So we conclude that we do not know what immaterial forms are, but only that they are, whether by natural reason based upon created effects or even by revelation, by means of likenesses taken from sensible things.

It should be noticed, however, that we cannot know that a thing is without knowing in some way what it is, either perfectly or at least confusedly, as the Philosopher [Aristotle] says we know things defined before we know the parts of their definition. For if a person knows that man exists and wants to find out what man is by definition, he must know the meaning of the term 'man.' And this is possible only if he somehow forms a concept of what he knows to exist, even though he does not know its definition. That is to say, he forms a

The remaining strength of the Anselm argument comes from its being a sort of backwards proof. Our minds cannot rest in contingent, non-permanent being, so they spontaneously move to Necessary, Permanent Being, Being Himself, although our minds may do so in an inchoate and more or less unconscious manner, in what we've called an infra-scientific way. We've seen this in Hawking and Wheeler's remarks. Anselm's argument starts at the conclusion of the proof, the Supreme Being, and then tries to work to "ground" that Supreme Being in *actual* existence. A major force of the argument, invalid though it is (because backwards), comes from the infra-scientific realization that contingent being *alone* is irrational.

Objections

We now deal with two objections to the proofs. One, at this point, is fairly easy to answer; the other is the most difficult that can be offered.

An Interested God

Physicist Steven Weinberg brings out the general intuition of many scientists in his implicit argument against God's existence given below:

> *Will we find an interested God in the final laws of nature? There seems something almost absurd in asking this question ...because it is difficult even to imagine being in the possession of ultimate principles that do not need any explanation in terms of deeper principles. But premature as the question may be, it is hardly possible not to wonder whether we will find any answer to our deepest questions, any sign of the workings of an interested God, in a final theory. I think that we will not. All our experience throughout the history of science has tended in the opposite direction, toward a chilling impersonality in the*

---

concept of man by knowing a proximate or remote genus and accidental characteristics which reveal him externally. For our knowledge of definitions, like that of demonstrations, must begin with some previous knowledge." From *The Division and Methods of the Sciences* p. 84.

laws of nature. The first great step along this path was the demystifications of the heavens...[501]

In the first sentences, we see the operation of some of the reasoning of the third and fourth proof; he is looking, pushing back for the explanation of things. Yet, he does not see that a qualitatively different step is required and this keeps him from seeing the way out. No, it's more than that; he is within the mathematical realm *(mathematica)* and does not choose to leave or is no longer conscious that he can leave.

Still again, we see the misuse of the narrow empiriometric world. The same is true of the second half of the quote. As a scientist, one lives in this world, one breathes in this world; it is one's job. Everyone or many[502] around the scientist is/are devoted to (empiriometric) science. It is very hard to think outside the narrow pathways and remember that the real world is much bigger than the empiriometric. As we've said, the empiriometric is the study of the physical world as quantitative; its explanations are of the quantitative interrelations that obtain among measured aspects of things. It is formally mathematical. Hence, relative to the second half of the quote, although the real world contains final causality (purpose), it will not capture it. Although the real world has men, like himself, who think (and thus have an immaterial substantial form[503]) and act for the end (purpose) of understanding the physical world, he will not see it in his empiriometric work. The more successful the mathematization becomes, the less he will see it; it will only get more "chilling." The great physicist and mathematician Blaise Pascal (1623-1662) warned of this, when he commented that the infinite spaces are frightening.[504] He did not mean to him, but to those who think all is mathematics. By

---

[501] *Dreams of a Final Theory,* p. 245, Pantheon.

[502] In doing a job well, one spends time with and interacts with those who share the enthusiasm and see the same goal as oneself; it is a self-selecting environment.

[503] See Chapters 4 and 5.

[504] This quote is often used in such a way as to imply that Pascal was frightened by these spaces. In fact, Pascal has the paradigm of a useless man say this. (See *Pensees,* Penguin Classics 1995, p. 130) In his own voice, he says that man is a thinking reed, so not measured by space.

contrast, the proofs show God is infinitely more interested than we are.

The Problem of Evil

This leads us to the second objection to God's existence. It is the only objection that can be raised that has force to it. What of evil? If God is infinite Goodness, why is there evil? Although we have saved it for last, this objection is actually the first objection raised by St. Thomas in the *Summa Theologica*.

Well, the proofs go through despite our difficulties, so we must say God is pure Goodness. Hence, we must attempt to understand evil to the extent we can. Remember we do not expect to understand everything, God is infinite and we are finite. We only expect to gradually increase in our understanding at the rate that we can, and we expect complete understanding to be always beyond our grasp. Nonetheless, we can understand at a fairly deep level. The evils that we see are of two major types: physical evil and moral evil. Let's handle these separately.

Physical evil is when a material thing is absent something that is proper to its nature. Examples are helpful: an animal missing a limb or its eyes, a tree missing a large part of its bark, an apple eaten out by worms of its fruit core, and the death of animals and plants.[505] This type of evil is explainable by the fact that these things do not have ultimate value in themselves, but in their broader environment only. Each individual of ontological species of animal is part of that species and in a way only exists for that species, because each form is a material form. Hence, the good of the species, the propagation of the species is the ultimate good in this case. And in turn the species can be subordinated to another good, say the stability of the whole ecosystem. This is even truer of lesser beings such as plants. This solution, though it needs much more filling out, easily solves the problem of physical evil as long as one never finds a case where the goods are not subordinated properly. We will return to this pregnant statement. However, it

---

[505] As one descends lower in being, it becomes harder to identify evil because less is there, so less can be distorted, but also because, for example, an electron or atom we only know in the very indirect ways we've discussed. Their privations tend to appear as probabilities in our empiriometric theories.

will fall infinitely short when we come to the problem of physical evil in human beings.

The fact that innocent children can be shot in their schools or that millions of Jews can be killed in horrible camps *can certainly not* be explained by simply saying that the good of the species is served by it. Each individual human being is an immortal substantial form animating a body. As such, each man is of infinite value. Because of his nature, no human person can be used as a mere tool for the good of another without creating an absolute evil for which God, Goodness, would have to be ultimately responsible for (as the Act of everything).[506] These questions are very deep. As such,[507] we can only say that the physical evil allowed to these people must be used, as hard as it may be for us to see, in the end for their own eternal good. Remember that a finite lifetime "in this world" is only an infinitesimal part of an eternal existence. We will have to leave this answer in its rudimentary but inescapable form. Restated, God allows evil that good may come of it.

Now, what could create such an odd situation? Only God's making creatures so like Himself that *they can will what they want*; they have free will. Such creatures can thus choose to do things contrary to the order established in things. This is moral evil in its most general sense.[508] Men can choose to ram two jet planes into the World Trade Center and one into the Pentagon, killing thousands of innocent people. They can do things that will only much later have horrible effects, like doing nuclear testing above ground and allowing schoolchildren to watch.[509] One can go on, but it is clear that if one is to really have a free will, such things must always be possible.

---

[506] Here we must make a distinction between the *ordaining will of God* (that which God directly wills) and the *permitting will* (that which God allows but does not directly will).

[507] Here we feel the strong need for revelation from God on such an issue, but we proceed without investigating revelation, using only reason--that's what we are doing in this book.

[508] There are distinctions relating to culpability for evil actions that must be made; we will do this in Chapter 9.

[509] This was done during the testing of the first atomic bombs. It is a case of not being careful enough and not knowing what you're doing before you do it.

However, some evils cannot be explained by man's inhumanity (intentional or otherwise) to man. The apparent evil in physical nature, such as the apparent non-optimum nature of the genetic code and the non-optimal position of the optic nerve in the eye[510] may turn out to be just our lack of knowledge of the overall scheme of how everything works together. However, when a child is born blind or lame, or when a young woman gets cancer and dies a painful death in the prime of her life, it seems these cannot be explained by moral evil, that is, by the evil actions of men. How do we explain them? Before answering, we should emphasize that we are not abrogating material causality or empiriological laws. DNA errors, for example, are still the proximate cause of genetic diseases. We are only asking how the DNA errors came about; that is, what is the reason that the DNA is not the way it should be?

It *seems*[511] we have no choice but to hypothesize the existence of other intelligent beings (who will thus have a free will) at work. Recall from the end of Chapter 5 that angels are such beings. They are immaterial beings. Further, note that the order in the universe is enhanced by the presence of a diverse array of

---

[510] The position of the optic nerve causes a blind spot in the eye.

[511] The introduction of free will helps us understand the order God has put in the world, but does not give us the total view of why or how He causes what He does (and He causes **all, including** *free will*). When I was an undergrad at MIT, my history class on the Middle Ages discussed (very briefly) St. Thomas. We talked about St. Thomas's answer (the short form, cf. his *De Malo* for the book-length answer) to the problem of evil: i.e., God allows evil so that good may come of it. The professor, who was in general very good, told us at that point to stop and consider the complete folly of such a thought. It was part of our natural (*not* planned) indoctrination into the culture of the university. As we've said, every cult (the center of a culture) implicitly or explicitly teaches a worldview or belief system. The truer such a system is, the more facility and success one will have in reaching truth. In this class situation, what the cult taught was completely wrong. For as we've seen, evil is not a being, but a privation of being. So when a being X is lacking something it needs, it's only because God, who owes it to Himself to give X something, does not. This He does for a reason that in the case of material being is for the good of some super-ordinate being and in the case of an intellectual being for X's own good. In any case, all goodness comes from Pure Goodness, and the finite creature that only participates in that goodness should not expect to be able to see the totality of that infinite Goodness. In metaphor, sometimes a master sculptor will chisel off a piece of marble that an apprentice cringes at the loss of.

beings, from quarks and electrons to amoebae to insects to worms to geese to bears to man. It certainly is reasonable to think God has chosen to create the full chain of beings possible to this universe. For any such beings to be part of the universe, part of the being, the unity of the universe, they must then have an intrinsic role in it. We thus hypothesize that they are given the role of orchestrating the various general actions of God discussed in the last chapter in the evolution section, specifically the second general action of God directing evolution.[512] How does this help our problem of evil?

Angels have free will and so can obviously, like us, turn against the created order (and thus against God).[513] Hence, we further postulate that some of the angels are in the state of deliberately turning against the created order. Thus, they are responsible, in this hypothesis, for the evil in the world not explainable by human evil actions. We therefore have a plausible argument for the existence of angels, but not a proof.

The question of moral evil raises a question for us: "What should we do with our knowledge?" This brings us to "truth in action," the second of the three categories of science (pure sciences, *applied sciences,* and methodological sciences) shown in figure 6-2 (Chapter 6). To make use of what we have learned up to this point, we must study the science of moral philosophy, even if ever so briefly. We will then be able to turn to the question that will culminate our explorations: "How then should we do science?"

Before turning to action, note that the above proofs of the existence of God can only be rejected in one way, by rejecting reason itself. Follow them carefully, for they have much depth and much food for thought that can lead to more depth. As Jacques Maritain says, quoting the renowned philosopher, Garrigou-

---

[512] Of course, their direction is confined to limits so as to be acting through the material order, not violating it, and hence this will not upset the overall order of things, just displace it somewhat. We've seen in the last chapter that such actions will be manifest in the empiriological as chance.

[513] Unlike creatures like us who live in time--we are amphibians (immaterial substances that are forms of bodies (material being))--angels are purely immaterial. Thus, they are not subject to change and thus make one clear decision at the moment of their creation that eternally sets the direction of their will.

Lagrange, "The mind has no other choice than between the alternatives: 'the true God or radical irrationality.'"[514] The history of philosophy is one long testimony to this fact.[515]

---

[514] From *An Introduction to Philosophy* by Jacques Maritain, where he is quoting Garrigou-Lagrange in *Dieu, Son Existence, Sa Nature*, Paris, 3rd ed., 1920.
[515] Again, see *The Unity of Philosophical Experience* by Etienne Gilson.

Chapter 9

A Mathematical Morality?

The applied science of ethics, also known as morality, is at issue now. What should I do, what ought I do? Many say, "There is no absolute answer; all things are relative; indeed, no one should impose his morality on another." Few professional journals print such explicit comments on this subject, but they are commonplace beliefs often stated in various ways. Indeed, many academics accept them implicitly and explicitly. Nobel laureate Steven Weinberg, for example, when asked about ethics (morality), said that it is unlike science in that there is no way to determine what is morally right.[516] He said the best one can do is to try to find and surround oneself with like-minded people. And again, a friend and academic colleague of mine from the humanities said once that one couldn't just live by the truth, because reality is too complicated. This reasoning, according to him, justifies performing public actions with which one privately does not hold.

Moral relativism has not always been so blithely accepted. Even relatively recently this was not the case. In 1963, another Nobel laureate, Richard Feynman, said that he thinks all can agree on practical morality.[517] He wanted, in parallel to modern physics (empiriological science), to have a science of the externals of

---

[516] CNN interview (1/23/02).
[517] *The Meaning of It All: Thoughts of a Citizen-Scientist* by Richard Feynman, published from lectures given in April, 1963, by Perseus Books.

morality, one's actions. He thought all reasonable people pretty much agreed on the basics of morality at that level. He says:

> *But my atheistic scientific colleagues, which does not include all scientists--I cannot tell by their behavior, because of course I am on the same side, that they are particularly different from the religious ones, and it seems that their moral feelings and their understandings of other people and their humanity and so on apply to the believers as well as the disbelievers. [sic] It seems to me that there is a kind of independence between the ethical and moral views and the theory of the machinery of the universe. Science makes, indeed, an impact on many ideas associated with religion, but I do not believe it affects, in any very strong way, the moral conduct and ethical views.*[518]

He also discusses how science students who stop believing in God maintain their moral principles nearly unchanged.[519]

---

[518] See pages 40-41 of *The Meaning of It All: Thoughts of Citizen-Scientist,* 1963. Feynman at one point implies that God and man and good and evil are too small! Apparently, he had little understanding of what these words signify.

[519] He (Feynman) claims, in a very roundabout way, that the loss of belief in God happens because of their unique education. He says they are taught to doubt, and he implies that the science they learn is not amenable to belief in God. The first of these statements has some merit, because science teaches one the importance of respecting facts, not opinion, and critically analyzing data. However, the age of the college students is *also* the natural age for questioning. Further, questioning--serious questioning--as we've seen in this book, was done long before modern science. Further, as we can appreciate by our philosophical background, the apparent disagreement between modern science and philosophy (i.e., what Feynman in broad strokes calls religion; in his use of the word "religion," he includes conclusions reachable by natural philosophy alone) is largely an artifact of what is taught and how. In general, he tacitly assumes that the prevalent thinking of science students in our schools (in particular our technical schools) is a natural result of *learning science.*

There appears to be an element of disingenuousness here, one that has built up, no doubt, over years of living with the status quo. Specifically, he neglects to bring up what is not taught. What is omitted is just as important as what is taught. The budding scientist is not taught to properly place his new particular knowledge in the whole of his knowledge. Further, the school environment is solely focused on the narrowly empiriometric in its daily activities and studies. No institutional time is spent inculcating prayer or religion

He sees "possibly of a new future where we forget, perhaps, about the theories of why we believe things as long we ultimately in the end, as far as action is concerned, believe the same thing."[520]

What are we to make of this? Are morals completely relative or are they accessible by empiriological methodology or in another way?

Moral Relativism

To answer, let's examine the statement at the beginning of this chapter: "All things are relative; indeed, no one should impose his morality on another," for this is the main manifesto of moral relativism in daily life. More accurately said: many believers in moral relativism, as well as unbelievers, take this statement as the fundamental "self-evident" starting point of moral relativism. Now, moral relativists by definition think that there are no morals that are universally true for everyone. After all, is this not what someone means when he says, "One should not impose one's morals on another?" More sharply, it means that there is no reason that would give one the right to tell me I am doing wrong.

In fact, this is clearly self-contradictory. It is saying, one *should not* say, *"should not."* The very fact that one is telling someone he "should not" means that he is imposing a moral view as if it were an absolute to be obeyed. It is an outright contradictory statement. This is significant because one is left with two alternatives: either there is no way to tell others that they misbehave--including forbidding them from passing judgments--or one must admit moral law of some type. In either case, one *no longer* has the "No one has the right to tell me I am wrong in what I do" argument. Again, there is no such thing as half of a principle.

---

on campus. Much time is spent inculcating a discipline of doing calculations, as if these two things are necessarily lived in two different worlds. One gets reinforcement for conforming to this behavior pattern and mild disapproval (as if it's a waste of time) for the other. This is what is disingenuous. He does not point out that the school acts and thinks as if God-- no even more, as nearly all outside the empiriometric (or empiriological) and its applications-- is unimportant. Is it a surprise that those that come out think that they are unimportant?

[520] Page 122, *The Meaning of It All.*

Once we've shown the above is a contradiction, there is no longer an option to use it.

So, is there absolute morality or not? Is morality purely relative? Though many will *tell* you they think so, I've never met anyone *who acts as if they think so.* If those supposed moral relativists[521] were charged double price in the grocery store because they were moral relativists, they would proclaim, with the greater mass of men, "That's unfair!" Can anyone imagine an editor professing, in his journal's rules for its authors, that there is no ethical duty to print the articles in the way their authors intended them, that he had the right to freely change their content? Or, again, can anyone imagine a "relativist" not raging against the evil of the criminal who steals his car from the office parking lot, or, God forbid, against the man who kidnaps his child? Moreover, most of that same group would express regret if they had it in their power to stop one of these actions and did not. Indeed, all spontaneously recognize some moral rights and duties.

In the larger realm, how does a moral relativist organize society? If he says nothing binds one's conscience, then he can only control by force. One can say all kinds of things to cloud the central issue; in the end, either one obeys a moral law or any law for an internal reason or an external reason. Leaving behind the internal leaves "might makes right" as the only way to maintain order.

All of this shows, in an indirect and inchoate way, how repugnant to reason it is to suppose that there is no moral law. There seems to be a moral base or foundation; is there indeed one, and what is it?

Empiriological Morality

Kant says there is. However, since, as we've seen, he has inadvertently locked himself in his head by his philosophical

---

[521] We hardly need to recall that Einstein's relativity theory is an empiriometric theory that, as such, does not address the full reality, but only the reality as quantitative. Yet, even from that point of view, its dependence on absolutes of a different sort (such as its invariant equations and the invariance of the speed of light) makes it of no real use to moral relativists, even as a metaphor.

idealism,[522] it will be no surprise that he bases his moral system on ideas, not on reality. In the end, as with the empiriometric system (Newtonian physics) that he tried to justify with his philosophy, one is only left with logic as a rule.[523] Logic of itself is content-less.[524] So, in this view, one can invent whatever moral system he wants as long as it is self-consistent.[525] Thus, Kant's philosophy has set the framework in which moral relativism operates to the degree it does.

Feynman's solution cannot succeed either. Recall that anything treated empiriologically leaves out the large parts of reality. The empiriological approach implicitly presupposes the overarching science of which it is a tool; for example, empiriometric science is part of the science of *physica* (wide sense). In the same way an overarching science of ethics is needed if one establishes an empiriological science of morality. Otherwise it has no grounding in the real, but only a sort of metaphor (beings of reason or models) of the real. What's more, in physics one studies material being whose first accident is quantity (extension—parts outside of each other). Hence, we expect the empiriometric, which is formally mathematical (study of universal quantity), to be of essential value. Now, morality, as we'll soon recognize, is a science of the immaterial realm. As we've seen, material things, even the least substances among them are more than pure quantity; how much more will this be true of the immaterial realm? Remember, immaterial means, among other things, "lacks extension." Hence, to attempt to understand something immaterial by means of pure quantitative modes of explanation is to ask for something to be explained in terms that don't relate directly to it.[526]

---

[522] See Chapter 4.

[523] Kant himself tried to assert a categorical imperative that would make man the end of all morality; of course, like all things that *begin* and end in one's head, their reality can not be affirmed.

[524] For example, I can say, "When X and Y are true, if X then Y is true" and still have said nothing about reality.

[525] As seen in Chapter 4, Gödel's theorem, of course, prevents one from ever knowing this within the system you create.

[526] Of course, even in the immaterial realm number applies; for example, I can specify the number of ideas that were brought up in a given conversation. Still, it

How does all this resolve itself in the practical realm? That is, what happens if we try to find a morality based on an empiriological science? Take an example. Say you, in trying to decide a moral question by empiriological means, do a careful study of the number of people who get murdered and the number of jobs that are available. You find a very high correlation between an increase in the number of murders and a drop in jobs available. Well, first, whether a correlation is real or not is itself a question of probability, not certainty. Second, given the correlation, it does not imply a direct causal connection. Third, assuming that you somehow convince yourself that there is a direct causal connection, how does one go from that fact to what one should do and not do? It cannot be done without **non-**empiriological input. One must first decide what is good and evil and, in this barren land of beings of reason (where either one is just as well taken as the negative of the other), even which he should do. If one uses an idea of efficiency or maximizing (empiriometric and practical) scientific benefit (such as J. Bronowski appears to want),[527] this becomes one's idea of good.

---

is clear that the number (quantity) of ideas I had, for example, is bound to be of minimal use in understanding ideas and the intellect.

[527] Bronowski, in *Science and Human Values* (Harper and Roe, 1965), tries to unwind the split that C.P. Snow talks about in his two cultures. He unfortunately goes astray because he tries to make modern specialized science the first science. He tries to build everything around it. He lumps all things into the same category of "science" (knowledge), which in itself is correct. However, his definition of "science" or knowledge is a very narrow (narrower than even the modern sciences that he starts with) but common one. He defines science as "the organization of our knowledge in such a way that it commands more of the hidden potential of nature. ...It admits no boundaries between use and knowledge" (cf. p. 7). In so doing, he leaves out much; for example, if we find that gravity waves have no application, are they not still objects worthy of knowledge? Or, if we cannot manipulate God, does that mean He's not worth knowing? More to our point, "How should we use things," (that is, what do we do with these things we get and why), is not in the category of things "useful," in his sense. One can always give an extended meaning to the word "usefulness," but he obviously means technological advances when he says useful in this way, which he has assumed (chosen) implicitly but never justified. In his respect for technology and the implicitness of his assumption, he is fairly representing a portion of our present cultural milieu. In the end, he, following the same pattern as Kant, gives us a categorical imperative based on his belief in modern science.

Why pick this one? And what is this idea of good and what does it have to do with morality? It is, in fact, a pick-your-own system, like Kant's is in the end;[528] we'll discuss this more later. None of this by itself brings us any closer to morality. So, we return to our question: Is ethics a real science?[529]

The Foundation of Morality

Finally, the answer: yes, there are indeed moral absolutes, and they are founded on reality and can be studied and understood, giving real knowledge of how we should behave. Let's start with first things first. We first know things; so we start with them and expand on what we've learned about good and evil. In short, we must return to the transcendental, good, to understand what morality is. Now, good is, in turn, related to order and final causality.

Order and Good

Start again from our perception of change, which is evident to all. Recall that change is the process of reduction of potentiality to act; an agent in act brings a patient in potentiality to the state of act. Potentiality only means something to the extent that it is referenced to something that actually is. Hydrogen and oxygen gas, as mentioned in the last chapter, are only potentially able to become water because the potentiality is ordered towards this

His system, being fundamentally Kantian, fails for the same reason. If one starts in one's head, there is no way back to reality. We must put first things first.

[528] To his credit Kant recognizes that people should not be treated as a means, but having locked the thing-in-itself (the real world) outside of his mind, he can never really justify or give content to this duty.

[529] St. Thomas gives the following order for studying the various sciences. He says, "So the proper order of learning will be the following. First, boys should be instructed in logical maters, because logic teaches the method of the whole of philosophy. Second, they are to be instructed in mathematics, which does not require experience and does not transcend the imagination. Third, they should be trained in the natural sciences which, though not transcending sense and imagination, nevertheless require experience. Fourth, they are to be instructed in the moral sciences, which require experience and a soul free from passion, as is said in the first book. Fifth, they should be taught matters concerning wisdom and divine science, which go beyond the imagination and require a vigorous mind. (St. Thomas in VI *Ethics* lect. 7.)

happening every time.[530] We describe such things in empiriometric terms by explaining that the fields act in *specific* predetermined (i.e., preordered, or preordained) ways on bodies such as electrons. Hence, as we've said multiple times, ordination implies foreordination. Or said another way, *every agent[531] acts toward an end.* As St. Thomas says "if the agent were not determinate to some particular effect, it would not do one thing rather than another; consequently in order that it produce a determinate effect, it must, of necessity, be determined to some certain one, which has the nature of an end."[532]

Now, look at our own human nature. We know it intimately, from the inside and we've discussed it in some detail. We know we are rational animals. Man is material being with nutritive, sensorial, and intellectual powers. With any kind of knowledge comes an appetitive power. The appetitive power of the intellect is called the will. When we judge something good to be good for us, we are attracted to it.

Now, all things are good insofar as they are. Evil, we saw in the last chapter, is the privation, it is the absence of some good that a thing should have for its proper operation. Now, we can say ontologically all things have a natural "appetite" for their completion, for their good. They strive for them or "love" them. Why so? At the inanimate level, an agent (insofar as it is agent) is oriented towards the completion of the potentiality in another. "Appetite" and "love" are used analogically here, for their use obviously does not imply that the inanimate things actually have a will, a volition in the matter. But the usage is not merely metaphorical. If one thing constantly acts to move toward something, there is an ontological predetermination between them.

Now, *good cannot be defined,* for as we've emphasized, the primary things are just seen, not defined. They are the things

---

[530] In the material world, substances act on each other, but this does not in any way change our argument. Take another example. Sugar and water have certain actualities and potentialities such that when they are combined, below a certain ratio, the sugar is completely dissolved in water. This, like mixing hydrogen and oxygen and our example of the rock throwing in the last chapter, will always happen, given the same circumstances.

[531] Insofar as it is an agent.

[532] *Summa Theologica*, Pt. I-II, Q 1, Art. 2

through which we define other things.[533] Yet, we can describe them. In the *pointing to* and *descriptive* sense, good is--in a broad analogical sense--the "desirability" of a thing. It increases in its amplitude, in its meaning, as we ascend the scale of being, for good is being under the aspect of desirability. At a low level of being, hydrogen and oxygen "tend" toward, are attracted toward,[534] the perfection (good) called water. [535]   A good of plants is to assimilate chemicals into their leaves and stem, thereby completing in some ways the potentiality in those substances, in their substance. In this analogical sense, every created thing acts both to perfect itself and to perfect another. Of course, we must say again, this only applies to real being. So, one cannot apply it to the evil that we find in the world, for evil is lack of being. Only what is, is good. The more it is, the better it is.

Hence, we can reformulate the principle of finality, as all things exist for themselves in operation, to overflow themselves by action.[536] Or again, using a phrase of Maritain, *every being is love of a good and this is the ground of its action.*[537] Hence, we have further cleared the view to the transcendental that we call "good" and revealed its multi-layered, polyvalent and analogical character. Now, we are ready to formulate our moral principles.

The First Principles of Morality

We see that man's will seeks the good. Hence, we can immediately enunciate the first principle of ethics. One should:

Do Good and Avoid Evil

Once we know what good is, this principle is self-evident. It cannot be denied. Bring this point home. The good is the end for which an intelligent agent *should* act. Now consider that an agent

---

[533] See also Chapter 4.
[534] In the modern (empiriometric) physics, we borrow the language of human attraction (and repulsion) to describe the action of the electric field. So, even there, we glimpse this analogical nature of the good.
[535] Of course, conditions must be made right for this to happen.
[536] In God, the action of the agent does not differ from agent, but they do in all created things.
[537] Page 110 of *A Preface to Metaphysics*.

that acts with evil as its end acts towards no end at all, for recall: evil is the absence of something. What acts towards *no* end, acts not at all; that is, there is no action, no "do", to do. This clearly absurd conclusion is the result of denying the above first principle of morality. But, how can this be, since men do evil all the time? Are we really saying it is impossible for us to do evil? *No.* We are saying what we choose to do must, at least, have the appearance of good to us. If it is a *real* good we've chosen, it increases our being; while if it is not, it contracts being (increases disorder). How the latter affects *us* is complex and we'll come back to it. Some distinctions need to be made to elucidate these important issues.

Think about what moral action is. Moral action takes place in two realms. Its primary (formal) sphere of action is internal, in the intellect together with the will of the individual man, that is, in the chief power of his immaterial substantial form. Its secondary (material) sphere of action is external, whereby the man acts out what he decides, brings into existence what he wills to happen. When he *thinks* that something is good for him, he is attracted by it. It has the aspect of good. He concludes the action is a good. The action that he has judged to be good for him is a predicate waiting for a subject to do it.[538] We can therefore rephrase the first moral principle as: the morally good (what you should do) is that which is really good for you. In this form, one can see it is self-evident because what is good for you implicitly contains the subject "what I should do."

Now, I only come to know what is good for me by the action of my intellect.[539] Hence, since we are not infallible, we can be mistaken about what is good for us; we can choose something that is only apparently good, but in actuality is not. In this case, *to the degree* that the error is not really our own,[540] what we do is morally (internally) good, but externally evil.

---

[538] St. Thomas says self-evident propositions that get their self-evidence by the predicate implicitly containing the subject rather than vice-versa are true by the second mode of being per se, or the second mode of perseity.

[539] That act consists of multiple steps: 1) the abstraction of ideas from phantasms, 2) acts of judgment whereby I realize X is Y, and 3) the act of reasoning whereby I draw conclusions from multiple judgments.

[540] In reality, the situation is complicated. We will discuss later in this chapter how one can intentionally (and thus with full responsibility) habituate oneself to

For example, if I come to think, after much experience, that pushing a button *only* dispenses stamps, then I am *not* morally responsible if I later find that pushing this button also causes the release of toxic material that causes cancer to the repairman who maintains the machine. My actions were morally good, but an external result was not.

One can also do deliberate evil. This, of course, is a manner of speaking; what we mean is that we can choose a good despite the evil it brings (or demands) with it. For example, we may know that stealing something from a store is wrong, but want the benefit of that item, and so choose to do it anyway. In this case, as in every deliberate choice for evil, we deaden our reason so that we may do what we please, and an element of deliberate irrationalism enters. We always do evil under the auspices and attraction of the good. Even the man who commits suicide illustrates the principle, because he *thinks* and then *decides* it is good for him to be released from life. This does not make it any less evil, it only manifests the inherent nature of the appetitive power associated with the intellect, called the will.

One cannot deny the first principle of morality: do good, avoid evil. The rule of reason, in turn, is how we determine what is good for us.[541] This special application of our mind, "the mind of man as it makes moral judgments" is given the name "conscience." It literally means "with knowledge" (Latin *con scientia*).

What Is Good for Us?

Every act we do involves *ontological* good. We must work with real things, real being. When we do evil or good, it involves

---

doing certain evils and thus become numb, even virtually unaware of their evil nature.
[541] Because of this, the moral laws are, in principle, accessible to all. However, of course cultural as well as material conditions can make some of the finer points hard or impossible to reach and some of the big ones harder to see. However, one does not necessarily expect to see recognition of even the big moral points such as not killing the innocent manifested in every culture, because choosing evil as a means to something a culture wants is always an available choice. In other words, because someone does evil does not mean he does not know it is evil.

being. But what specifies what is good for us? Reality does, both our human nature and all of being. We should conform ourselves to reality; in the process we do not lose ourselves but find ourselves. We see again that morality is living the truth.

To provide appropriate images of what we mean,[542] consider two related metaphors. The world is like a tuning fork; if we sing the right notes, it will sing with us. It will resonate with us. Or again, given a music score, words, and a chorus of people, one can sing according to the score and words along with the chorus, thereby increasing the harmony; one can also act against them and decrease the harmony. The metaphor limps severely because these situations implicitly imply that one can go somewhere else and do something else or do nothing at all. The situation is infinitely more profound in our moral life. Our moral life involves not some part of reality or some part of ourselves; it involves our whole self, acting in the whole of reality open to us.[543] We either choose to use our reason to act in accord with reality or against it.[544] Moral evil, like all evil, is then inscrutable because it is, in the end, irrationality. Recall, physical evil like that found in the animal kingdom can be shown to be good relative to a higher plane. Moral evil however is *not* a disorder that is a good relative[545] to a larger *created* order.[546]

---

[542] Recall, by nature our human intellect associates images with what we think and vice-versa. In topics such as morality, the images should be dropped as the focus of our attention as soon as they have done their job of aiding us in understanding the thing in question.

[543] Because what is good for us is that we act in a way fitting to our place in the created order, the rules that arise from such consideration is often called the natural law.

[544] Note, not acting also constitutes a moral choice that either works along with or against the truth of acting things. If I am witness to a robbery, for example, my not telling what I saw could lead to further loss of property by others, in which case I have then contributed to it (though indirectly) by my silence.

[545] By contrast, in Chapter 8, we discussed how physical evil is relative in this sense.

[546] It is only resolved in Being Himself. Moral evil is where the absolute need for revelation and help from God hits us hardest. We ask, why does this happen to my children, my family? Why does this evil happen to that innocent person? Even more, we each ask, what about the evil I have done, what is to be done about it? We feel these questions in the deepest part of our being. These cannot

The Big Picture

To further probe the nature of what's good for us, note that there are accidental goods and substantial goods in direct analogy to accidents that inhere in substances. An accidental good is one that is used to get one to a substantial good. Let's call it a useful good; it is like a rest stop on our way to our destination for the day. There must be a substantial good, things that are ends of moral actions in themselves, because otherwise there would be no bottom, no reason why we did a particular series of acts.[547]

Before we explore these types of goods, there is one more to mention. Although there are terminating points called substantial goods for our useful actions, there must be an end for which we order these individual goals; otherwise they will have no foundation. We saw in the last chapter that proceeding to infinity in this type of series only infinitely pushes off the answer. We know by that same chapter that all these goods must be ordered to Goodness itself. In short, like all of creation, we are ordered to God. He is our ultimate end. We should avoid an easy-to-jump-to mental picture. We might tend to picture God as a human being like us, seeking our attention: in other words, as selfish. Recall, God has no lack, no needs; He acts only as pure goodness, out of generosity. St. Thomas summarizes it in his usual penetrating way: "God seeks His glory not for His own sake but for ours." (*Summa Theologica* II-II 132, I, ad I.)

The Specific Goods

What specifically is morally good for me? By now, it should be clear that, while everything is good (insofar as it *is*), everything is not morally good. Cyanide is ontologically good, but it is not good for me to eat it. The order of moral goodness is a subset of the whole of ontological goodness. Now, to discuss the

---

be answered in the created order, and so we have no access to them except what God chooses to tell (reveal to) us.

[547] This argument applies also, of course, to the existence of substances.

specifics, we must identify the specific needs (as opposed to wants) we have. We have two sets of needs, one of body and one of soul (our immaterial substantial form).

Our body, which includes nutritive and sensorial powers, needs food, air, the right temperature range, and like things. Without these we will die. Our sensorial powers need exposure to things so that, through them, we may gain in that type of knowledge. There are other physical desires, such as sexual pleasure, that are not needs in an absolute sense for the individual, but only relative to some greater setting such as that of the family. Now, turn to the immaterial aspect of man. The needs of the soul are for truth and love, which are for intellect and will respectively. We saw in Chapter 5 that for all these different aspects to work together, for them to be the unity that they are, there must be an order. Among them, we saw that intellect was first, then sensorial and nutritive powers respectively. These then are the order in which we must keep them if we are to do good to ourselves. We also saw in Chapter 5 that to the degree which these powers are in order, that is the degree in which they are one; that is the degree to which we "are." Increasing the disorder among these powers diminishes our being.

Once we see this fact, we see clearly that when we act like animals, ignoring the needs of the intellect, we diminish ourselves, no matter what rationalization we might use to justify it. This is not to say that we should not enjoy sensorial pleasure of eating or any sensorial pleasure (for they, in themselves, like all things are good), but that they should be directed by reason, and that means kept in right order.

So, what should we do? To really get to the details, let's subject the Ten Commandments to the scrutiny of reason. Although our culture received them through a single group, the Jewish people, we'll see they have the universality of all true morality. Note that we are not introducing religion here, only making use of a culturally available reference point. We (Americans) have incorporated all of them in civil law and practice to one degree or another. We will only cover them in a generic way appropriate to our modern science theme. They, like all such principles, have the character of a "command," because once the principle is understood, it comes implicitly with an "I ought to do this." Because of its implicit command character, we often call such principles "duties." The first three of these are about our duty to God and the last seven are about our duty to our fellow man. Take the latter first.

Our duty to our fellow man stems from his nature. Any needs that we have, he will obviously have as well, because, by "fellow man," we simply mean one who shares our human nature. In sharing our nature, he shares our dignity. We know that our dignity, in turn, comes from our having an intellect and a will. This fact (cf. Chapters 4 and 5) means that we have an immortal substantial form that was created directly by God, which again manifests man's dignity. Our intelligence is a shadow of Pure Intellection. Hence, we say human beings are made in the image of God, and this gives us a value infinitely above all the things of the material realm put together, including the highest *non*-rational animals. Man can contain all these in his mind.[548] The golden rule: "Do unto others as you would have them do unto you" is an expression of the truth of our common human nature.

What does it entail? It obviously reinforces the truth that we must value ourselves. What more? Many things. For example, taking one of the commandments, we must not steal from our fellow man. Why? Because their dignity requires their needs be respected, and one of their needs is to have control over some part of the world, so that they may be true actors in the world, utilizing their freedom for good. Without some number of things that are one's own, one's freedom would be reduced to a practical non-reality. Anytime someone tried to do something, someone else could take the necessary instruments away and do it or not do it the way he wanted to.[549] We obviously have this need for personal property, and therefore this order belongs to the world as made; and thus, if I do not respect it, I--in the end--am trying to take a place in the world that is not my own. I am trying to fit a square peg in a round hole. Or, to use our metaphor above, I am trying to sing a different tune than is on the program. Hence, one should not

---

[548] Of course, if we were to encounter other races with intellects, the same reasoning would require us to treat them, respecting their character, as made in the image of God in the above sense.

[549] We would be returning to the "might makes right" theme discussed earlier.

steal. A civilized culture, therefore, will have laws against stealing, whose force will ultimately come not from the penalty,[550] but from the moral duty inherent in this principle that all rational men will be able to understand and feel the force of.

Similarly, even more forcefully, we can feel and see the truth of the command or duty that one should not kill an innocent person. Since each individual is created directly by God, only God has sovereignty over an innocent man's life. One can understand that a man might lose his right to bodily life, say by brutally killing and torturing many innocent people with no willingness to stop. Or again, say he attacks an innocent child on the side of the road, and the only way to stop him from killing her is to kill him. By sharp contrast, killing a man who has committed no such offense is equivalent to trying to usurp God's sovereignty.[551] Why? Such a man has the same essential status with respect to the moral realm that he had at the moment of the creation of his soul by God. Thus, in deliberately killing an innocent man, one is attacking the state that the man was in as he came from the hand of God. The offender is trying to undo the decision of God to create that man. In other words, he is attacking the order of the universe at its core through his attack on the intrinsic dignity of the man. Such a state clearly puts one at odds with the Ultimate Good, which can only lead to one's unhappiness.

There are many more moral laws, general principles that should guide our actions. There are some for every sphere of life. Some of these, like sexual moral principles are extremely important, but this arena and others will take us off our course, which is to understand the generals of moral philosophy with an eye toward how we should do science. We will thus cover only one more command with respect to our fellow man. This last duty is especially relevant to our problem because it contains, in a way, all the other moral principles.

---

[550] Though the penalty and threat of penalty will help those who choose not to obey to change, and those who would otherwise not think seriously about fixing their moral compass to do so.

[551] Of course, one cannot *in the end* do this, but he can make the choice at that moment that goes against it.

"Thou shall not bear false witness," implies a broad prohibition against lying. It is about our need for truth. The command is couched in terms that make clear the reason why truth is so important to us. Because man's chief power is his intellect, his most important need is the need for truth. If someone lies about you in public or court, the effect on you will clearly be evil. More broadly, anything that is told you wrong about anything will end in mistaken steps. Every thing we do depends on having correct knowledge; those who lie to us deliberately put us on the trail away from our own end. Truth is essential for us; an intellect only exists to understand. In short, we are made for truth. While bodily integrity and the like are necessary for our ability to find truth, integrity in our chief power (the intellect) is what makes our bodily integrity mean something. Indeed, bodily integrity without intellectual (moral) integrity puts us lower than the animals, because we are by nature above them, yet, in such a state, we act as them. No, it's worse than that; we can use our minds to deliberately act against the created order, but they cannot. The more ontologically good something is, the more evil it can be; only order is subject to disorder, so with more order (unity or good) comes the possibility of more disorder (evil).

This leads us naturally back to our duty to God, for we've seen God is Truth Himself. Before we speak of this primary obligation, we should note that everything we do is either good or evil. Though many things are morally neutral in themselves, each of our free acts, insofar as they are such, are either moral or immoral. They are either consistent with the reality of our nature and our place in the created order or not. Most of those daily choices are of the minor variety, but these are the stuff out of which our lives are made. All the little acts of our life contribute to those few big acts at the moment of decision for those acts.

A serious question arises: How can we possibly, at each moment of our lives, be thinking about these and all principles? We are not angels and thus we don't have effortless views of the truth. We have to work to get to truth by hard reasoning and careful observation. How can we possibly live up to the moral law that will give us the good we seek? Before we answer, note the problem is further compounded by another fact.

We are meant to act to seek the good, the right order of things, yet we all are, to a serious degree, lacking in this order ourselves. We have some level of disorder in our structure right from the start; we are born with it.[552] A child does not naturally want to listen to his parents, despite repeated experience with severe harm that he may undergo in not listening. You tell him not to climb onto the countertop and you even stop him multiple times. You explain that he will get hurt. He's seen you were right nearly every other time. He's fallen off of other things and been hurt. Yet, he does not listen and he falls and needs stitches. We see the disorder in ourselves, and even more clearly in others.[553] It is apparent that we all have a sort of inclination to disorder.[554]

So, how can we cope with so many small decisions with such a damaged nature? The answer is known by all through experience. We develop habits. Such habits of action come in two categories: voluntary and involuntary. Now, the involuntary ones are part of our sensorial and nutritive natures; when in proper order, these involuntary actions are at the service of the voluntary ones through our actions. The pumping of blood and breathing of air, for example, serve the bodily life so that we can do the actions we choose. More importantly for us, the subconscious is formed or deformed by our voluntary action. Scientists become accustomed to how to solve experimental and/or theoretical problems; it becomes *second* nature. Liars become good at lying; it takes no effort for them to become convincing. If they ever want to change and become truthful, they will have to undue a natural tendency to tell a lie to get what they want; it will not be easy. Similarly, with our somewhat disordered nature, it takes effort to establish habits to counter that inclination. The coach's saying, "no pain, no gain" is applicable here. Each person knows that in his own field that

---

[552] What the source of this disorder is in detail can only be answered by revelation from God.

[553] Again, something is not quite right in us, for where disorder should be easiest to see, that is in the most accessible spot, ourselves, we don't see it. That is, in the thing we have the most intimate experience with in this world, which is ourselves, we often miss a disorder that we spot with ease in another whom we barely know.

[554] This disordered inclination "that is in our bones" is called by Christians "original sin."

understanding and facility, to the degree they come, come only with practice and experience. In short, it is through habitually forming our little decisions by discipline that we build the character, the order in our nature, to make the decisions that will make us happy.

Habits (or, more accurately skills) that help one live a good life are called virtues. There are four cardinal habits or virtues: prudence, justice, fortitude, and temperance. One habit is for each power in the soul. Prudence is the virtue that regulates our actions in the mind when we are thinking about what we should do, and justice is for the will. The last two of the four virtues are habits that aid us in right use of our emotions. Fortitude or courage is to order our emergency emotions or those emotions, such as anger or fear, that push us toward action in response to approaching danger. Temperance regulates our emotions that attract us toward simple goods, like the hunger we feel when we have not eaten all day, and smell the freshly roasted Thanksgiving turkey coming out of the oven.

The degree to which my involuntary actions are in right order under the voluntary ones together with the degree that my voluntary actions follow right reason is a measure of my integrity, the degree to which I am one, a unity, and hence (by the convertibility of unity and being), the more "I" there is. Furthermore, in Chapter 5, we mentioned that man's chief power is his intellectual power (including the appetitive power of the will), but one might have wondered how the various powers were ordered with respect to each other. Now we know. The virtues, the second nature, is what establishes the order, the ordination, and hence the subordination, and finally therefore, the degree of being.

Right Desire

The virtues are extremely important. By them we order ourselves, including our passions. Ordering our passions *does not mean* suppressing them or using them sparingly or at low intensity; it means *not* using them *inordinately*, out of order. The image of a train depicted in Figure 9-1 may be helpful in understanding the proper order.

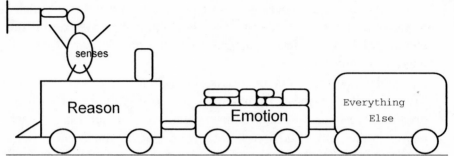

Figure 9-1: The train metaphor helps place the proper role of our various powers. Everything comes through the senses, from which our intellect spontaneously apprehends, through abstraction, simple essences in the world. Judgements are then made, which are analyzed by reason, resulting in further understanding, which in turn leads the emotions to respond in accordance with the understanding reached. If, for example, the conclusion is that something will be dangerous, fear or anger will arise moving one to flee or fight respectively.

Desire is the fuel of the engine of our actions,[555] which are directed by reason; the intellect, in turn, gets its input from the senses. Living a good life leads to right desire, desire that is in tune with our own best interest. The more our desire is what it should be when it should be, the less work we have to do to respond to average daily events. Despite its importance, "right desire" is seldom discussed. Why? Part of the reason is the abandonment of reason and hence the concept of "right" or "order" connected with desire. However, more hidden and in many ways insidious, because it is partly responsible for the former, is the implicit belief that passions are bad when connected with intellectual work. Like all such errors, it is only their element of truth that powers them; the element of truth in this error is that *inordinate* (again, it does not mean "intense") emotions do cloud reason both in oneself and in others. This is especially true of anger. Furthermore, emotions, especially anger, tend to cause an intensity that wears one out. What then is the error? The error consists in thinking that because inordinate emotions cloud reason and wear one out, they, especially anger, have no place. Of course, in true intellectual work, it is the proper expression of these emotions, not the

---

[555] In the metaphor, *right* desire can be thought of as choosing to stay on the tracks.

elimination of them, that is important. The proper balance is needed. Of course, emotions should not, in most cases, have the intensity of expression in intellectual work that they would in other places, yet even when not as intense, they should be there in such a way as to order one to the task at hand and to one's final end.[556]

Because of the prevalent implicit thinking that leaves emotions out completely, a two-fold problem results in our culture. First, many conclude that he who appears the most devoid of emotions is the most intelligent, knowledgeable, and wise. Second, one who is *not* integrating his emotions correctly in one portion of his life will develop habits that lead to *inordinate* use in *other* parts as well. As Aristotle said, balance is what is needed.

Furthermore, whenever one extreme is present, it will not be long before someone reacts with the other extreme. If reason is what we get when we extract all passions, then sooner or later someone will say, "Well then, reason is the enemy."

This is precisely the position I saw taken on Bill Moyers' PBS show *Now* on April 26 2002.[557] His guest, Herman Gollob (and Moyers seemed to agree) points to a dichotomy between reason and the heart, and says that one should go with the heart because thinking too much will lead you to egoism. He gives examples from Julius Caesar. Since reason of itself is a power that is good of itself, such a diagnosis must come not from looking at reason per se, but from a life of exposure to those who have lived in such a way that their reason was opposed to their heart.[558] In particular, the men he saw and knew must have been intelligent in some way, but lacking in a certain moral character and also have had, according to him, a large element of, at least apparent, egoism in their character.

In any case, the answer to this dichotomy between reason and heart is in the right ordering of the passions and the intellect,

---

[556] These two are not in conflict in any way, because the first should be done only toward and in line with the second.

[557] See transcript at *http://www.pbs.org/now/transcript/transcript115_full.html.*

[558] "Heart" is used here in a way suggestive of emotions only. In fact, heart can be used in a more complete sense, which would more accurately capture what one means when he speaks of the heart. The heart is the center of human activity. In a good man, the heart will be the proper ordering of will, intellect, and passions.

not in the rejection of either. We do not want to be men whose hearts are divorced from their heads, or vice-versa. The profound medievalist C.S. Lewis rightly called such people, "men without chests," men without that intermediate connection that allows their reason to act rightly within the world. Let's consider for a moment more this right desire.

Except for those who have so abused their freedom as to lose nearly all of their ability to distinguish their own innate right desires, most can pick out the general trends of their passions and loves. We have a deep desire for truth. The more *right* our desire, the greater our desire for truth. Now, it's not just any truth we desire, we want Truth Himself. C.S. Lewis, using these desires, backs into our Ultimate Good:

> *Most people, if they have really learned to look into their own hearts, would know that they do want, and want acutely, something that cannot be had in this world. There are all sorts of things in this world that offer to give it to you, but they never quite keep their promise . . . [Now] ... "Creatures are not born with desires unless satisfaction for those desires exists. A baby feels hunger: well, there is such a thing as food. A duckling wants to swim: well, there is such a thing as water. Men feel sexual desire: well, there is such a thing as sex. If I find in myself a desire which no experience in this world can satisfy, the most probable explanation is that I was made for another world. If none of my earthly pleasures satisfy it, that does not prove that the universe is a fraud. Probably earthly pleasures were never meant to satisfy it, but only to arouse it, to suggest the real thing...* "[559]

This is not and does not purport to be a *philosophical* proof of the existence of God; it is what one might call a pre-philosophical or infra-scientific precursor to such a proof; it is one's mind in the state of glimpsing the necessity of God's

---

[559] *Christian Behavior*, Macmillian, 1943 pp. 55-56.

existence, but only in an inchoate and confused way.[560] The philosophical proof from finality (the fifth proof in the last chapter) is the result of the mind's consideration of the facts on a strict philosophical level. By contrast, Lewis only wants to bring to mind our natural desire for the Ultimate Good. St. Augustine says it another way. He says, "For Thou hast made us for Thyself and our hearts are restless till they rest in Thee [God]."[561]

Now, despite this fact, many do not seek Truth. They seek to be known as seeking and even as having found truth without really seeking, let alone finding. Such people are known as sophists. They were responsible for killing the great Socrates by poisoning him with hemlock. Socrates was the teacher of Plato who, in turn, was the teacher of Aristotle. Socrates was showing up their lies, and they could not tolerate the loss of their one "good," which was their *appearance* of knowledge.

Commenting on a similar remark by Aristotle, St. Thomas says,

> But the philosopher differs from the sophist "in the choice," i.e., in the selection or willing, or in the desire, of a way of life. For the philosopher and sophist direct their life and actions to different things. The philosopher directs his to knowing the truth, whereas the sophist directs his so as to appear to know what he does not.[562]

St. Thomas More, the man who was executed by King Henry VIII for defending the supremacy of the pope in the Church, encountered a different sort of opposition to his unwillingness to lie. The widely-acclaimed play and Hollywood movie, *A Man for All Seasons,* depicts his life. In one scene, his daughter Meg asks him why he would not just sign the oath against the supremacy, but not really mean it in his heart. He explained that in signing such a

---

[560] One indeed has to be very attentive in one's understanding of the thought "Every desire has a fulfillment." It means somewhere in the desire is the desire for the good. For example, if a man has the desire to kill someone, it is because he wants what results from that death, not the death itself. For example, he may want the feeling of revenge or the freedom from his control that results. Thus, it is that feeling and that freedom he really seeks.

[561] *Confessions* by St. Augustine, Book I-I

[562] *Commentary on Metaphysics* Book 4 Lecture 4, 575.

document, he is holding his very self in his cupped hands. It is he who hangs in the balance. It is he himself, he explains, that will spill out if he opens his fingers and lies. Even his own daughter, educated by him, had the strong tendency to think truth a sidelight.

Lest anyone think that such thinking against truth is for days past, I have been told by a scientist in good standing--no, a world-renowned scientist--that "it does not matter what the truth is." Mind you, such men do want to get their experiments to work, but they do not care much how they do it or about much else. This is where the problems come in for modern science. For example, Werner Heisenberg,[563] in Germany, willingly adopted the Nazi thinking.

Before going into a little more detail on relatively recent ethical thinking by modern scientists, let's summarize what we've found about moral philosophy.

Happiness

It can all be summarized by saying, as St. Thomas does, that we all seek one final end, and that is happiness. We all want to be happy. No one can deny this. However, as Aristotle says at the beginning of his work on ethics (called the *Nicomachean Ethics*), all agree on the name, but not all agree on the content. We, after

---

[563] Apparently, Heisenberg tried to avoid his moral obligations by pretending science was "above" politics. Such a position amounts to identifying empiriometric science with God, the Ultimate Good. A perfect recipe for the Nazi's who used horrific experiments on living Jews for advancing their medical knowledge. Such a position is also utilitarian, given Heisenberg kept a job, a job that included helping the Nazi war machine, while those more upright men would leave theirs. Heisenberg says in 1942 about the war, "For us there remains nothing but to turn to the simple things: we should conscientiously fulfill the duties and tasks that life presents to us without asking too much about the why or the wherefore...And then we should wait for whatever happens...reality is transforming itself without our influence." published as Ordnung der Wirklichkeit (Munich: Piper-Verlag, 1989), quote on pp. 171-172; reprinted in Heisenberg, Collected Works, volume C I, W. Blum et al., eds. (Munich: Piper-Verlag,1984), pp. 217-306, on p. 304, which I quote from "A Historical Perspective on "Copenhagen'" By Dr. David C. Cassidy, Hofstra Univ., 2000. cf. http://web.gc.cuny.edu/ashp/nml/copenhagen/Cassidy.htm#8

careful analysis, now know what happiness consists of. It consists in seeking and finding Truth Himself. We do this in our daily actions in a thousand little and a few big ways throughout our lives.[564] Every human act is determined by its object, what one aims at doing. If the object is good, the act will be good. If you are correct about the goodness of the object, you align yourself properly in the entire ontological realm, both moral and physical. Therefore, when a man does something that is truly good, he makes himself better (if you'll excuse the poor English, for emphasis we can say, "it makes him more good"), because he "is" more. Aligning oneself with what is really good for oneself can only increase one's degree of perfection. This does not mean he will feel happy all the time, but that he will be doing things in such a way as to bring himself to what he needs, including the Ultimate need that will fulfill him.

As we've seen, if one is mistaken about the goodness of the act, to the degree he is mistaken is the degree that he will not be morally responsible and thus, will not, to that same degree, distort (i.e. diminish) his being in the moral realm. Yet, the ontological realm still suffers an evil. In the case of our stamp dispenser, poison is released that kills someone. From what we've said about habits, we see that we can be responsible for acts without at the particular time having made a direct decision to do a particular evil. In the case of the stamp dispenser, I may have made many small decisions to not pay attention to things that could cause me any distraction, even though they are important. Hence, I may have seen fluid that looked dangerous coming out of the dispenser one time. Another time, I may have smelled something unhealthy at the push of the button. Hence, I would have some, though possibly small, guilt in causing the repairman's death.

Finally, we can deliberately do evil because we want some good. We may do the evil because it is part of, or on the way to, the good we want. For example, a man may argue, as apparently a

---

[564] To have complete happiness we must turn to revelation, which is outside the scope of this book. Again, this book confines itself to discussing what we can know by reason alone, but revelation is not outside the scope of philosophy as love of wisdom, all wisdom.

Princeton University philosopher is arguing, that a child of less than one year of age can be killed if he is not wanted, an inconvenience. He wants the good of quiet and peace or freedom from responsibility so as to do his "vocation," but at the expense of killing an innocent person. A politician may decide that it's worthwhile to cheat someone out of his position so that he may get a much-needed bill passed. In these cases, one puts one's self in a role of Cosmic Fixer, trying to work in a mode that he is not made to work in. He puts himself in the place of God, implicitly saying "I know, better than the First Cause, how things should happen." Although his nature is made to act within the created order, the "cosmic fixer" acts as if he can create (in philosophical sense) a new, better one. In the end, he is in the state of disorder with respect to the created order, and thus he is lessened; [565] he will be less happy, and will have made some others miserable as well. The Confucians call the rebalancing the Toa,[566] the way; the common man says, "What goes around comes around." The first principle of morality: "Do good, avoid evil" takes on the form: "One cannot do evil that good may come of it." In other words, against Machiavellians, "The end never justifies the means." We saw in St. Thomas More's explanation to his daughter what deliberately doing evil does to one's own being immediately upon the doing; one lets out one's very self.[567]

Now, one may argue, "Are you really saying that atheists are not moral and will not be happy?" Well, it depends on what is meant by "atheist." If they truly reject God, including any implicit accepting of Him by an acceptance of the order He established, the answer is absolutely yes.[568] However, the reality is not so simple. Many atheists are denying not God, but some conception that they have of God. Further, many do not allow themselves to become

---

[565] In short, despite the cosmic fixer's apparent opinion, God is good and He is in control.

[566] However, unlike Confucians, we see that the order does not have to be resolved in the created regime; it can and is resolved finally in God Himself.

[567] For this reason, Plato said it was better to have evil done to you than to do it to others. The first affects only the exterior, the latter destroys one's very self.

[568] It is no accident, for example, that the countries that specifically denied God--the Soviet Union and Nazi Germany--were the ones guilty of the most heinous crimes against humanity.

conscious of their last end, yet recognize the truth of what's in front of them. Like all error, this error is hard to discuss because it is only discussable in the context of what in it is not error, i.e., what is true in it. So, though such atheists have no final reason for it, they do see the good in front of them, and they, for example, will not allow the killing of innocent people. They see the good, but do not allow final integrity to their thinking, for they do not admit the Ultimate Good that grounds it all. They are like a man who recognizes all the laws and particulars of plant growth and is thus able to grow some great outdoor gardens, but never acknowledges, in words or speculative thought, the sun's central role in their growth. Of course, he must acknowledge its role implicitly by where and how he places the plants. It is the same for the good "atheist." As Nietzsche says, the will to truth--for example, the witness of the scientist searching for the hidden realities of the world--is witness to God of Truth.

Scientists and Morality

Modern scientists have at least an implicit respect for truth, because they seek, at least, to understand the quantitative interrelations among things as they really are. Yet, we've seen an infection of moral relativism and even some relativism with respect to truth itself. What made Feynman, a genius of first order in (empiriometric) physics,[569] think that external morality would be more or less unaffected by changes in science and religion? Furthermore, Feynman is not alone; he is simply an exemplar of a dominant class. So, what leads him (and them) to his (their) thinking? Partly it's from ignorance of sound philosophy and partly from an interest in empiriometric science that is all-consuming, leading him to think of everything in terms of it.[570] It's also partly

---

[569] Feynman has impacted that field, my field, in marvelous and important ways.

[570] Recall that the empiriometric science is formally mathematical and thus leaves out final causality. Without final causality, one cannot see the concepts of good and evil. This, indeed, is why most of the academic culture misses them. Most of that culture is either immersed in the empiriometric or in reaction against its claims to have the whole truth. The latter group, partly because it does not understand completely what it is reacting against (this requires philosophical analysis like we've done in this book), overreacts and denies all truth. In so

from his experience, for that is what he says his reason is. But, what explains his experience?

Well, perhaps each individual just figures out what external morality is on his own. After all, we have seen that moral principles are based on reason, so one can figure them out by experience and thinking. Leaving aside the extreme difficulty of doing that by oneself, note that Feynman has revealed to us that, in his academic milieu, there was a strong belief that morality is not something to be thought about and figured out.[571] Now, since our hypothetical student is under considerable pressure to adopt this belief of his educational milieu, especially given the substantial intellectual authority it carries, it is probable that he will indeed adopt it.[572] Now, one who rejects the possibility that morality can be thought out objectively will not seek to do so. Just as no one will seek to learn general relativity if he believes it is impossible to learn, so no one will seek to learn ethics if he thinks the subject not approachable by reason.

We're back to where we began: "What explains Feynman's experience that students return to what Feynman thinks is good moral behavior on their own?" If it is not internal (from reason), it must be external. It comes from the same place as the belief that morality is impossible, but from a different sector. It comes from the broader culture. It is our moral capital handed to us by our larger cultural setting.[573] Hence, the short answer is we do it because we have not quite yet taken seriously our new doctrines and still implicitly believe the old ones. This is what makes the radical shifts in thought seem benign. We don't see them all at

doing, they make mockeries of their own fields, which, of course, should be about truth (being) in some respect, in the process. In short, such empiriometric rationalism breeds irrationality.

[571] At best, it was empiriological morality, which we've shown is equivalent to pick-your-own morality.

[572] It is true that some students will reject the culturally imposed belief and seek objective morality despite the pressure, but, on the whole, most will follow the ruling culture. That's effectively what one means by "culture."

[573] In Chapter 6, we discussed how practically everything in our Western culture is born from or mediated through the Catholic Church (Europe and Catholicism were synonymous for a long period of time). So, the base of our current Western cultural values are passed down from the Catholic Church and maintained in various ways by various break off institutions and ideologies.

once; we see them only gradually and thus don't feel their effect. It's like the proverbial frog, of which it is said if he is put in hot water, he will immediately jump out, but if put in cool water and the temperature only gradually raised, by the time he realizes what's happening, he will be unable to escape.

Metaphorically, we are living on our inheritance money. It will not last forever. If we adopt the idea that morality is empiriometrically discovered or is relative, we will not, at first, see the full consequences in practice (because of our inherited beliefs), and so we will not be alarmed by the consequences, as we might otherwise be. To see the drastic change, just think how the average man of 1963 would view our twenty-first century culture. He would come from one world to a markedly different one: from a world with low tolerance for divorce and a (relatively) miniscule divorce rate to one where it is accepted and commonplace, from universal rejection of abortion at all stages of pregnancy to universal acceptance during all stages up to and including birth,[574] from a world where a family was a man, a woman and (usually) children to one where a family is self-defining, from a world where a child's biggest problem in school was tardiness to one where the daily worry is whether the children have deadly weapons.[575] Can one really say that morals are not affected by science and prevailing cultural (religious) beliefs? Of course not. The point here is to see the importance of our ideas and of our cultural inheritance. We can lose all of the latter without intending to, by not acknowledging the full consequences of our thinking. Whether we like it or not, there is no such thing as half a principle.

Current Issues

We should not leave such a chapter without noting several pressing moral problems of our times that are associated with modern science. Should we clone human beings? Should we use embryos for research? Should we genetically engineer new animals

---

[574] This procedure is the so-called partial-birth abortion.

[575] This last, rather than being directly about the change in moral thinking, is more about the symptoms that accompany a shift to moral "opinions," excluding more and more a basis in reality which only can ground moral reasoning.

and plants? If so, what are the limits? What limits should be put on technology, in particular its use of environmental and physical resources? What, if any, limits should be put on technology to avoid violation of individual privacy and state control of individuals?

And we have more mundane questions. What are my obligations to family and friends? What are the obligations of my profession? For example, in the case of a professor (like myself): What is the proper balance between research and teaching? What obligations does one have to post-doctorial and junior colleagues in general?   On a different note, as the Judeo-Christian cycle of resting on Sunday[576] passes out of use, what is a reasonable work schedule? How often should one rest from his work and give time to God and others? More generally, should our curiosity be the only limit to what we do and don't do?

We can answer some of these questions relatively quickly with the solid base we've established. Case in point: we now know the answer to the hotly debated problem of embryo research and so-called therapeutic cloning.[577] We know killing an innocent human person is wrong, and we know human life begins at conception,[578] so *we now know deliberately killing embryos for research, or any other reason, is wrong.* Other problems, on the other hand, involve further reasoning and investigation.

In any case, what we have done is quite significant. Among other things, we have set both the base and the method for approaching all such problems. Like the other areas of philosophy we have discussed, we should realize that moral philosophy requires the hard work of reasoning, applying and contemplating its truths. Such a process, as before, means, especially in the beginning, several re-readings of the material. What's more, since moral philosophy is about *living the truth,* it is imperative to have

---

[576] Saturday for non-Christian Jews.

[577] This is a deceptive description of the process of cloning a human embryo, doing research, and in the end, taking the life of the human embryo.

[578] Even if one were to refuse to acknowledge the validity of the arguments given above, he would be confronted with the fact that one should not kill what might be human. For example, if one is going to rip down a building, and he has any reasonable doubt that someone might still be in the building, he should first dispel that doubt before acting.

our thought change our will, change how we act, and in general change what we are. Indeed, one can readily discern that living the truth puts us in intimate contact with it. Such a life gives us what scholastic thinkers call *connatural knowledge* of the subject. It enables us to answer moral dilemmas, such as the ones above, with greater felicity and accuracy.

Although we will answer some of those types of questions in our culminating chapter, our major goal in turning to this final chapter is to bring all we've learned to bear on the problem: "How should we do science?"

Chapter 10

How Then
Should We Do Science?

*I*n considering the answer to the question of the chapter title, another question cannot be avoided. It makes us ask what we mean by "science" and thus forces us to consider the full meaning of science. Of course, considering how science should be done in the full sense still leaves the more specific and ancillary question: "Does the answer to the broader question change the way modern specialized science should be done and will it give better modern science?" This is an extremely important question that we will discuss in some detail later. For now, we emphasize that science is bigger than just the modern sciences, that is, the empiriological sciences. As we saw in Chapter 6, science (philosophy),[579] properly speaking, includes all knowledge.[580] Furthermore, the science that studies the first principles of things, which is also called philosophy (narrow sense), in fact in the common usage of the word, precedes modern science.

Hence, philosophy, in its wide sense, includes modern science and thus is before modern science as whole is before part, and philosophy in its narrow sense precedes modern science because it is implicitly *required* by modern science. In

---

[579] We identified science in the wide sense with philosophy in the wide sense. Both are seeking knowledge in the general sense. Recall that PhD's (which means doctor or teacher of philosophy) are given in a much wider range of subjects than what we now narrowly call philosophy.

[580] Recall as well that the Latin root *"scientia"* means knowledge.

short, philosophy is "the science before (modern) science." Therefore, we should do modern science by being cognizant of its setting in the larger realm of knowledge, and its implicit (and sometimes even explicit) dependence on philosophy (narrow sense). For example, the modern sciences of physics, chemistry, and biology should be cognizant of their being a part of the larger science of *physica.*

Now, what does this "before" consist of? Let's see chapter by chapter.

We saw in **Chapter 2** that one can use the word "knowledge" to signify all those things we think we know with a reasonable degree of certitude. We then defined *proper* knowledge as that which we have direct sensorial knowledge of, and have ourselves done the intellectual work necessary to come to the relevant conclusions, rather than relying on others. We also saw that all other knowledge, which we call improper knowledge, is really at bottom a species of belief that we obtain from the culture around us that we trust.

These distinctions come before science (the modern specialized sciences) both in time and in principle. If we are not cognizant of the distinction between proper and improper knowledge--where knowledge is taken in the broadest sense, not just in the empiriological sense--we will sooner or later mistake one for the other. Without an understanding of the role of improper knowledge in our thinking, one takes, as we discussed using the example of the rotation of the earth, one's cultural presuppositions on *blind (unexamined)* faith. In addition, these cultural presuppositions are often foundational ones; if they are wrong, the very substructure supporting and encouraging knowledge will fall. Furthermore, by such a blind faith, we will *unconsciously* narrow our view of the world to that of our particular culture and subculture at work and at home. Now, under these circumstances, if a fertile culture changes in such a way as to undermine science itself, one can easily miss the gradual trend. We are currently seeing some evidence of such a shift in the physics community.

Take a prominently featured letter in *Physics Today,* a reputable general journal for physicists, by Mano Singham, a physicist from Case Western Reserve University. He thinks both science and evolution are "undirected."[581] He says that like evolution,

> ... *scientific theories evolve according to how well they answer, at any given time in history, the immediate questions of interest to scientists. As a result, the present impressive array of theories has developed to satisfactorily answer the questions that interest us now. But* **that does not mean that science is goal-directed** *and thus progressing toward the "truth"*... **to be valid, science does not have to be true.**[582]
> [Emphasis added]

He *apparently* thinks science is a cultural phenomenon,[583] defined by the whim of scientists, not by reality.[584] Now, most scientists enter science because they are fascinated by physical reality and want to understand it more deeply. Indeed, if people ever really believed that science was not in any sense about truth, then sooner or later, real science

---

[581] Compare this current thinker, for example, with Bronowski's previously mentioned 1965 book *Science and Human Values,* where he assigns a central place to the search for truth modeled after the sciences. Cultural norms are changing.

[582] *Physics Today,* June 2002, p. 51.

[583] It is, of course, true that scientists do not work on everything at once and thus they make decisions about what's important. They decide what they should do now and what should wait for later. Some of those decisions are wrong; some even spring from objectively immoral considerations, but one does not define something by the exceptions. Because some accidentally veer off the road or even drive off purposely does not mean that there is no road. And even less does it mean that one has no final destination.

[584] How long will Americans support pure science if they really believe it is only this? Applied science might be given some money, if Americans are not too impatient for its results. But if Americans believe pure science (such as finding gravity waves or searching for the Higgs boson that have no clear application) is only about scientists' own questioning and answering of each other because it's interesting to them, then Americans would no doubt rather use more of their money for football or movies. After all, many more people think these latter are better entertainment than making up physics laws and equations and spending long frustrating hours in a lab that presents manifold risks of injury. In fact, these experiences are rewarding *only* because of the times that one learns or sees something new (at least for himself) about *reality*. It is the truth of science that excites scientists.

would stop, as there would eventually be no new scientists to replace the current ones. Here's how it *could* happen.

At first, students would be taught by physicists who say such things as "Science is not about truth" but *act* differently. That is, despite their professed beliefs, they continue, to some extent, to do their experiments and argue their case based on the hidden supposition that there is truth of some type in their work. Now, the students will not know as much about their professor's actions as about his articulated belief. Furthermore, actions have to be interpreted, and they are usually interpreted in light of the professed beliefs of those acting. Hence, students will tend to adopt the belief expressed by the professor. If many professors started teaching in such a way,[585] the number of students wanting to become physicists would decrease, for who wants to *dedicate his* life[586] to a game[587] in which the participants determine what is important by no objective standards but those imposed, say, by random choice or by the most powerful? Recall, their standards could not be obtained by conformity with reality, for truth is conformity of the mind with reality, and they've rejected truth. Such the trend thus leads finally to the destruction of science. Science may return, but only when it is culturally allowed that such truths are worthy of being explored.

Of course, science could be transmuted into a purely practical technology in which one is only interested in predictive theories for the potential control (real or imagined) they give over nature. However, we have just admitted this is not science, but really a technique for getting some end. The relation of this transmuted "science" to true science would be like what a robot is to a man: a mechanical imitation.

Chapter 3 showed us that sensorial knowledge comes first *for us*. We found that sensorial knowledge is a real form

---

[585] It seems to me that such thinking is on the margins now, but the fact that such an article as described above could be given a prominent place in a mainstream journal is not a healthy sign.

[586] Monetary compensation is not high for physicists as compared to other professions.

[587] Under Singham's above account of science, science does not even rise to the level of a game, for a game is goal-oriented.

of knowledge. It is direct awareness of the sensible things around us. As such, it is partially immaterial because--by our phantasms--we know, for instance, the color of a thing or the coldness of it.

We further found in Chapter 3 that our sensorial powers are limited and there can thus be errors in perception, but in the end it is our senses that provide the means for the correction of those errors. In short, the senses are reliable[588] and we must rely on them for all we know. Thus, illusions can be identified as such and understood to give proper knowledge of the thing(s) under consideration. For example, I was asked by a friend who knows science, "What if someone has two cans of primary yellow paint and one can of primary blue (cyan) and he mixes one yellow and one blue to make green?[589] When I walk into the room, what is my proper knowledge?" Answer: You know that there is one yellow can and one that is green; the latter could be "rainbow" green (i.e., *not* composed of multiple color wavelengths)[590] or may be a "mixed"[591] green composed of multiple "rainbow" colors.[592] You have to test to learn more, to increase your proper knowledge.

We saw what happens if we forget the primacy of the senses. I gave an example of a student who, in fact, despaired of the existence of the world; he thought everything unreal.

---

[588] This statement is not to be interpreted to mean that one cannot damage the senses, but that in their natural state, along with the unifying sense, they function to put us in contact with reality.

[589] Note in "mixing of colors," (the subtractive mode) the primaries are yellow, magenta, and cyan, but red and blue can be substituted for the latter two with some success.

[590] Recall, the rainbow colors come from a splitting up of the "white" light from the sun.

[591] Again, beware of reductionist tendencies; just because something is composed from pieces (colors) doesn't mean it isn't a whole. Also, remember the senses are trustworthy, but they don't tell us everything; they have limits in their ability to distinguish. For example, two apparently identically-shaped objects that are at a distance may (under detailed experiment) turn out to be somewhat different, and likewise two very similar appearing colors may turn out to be somewhat different.

[592] Of course, this assumes one knows something about colors and paints and the way they are mixed.

The Kantian error of thinking that we know only what's in our mind leads to this thinking. So much for science, if people let this part of the "before" go.

In Chapter 3, we also discovered that all material things are composites of potentiality (matter) and actuality (form). Everything we have direct experience of *is* something (form), but can *potentially be* (matter) something else. This composition is evident because of the undeniable existence of change. This important point is often lost because it seems trivial, but it is not.[593] It is a *necessity* imposed on us by the fact of change.

Now, if we deny potency and act, physics ceases, for physics is about observing and understanding how and why things happen. Physics (*Physica*, as well as its empiriological tools) is the study of changeable being.

In **Chapter 4**, we saw more of the consequences of Kantian thinking.[594] We saw that Gödel's theorem is a depressing thing that leads to the end of science for those who do not respect the fact that all of our knowledge comes from things in the external world through our senses. By the time of Gödel, more than a few were under the illusion that mathematics was all truth,[595] since for them it is the form of all science, and that sooner or later it was going to come to its glorious victory in complete self-consistent systemization. Mathematicians were among this group, but so were physicists who took the empiriometric science as the exclusive science

---

[593] Garrigou-Lagrange emphasizes, in *Reality--A Synthesis of Thomistic Thought* (in Chapter 5), the importance of understanding potency. He says, "When potency is conceived as really distinct from all act, even the least imperfect, then we have the Thomistic position. If, on the other hand, potency is conceived as an imperfect act, then we have the position of some Scholastics, in particular of Suarez, and especially of Leibnitz, for whom potency is a force, a virtual act, merely impeded in its activity, as, for example, in the restrained force of a spring."

[594] Kant's system, by making the categories the forms imposed by our mind, is thus philosophical idealism, leaving us only contact with our own thoughts, not with reality by those thoughts.

[595] Though nods were given by some of these to the empirical, it was usually in the fashion of Kant, whereby these were really, in the end, part of our mind, which in turn was oriented solely to the mathematical.

and thus considered all things as explained by mathematics. David Hume (1711-1776) stated the belief succinctly:

When we run over our libraries, persuaded of these principles, what havoc must we make? If we take in our hand any volume: of divinity or school metaphysic, for instance; let us ask, Does it contain any abstract reasoning concerning quantity or number? No. Does it contain any experimental reasoning concerning matters of fact and existence? No. Commit it then to the flames: for it can contain nothing but sophistry and illusion.[596]

The finding of Gödel profoundly saddened such people. It attacked their hope at its core. But, for someone who understands the issues in Chapters 3 and 4, such a belief system and enterprise was clearly foolish.[597] Only those who conceive man in the model of an angel, as Descartes and ultimately Kant do, can be grief stricken by finding that one must have reference to something outside of his mind to obtain truth. Our minds are not the source of truth; we know reality only through the means of our senses.

We also saw in Chapter 4 that we abstract our intellectual knowledge (our ideas) from sensorial knowledge (phantasms). This crucial point is lost on many. They deny the immaterial because they don't realize, as philosopher Jude Dougherty aptly points out: *"...more is given in the sense report of reality than the senses are able to appreciate."*[598]

Briefly we recap what we have learned of ideas.

We found that ideas are that *by which* we know things, **not** *that which* we know. So, when we talk of an object that we

---

[596] The last paragraph of *An Enquiry Concerning Human Understanding*, Harvard Classics Volume 37, copyright 1910 P.F. Collier & Son.
[597] Such statements are not even self-consistent; where, for example, is there mathematics or the experiment in the statement "for it can contain nothing but sophistry and illusion?" Hume is the first victim of Hume. It is no accident that Hume's own thinking ends in its own destruction; such a self-destructive feature is characteristic of philosophical idealism, even when masquerading as empiricism.
[598] Thomistic Institute 2001, *Maritain on the Limits of the Empiriometric* by Jude Dougherty, the last paragraph.

know, we should speak of our idea *of* that object. We further saw our ideas of things, like that of a circle, are general, so that they cannot be material, which is specific. Material things are specific things but can be other things. Ideas present to us general things, and ideas cannot be anything but what they are. For example, the *idea* of a nut-bolt type fastener cannot be changed. Even if, in my imagination, I take away the nut, it's implicitly called for in the threads on the bolt; if I truly exclude the bolt, then I abandon, not split, the *idea* of the fastener; it's no fastener at all, not part of a fastener. Furthermore, we noted that many of our ideas present objects that have no sensible aspects at all. We pointed out that justice has no color, weight, or any other material property. We further pointed out that ideas have no extension; one cannot chop an idea in half. Since quantity (extension) is the first accident of material (changeable) being, that is what makes them material (able to change), ideas are immaterial (not material). From this, we necessarily concluded that the intellect, and hence the substantial form of man, is necessarily immaterial.

Now, these facts are essential for science as well. First, if one thinks ideas are that which he knows, he is trapped inside his mind with no contact with reality and thus must abandon hope of learning about the world external to himself. In short, modern science takes for granted that ideas are that *by which* we know things. Second, if one is ever really convinced that his mind is material, he must distrust his mind, because material reality is determined by the outside, which could just as well make one think logically as not logically, think falsely as soon as truly.[599] Such absurd thinking leads one to *think* that one *should stop thinking!* It is hard to fathom holding one's sanity in the midst of such an absurd belief structure that fundamentally denies truth.

---

[599] In such thinking and speaking about true and false and logical and illogical, one is already betraying that one either does not really take seriously the materialist belief or does not really understand it. They already implicitly involve the immaterial mode of thinking where one thing can be another. A bird, for example, can *be* black.

Friedrich Nietzsche (1844-1900) tried the "there is no truth" experiment.[600] I don't mean try it in circumstances where the experiment is kept at a distance so the results cannot be seen. Many today claim to do the experiment, but they only do it in this unreal way. Specifically, when it is their part of reality that is at stake, the part they like and value for whatever reason, they drop the game and defend it as true. Unlike these sham experimenters, Nietzsche really tried the "there is no truth" belief and in the end lost his sanity; in fact, he really lost the battle once he started the experiment.

We also saw in Chapter 4 the concept of being. We saw that the first thing that we know is that "there is an 'is.'" Being is primary. Being, we saw, is multileveled, not univocal. We cannot write a sentence without implicitly referencing being. Everything we discuss and study, including science, implies a reference to things that really are. Even logic, which we discussed in Chapter 4 as well, references the real world implicitly; for example, in every proposition or implication, we are forced to recall, "this *is* that" or "if this *is* that, then something *is* something else."

Of course, logic itself is also a prerequisite to science. In spite of claims to the contrary by "quantum" logicians, who use (standard) logic to obtain their conclusions, logic is absolutely necessary for doing science.

Truth was the central topic of Chapter 4. We found the following. All things insofar as they are, are intelligible. Intelligibility is *being* looked at from the point of view of understanding. The essence of a thing is made present to us by our idea of it. The intelligibility (the actuality or form) of the thing is freed by our intellect from the existing thing, which is a form-matter composite. In brief, the intellect forms an idea by which one becomes the thing; one is conformed to the thing in its essence.[601] If we deny this conformity of the mind with the thing, i.e. truth, we have joined the anti-truth war of

---

[600] Of course, no one can really do this experiment.

[601] As we noted, our first ideas of things are confused and unclear. It is only after more observation and thinking that one comes to better understand the essence of a thing.

Nietzsche and will thus share his fate. We must at least implicitly accept it. Obviously, science certainly *presupposes* these facts, though it seldom, if ever, needs the details we've described in its daily work.

We saw in this chapter that thinking is a multi-step movement to truth. First, we abstract ideas from our phantasms, then we make judgment of what is what. We may note, for example, that a crow is black. Finally, we reason; in the process of reasoning, we link together propositions, look for commonality among things, and come to conclusions. Usually this process is implicit and spontaneous. This is why those who seek and live the truth are known to have common sense. Such people do not skirt obvious realities in the name of systems of thinking. Now, there are two ways to look for commonality. One is to take a sort of average. The other is to look for formal causes, really look at the essence of things. The first way is the way of rough common sense; the second is the way of, what we might call, the refined common sense known as proper knowledge. Too many settle for the first without even recognizing the existence of the second; true science cannot.[602]

In **Chapter 5**, we made use of our new understanding and discussed the difference between animals, men, and robots. We saw that animals have sensorial knowledge and nutritive life, man is a rational (i.e. has an intellect) animal and robots do not even have a nutritive life. Science needs these conclusions as well. In the pure science of, say, the psychology of animals and men, one needs to know that animals have sensorial knowledge and man has sensorial and intellectual knowledge to avoid huge errors in understanding and interpreting empirioschematic data, such as saying animals and

---

[602] Maritain says in this regard, "You know that according to certain idealist theorists concerned with the diverse ages of the intellect, Thomism corresponds to the mental development of a seven to nine year old child. Well, their own conception of the life of reason applies exactly enough to the mental development of a child who has grown up without becoming an adult and who nevertheless pretends to science, to the activity of a grown man without ever having attained,-except in mathematics,- to the proper means of science, that is the typological [formal] visualization [abstraction] ..." *The Philosophy of Nature*, 1951, pp. 23-24.

men are really degrees of the same thing. Similarly, in biology it would be essential in understanding the animal as a whole organism, such as moving beyond the empirioschematic analysis of his habits and daily activities. In cybernetics, one needs the conclusions to prevent wildly erroneous conclusions about artificial life and intelligence.

Science needs the conclusions of Chapter 5 in an indirect way. For example, if man is not qualitatively different from robots and animals, how can we justify, other than by might makes right, that we build and use robots at our discretion (especially when they reach a certain sophistication)[603] and that we examine and study animals, confine them, and eat them. The answer is, we cannot. On one account, we raise the scale for animals and thus we stop using animals. However, most of the understandings of modern biology have depended and depend on animal studies. On the other end of the scale, why not lower the scale for ourselves; why not use our fellow man for experiments? That's already happening with "therapeutic" cloning. Could it go further? Why not, if we really think there is no radical difference? Will

---

[603] The fact that someone may not mind this dilemma at some point, only means that he is willing to consider that robots might be treated with the same rights as men. This, in turn, either means he assumes that the robot has an immaterial substantial form, in which case he is no longer speaking of a robot, or he means that neither robots nor we have one. This latter stance means that we are all equal, but equally unimportant. Cultural capital will eventually run out and it will be realized that this belief means that individuals can be treated as things. Not in some ways, but all ways. Similar logic follows for the case of animals.

Someone may think he has a way around this difficulty by simply putting things on a quantitative scale and then assigning rights based on where on the scale they fall. Such an empirioschematic program can work as long as one is willing to acknowledge that it is ad hoc. It is open to someone else picking a different scale with different rights and, in any case, the "rights" can be circumvented. In other words, as long as the difference that defines one's rights is not a qualitative one, it is in fact not a question of an absolute right but a relative one, for that is all a difference of degree allows of itself, without an arbitrary proclamation of one's will. So, for example, for the sake of enough amoebas, one would be allowed (sometimes required) to kill an innocent child, say your neighbor's five-year-old daughter. How many really would allow this to happen? Well, that's where the reasoning leads. We may emotionally object, as well we should, but what's our reason?

we allow fetus experimentation next? How about those less than one year old?[604] Such thinking (and the resulting acting) may not destroy science, but would certainly destroy any real worth in doing it.

In **Chapter 6**, we uncovered the profound differences between the sciences (wide sense). We found that there is a three-fold top-level division: 1) pure sciences, those that study *truth as truth;* 2) applied sciences, those that study *truth as lived;* and 3) methodological sciences, those that study the *human tools for obtaining the truth.* We also discussed in detail the three levels of abstraction: 1) *Physica,* the study of changeable being; 2) *Mathematica,* the study of being as quantitative; and 3) *Metaphysica,* the study of being as being. Each of our ideas presents to us an object on one of these levels. These levels, in turn, divide the pure sciences into three categories.

The truths of this chapter are necessary for each specialized science to learn its limits, and locate the source of its first principles. Without an awareness of the mentioned divisions, one inevitably limits one's view to a narrow swath of the world and simultaneously hopelessly confuses the domains. In particular, scientists can start to think the world is empiriological. That is, they start to believe that the world is only empirical data and the logical constructs made up in our head.

We also learned that modern physics is largely empiriometric science, which is a mixed science that studies mobile being as quantitative. It is materially physical *(physica)* and formally mathematical *(mathematica).* Without this understanding, physicists tend to adopt contradictory points of view. As experimentalists, they tend to be materialists, not believing in the immaterial; as theorists, they tend to be Platonists, thinking ideas (immaterial), specifically mathematics, as the only reality.

For the average practicing scientist, the contradictory nature of these beliefs will never come to his direct attention;

---

[604] Recall in Chapter 9 we discussed a Princeton professor who thinks one-year-olds don't have full rights.

they will remain a vague set of notions that he articulates now and again, but are resolved in the end by his implicit realist (Thomist-Aristotelian) philosophy. In short, when the scientist appears to adopt materialism or Platonism, it is really only a vague pragmatic (what he might call "heuristic") way of talking; it will have no real rational consistency. While the scientist himself may learn to live with it, without too much damage[605] to his humanity and his work, the error of thinking that all is empiriological will be let loose in those who *really* take the thinking as seriously as the scientist may *say* he does. Eventually, without correction by other forces, such as cultural norms, the error will come home to roost in the scientist himself when he cannot answer the subjectivist at his door using his very arguments, in a refined form, against science.

Indeed, it is such a discussion on the importance of having a culture that is imbued with truth that we took up in Chapter 6, for such a culture is necessary in order, among other things, to have healthy soil[606] for activities such as science. Linking up to the fact, discussed in Chapter 2, that we depend heavily on our improper knowledge in advancing our proper knowledge, we saw how important culture is. Indeed, we saw that because of our limited nature and time, most of our knowledge is improper knowledge. Hence, if our culture feeds us lies, most will obtain some level of despair about knowledge as they test the things they think they know, and find them to be false.

In this vein, we saw that an anti-Catholic prejudice has hidden from us the important truth that Catholic culture did not stifle science. Indeed, it fostered, protected, and finally provided Galileo--who was no less a Catholic in a Catholic environment than his predecessors--with the education, information, and technology[607] he needed to crown the efforts

---

[605] This is also open to question, depending on what one considers too much is.

[606] As well as safeguard it.

[607] Clocks, lens making, and the printing press were all technologies invented in the Middle Ages in Catholic Europe. For example, in 1267 AD, the Franciscan Roger Bacon wrote, in his *Perspectiva,* "Great things can be performed by refracted vision. If the letters of a book, or any minute object, be viewed through

of gradual growth of scientific knowledge in the Middle Ages with his great discoveries and synthesis, which were later brought to fruition by Newton. To forget the importance of this cultural inheritance can be catastrophic. We lean on it every time we inadvertently pull out the rational basis of our science. It is only those ingrained cultural beliefs, sustained by centuries of reinforcement, that keep us from following the logic of our erroneous positions to the inevitable conclusions. Indeed, if we are not aware of the power and content of our culture, the implicit cultural beliefs imbedded in us can give us a false sense of security about our fate. This false sense of security, in turn, numbs our sensitivity to the effects of erroneous first principles, thereby facilitating their corrosive effect on society and eventually science.

In **Chapter 7**, we saw results of one such error: taking empiriological thinking as philosophical thinking, as if modern science (empiriological science) was inclusive of all sciences, including philosophy. Modern thinking has no awareness of the division of the sciences discussed in Chapter 6. By taking the empiriological as the fundamental or only science, one is effectively adopting Kant's philosophy. Recall, the reason he created his system was to justify Newtonian empiriometric physics. If one starts in one's head, one can only end there. Indeed, we saw, by a sort of lived Gödel's theorem, Kant ended by showing that we couldn't really know anything. This, ironically, leaves Newtonian physics and all science with no basis.

By contrast, we saw that the precursors to Newton and Galileo used Thomist principles, and that they flowered in the cultural atmosphere of Catholic Europe that respected and fostered such sound philosophical understanding. In particular, we saw in Chapters 6 and 7 that the culture held that: 1) the world exists independent of us and is orderly; 2) we can

---

a lesser segment of a sphere of glass or crystal, whose plane is laid upon them, they will appear far better and larger." Eyeglasses were invented circa 1280 and spread widely. It was only in the Catholic realm that these inventions obtained a cultural hold that allowed them to both be used pragmatically and for scientific research. As with science, it's not that technology does not appear in other places (notably China), but what appears ends by being stillborn.

understand it; 3) the world is good, and thus we should have no aversion to experiment, i.e., to observing and working directly with the material world; and 4) the world is not necessary. Further, Galileo and Newton both used Aristotelian methodologies. Newton used Thomist principles. Case in point: he recognized the empiriometric nature of his work. In the *Principia* he said:[608] "For here I design only to give a mathematical notion of those forces, without considering their physical causes and seats."[609]

So, in Chapter 7, we considered what happens in six cases when the empiriological is taken philosophically. For example, we looked at Newtonian mechanics. Despite the above warnings of Newton, we saw some considered inertia as having ruled out needing a cause for motion, as if something could change itself.

We saw that the concept of inertia originated in the Middle Ages; the medievals noted the fact of inertia in the physical world and understood it at a deep level. They refined the concept by thinking about it physically, not excluding efficient causes. We saw they surpassed Aristotle because culturally, unlike Aristotle, they were free to think about the world as non-necessary, free to notice that the universe could be another way or not at all. They were able to take what is implicit in Aristotle explicitly and without fear of cultural reprisal.

---

[608] This is not to say that Newton understood Aristotelian principles at a deep level, for soon after these comments, he begins his discussion on time and space as if he is correcting philosophical errors, when he is really doing empiriometric modeling. However, he understood them to some degree and followed Aristotelian methodologies. Most significantly, he--like Aristotle--did not let conceptualism drive science; he let the real world do that. Even more so, because his Christian culture freed him from having to struggle with some of the tendencies Aristotle inherited from his cultural milieu. This included, like his medieval predecessors, rejecting the parts of Aristotelian physics *(physica)* that the data rule out. Again, it did not, and could not rule out the foundational parts of *physica,* but only the parts that come after. That is, it could only affect conclusions within the specialized science that, by Newton's time, was already quite mature.

[609] Newton's *Principia*, Motte's translation, revised by Cajori, 1962, p. 5.

Furthermore, free of the pagan belief in a plurality of gods with its conflicting and random elements, they were able to think of the universe as a whole and take seriously the rationality of *all* things. In particular, the Greek idea of the *divinity* of the heavens (the bodies in the sky) is profoundly contrary to the medieval (Catholic) cultural environment, for it is part of the same world God created.[610] Again, all particular truths are implicit in Aristotle, but never brought out by him because, I argue, of his cultural milieu.

Further, we discussed the proof of the existence of the universe, which is implicit in St. Thomas, and explicitly believed by the medieval Catholic culture. Absurdly enough, the understandability and thus existence of the universe was put into question during the Enlightenment period, after Newton, by certain thinkers. Accepting the universe as a "universe", *one turn* ("one world"), a unity, was necessary for Newton's great insight of treating the motions of the planets and stars in the same way as the bodies on earth. It continues to be necessary to do modern science; it is what we do every time we do an experiment directed at a different part of the universe, expecting that the laws we already know can be applied.

We also revealed the profoundly irrational positions that can be held if one does not remember the nature of the empiriometric. We found that one can, and many do, argue that something is not there when one is not looking at it (quantum mechanics). We found that Bell's theorem, which is used to back up such claims and thus has been *called* the most profound discovery of science, is actually based on a simple

---

[610] This brings up an interesting fact that distinguished philosopher Fr. Benedict Ashley points out. In the Aristotelian cosmology the "earth is the dregs of the universe" (p. 55, *Aristotle's Sluggish Earth: The Problematics of the "De Caelo"* by B. Ashley, Abertus Magnus Lyceum, 1958). This calls into question the standard "egocentric" interpretation of the pre-Copernican theory. According to this interpretation, it is thought that the ancients put the earth in the center and wanted to keep it there, because that was a way of emphasizing man's importance in the cosmos; however, if, as it was often stated by the ancients, the lower regions are lower also in importance, the interpretation cannot stand. In fact, a key reason why the earth was put in the center is that it seemed to be true.

but fallacious ontological interpretation of the empiriometric. The errors one makes do not have to be complicated if one is insensitive to ontological issues, insensitive to what is. What Gilson said of metaphysics is also true for the foundational principles of *physica;* he said, "Don't pose questions to metaphysics, if you don't want answers from it."

Neglecting ontology, we further found, can lead one to statements like the following. Noted MIT physicist Alan Guth's empiriometric work is taken to say, on the front page of *Discovery* magazine,

> *The entire universe burst into something from absolutely nothing--zero, nada. And as it got bigger, it became filled with even more stuff that came from absolutely nowhere.*[611]

Two profound irrationalities are present in these statements. First, it says something (the whole universe) comes from nothing. Being from non-being. One cannot get more directly irrational than this. Note, the *Discovery* article does not say God created the universe *ex nihilo,* but that the universe is explained--yes, you read that right, *explained*--by saying it came from nothing.[612] Secondly, we saw in Chapter 7 that one cannot argue from existence at one point to complete non-existence at some earlier point, and thus one cannot prove the universe had a beginning, although one can have probable, even highly probable, evidence, such as the big bang provides.

Now, the article later says, in physics, nothing is really something! The convoluted nature of such statements can make it appear profound to some, but such statements actually have exactly the type of ambiguity required to maintain error. Recall, error is not something of itself; it is only something

---

[611] April 2002 issue.

[612] It looks like this conclusion is reached by identifying the empiriometric concept of energy with being itself. In this way, one can turn the crank and act is if "negative" being cancels "positive" being. As if non-being and being are interchangeable. We examined this interesting error using light and darkness in Chapter 6. It boils down to treating everything as beings of reason.

with respect to the truth it distorts, so it needs convoluted statements to be maintained.

In Chapter 7, we went further than pointing out the errors; we gave examples of how one should go about interpreting the empiriometric and, in one case, the empirioschematic. We were not so much interested in giving an exhaustive or even, in most cases, a necessarily correct ontological interpretation, but a reasonable one. In this way, we clarified the distinction between the empiriometric and the properly explanatory, which gets not just at the quantitative interrelations of things coordinated by beings of reasons that is empiriometric theory, but gets at what things *are*. Specifically, we revealed what one might say about the real essence of things using some key modern scientific discoveries (empiriological findings). In so doing, we also set a pattern by which one should think about the empiriological in the larger context of *physica* and thus all of our knowledge.

In **Chapter 8**, we discussed the existence of God and what we can know about Him. We found that if we deny His existence, we implicitly deny the foundational truths that science rests on, for the foundational things we discussed above all lead inexorably to His existence. Indeed, those touchstones of sanity must be denied if one wants to deny Him. We also found that one can avoid making one's understanding of His existence explicit by keeping the first principles of science implicit only, never acknowledging them directly.

We've already discussed what is in store for the culture when one speaks and believes one way and acts another.

For the individual, such inability or refusal to acknowledge first principles and their necessary consequences can lead to the many problems also previously discussed. Among them is the searching for causes in places where they cannot be found. For example, take Guth's implicit belief that we can find a reason for laws by empiriometric science. He says, "Where do the laws of physics come from? ... We are a long way from being able to answer that one."[613]

---

[613] *Discovery* magazine, April 2002, p. 38.

The study of being as being, metaphysics, protects us from falling into these and other errors. More than that, metaphysics brings forward the first principles of all knowledge in their full generality. Metaphysics is the first philosophy; it is the most certain because, by it, we grasp the intelligible reality in things at their core. The transcendentals, namely being under its different aspects, is the prime intelligible. We must remember that being is true, is good, is one, is real, etc. Maritain says in this regard:

Being is, indeed, the proper object of the intellect; it is embowelled in all its concepts; and it is to being, wrapped up in the data of the senses, that our understanding is first of all carried.

Should it set this object of its concept free so as to look at it in itself, insofar as it is being, it sees that it is not exhausted by the sensible realities in which the intellect first discovered it; it has a supraexperimental value. So, too, have the principles based on it. In that way, the intellect, if I may say so, "loops the loop," in coming back, to grasp it metaphysically and transcendentally, to that very same being which was first given to it in its first understanding of the sensible.

And so, because it has in its metaphysical concepts, such as being and the transcendentals, an intellectual perception of objects which can be realized otherwise than in the matter in which it perceives them, it will also attain these objects (this time, without directly perceiving them, and, as it were, by the mirror of sensible things) wherever they are realized without matter, as facts established in the world of experience compel us to infer. Thus, the suprasensible cannot be, at least in the natural order, the object of an experimental science. Nevertheless, it is the object of a science properly so called, and indeed, of the science par excellence. For if the universe of being as being, set free by the mind when it delivers its objects from all materiality, does not fall under the senses, intelligible necessities, on the other hand, are discovered there in the most perfect manner. Thus, the knowledge ordered to such a universe of intelligibility is most certain in itself even though we find it difficult to acknowledge it. For we are an ungrateful and mediocre race which only asks to fail in the highest in what it is capable of, and which, of itself, even when higher gifts have strengthened its eyes, will always prefer the dark.[614]

In the next chapter, **Chapter 9**, we find that "what we should do" is based on what is in accordance with our own nature as it is meant to be part of Nature. We found that God is our ultimate end. If we don't acknowledge this fact, we are left in the practical order, as in the pure sciences with thought, with no ground, no basis for our actions. We are left with "willing" for our own happiness, which makes no sense if we have no final end. Hence, inevitably, one substitutes another last end either implicitly or explicitly. If Truth, Being Himself, is not our end, then, to the degree He is not our end, an element of disorder, of "nothingness," is involved in our purpose, and we are thus bound to create havoc for ourselves and for others. Another way of saying this is: to the degree we leave Being out, even implicitly, that is the degree we allow irrationality to reign. Within a social unit, we saw this amounts to "might makes right."

The natural result for modern science deprived of this particular aspect that comes "before science" is that the empiriological science becomes our last end, our god. It becomes that for which we live. If someone takes this substitution seriously, his family and loved ones become tools for advancing that narrow field and his position in it. Recall that the narrow field of empiriometric science is not even a stand-alone field, so people become *tools for a tool that is deprived of what it's meant to build, physica.* Thus, the necessary result of leaving God out, even implicitly, is that people become mere means for the ends of the powerful; they are thus deprived of their dignity as human beings. Again, even though one may not follow the logic to the end and thus not

[614] *The Degrees of Knowledge*, Maritain p. 67.

make the last step of acting on the inevitable conclusions of the reasoning, it remains true that these consequences are implicit in what we think and say when we deny our last end, Goodness Himself.

We must also remember that modern science, for the most part, is the one place where one finds respect for truth both among the public and among academics. In short, wherever and whenever it humbly works to discover reality, science is defending truth. It would be a shame if this important defense of truth is destroyed by those who attempt to assign modern science a greater importance in the order of knowledge than is justified. By the same insight of proper order, one should not let the humanities--by which I mean the methodological sciences (such as poetry and literature, language arts and many of the social study fields[615]), which are legitimately concerned with the subjective elements in communication--take more than their due by allowing them to eclipse the pure and applied sciences (extended sense).[616] Recall, the methodological sciences only exist to serve the pure and applied sciences. This does not mean they are unimportant. Indeed, they are essential; no field can, without harming itself, deny it. Ethics, for instance, needs literature to give food to the imagination to aid one in living as one should. Or again, *physica* needs literature to transmit the beauty of science to contemporaries and to posterity.

In short, the work of all sciences should be respected in their proper place and sphere. Those with a traditional bent, few indeed now, should remember the real advances that modern science has made and resolve to lose neither the new methods that have brought it such success nor the many new findings, but to value them properly. Those with a modern bent, which is all of us to some extent (because we live now), should note and remember the many severe problems that accompany modern science when it is loosed from its proper setting.

---

[615] At least in the way they are currently approached.
[616] See Figure 6-2 (Chapter 6).

So "How then should we do modern science?" The first answer is already given above. That is, keep in mind that *physica* is larger than modern empiriometric science, and furthermore that there is a whole arena of other fields that interact with *physica*. Some of these fields need *physica*'s results, and others give *physica* some of its foundational principles. In all of this, we remember that being is primary. Knowledge is about reality, not about knowledge. Thinking the latter is the error of philosophical idealism.

But you say, "Specifically, how do our philosophical insights change modern science, and how it should be done? Or does it?" They change it only in one way. They require it to broaden to some degree. How? Simply and seamlessly, it just means replacing the current implicit philosophical basis with an explicit, sound, thought-out one. This does not change the empiriological basis and methodologies of modern science much, except possibly in the moral realm. Putting one's proper final end in place does mean that some will have to make profound changes not in technical method, but in priorities. For example, some may have to cease to use faculty and students and staff merely as tools; these things most know already, whether they act on it, and how often, is a different question. Furthermore, the decay of cultural norms cannot be dismissed, for it causes the serious problems already discussed. In any case, the technical and methodological approaches change very little; we saw in Chapter 7, and we'll get more idea from an example below, when and how such changes might occur. Correct philosophical understanding will also keep one from trying to force ontological considerations into an empiriometric theory. For example, one can accept the theory of relativity, because he clearly sees that it is empiriometric, not directly ontological. One will be clear what belongs where and why. Students will no longer, for example, put up resistance to the ideas because they will know their natural place. Finally, in the great upheavals where one empiriometric paradigm is replaced by another, sound philosophy knowing its limited place will likely be as helpful as pure empiriometric thinking in sparking ideas for larger theories.[617]

By contrast, the explicit philosophical underpinning *greatly changes* what one does with the empiriological work *after it is completed*. That is, once a new theory is complete, it affects how one uses and understands it.

Now, empiriometric science should remain the main tool and task of modern science. It cannot be replaced; it is bound up with our natural ways of acquiring knowledge by abstraction from sense experience and by the material nature of the world. Yet, it must be recognized for what it is: mobile being as quantitative, a tool of *physica*. We must not stop once a theory is complete; once the tool is made, we must be willing to use it. Tools are for building. We should use the theory we obtain to understand, to the degree we can, what it tells us about the world.

The Nothingness of Atoms and Us?

To see how all this manifests itself concretely, let's take one last example in the manner of Chapter 7. In this example, we will see some of the process of empiriometric discovery, and its lack of logical certainty in such cases. We will see, in this case, that we obtain, nonetheless, practical certainty (that atoms exist) and that it is, as we've stressed above, in the interpretation of the empiriometric theory that the real problems can be circumvented. So, let's return to the nothingness of the atom dilemma introduced in Chapter 1.

In that chapter, we saw that if we reduce everything to the arrangement of inert atoms and say atoms are mostly empty space, then we must conclude that we are mostly nothing. As we saw in Chapter 2, there are severe problems with this line of argument. The most manifest problem with the argument is that it implicitly assumes that we know atoms before we know ourselves. This is clearly not true. As we've emphasized, in trying to understand things, *we must start with what is more*

---

[617] In Chapter 7, we noted several points where such considerations might be helpful.

known and proceed to what is less known. However, it is an occupational hazard of physicists, chemists, and scientists and engineers of all types to think of atoms as known first, for in their work, they often think in terms of atoms and not at all about those things that allow them to access and deduce the existence of atoms. These things include the scientists themselves, many other macroscopic things, as well as many significant ideas passed on to them by others. They also see the successful results that they obtain by applying their understanding of atoms in their work domain. A first-rate philosopher professor recently told me what happened when he explained to a science student that knowledge of atoms comes after knowledge of other things. The student then explained that this is not how scientists view the matter. Yet, it remains true that we learn about things by our senses, and we cannot sense atoms; no one has seen[618] or heard an atom. So, we must and do learn about them through things we know directly.

Second, as we pointed out earlier in this book, the concept of "mostly nothing" is an empiriometric one that begs to be interpreted ontologically. When I say my grass is mostly green, I am identifying some fraction of my whole existing lawn as green. There is no way to do this with being. One cannot say a fraction of something is non-being, because the non-being is not part of the something. Hence, properly

---

[618] In 1979, W. Neuhauser, M. Hohenstatt, and H. Dehmelt (cf. David Wick, *The Infamous Boundary*, p. 123), observed, after years of thinking and experimenting, a blue star-like object floating in their vacuum system. They identified it as a Barium atom (ion). They had "seen" an atom. Well, *seen* is here used in an equivocal way. If, by seen, one means seen in a way commensurate with the senses, that is, seen in a way that allows one to say enough about what the thing is to know its an atom, then we must say they did not "see" an atom. To know it's an atom depends on a series of deductions hanging from a web of empiriometric concepts. If someone without scientific knowledge were to walk by and look at the blue dot in their apparatus, they would say "How funny, a blue dot," not "There's a Barium atom!!" If the observer is then told, as you are now, that it is an atom, that identification, for the observer, is improper knowledge accepted on the authority of the scientist. Of course, it is awe-inspiring to see the usefulness of the empiriometric in bringing us reality at such a small level. But we must still keep in mind what comes first and what comes later.

speaking, one should say that if the atom is nearly nothing, then juxtaposing many things that are nearly nothing does not give one something qualitatively different than what one starts with. As we've seen, any number of bad arguments doesn't make a good argument, any number of mediocre mathematicians doesn't make an Euler or a Gauss; one cannot add qualities and get a different quality, as one can do with quantity. As Duhem said:

> *The essential attribute belonging to the category of quantity is therefore the following: each state of a quantity's magnitude may always be formed through addition by means of other smaller states of the same quantity; each quantity is the union through a commutative and associative operation of quantities smaller than the first but of the same kind as it is, and they are parts of it.*[619]

In short, recall, the first accident of things is quantity; the second is quality. We cannot do without qualities. The world has them. Qualities are what allow for relations and actions between things. Nonetheless, the empiriometric tendency is strong; Cartesians,[620] those who thought everything was quantity, and others roundly criticized Newton for introducing an occult[621] *quality*; Newton called it gravitation. One cannot stack inert "atoms" side by side and get a man. Aristotle, though he is often censured for criticizing Democritus' idea of atoms, is on the side of modern science in this, because Democritus had the idea of atoms as inert (totally non-reactive), and in principle unbreakable.[622] Though it is rarely, if ever, pointed out that, at the most important level, Democritus' notion is opposed to modern discoveries. Indeed, the empiriometric science, when rightly (ontologically)

---

[619] See p. 110 of *The Aim and Structure of Physical Theory* by Pierre Duhem, 1991, Princeton University Press.

[620] Followers of Rene Descartes.

[621] So called because they are not directly seeable.

[622] Etymologically, the Greek and Latin words mean "not cut," in other words, indivisible. That is, etymologically "atom" means "not divisible," but this is not the modern usage of the word.

understood *does not imply* a mere stacking[623] of atoms, but without proper philosophical understanding, such a conclusion appears natural. We will return to the details of modern science's study of atoms shortly.

For now, we have opened the issue of reductionism; let's continue further in. Reductionism is helpful in its proper place in the *empiriometric* science. It facilitates one in building models and finding quantitative relations, **but** it is *untenable* to use it as ontology--that is, to use it to understand what is really happening. A man cannot be understood by just understanding an isolated atom, whatever that might mean. It is "more impossible" to do this than to understand a sentence by means of the *isolated* letters, or a song by means of understanding the *isolated* notes. Why more impossible? Well, impossible is impossible, no adjectives can change that; indeed, to put the "more" is really an instance of attempting to reduce quality to quantity.

However, I did have a reason, other than giving the opportunity to point out this type of blunder, for saying it this way. What? There is a real difference between the case of man and his atoms and the book and its words. With man, we are dealing with real ontological unity, not unity based on signs, which is a unity imposed from the outside, but the interior unity of a thing. In the case of the book, one may cheat by sneaking the isolated words together; one cannot cheat with the man. If he is nothing more than what each atom is individually, then that's what he is. If a man is not a unity, is not one thing, just a stack of atoms, he is nothing better than the individual atoms that are stacked up. Stacking them up will not make him anything more than the atoms already are. There's nothing to sneak in.

But man is much more than a stack of atoms. Even a non-rational animal is much more than a stack of atoms. Even a plant, even an inanimate substance is more, though at this later point it's not much more. What's the resolution of the dilemma?

---

[623] Even stacking requires some sort of active quality to keep one from falling into the other.

Atoms are *neither* inert things *nor* unbreakable things. They are secondary matter that can receive a higher form. When atoms, say of silicon, come together to form a crystal under the right conditions, the atoms interact with each other, and changes occur (potentialities are reduced to act). Indeed, we would not know anything about an atom, unless we were able to do something to it or observed it in something as it did something. It cannot be inert, not subject to change. In summary, if the atom did not have qualities it could not be observed, because it could not act on anything. Qualities are, after all, that which issues from a substance and allow it to act on other substances.

When we construct an empiriometric theory of atoms, we use measurements from many different types of experimental setups and study atoms in many varied chemical settings (i.e., in different substances). In this way, as we've said, we leave behind the qualities as they really are and replace them with a mathematical system and beings of reason (models) to interpret that system. In short, many different actualities and potentialities of both the atom and the things used to probe it are included in the empiriometric theory in hidden--and don't forget, usually averaged (thus leaving out the individual)[624]--ways. Thus, although we know that the atom has qualities, to know what they are is a completely other and potentially extremely hard problem. This recalls our original statement that we do not even directly know atoms themselves. So, before trying to give a final answer to the atom dilemma, let's recall how far removed the atom is from our direct experience. Indeed, how do we even know atoms exist? And, what do we know about them?

---

[624] Note, it is often said atoms are identical in every way except for where they are. Again, this is leaping way beyond the empiriometric implications, for we are forced, for various reasons, into a statistical description, which of its nature leaves out individuals and only talks about average traits. Two "identical," in some empiriometric sense (say they are same isotope), aluminum atoms (e.g., isotope mass 26) could be significantly different ontologically; they can clearly manifest this by behaving differently. For example, at one moment, one may undergo beta decay and the other not.

John Dalton (1766-1864) was the first to successfully bring out the experimental evidence for atoms, in a meaning close to the modern one.[625] Fundamentally, he and others found (within in some numerical error, like all experiment) that the results of reactions between various chemicals led to integer ratios of the reactants' and products' weights.[626] Dalton stated that the elements always combine with each other in small whole number ratios. He and others found that these integer ratios could be explained by assuming that there were pure elements composed of small parts called atoms.[627]

Such reasoning did not convince everyone. However, evidence confirming the atomic hypothesis from many sectors began to build toward the end of the 1800s and beginning of the 1900s. While the first experiments were more direct, the later ones were more theory-laden. None by themselves was convincing. Yet, when considered together, the interlocking of one experiment and its interpretation with another, one becomes more and more convinced that there are indeed atoms. At some point, the evidence becomes so overwhelming, a scientist, such as myself, takes it for given. What of the nature of atoms?

Ernst Rutherford (1871-1937)[628] postulated the structure of the atom in 1911. He did so using the results of the following experiment. The experimenters took a material that spontaneously emitted particles named alpha particles. These particles cannot be seen, already making it one step removed

---

[625] He and others obviously saw and understood, unlike Democritus, that atoms interacted. They did (falsely) hypothesize that atoms were, in principle, unbreakable. Yet, as an empiriometric assumption, this was helpful, because for the range of conditions that they were working under, atoms did not break up enough to affect the creation of their empiriometric theory. Note that atoms do and are breaking up all the time, for certain forms of natural radioactive decay are nothing other than atoms "breaking down" from one type of atom to another. Americium 241 decays naturally by alpha decay, for example, to Neptunium 237.

[626] And, for gases under the right conditions, it's true for volumes as well.

[627] In other words, given a chunk of such a pure element, one can, even in principle, only cut it into so many pieces; the smallest piece is the atom.

[628] Geiger and Marsden carried out the experiment at the suggestion of Rutherford.

from direct observation, so one must use a film or other screen that shows a spot visible to the naked eye when an alpha particle strikes it. A thin layer of gold was placed between the source of alpha particles and the screen. The source was directed at the gold. As expected, many marks were seen on the screen directly on the other side of the gold, apparently implying that the particles went straight through,[629] but surprisingly some few appeared to bounce straight back (appearing, for example, as marks on a second screen placed on the back side of the source). It was as if one shot a cannonball, as Rutherford later said, at tissue paper and it came back and hit you. This led to the conclusion that the atom is mostly "space" with something very heavy, the nucleus, in the middle.

Using all the things we know empiriometrically about the atom, what can we say about the atom besides it exists? We've already noted that the atom has qualities, but what do we know about those qualities? Before answering, note again, the ontological analysis of empiriometric theories, in general, leads one to only probable knowledge. The more theory-laden and indirect is the theory, the less certain are any ontological conclusions, but let's say what we can.

First, the empiriometric theory describes electromagnetic interactions between the electrons. We can interpret this ontologically to mean that electrons have at least one quality that is able to act on other electrons and the nucleus. The empiriometric theory further supports the idea that this active quality is present throughout the atom at various intensities and changes with time. We could say that the active quality is manifested by the intensity of the electric field at a given point in the atom. In short, between the

---

[629] This is, of course, not a direct observation, but a hypothesis. Compare this, for example, with a metaphorical parallel experiment. Consider a perforated wall that you throw colored baseballs at. In this experiment, unlike the one above, one can watch the ball, for instance, go through the wall and hit the facing wall. One can also go pick up the ball and verify that it was the one thrown. In the Rutherford experiment, one sees spots appearing on the other side of the gold "wall" when one puts the source in, and few if any when one does not put the source in. One has to make hypotheses and test and convince oneself that the above model makes sense.

electrons and the nucleus, there is something, not nothing. Qualities are accidents, which mean they can only inhere in another. This ontological description is backed up by the empiriometric theory known as quantum electrodynamics, which predicts that even within the "empty" section of an atom, there are fluctuations and changes occurring. For example, the Lamb shift is a shift in energy levels that is believed to result from such fluctuations interacting with the electron. So, empiriometric theory with a reasonable ontological exposition belies the idea that an "isolated" atom is "mostly empty space."

In summary, even isolated atoms are more than we may have previously thought. Further, when atoms interact to form an inanimate substance, say for example hydrogen and oxygen, they become part of an ontologically higher substance, water; they are virtually present in the new substance. Virtually does not mean the atoms are not really there; they are. It means their actuality is subsumed into the more full actuality of the new substance of water. Similarly, when a plant ingests an inanimate substance, like water, the nutritive life of the plant subsumes the water into its activity. The water is virtually present in the plant; *the plant is one thing, not thousands* numbered by the different compounds in it; the water is a part of the plant, but its actuality is subsumed under the higher actuality of the plant. Hence, in the case of man, he is composed of atoms; the atoms are really there, but their actuality is contained by the greater actuality of the man. Again, as mentioned in Chapter 2, you are one substantial being, not 10^{28} beings (atoms). You cannot be both. The paradox is resolved because being is not univocal, like much of the mathematics that we are so habituated to; it is many-leveled. It is analogical.

It is only when an atom is stripped off, say the surface of one's fingertip, that it takes on its own substantial existence. Similarly, we can make the same statement about protons, neutrons, and electrons. They are actualities in the atom, but they are not substantially present, only virtually present in the atom. Once they are stripped out of the atom, they take on a substantial[630] existence of their own. To further appreciate the idea of "virtual," consider the following. The properties of hydrogen and oxygen are radically different from that of water that contains (virtually) them both.

What does this mean for the nothingness of the atom paradox? It means that the atom takes on a new level of being when present in man. Potentialities are actualized that were not in the isolated atoms. The form of the man is something qualitatively different than that of the isolated atom, which is what we knew already, because it is what we know first.

The Love of Wisdom

We see that philosophy can save us from many fatal mistakes like the "nothingness of the atom" canard. However, we do not study philosophy *primarily* to save ourselves from mistakes. We study it because that is what we are made for. Philosophy is the love of Wisdom; it is love of Truth.

Philosophy, unlike mathematics, is not simply working within a more or less predefined mental framework. It is a series of insights into reality; as such, it probes inward deeper and deeper into reality, rather than scampering around on the surface. Philosophy requires one to stop and stare at reality; it requires receptiveness to reality. For to access truth, one must conform oneself to reality. It needs a certain stillness and patience with what appears to be obvious, but is more than just obvious, it's profound.[631] It is like staring at a beautiful landscape during sunset; if one is used to busyness, he can initially feel like he is wasting time. His decision to stay will

---

[630] We are here assuming that they are not accidents of the atom.

[631] An example of this is found in physicist Pierre Duhem's comment, "If we rid the physics of Aristotle and of Scholasticism of the outworn and demoded scientific clothing covering it and if we bring out in its vigorous and harmonious nakedness the living flesh of this cosmology, we would be struck by its resemblance to our modern physical theory: we recognize in these two doctrines two pictures of the same ontological order, distinct because they are each taken from a different point of view, but in no way discordant." (Page 310 of *The Aim and Structure of Physical Theory* by Pierre Duhem, 1991 Princeton University Press.)

likely be amply rewarded, but his decision to leave will mean he will be unaware and thus ambivalent to what he missed. Philosophy is a meditating on reality; empiriological science can sometimes be a substitution of action and thought for reality. These differences, along with our somewhat impatient cultural tendencies, partly explain the widespread ignorance of sound philosophy in our culture.

The formerly self-professed "pagan" and renowned philosopher Mortimer Adler, when on TV (on PBS) not so long ago, was asked how so many have made such fundamental philosophical mistakes. Specifically, how was it, he was asked, that so many did not understand the truths that St. Thomas enunciated so clearly? Adler shook his slightly bowed head, with a pained look on his face and said, (and I speak from memory so it is paraphrased), "I am afraid I have to say something unkind here," and, after a pause, still pained: "These men simply have not submitted their minds to the literature [of St. Thomas and his disciples]."

We see that the science before science is indeed so. We deny it at the peril of the second science, modern science, and our own happiness.

Books of Interest

Adler, Mortimer. *Ten Philosophical Mistakes.* New York:
Macmillian Publishing Company, 1987.

_____. *Truth in Religion.* New York: MacMillan Publishing
Company, 1990.

_____. *The Angels and Us.* Collier Books/MacMillan Publishing
Company, 1982.

_____.*How to Speak, How to Listen.* New York: MacMillan
Publishing Company, 1997.

Apostle, Hippocrates George. *Aristotle's Philosophy of
Mathematics.* Chicago: The University of Chicago Press,
1952.

Aquinas, St. Thomas. *Commentary on Aristotle's Metaphysics,*
translation by John P. Rowan. Dumb Ox Books, 1995.

_____. *Commentary on Aristotle's De Anima,* translated by
Kenelm Foster, O.P., and Silvester Humphries, O.P. Dumb
Ox Books, 1994.

_____. *Commentary on Aristotle's Physics,* translated by Richard
J. Blackwell, Richard J. Spath, and W. Edmund Thirlkel.
Dumb Ox Books, 1999.

_____. *Summa Contra Gentiles, Book One: God,* translated by
Anton C. Pegis, F.R.S.C. University of Notre Dame Press,
1975.

_____. *Summa Theologica, Complete English Edition in Five
Volumes,*translated by Father of the English Dominican
Province. Christian Classics, 1981.

_____. *On Being and Essence,* translated by Armand Maurer.
Pontifical Institute of Medieval Studies, 1968.

_____. *The Division and Methods of the Sciences,* translated by
Armand Maurer. Pontifical Institute of Medieval Studies,
1986.

_____. *On There Being Only One Intellect / Aquinas Against the
Averroists,* translated by Ralph McInerny. Purdue
University Press, 1993.

_____. *Commentary on Aristotle's on Interpretation and Posterior Analytics.* 2002.

_____. *Commentary on Aristotle's Nicomachean Ethics,* translated by C.I. Litzinger. Dumb Ox Books, 1964.

_____. *Truth, Vol. I-III,* translated by Robert W. Mulligan. Hackett Publishing Company, Inc., 1994.

_____. *The De Malo of Thomas Aquinas,* translated by Richard Regan. Oxford University Press, 2001.

_____. *Thomas Aquinas On Being and Essence,* translated by Armand Maurer. The Pontifical Institute of Medieval Studies, 1968.

_____. *Aquinas on Creation,* translated by S. E. Baldner & W. E. Carroll. Pontifical Institute of Medieval Studies, 1997.

_____. *An Exposition of the "On the Hebdomads" of Boethius,* translated by J. L. Schultz and E. A. Synan. The Catholic University of America Press, 2001.

_____. *How to Study* (being the letter of St. Thomas Aquinas to Brother John De Modo Studendi), translation by Victor White, O.P. Oxford, 1947.

Aristotle. *The Complete Works of Aristotle (Two Volumes), The Revised Oxford Translation,* edited by Jonathan Barnes. Princeton/Bollingen Series LXXI.2, University of California Press, 1984.

Ashley, Benedict. *Aristotle's Sluggish Earth: The Problematics of The De Caelo.* Albertus Magnus Lyceum, 1958.

_____. *Theologies of the Body.* The Pope John Center, 1995.

_____. The Search for Wisdom: An Interdisciplinary, Contextual Introduction to Metaphysics (to be published)

Baum, David. *Quantum Implications: Essays in Honour of David Bohm,* edited by B.J. Hiley and F. David Peat. New York: Routledge & Kegan Paul, 1988.

Brody, Thomas. *The Philosophy Behind Physics,* edited by Luis de la Pena and Peter Hodgson. Springer-Verlag, 1994, California Press, 1962.

Cao, Tian Yu. *Conceptual Developments of 20th Century Field Theories.* Cambridge University Press, 1997.

Chesterton, G. K. *The Life of St. Thomas Aquinas "The Dumb Ox".* Image Book, 1956.

_____. *The Everlasting Man.* Ignatius Press, 1993.

_____. *Orthodoxy.* Image Book, 1959.

Claggett, Marshall. *Greek Science in Antiquity.* MacMillan
        Publishing Company, 1963.

Crombie, A. C. *Robert Grosseteste and the Origins of
        Experimental Science 1100-1700.* Oxford University
        Press, 1955.

Cushing, James T. and McMullin, Ernan editors. *Philosophical
        Consequences of Quantum Theory: Reflections on Bell's
        Theorem.* University of Notre Dame Press, 1989.

Dales, Richard C. *The Scientific Achievement of the Middle Ages.*
        University of Pennsylvania Press, 1973.

Darwin, Charles. *The Origin of Species.* Prometheus Books, 1991.

Davies, Paul. Various works.

De Koninck, Charles. *Natural Science as Philosophy.* Quebec,
        1959.

_____. *Introduction to the Study of the Soul,* translated by Bruno
        M. Mondor, O.F. Dominican House of Philosophy, 1951.

_____. *Abstraction from Matter.* Laval Theologique Et
        Philosophique, 1957, 1960.

_____. *Random Reflections on Science and Calculation.* Laval
        Theologique Et Philosophique, 1956.

DeMarco, Donald. *The Heart of Virtue.* Ignatius Press, 1996.

Dugas, Rene. *A History of Mechanics.* Dover Publications, Inc.,
        1988.

Duhem, Pierre, *Le Systeme Du Monde, 10 Volumes*

_____. *The Evolution of Mechanics,* translated by Michael Cole,
        Sijthoff & Noordhoff, 1980.

_____. *Medieval Cosmology: Theories of Infinity, Place, Time,
        Void, and the Plurality of Worlds,* edited and translated by
        Roger Ariew, The University of Chicago Press, 1985.

_____. *The Aim and Structure of Physical Theory,* translated by
        Philip P. Wiener, Princeton University Press, 1991.

Eddington, Sir Arthur. *The Nature of the Physical World,* Folcroft
        Library Editions, 1935.

_____. *The Philosophy of Physical Science,* University of
        Michigan Press, 1958.

Feynman, Richard P. *The Meaning of It All.* Perseus Books, 1998.

Garrigou-Lagrange, Reginald, *God: His Existence and His Nature.*
        St. Louis: B. Herder Books, 1946.

_____. *Reality: A Synthesis of Thomistic Thought.* St. Louis: B. Herder Books, 1950.

Gell-Mann, Murray, *The Quark and the Jaguar.* W. H. Freeman and Company, 1994.

Gilson, Etienne, *Methodical Realism.* Translated by Philip Trower, Christendom Press, 1990.

_____. *The Christian Philosophy of St. Thomas Aquinas.* University of Notre Dame Press, 1956.

_____. *Elements of Christian Philosophy.* Doubleday & Company, Inc., 1960.

_____. *The Spirit of Medieval Philosophy,* translated by A. H. C. Downes. University of Notre Dame Press, 1936.

_____. *God and Philosophy.* Yale University Press, 1941.

_____. *From Aristotle to Darwin and Back Again: A Journey in Final Causality, Species, and Evolution,* translated by John Lyon. University of Notre Dame Press, 1984.

_____. *Methodical Realism.* Christendom Press, 1990.

_____. *Being and Some Philosophers.* Pontifical Institute of Medieval Studies, 1952.

_____. *The Unity of Philosophical Experience,* Ignatius Press, 1999.

Grant, Edward (editor). *A Source Book in Medieval Science,* Harvard University Press, 1974.

Hawking, Stephen W. *A Brief History of Time: From the Big Bang to Black Holes.* Bantam Books, 1988.

Heisenberg, Werner. *Philosophical Problems of Quantum Physics.* 1979.

_____. *The Physicist's Conception of Nature.* 1958.

_____. *Problems of Nuclear Science.* 1952.

_____. *Physics & Philosophy; The Revolution in Modern Science.* 1962.

Herbert, Nick. *Quantum Reality: Beyond the New Physics.* Anchor Press, 1985.

Hofstadter, Douglas R. *Gödel, Escher, Bach: An Eternal Golden Braid.* Basic Books, Inc, 1979.

Jaki, Stanley L. *Means to Message: A Treatise on Truth.* William B. Eerdmans Publishing Company, 1999.

_____. *God and the Cosmologists.* Scottish Academic Press, 1998.

_____. *Science & Creation.* Scottish Academic Press, 1986.

_____. *The Origin of Science and the Science of Its Origin.* Scottish Academic Press, 1978.

_____. *The Relevance of Physics.* Scottish Academic Press, 1970.

_____. *Giordano Bruno: A Martyr of Science?* Real View Book, 2000.

_____. *Brain, Mind and Computers.* Regnery Gateway, 1989.

_____. *The Purpose of It All.* Regnery Gateway, 1990.

_____. *Angels, Apes & Men.* Sherwood Sugden & Company, 1983.

_____. *The Road of Science and the Ways of God.* Scottish Academic Press, 1978.

_____. *Miracles and Physics.* Christendom Press, 1989.

_____. *Is There a Universe?* Wethersfield Institute, 1993.

_____. *Bible and Science.* Christendom Press, 1996.

_____. *Scientist and Catholic: Pierre Duhem.* Christendom Press, 1991.

_____. *Reluctant Heroine: The Life and Work of Helene Duhem.* Scottish Academic Press, 1992.

_____. "The Inspiration and Counter-Inspiration of Astronomical Phenomena." *The Asbury Theological Journal,* Fall 1996, Vol. 51, No. 2.

_____. *The Paradox of Olbers' Paradox.* Real View Books, 1969.

_____. *Uneasy Genius: The Life and Work of Pierre Duhem.* Martinus Nijhoff; 1984.

_____. *Chesterton: A Seer of Science.* Univ. of Illinois Pr (Pro Ref), 1986.

_____. Chance or Reality and Other Essays. Rowman & Littlefield, 1986.

_____. *Planets and Planetarians: A History of Theories on the Origin of Planetary Systems.* Books Britain, 1978.

_____. *Word: Blocks, Amoebas, or Patches of Fog? Artificial Intelligence and the Conceptual. SPIE* Vol. 2761, 1996.

John of St. Thomas, (also called John Poinsot). Various writings.

Kant, Immanuel. *Critique of Pure Reason.*

_____. *Universal Natural History and Theory of the Heavens,* edited and translated by Stanley L. Jaki. Scottish Academic Press, 1981.

Kneller, Karl A. *Christianity and the Leaders of Modern Science.*
     Real View Books, 1995.
Kuhn, Thomas. *The Structure of Scientific Revolutions.* University
     of Chicago Press, 1962.
Lewis, C. S., *The Abolition of Man.* Macmillan Publishing Co.,
     1955.
_____. *Mere Christianity.*
Maritain, Jacques. *Distinguish to Unite* or *The Degree of
     Knowledge,* translated under the supervision of Gerald B.
     Phelan. Charles Scribner's Sons, New York, 1959.
_____. *An Introduction to Philosophy.* Christian Classics, Inc.,
     1989.
_____. *Philosophy of Nature.* New York: Philosophical Library,
     1951.
_____. *Untrammeled Approaches,* translated by Bernard Doering.
     University of Notre Dame Press, 1997.
_____. *The Person and the Common Good,* translated by John
     Fitzgerald. University of Notre Dame Press, 1985.
_____. *Approaches to God,* translated by Peter O'Reilly. New
     York: The Macmillan Company, 1954.
_____. *A Preface to Metaphysics: Seven Lectures on Being.* Ayer
     Company Publishers, Inc., 1987.
_____. *An Introduction to the Basic Problems of Moral
     Philosophy.* Magi Books, Inc., 1990.
_____. *Three Reformers: Luther, Descartes, Rousseau.* Charles
     Scribner's Sons.
_____. *The Collected Works of Jacques Maritain, Vol. I & II.*
     University of Notre Dame Press, 1997.
_____. *The Range of Reason.* Charles Scribner's Sons, 1952.
_____. *Formal Logic,* translated by Imelda Choquette. Sheed &
     Ward, 1946.
_____. *Reflexions Sur L'Intelligence.* Nouvelle Librairie
     Nationale, 1926.
_____. *The Dream of Descartes,* translated by Mabelle l.
     Andison. Philosophical Library, 1944.
McInerny, Ralph, *Characters in Search of Their Authors,*
     University of Notre Dame Press, 2001.

_____. *Aquinas Against The Averroists / On There Being Only One Intellect,* translated by Ralph McInerny, Purdue University Press, 1993.

_____. *A Student's Guide to Philosophy.* ISI Books, 1999.

Melzer, Weinberger, and Zinman. *Technology in the Western Polictical Tradition.* Cornell University Press, 1993.

Misner, Thorne & Wheeler. *Gravitation.* W. H. Freeman and Company, 1973.

Newton, Sir Isaac. *Principia, Vol. I & II,* Motte's translation revised by Cajori. University of California Press, 1962.

Oresme, Nicole. *Nicole Oresme and the Kinematics of Circular Motion,* edited by Edward Grant. University of Wisconsin Publications in Medieval Science, 1999.

Pascal, Blaise. *Pensees,* translated by A.J. Krailsheimer. Penguin Books, 1995.

Patterson, Francine & Eugene Linden. *The Education of Koko.* Holt, Rinehart and Winston, 1981.

Penrose, Roger. *The Emperor's New Mind: Concerning Computers, Minds, and the Laws of Physics.* Oxford University Press, 1989.

Pieper, Josef. *The Four Cardinal Virtues.* University of Notre Dame Press, 1966.

_____. *In Defense of Philosophy,* translated by Lothar Krauth. Ignatius Press, 1992.

_____. *Guide to Thomas Aquinas,* translated by Richard and Clara Winston. Ignatius Press, 1986.

_____. *Living the Truth.* Ignatius Press, 1989.

Plato. *Complete Works,* edited by John M. Cooper. Hackett Publishing Company, 1997.

Poincare, Henri. *Science and Hypothesis.* Dover Publications, Inc.

_____. *Science and Method.* St. Augustine's Press, 2001.

_____. *The Value of Science.* Dover, 1958.

Sebeok, Thomas A. & Robert Rosenthal, editors. *The Clever Hans Phenomenon: Communication with Horses, Whales, Apes and People.* The New York Academy of Sciences, 1981.

Sheed, F. J. *Theology for Beginners.* Servant Books, 1981.

Simon, Yves R. *The Great Dialogue of Nature and Space, A Carthage Reprinting.* St. Augustine's Press, 2001.

St. Cajetan. Various works.

Sullivan, Daniel. *An Introduction to Philosophy.* Tan Books and
     Publishers, Inc., 1992.
Thorne, Kip S. *Black Holes & Time Warps.* W. W. Norton &
     Company, 1994.
Wallace, William. *The Elements of Philosophy,* Alba House, 1977.
_____. The Modeling of Nature. Catholic University Press, 1996.
Wegemer, Gerard B. *Thomas More: A Portrait of Courage.*
     Scepter Publishers, 1997.
Weisheipl, James A. *The Development of Physical Theory in the
     Middle Ages.* University of Michigan Press, 1971.

Glossary

accident:
    a) Generically, *an accident* is a property (in the widest sense). It is that which inheres in another, that which must exist in a substance, but is distinct from its essence. For instance, when one says, "there's a red..." all know the speaker must continue and tell us "a red" something. There are nine categories of accidents (*see* Chapter 3).

    b) A *proper accident* or *property in the strict sense* is an accident whose existence is necessarily caused by the substance. The substance can, of course, be impeded in its causing of a property by the action of other causes. For example, chemical or radiation damage can cause genetic damage to an animal fetus while in its mother that leads to it being born lame. The animal remains an animal, that is, it is *essentially* the same (same essence), but is missing a leg, a proper accident.

    c) A *mere accident* is an accident that does not spring from the essence of a thing. It is received in the substance from some external cause. For example, water may be found at 40 degrees or 80 degrees, the temperature at either moment is a *mere* accident of the water.

accidental form: See *form*.

act: Something "in act" is something which is. *The actuality of a thing is that which it is at a given moment, as opposed to that which it may become.* The *act* of existence is the most primitive, the most primary, action in that all other actions come from the act of existing, from things that are as they are. "Act" is an expression of the *verb* form of being. It is what "be s" in being. Something *is* to the degree that it is "in act." For example, the shape of an apple is part of the actuality of the apple.

animal: (philosophic sense) A living organism with the capacity of sensorial knowledge.

animalae: Category of the modern biological (empiriological) classification scheme that is probably composed completely of animals in the philosophical sense above. Some animals (philosophical sense) are put in the other empiriological categories.

being: The first thing we know is that "there is an is." Being is primary. Being is analogical; it is heterogeneous, not homogeneous, on many levels, not one. Its primary meaning is to exist; other meanings flow from this one. Being is first in importance in philosophy; the transcendentals are being as viewed from various aspects. We divide being into two pieces:

    a) Noun form, anything that "be s", anything that is. In Latin, *"ens."*

    b) Verb form, "to be," the act of existing. In Latin, *"esse."*

beings of reason: Those objects of thought that can only exist in the world of the mind, not in the world outside of the mind. Dark, for example, is a being of reason; it is the absence of light. Darkness, of itself, cannot exist. From logic, for example, propositions are beings of reason. From mathematics, the square root of minus one is a being of reason; it cannot exist as conceived outside of the mind. Where, show me, are there $\sqrt{-1}$ cows? It is not possible, for $\sqrt{-1}$ is a being of reason. Mathematical objects are reductively real (*see mathematics*).

Most strictly, they are second intentions, including the purely mental relations created by the mind which manipulate them. Second intention are those purely mental objects that the mind creates in order to aid in understanding the world. For instance, one can consider an object not as it is originally given, i.e., as a reality abstracted from the sensible realm, but as it is considered by a reflexive operation of the mind (i.e. secondarily), that is, considered *as a thought in one's mind, as existing in one's intellect (abstractly)*. The existence of such beings and the purely mental relations established to manipulate them are obviously wholly dependent on the mind, and they are spontaneously generated during the activity of reason and thus can be most properly called beings *of* reason.

belief:

    a) Belief in the generic sense means having a level of probable, but not certain, conviction that is usually largely based on the word of another. In this sense, improper knowledge is thus a species of belief.

b) <u>Belief</u> in the proper sense means trusting the word of another.

c) <u>Levels of belief</u> refer to the chain of beliefs from which a given belief hangs. For example, one may believe something because he learns it from someone who told someone else, who in turn was told by someone else. Similarly, one can have a belief, in the generic sense, that hangs from a chain of probable reasons (likely backed up by the word of another) based in its turn on some previous probable reasoning. Of course, combination chains that consist of proper beliefs and beliefs in the generic sense are also possible.

body: A material substance. Any form-matter composite (or group of such composites); that is, a substance that has quantitative properties. Because of their composite nature, all bodies are capable of change. They have at least the nine categories of accidents listed by Aristotle, given below. Sometimes used to indicate a group of material substances that are clumped together.

categories: The nine kinds of accidents possessed by all changeable substances (bodies).

   <u>Those properties intrinsic to a material substance:</u>

1) *Quantity* (extension)

2) *Quality* (what issues from a substance, such as color, temperature, pressure, sound, smell, hardness and consistency)

   <u>Those properties involving relations in a strict sense:</u>[632]

3) *Relation* (pure relations such as equality, similarity, and causality)

4, 5) *Action* and *reception* (often translated "passion" or "being acted on" or "affection") Respectively, changing and being changed

6-8) *Place, orientation, environment*

9) *Time*

(see next page)

---

[632] Because of the oneness of the reality, everything is related to everything else in some sense.

To be more complete, one can note that **substance** is the first category, followed by the nine kinds of accidents above, giving ten total categories that make up the broadest genera in the classification of changeable being.

change: Potentiality in the *process* of becoming actuality. Technically, it is the actualization of the potential as such.

changeable being: *See material being.*

color: Generically, a primary quality of a body observable by sight. Reductively, its species are hues of the spectrum such as red, orange, yellow, green, blue, indigo, and violet. However, there are many colors besides just the spectral ones. White is composed of colors. Black is the absence of color. Our eye is limited and doesn't see all colors equally well. One can, by analogy, call non-visible parts of the electromagnetic spectrum, such as ultraviolet and infrared, colors.

common experience: Those experiences that we all accumulate by daily living that require no special training or techniques in thinking (such as predicate calculus). They are "common" not because we all have many, or even some, identical experiences, but because we are learning of the same world through a common human nature.

concept: *See idea.*

connatural: Those things that are consonant with our nature. Connatural knowledge, for example, is a knowledge that comes from lived experience correctly incorporated. Mathematics is connatural to us because it uses both our imagination and our intellect. Case in point: we abstract the concept of circle, but we can still make use of images in our understanding it.

conscience: The mind of man in its role of making moral judgments. Literally, from Latin, *con scientia*, which literally means *"with knowledge."*

corporeal being: Same as *body*.

create: To bring into existence from nothing, usually made explicit by saying, "creation *ex nihilo*," which literally means "creation from nothing." Creation is contrasted with *making*, whereby a material thing loses a given form and acquires a new one. For instance, one makes water from hydrogen and oxygen. In the reaction of hydrogen gas and oxygen gas when exposed to heat, the forms of hydrogen and oxygen gas are lost, and that of water educed, but the (secondary) matter is conserved. The water is ***not*** made from nothing; it is made when one causes the actualization of already existing potentialities in the hydrogen and oxygen. Oxygen and hydrogen atoms are subsumed under the new form of water. Another example is the making of a house; the builder starts with certain materials and *uses them* to make the house.

Another example is the making of a house; the builder starts with certain materials and *uses them* to make the house.

degrees or **levels of abstraction:**

1st *Physica* (leaving behind only particular matter behind). Example: the general idea of a dog.

2nd *Mathematica* (leaving all accidents, but the first accident quantity). Example: circle.

3rd *Metaphysica* (leaving behind all features that belong *only* to material things). Example: the concept of substance.

difference: *See genus.*

empiriological: That tool of a broader science, e.g. *physica*, that makes heavy use of beings of reason to bring sensorial data under certain organizational principles, especially in such a way as to maximally predict outcomes. It both reflects and hides in varying degrees the underlying real being which is the ultimate cause of the relations and properties seen. It usually considers the average of features of many things, rather than the essential features of a given thing. The empiriological methodology contrasts with ontological methodology, for the latter has the aim of understanding the essence of things; what things are. The result of empiriological science is usually a puzzle waiting to be understood ontologically.

a) ***Empiriometric*** science is the primary mode of operation of modern physics. It is the mixed science that is formally mathematical and materially physical. It takes as its mode of explanation the mathematical, but it is trying to explain the physical. St. Thomas and Aristotle use optics as an example; it's formally geometry, but materially about light. It makes use of two different levels of abstraction: *mathematica* and *physica*. In modern usage, empiriometric science has developed highly refined techniques of quantitative measurement and development of theory. At this advanced degree of empiriometric, one interprets the measurements using sophisticated theoretical understanding where one concept hangs in the middle of a web of others.

b) Empirioschematic science is the science (extended sense) that organizes measured and observed sensorial information into the beings of reason of schema rather than mathematics, in order to better see the common features. As one recedes from the simplest types of matter, ones that are lowest in the scale of being and therefore more closely pure quantity, the empiriometric method becomes harder and harder and less and less probative. At the level of the many chemical reactions already it starts to become helpful to use schema rather than mathematics. By the time one is in the biological realm, the empirioschematic becomes the rule. The empirioschematic is not properly a mixed science because while it remains materially physical, it is *also* formally physical, in particular sensible. However, it does tend toward the philosophical, toward making use of real being, but in a mode amenable to the sensible, so that the philosophical principles are distilled out of the *physica*, leaving only a being of reason that can serve the purpose of keeping account of all the sensible phenomena primarily as sensible, not as understood.

essence:
a) In the *wide sense*, <u>essence</u> is what a thing is as intelligible.
b) In a *restricted sense*, the <u>essence</u> of a thing is what the thing is necessarily and primarily as the first principle of its intelligibility (Jacques Maritain)
c) In the *most restricted sense*, <u>essence</u> is the form of the thing; this implicitly includes reference to matter, in the case of material beings.

evil: The privation of a good. It is a lack of a being that a thing should have but does not. We say that a given food is bad, because it should be edible but it is not. We say that a man is evil because he does what he should not. Note, the more something is, the more evil it can be, because it has more to distort, more to become disordered.

form:
   a) **_Substantial form_** is that which actually is in what exists of itself.
   b) **_Accidental form_** is that which exists in a substance.
   c) **_Form_** is generally that correlative of a material being (form-matter composite) by which it actually exists, as opposed to what the material being may become, potentiality (matter). An apple is primarily its "appleness" (its substantial form), but it can become part of me when I eat it, because it has the potentiality to do so. Wood does not have this potency.

genus: A class of things made up of subordinate classes, called *species.* What defines--specifies--a group or subordinate class in the genus as a species is called *specific difference* or simply *difference*.

God: That being whose existence is its essence. He is who Is. He is Pure Act, Pure Being, Necessary Being, the Uncaused Cause that is responsible for the existence of everything. He is the root of all, that is, the "Is" that permeates all contingent beings and gives them their "to be."

heterogeneous: Non-uniform, not consisting of the same qualitative type throughout. Being is heterogeneous. That is, the nature of being admits various analogous states, not all of one type; for example, not all being is mathematical.

idea or **concept:** That by which we know things in the mind. Ideas put us in contact with the general rather than particular and are distinguishing characteristic of intellectual knowledge. *Phantasms*, by contrast, unite us with the particular and are associated with sensorial knowledge.

imagination: The imagination is our ability to recall and manipulate our sensorial knowledge. In common usage, it often only means the ability to manipulate phantasms (images). For example, one who thinks of a cat with three eyes that smells like a rose is called imaginative. Whereas one who recalls, by way of phantasm, the exact state of his house cat is not, in most common speech, said to be using his imagination. There is a more general use of the word that includes any use of phantasms (images), whether manipulation or just representing an object no longer present. In this definition, imagination is simply use of images (phantasms). To show this usage is not as unusual as one might think, I give in a footnote, [633] in order, Webster's 1995 CD Dictionary's first two entries for imagination."

immaterial: Not material, also called spiritual. Material things are subject to change because they have a potentiality, which we call matter, to be something other than they are. The first accident of material things, quantity or extension, is what makes material things capable of change. Immaterial things cannot be other than they are.

infra-scientific experience: Experience that has not been philosophically examined. It is common experience that has been sifted some by one's spontaneous thinking processes, but not enough to rise to the level of science properly called. It derives from: *infra* (meaning below as in *infra*red, below the red) and *scientific* (meaning knowledge of some type and degree.) Infra-scientific experience is the experience of daily living; the older we are, in general, the more of it we have. Those who live more deliberately and consciously will have more of it at any given age. Each of us has it; one may have thought about certain experiences here and there in a haphazard way but have never subjected them to the type of rigorous analysis that would qualify it properly as "science *(scientia),*" as proper knowledge.

intellect: Philosophers distinguish two aspects in the human intellect: 1) the *agent intellect* (in Latin, the *intellectus agens*), which draws what is essential (in various degrees) from the phantasm of the thing under consideration, and 2) the *passive intellect* which then forms a *conscious* idea of the thing. The act of sensorial knowledge and intellectual knowledge are spontaneous, and we are *only* directly aware of the resultant act of the passive intellect which presents us with a general thing, the general idea of man say, rather than the particular man, say,

---

[633] 1. *a*) the act or power of forming mental images of what is not actually present *b*) the act or power of creating mental images of what has never been actually experienced, or of creating new images or ideas by combining previous experiences; creative power; 2. anything imagined; mental image; creation of the mind; fancy. (©1995 ZCI Publishing, Inc. ©1994, 1991, 1988 Simon & Schuster, Inc.)

John Doe. The intellect is of necessity not material (immaterial), because the material world changes by loosing its form and acquiring another, whereas the intellect acquires the form of an object *as* the form of the object in such a way that I am united with the form of the object while remaining myself. If my intellect were material it would loose itself in the process of understanding. Furthermore, matter is specific and ideas are general.

knowledge:

a) <u>Proper knowledge</u> is *knowledge* that is obtained and based on one's own *correct* application of reason and experience. Improper knowledge includes those things we think we know, usually based on some level of trust in another. Improper knowledge is a species of belief in the generic sense. Proper knowledge is certain knowledge, not probable. In an extended use of the word, one can include probable knowledge that is beyond reasonable doubt in its definition.

b) <u>Levels of knowledge</u> refer to the chain one creates as he starts from experience and builds conclusions that he then uses to draw other conclusions that, in turn, are used to derive other conclusions. Each such layer is called a level. Such layering also happens with improper knowledge as well, when, for example, one learns something from someone who told someone else.

c) <u>Knowledge</u> is the unity of the knower and the known. When I know something, I conform myself to the thing, so as to "see" it from the inside.

levels of abstraction: *See degrees of abstraction.*

logic: That branch of the methodological sciences that deals with the proper understanding of the reasoning processes, which enables us to reason correctly, with facility and order. (cf. St. Thomas Anal. Post. Lib. 1 lect 1 n1.)

material being: Same as *body*, though may be used when one is referring to material substantial being as opposed to a group or "tied" together group of substances that move as one.

mathematics: Second level of abstraction that leaves behind all accidents of material things, save their extension. It consists of geometry, which leaves behind universal quantity, and arithmetic, which leaves behind all qualitative aspects of figure. By making analogies, the mind comes to understand the field of analysis, which builds the bridge between the two arenas.

Since they are abstracted from the real world, mathematical entities are real, even though they are conceived in an idealized condition not found in the world (they are, after all, abstracted from the particular). Following Jacques Maritain's excellent terminology, we call the world of mathematics the world of the mathematical preter-real. However, mathematical beings can be conceived in ways in which they cannot exist in the real world; in such cases, they are beings of reason. Asking, "Where are those –2 cows?" manifests such a case. Again, all mathematical entities are reductively real; that is, they can be decomposed into real pieces, but as entities they can be beings of reason. "–2" is an operation of taking away followed by a number. (Note, it is not the idea that is decomposed but the mathematical form that the idea brings to us which can be decomposed).

Thus, there are three ways of conceiving mathematical entities:

a. As they exist in the material world.
b. As they exist in the mind abstracting all accidents but quantity and its limits such as figure. This is called preternatural domain.
c. As considered reflexively, usually regulatory or symbolically. In this case, they are beings of reason, logical operations.

matter:

a) Matter is generally that part of a form-matter composite that is its potential to become something else, that is, to lose its current form and taken on another.
b) Prime matter is pure matter, pure material potentiality, material potentiality conceived without the act of any specific thing or things as the capacity to become any other kind of material substance given the right sequence of causality. Note, however, that potentiality (matter) only exists with respect to something that actually is. Indeed, since only something that is can be changed, that is, has the potential to be something else, pure potentiality is really nothing if isolated from actuality. Prime matter is a relative

concept that *requires* its correlative of actuality. Thus prime matter, pure potentiality viewed as an entity in its own right, separated from actuality in conception, is a *being of reason* made by one's mind, as one can never find prime matter in a state separated from an actual existing thing. Although such a concept is not prime matter at all, it is a common mistake to think of it so.

Prime matter taken in its proper, relative sense is a real being, for material things really have the capacity to change. Material things are actually something and are potentially something else.

c) <u>Secondary matter</u> is any changeable (material) being or beings that one considers as undergoing an *accidental* change. For instance, the marble blob that gets carved into a statue is the secondary matter in the making of a statue.

metaphysics: The first philosophy. It is first in the sense of ultimate in our knowledge, since it is meta-science or a reflection all things to consider what is common to all of them and how they differ. Hence, it studies being as being, considering all things as a system of causes and effects ultimately caused by God. It involves the highest level of abstraction, called the third level of abstraction, since it is not limited to material substances, but also considers non-material substances from their material effects. Examples of what metaphysics studies include are: angels, man's immaterial substantial form, substances, and accidents.

moral philosophy: The study of the first principles of applied science, truth in action. It answers "What should we do?" The first principle of moral philosophy is self-evident: "Do good, avoid evil." It is directly related to the basic undeniable principle: everyone desires happiness.

motion: *See change.*

natural state: The state(s) of a thing as it is naturally ordered to be, that is, the thing as it should be, as opposed to the thing in a pathological state, in which it is missing something(s) that properly belongs to it. For example, a lame or sick animal is *not* in its natural state. In the case of an engineered thing, the "natural" state is the state which we designed the thing to be in. For example, a bicycle wheel bent in half is *not* in its natural state.

One might think a natural state would be any state of a thing found in the world. This broad use of the term refers to the larger environment; by contrast, we focus on the thing and its nature.

natural and **supernatural:**

  a) Natural (thing) refers to any member of or the whole of the universe, including the immaterial and material that act together to form a unity. The universe and those things that make it up have their essences distinct from their existence.

  b) Supernatural refers to any effect other than that due to creation, which cannot be produced by a creature, but only by God (whose essence is His existence).

nihilism: The belief that the universe is vacuous in a profound philosophical sense, that, at its core, reality is hollow. It includes the corollary that our existence is pointless.

nominalism: The belief that things have no essences, that everything is really an individual having no real common features with other things. It is a belief that mistakes all knowledge for sensorial knowledge. As Jacques Maritain says, and I paraphrase, a nominalist cannot forgive intellectual knowledge for not being knowledge of particulars actually in existence, like sensorial knowledge is.

ontological: Having to do with real being, as opposed to the output of the empiriological. *See* empiriological, empiriometric, and/or empirioschematic.

organism: Those substances that are organized heterogeneous parts ordered immanently (from within, interiorly rather than from the outside) toward the whole, with at least nutritive and reproductive functions.

phantasm: That by which we know things as they are in particular, also called *images.* Phantasms are pure signs used in sensorial knowledge. When I pick up my glass of ice water, I acquire the coldness of my particular glass as the coldness of my glass by way of a phantasm.

philosophical idealism: The belief that one's knowledge starts with thought rather than things.

philosophical realism (moderate): The philosophical position that recognizes that things are individuated, but yet in our minds, our ideas of them are universal. I abstract the general idea of dog from the particular dogs in the world. Hence, dogs exist in my intellect as a universal idea, but in reality they exist only as this particular dog.

philosophy: (*See* Chapter 6 for more details.)

    a) In the *narrow sense*, as currently used, philosophy is the study of the first principles of various subjects and of all things. *physica, mathematica, ethics,* and *logic* would all thus be called philosophy with *metaphysics* being the first or ultimate philosophy. In this sense, one can also speak of the philosophy of a given discipline, meaning the first principles of that discipline.

    b) In the *wide sense*, philosophy is the love of wisdom, *all wisdom* and as such, includes all the sciences. This is the ancient use of the word.

physica: *Same as physics in the wide sense.*

physical thing: Same as *body*.

physics:

    a) In the **wide sense**, physics or as we call it, *physica*, is the study of changeable being. It involves the least abstraction, and as such is called the *first level of abstraction*. In it, one leaves behind only particular matter, not general matter: for example, it leaves behind Fido's flesh and bones but retains the flesh and bones generally. Looked at from how its conclusions are verified, it is being resolved in the sensible.

    b) In the **narrow sense**, as it is most often used today, it refers to the empiriometric science of physics, which is a *tool* used by *physica*.

plant: (philosophic sense)   A living organism that has nutritive and reproductive powers only. Note here we use infra-scientific meaning of the word "nutritive," not that of the specialized science of biology; biologists use the word nutritive to mean source of energy --which for *plantae* (as biologists define it) photosynthesis (direct conversion of energy from the sun). Here we mean the ability of the organism to assimilate "compounds" from its environment and make them an intrinsic part of itself and thus grow and/or maintain itself.

Plantae: (modern) Biological classification scheme that is closely related to the philosophical concept of plant.

potentiality: Generally, the capacity of a *being* to become.

principles:

1) *Contradiction:* something cannot be and not be at the same time in the same manner.

2) *Sufficient reason:* everything contains the reason for its existence in itself or in another.
   Note, this principle is the principle of causality viewed from the standpoint of intelligibility (one of the transcendentals).

3) *Causality:* roughly, nothing can change itself. More profoundly, *something can act only so far as it is in act.*

4) *Finality:* as all things exist for themselves in operation, to overflow themselves by action. *Or again, every agent, insofar as it is an agent, acts toward an end.*

quality: The second accident of material things. More generally, those things that issue from a substance. Color, for example, is a sensible quality. It is through quality that we know quantity. Quality is also distinguished from quantity in that from two given "quantities," a larger quantity can be made; however, from two qualities of the same type, one obtains only the same quality. For example, two, or even as many as you like, mediocre mathematicians do not add up to an excellent one.

quantity: Extension, the first accident of material being, that which remains of a material being when all else is taken away. Material beings are changeable because they have parts outside of each other, that is, because they are extended, have quantity.

reductionism: The belief that each thing is no more than the parts as seen in isolation from the thing. It is closely related to the belief that each thing is no more than what is manifested by the correlation of the measured quantities (and/or models) that represent the behavior of the thing after it is broken apart.

science:

a) Modern meaning usually includes only those sciences that are heavily empiriometric, often mistaking the empiriological for all of science.

b) Ancient meaning included all knowledge and made distinctions between the methodologies and material and formal nature of the various sciences.

self-evident: That which, once its terms are understood, cannot be denied. Some things are self-evident in themselves, but not to us till we truly see the meaning of the terms involved.

No proposition is self-evident from the words or "beings of reasons" to which words might refer, but only from the reality (real being) to which the words refer. Self-evident propositions are known by direct insight from sense observation, not by demonstration. All truths known by demonstration must ultimately reduce logically to such directly known truths.

senses: That through which we know everything.

   a) <u>External senses</u> are primarily the five senses of touch, sight, hearing, smell, and taste.

   b) <u>Internal senses</u> are the internal counterparts of the external senses that carry out specialized activities. Since these powers are part of the sensorial system, they can be called internal senses. The internal senses or powers are: 1) the *unifying sense* that brings together all the data of the individual external senses to fashion a phantasm by which I know the thing under consideration, 2) the *sense memory* that allows recollection of an experience accurately and in proper time, place, etc. context, 3) the *evaluative sense* that, in turn, controls the *appetitive power* which causes the animal to feel attraction or repulsion, depending on whether the evaluative sense determines the thing under consideration to be helpful or harmful to the organism, and finally 4) the *imagination,* which is the ability to recall and manipulate the phantasms.

sign: (pure and instrumental):

   a) An <u>instrumental sign</u> is a being that first presents itself and then in presenting itself also conveys a message. This is what one means by a sign in everyday life. A stop sign is first a piece of metal made into a hexagonal shape and painted red with some white. We recognize the white on the sign refers to another reality outside of the sign itself, because we have been taught meanings to associate with the white symbols. In particular, we learn that the symbols mean we should stop our cars before proceeding into the intersection.

   b) A <u>pure sign</u> is a being that unites a knower to object known.

Ideas and phantasms are pure signs. They put us in contact with forms of others. They are that by which we know things. By an idea, the knower is united to the known. I become by its referential existence, another form without losing myself. By contrast with instrumental signs, we only know of the existence of pure signs by reflecting back on the fact that we have come to know something. Not recognizing that ideas are that by which we know something, i.e., thinking that they are that which we know, leads to philosophical idealism. The latter holds or ends in saying that we only know our ideas, in which case there is no way to know any thing outside of our minds.

soul: An immaterial substantial form of a form-matter composite: in particular, since man is the only rational animal that we know of, the substantial form of man. Sometimes the word "soul" is used in an extended sense to mean the substantial forms of animals or even plants. Note however, that these substantial forms are qualitatively different from each other as well as from that of man; in particular, plants and animals do not have immaterial substantial forms.

specialized sciences:
  a) Generically, the <u>specialized sciences</u> are those sciences that study some narrow range of beings, often in a narrow view.
  b) <u>Modern specialized sciences</u> are the above sciences as currently practiced. As such, these sciences approach things, at least largely, (and viewed from what is usually considered satisfactory explanation by scientists practicing them) by a non-ontological mode of "explaining." They are usually seeking schematic and/or mathematical explanation (broadly called empiriological) and as such, are interested and focused on those levels of understanding and thus do not usually reach the essences of the beings under study except obliquely and inchoately.

species: *See genus.*

substance: That which exists by itself, per se, not needing to exist in another, as accidents must. *See accident.*

substantial form: *See form.*

transcendentals: Each of the transcendentals are interchangeable or, said another way, they are "being" looked at from various

viewpoints. They are, with the Latin in quotes:
a) *being* (ens),
b) *unity* (unum)
c) *reality* or *thingness* (res)
d) *identity as something apart* (aliquid)
e) *truth* (verum)
f) *goodness* (bonum)

Beauty is the "splendor of all the transcendentals together." (*See* last paragraph of this definition.)

To the degree something is, is the degree that it is one, is real, is something apart, is intelligible, and is good. God alone possesses these in their perfection; all else only shares to a greater or lesser extent in being and thus each of the transcendentals.

More completely, *beauty* is the "goodness of truth." Since truth is being as intelligible, being as related to a knower, and goodness is being as desirable, being as related to someone who wills or desires it, we can say the following: Beauty is truth as it satisfies one's desire or will to know by reason of its evidence or clarity. For man, beauty includes various types dependent on sensorial powers and intellectual powers considering the object. Of course, in all cases, all the transcendentals come into play in beauty because the good and true can only be such to the degree they are one, real and set apart.

truth: The conformity of the mind with reality. All things are true, in that they are intelligible, oriented towards a knowing mind.

univocal: Existing on one plane, homogeneous non-differentiated. Literally, univocal means "one voice."

universe: The sum total of all that exists in our natural world, including material and immaterial elements. It is a "republic" of natures. Since all that is, to the degree that it is, is one, the universe is a unity, a uni-verse, which literally means "one turn." It is derived from the Latin *universum,* meaning "all together." *Universe* is often used in a restricted sense to refer only to the material things of the universe, which we here call the *material universe.*

vices: Habits of (or skills in)[634] doing evil that make acting
wrongly second nature.

virtues: Skills in (or habits of) doing good that make acting
rightly second nature.

---

[634] "Skills in doing evil" is an even better definition provided the word "skills" is
loosed from any connotation of "proper discernment for the good."

Index

About the Author

Since Einstein first conceived general relativity over 80 years ago, physicists have sought a definition for angular momentum in general relativity. No satisfactory definition of angular momentum had been given. In 1997, Anthony Rizzi discovered the first such definition, thereby gaining worldwide recognition for his work in theoretical physics. (See *Science*, October 1998, Vol. 282, No. 5387, pg 249.)

He is uniquely established as both an outstanding theorist and experimentalist in general relativity, specializing in the cutting-edge field of gravity wave research, including LIGO (Laser Interferometer Gravitational-wave Observatory) related areas. He was the first scientist appointed to the California Institute of Technology's Louisiana LIGO observatory, where he was responsible for significant developments preparing the instrument for the detection of gravity waves. During this time, he taught graduate physics courses at LSU. He has also been a research scientist at Princeton University.

Industry is also no stranger to Dr. Rizzi. Earlier in his career, he was employed for ten years as a staff physicist and design engineer for Martin Marietta (later Lockheed Martin) in Denver, Colorado. His work included projects for the Manned Mars Craft and the Mars Observer, and he received the NASA Award, as well as a Martin Marietta New Technology Award.

In 1982, he received a BS in physics from the Massachusetts Institute of Technology (MIT), soon after his MS (physics) from the University of Colorado and later his PhD in physics from Princeton.

Dr. Rizzi has used in his study of philosophy and theology the same rigorous, in-depth questioning self-study style that he used throughout his physics career. Over the past 20 years, he gained an extensive background in philosophy, learning modern and ancient philosophy. In 2003, Dr. Rizzi founded The Institute for Advanced Physics (IAPweb.org); as Director, he is dedicated to implementing in science education and research the answers to the question "How then should we do science?" In addition to his ongoing research in general relativity and LIGO-related areas, he gives lectures and interviews as seen on *EWTN*, *FOCUS Worldwide Network* with Archbishop Hannan, *Catholic World Report*, *Zenit News Agency* and *Relevant Radio*. He is blessed with a lovely wife and three precious children.

Printed in the United States
41175LVS00004B/1-72